always up to date

The law changes, but Nolo is always on top of it! We offer several ways to make sure you and your Nolo products are always up to date:

1 Nolo's Legal Updater

We'll send you an email whenever a new edition of your book is published! Sign up at **www.nolo.com/legalupdater**.

2 Updates @ Nolo.com

Check **www.nolo.com/update** to find recent changes in the law that affect the current edition of your book.

3 Nolo Customer Service

To make sure that this edition of the book is the most recent one, call us at **800-728-3555** and ask one of our friendly customer service representatives. Or find out at **www.nolo.com**.

please note

We believe accurate and current legal information should help you solve many of your own legal problems on a cost-efficient basis. But this text is not a substitute for personalized advice from a knowledgeable lawyer. If you want the help of a trained professional, consult an attorney licensed to practice in your state.

4th Edition

The Complete IEP Guide

How to Advocate for Your Special Ed Child

by Attorney Lawrence M. Siegel

FOURTH EDITION	OCTOBER 2005
Editor	LISA GUERIN
Illustrations	MARI STEIN
Book Design	TERRI HEARSH
Cover Design	TONI IHARA
Production	MARGARET LIVINGSTON
Index	SONGBIRD INDEXING SERVICES
Proofreading	SUSAN CARLSON GREENE
Printing	CONSOLIDATED PRINTERS, INC.

Siegel, Lawrence M., 1946-
    The complete IEP guide : how to advocate for your special ed child / by Lawrence M.
Siegel.-- 4th ed.
        p. cm.
    Includes index.
    ISBN 1-4133-0199-1 (alk. paper)
    1. Individualized education programs--Law and legislation--United States--Popular
works. 2. Dispute resolution (Law)--United States--Popular works. 3. Special
education--Parent participation--United States--Popular works. I. Title.

KF4209.3.Z9S57 2005
371.9'0973--dc22

                                                            2005051824

Dedication

To the memory of Becky Luftig, my first client and a remarkable young woman, for whom "disability" was an attitude and nothing more

To my parents, and

To my wife Gail, for that first day on the Wheeler steps, and ever since, her joyous smile.

Acknowledgments

My appreciation to the entire Nolo staff which, to a person, has always been professional and friendly and never seemed to feel those two concepts were incompatible.

Special thanks to Marcia Stewart for her superb editing, her patience as we worked through and wrote about the complexities of the IEP process, and her clear goal of making the IEP process friendly to and useful for families of children with disabilities. And thanks to Spencer Sherman for his work updating the 2nd edition.

Several other Nolo staff deserve special thanks:

Jake Warner, for his enthusiasm about the project

Robin Leonard, for her extensive editing and excellent work developing the list of resources for families of children with disabilities

Stanley Jacobsen, for his helpful research assistance

Terri Hearsh, for her terrific design work

Mari Stein, for her delightful illustrations

Toni Ihara, for her delightful cover (and patience)

Michele Crim, Jennifer Spoerri, Jennifer Macko, and Kelly Rosaaen, for their kindness and marketing/PR expertise

Erin Douglass, for putting together clearly written cover copy and being a pleasure to work with, and

Karen Turk for her editorial assistance, especially on forms and checklists.

Thanks also to my colleagues and friends on the California Advisory Commission on Special Education.

Table of Contents

Appendixes

Index

1

Introduction to Special Education

Some years ago, a parent came to my office to discuss the difficulties her teenager was having in school. The parent was a kind and thoughtful person, but looked overwhelmed. Her child had learning disabilities and increasing emotional problems, and the pain of the child was etched on the face of the parent. Her child was falling further behind, losing the confidence she once had, and missing the academic skills and emotional strength she would need for adulthood.

My client sat quietly for some time and then asked in a whisper, "What in the world can I do for my daughter?"

Whether you and your child are entering special education for the first time or the tenth time, you have probably asked the same question. You have a dozen concerns and a hundred fears. You don't know where to begin. The problems seem insurmountable. There are more than 5,000,000 children with disabilities in the United States—that's one out of every twelve children and teenagers. At some point, their parents have felt the same way my client did—and you probably have, too.

Fortunately, Congress enacted a law called the Individuals with Disabilities Education Act, or IDEA, to evaluate children with disabilities and to provide special education programs and services to help them succeed in school. Before IDEA was enacted in 1975, public schools frequently ignored children with disabilities or shunted them off to inferior or distant programs. IDEA represents a long-overdue recognition that individuals with disabilities have the right to access public institutions and be served appropriately, with dignity and respect.

The detail and reach of IDEA are remarkable— no other law in this nation provides such clear and unique legal protection for children. Everything you do to help your child secure an appropriate education is connected to, and determined by, the legal requirements of IDEA.

A. What Is Special Education?

"Special education" is the broad term used to describe the educational system for children with disabilities. The term is used in this book to describe that portion of your child's school system that provides special services and programs for children with disabilities. There are three fundamental questions to consider as you begin the special education process:

- Where is your child now?
- Where do you want your child to be?
- What do you need to get your child there?

IDEA entitles your child to an "appropriate" education that meets his or her unique needs. You'll likely have a good sense of what is meant by an appropriate education as you read this book. Broadly speaking, an appropriate education involves the following educational components:

- The specific program or class (called "placement") for your child. Placement is more than just a classroom; it also includes characteristics such as location, class size, teacher experience, and peer makeup.
- The specific services (called "related services") provided your child, as well as the amount and frequency of those services and who provides them.
- Other educational components, such as curricula and teaching methods.

Special education provides a process for evaluating your child and developing an *individualized education program,* or IEP. The acronym IEP refers to several interrelated things:

- the meeting where the school district determines whether your child is eligible for special education (called the IEP eligibility meeting)
- the yearly meeting where you and school representatives develop your child's educational plan (called the IEP program meeting), and
- the actual detailed written description of your child's educational program.

"Disability" Is a Loaded Term

Webster's *New World Dictionary* defines disability as an illness, injury, or physical handicap that "restricts" or causes "limitations" and "disadvantages." Advocates in special education and disability rights understandably object to the term "disabled," preferring "child with disabilities"—this is the term we use throughout this book.

All human beings come into this world with a variety of qualities and characteristics. Having special education needs does not mean that your child should be treated as "different" or denied the care and respect that all children deserve. Human beings are complex, and a determination of who is able and "disabled" is an effort in futility. Franklin Roosevelt was president four times and could not walk. Stephen Hawking is severely disabled and understands the universe like few on this earth.

It is not a cliché to say that we all have some kind of disability, even as we realize that the difference in degree between one or another disability can be significant and life altering. Defining terms should not be judgmental terms. I have many colleagues who are deaf. They are, to be sure, without hearing, but to consider them ineffective or incapable would be ludicrous. They cannot hear, but communicate in a beautiful, complex, and effective way. In a meeting of deaf people, it is my halting sign language that is ineffective and disabling to me.

Special education laws give children with disabilities and their parents important rights not available to children in regular education and their parents. These include the right to:

- have the child evaluated
- secure information about the child
- attend an IEP meeting
- develop a written IEP plan, and

- resolve disputes with the school district through an impartial administrative and legal process.

While the specifics of any one child's special education needs may vary—one child may need placement in a private school while another needs a one-to-one aide for full-time participation in a regular class (called "mainstreaming")—mastering the IEP process is central to securing an appropriate education for your child. But equally important, the IEP process is entirely individual. The program developed by you and the school district must fit your child, not the other way around. What works for other students is irrelevant if it won't work for your child. IDEA does not tell you or the school district specifically how your child will be educated. Rather, IDEA provides rules to govern the process the IEP team uses to decide what is appropriate for your child.

B. Being Your Child's Advocate

Advocating for your child is easy: All of us want the best for our kids. Still, there will be bumps along the way. The IEP process is maze-like, involving a good deal of technical information, intimidating professionals, and confusing choices. For some families, it goes smoothly, with no disagreements; for others, it is a terrible encounter in which you and your school district cannot even agree on the time of day. For most people, the experience is somewhere in between.

Don't fall into the trap of thinking that teachers, school administrators, and experts know everything and that you know nothing. Right now, you may not have all the information you need, and you may not know where to look for it. But the law states that you and your school district are equal decision makers, and that the school district must provide you with a good deal of information along the way.

You do not need to be a special education expert or a lawyer to be an effective advocate for

Warning: Special Education Rules Are in Flux

Congress has reviewed and changed IDEA several times since the law was enacted in 1975 as the Education for All Handicapped Children Act. In 2004, Congress changed the rules again when it passed the Individuals with Disabilities Education *Improvement* Act, which made important modifications to IDEA. These changes became effective on July 1, 2005; you can find the text of key provisions of the new statute in Appendix A. While most special education rights and procedures remain the same under this new law, there have also been numerous and significant changes, all discussed fully in this book.

The Department of Education—the federal agency responsible for administering and enforcing the law—has not yet issued final new regulations interpreting the statute as this book goes to press. The role of regulations is to clarify the law, often supplying additional definitions, details, and rules intended to flesh out the language of the statute passed by Congress. Although regulations interpreting the old law are still valid and in effect, some of these regulations will change to address issues raised by the 2004 amendments to IDEA.

The Department of Education issued proposed new regulations on June 10, 2005. Proposed regulations don't have the force of law. Instead, they are like a first draft—agencies issue them, then ask for public comments on the proposal. Once the time period for comments ends, the Department decides whether to make changes before issuing a final version (currently, the Department anticipates issuing new regulations by the end of 2005). Many of the proposed new regulations simply restate the former regulations, although some of the citation numbers have changed. The proposed regulations also include new material on the 2004 changes to IDEA.

This book continues to refer to the existing regulations where necessary to explain how the law is currently interpreted; unless otherwise noted, these regulations are not expected to change in content (although the citation numbers will change). In areas where the proposed regulations break new legal ground, the book describes them as well. Remember, however, that both the existing and proposed regulations will be replaced by the final regulations adopted by the Department of Education. Because regulations often add requirements and rules that go well beyond the scope of the actual law, **it is very important to make sure that you have the latest regulations.**

To read the proposed regulations and find out whether final regulations have been issued, go to the website of the Department's Office of Special Education and Rehabilitative Services, www.ed.gov/osers. You can also contact your state's department of education (see Appendix 2 for contact information) or your school district for updates about the regulations.

your child. The general strategies for helping a child in the IEP process are not complex and can easily be mastered. The cliché that knowledge is power is absolutely true in the world of special education.

C. Using This Book

The purpose of this book is to help parents effectively proceed on their own through the IEP process, whether it's their first time or their fifth time. The book is for parents whose child has emotional difficulties, is deaf or blind, has other physical conditions, or has a multitude of disabilities. In other words, it's for the parents of every child with disabilities.

 If your child has learning disabilities: Nolo publishes a specialized version of this book just for parents of children with learning disabilities. *Nolo's IEP Guide: Learning Disabilities,* by Larry Siegel, addresses issues of particular concern for children with learning disabilities, including commonly used evaluations, special eligibility requirements, teaching methodologies, and more. If your child has learning disabilities,

you'll want to use this more specific resource. Nolo will be happy to exchange this book for a copy of *Nolo's IEP Guide: Learning Disabilities.* Simply call 1-800-728-3555 Monday through Friday, 7AM to 7PM PST, and one of our customer service representatives will be happy to help.

Specifically, this book can help you:
- develop an understanding of special education law
- understand eligibility rules and the role of evaluations
- gather current material and develop new information about your child
- determine your child's specific goals and educational needs
- gather current material and develop new information about various school programs, as well as options outside the school district
- prepare for the IEP meeting
- attend the IEP meeting and develop your child's IEP plan, and
- resolve disputes with the school district.

Mastering these tasks will require you to be generally organized (but not fanatically so), willing to ask questions, and make use of resources that are widely available. The suggestions and forms in this book will help you get—and stay—organized throughout the IEP process.

Detailed appendixes provide invaluable information, including:
- copies of key federal special education laws
- addresses and websites of federal and state special education agencies
- addresses and websites of national and state advocacy, parent, and disability organizations
- a bibliography of other helpful books, and
- two dozen tear-out forms, letters, and checklists to help you through every stage of the IEP process.

Some of the material will be very familiar to parents who have been through many IEPs—for example, you may already know too well the cast of characters and the basic legal requirements. Still, you should review each chapter, even the ones that cover familiar topics. You may find new insights or angles on old problems, and you will learn how new rules that went into effect in July 2005 have changed the special education landscape. Of course, you can skip material clearly not relevant—for example, if your child is already in special education, you don't need to prepare for an eligibility meeting.

If you are new to special education, very little in this book will be familiar to you. You might want to start by taking a quick look at the chapter titles and table of contents to become familiar with key ideas and how they relate to each other before you start reading. As you read, check the index and jump among chapters if that makes sense. Highlight points you want to remember.

The special education process has a discernible beginning and end. In general, it takes a year. There are similarities and differences between the first IEP year and subsequent years. For example, each year you will gather information and prepare for the yearly IEP program meeting, at which time you and the school district will determine placement and related services. But the first year always includes evaluating your child's eligibility for special education. In subsequent years, your child may or may not be evaluated. Eligibility is rarely addressed after the first year, unless you or the school district feels a change is justified—for example, if your child no longer needs special education or may qualify under a different eligibility category.

There is a certain chicken-or-egg quality to the order of some of the chapters. For example, the chapter on evaluations comes before the chapter on eligibility. You will soon learn that your child must be evaluated to be found eligible, but you need to know how a child becomes eligible before you arrange an evaluation. Which chapter do you read first? It really doesn't matter, as long as you read both.

What This Book Doesn't Cover

IDEA provides rights and procedures for children between the ages of three and 22. There is another procedure for children under three, but this book's fundamental focus is on children between three and 22. There are also certain IDEA issues that involve very complex and detailed procedures and are discussed only briefly in this book, such as transition services to help children over age 16 prepare for a job or college, including independent living skills. This book does not address in detail issues regarding discipline of special education students, including suspension and expulsion. This issue is complex; you should contact an attorney or at least a support group (see Appendix 3) regarding discipline issues.

D. Icons Used Throughout This Book

The icons listed below appear throughout this book to help you along.

 Books or organizations that give more information about the issue or topic discussed in the text.

 Related topics covered in this book.

 Slow down and consider potential problems.

 You may be able to skip some material that doesn't apply to your situation.

 A practical tip or good idea.

 A tear-out copy of the form discussed in the text is in Appendix 5.

E. Getting Help From Others

Other parents, local groups, and regional or national organizations can be of great help as you wend your way through special education. The amount of information these folks have can be amazing. Other parents and parent groups can be your best resource and certainly a source of support to help you through hard times. Others who have been through the process before can help you avoid making mistakes or undertaking unnecessary tasks. Most important, they can be a source of real encouragement. Chapter 15 provides further thoughts on making use of your local special education community.

Note: Reference is made throughout this book to parents, but the term is used to include foster parents and legal guardians. ■

2

Overview of the IEP and Special Education Law

As mentioned in Chapter 1, a federal law, the Individuals with Disabilities Education Act (IDEA), furnishes a formal process for evaluating children with disabilities and providing specialized programs and services to help them succeed in school. Special education is unique because of the central role parents play in determining their child's educational program. Under IDEA, the program and services your child needs will be determined through the individualized education program, or IEP, process. The term IEP is used to refer to a meeting about, and a written description of, your child's program. Your ability to understand and master the IEP process is central to your child's educational experience. Indeed, the IEP is the centerpiece of IDEA.

This chapter discusses the specific mandates of IDEA and how they apply to your child. It provides an overview of your child's legal rights to special education and the IEP process, so you can effectively advocate for your child.

As you read this chapter, keep in mind the following:

- Don't let the word "law" throw you. The actual language of IDEA, and more important, its underlying purpose, can easily be mastered. The legal concepts in IDEA are logical and sensible.
- Developing a broad understanding of the law will help you when you review later chapters on eligibility, evaluations, IEPs, and other key matters.
- The actual language of IDEA appears in the body of the book. While I provide plain English descriptions of special education law, you can find key provisions of the actual law as passed by Congress in Appendix 1. IDEA is found in the United States Code starting at 20 U.S.C. § 1400.

IDEA regulations are changing. The regulatory citations throughout this book are to the current IDEA regulations—those that will be in effect until the Department of Education issues final regulations interpreting the 2004 amendments to IDEA. The Department expects to release these final regulations at the end of 2005; many of them will be identical or similar to the existing regulations cited in this chapter (although the citations will be different), while others will be new. When you use this book, you should make sure that you have the most current version of the regulations. See "Warning: Special Education Rules Are in Flux," in Chapter 1, for information that will help you stay up to date. You can find the most recent version of IDEA, including the 2004 amendments, starting at 20 U.S.C. § 1400; the most pertinent sections are included in Appendix 1.

A. What IDEA Requires

IDEA was enacted in 1975 and reauthorized and revamped in 2004. The purpose of the law is to ensure that children with disabilities receive an appropriate education. To achieve this goal, IDEA imposes a number of requirements on school districts—the most important are discussed below.

1. Eligibility and Evaluations

Every school district has the legal duty to identify, locate, and evaluate children who may be in need of special education. This includes wards of the court, children who have no fixed address (such as migrant or homeless children), and children who may be advancing from grade to grade but nonetheless may need special education. (20 U.S.C. § 1412(a)(3).) Once a child is identified and located, the school district must find him or her eligible for special education through an evaluation and IEP process before specific programs and services can be provided.

IDEA defines "children with disabilities" as individuals between the ages of three and 22 who have one or more of the following conditions (20 U.S.C. § 1401(3) and (30); see also 34 C.F.R. § 300.7 of the current IDEA regulations):

- mental retardation
- hearing impairment (including deafness)
- speech or language impairment
- visual impairment (including blindness)
- serious emotional disturbance
- orthopedic impairment
- autism
- traumatic brain injury
- specific learning disability
- ADD (Attention Deficit Disorder)
- ADHD (Attention Deficit Hyperactivity Disorder), and
- other health impairment.

For your child to qualify for special education under IDEA, it is not enough that he or she has one of these disabilities. In addition, there must be evidence that your child's disability adversely affects his or her educational performance.

Your child has a right to an initial evaluation, with subsequent evaluations at least every three years. If you are not satisfied with the initial evaluation or you feel that your child's disability or special education needs have changed, your child is entitled to more frequent evaluations— and even outside or independent evaluations—if you request them. (20 U.S.C. §§ 1414 and 1415(b)(1).) You have the right to additional reevaluations upon request. If you ask for more than one evaluation per year, however, the school district must give its consent. (20 U.S.C. § 1414(a)(2).)

Evaluations and Assessments

IDEA makes a distinction between "evaluations," which are the tests and other methods used to determine your child's eligibility for special education and to design your child's educational program, and "assessments," which refer to the tests your state uses to measure the performance of *all* children in school. Prior to the rising popularity of statewide assessments, however, these two terms were often used interchangeably (even in previous editions of this book), so don't be surprised if your school district continues to do so. Chapter 6 provides detailed information on special education evaluations.

Eligibility for special education services is discussed in detail in Chapters 6 and 7. The very specific rules regarding the initial and subsequent evaluations are described in Chapter 6.

2. Nature of the Education

Under IDEA, your child is entitled to the following fundamental educational rights (20 U.S.C. § 1401(9) and (29)):

- **Free appropriate public education (FAPE).** Your child is entitled to an *appropriate* education at no cost to you.
- **Special education.** Your child is entitled to an education *specially designed* to meet his or her *unique* needs.

Chapter 5 discusses how to develop a blueprint of your child's program and service needs.

IDEA fundamentally requires that the educational program should fit your child, not the other way around. For example, it is not appropriate for a school district to place a deaf child in a class for developmentally disabled children or a learning disabled child in a class of emotionally disturbed students. These would not be individually tailored IEPs. The classroom setting, teaching, and services provided would not be appropriate for the deaf or learning disabled child. "Appropriateness" is the standard for evaluating all IEP components—the goals, services, and placement.

Appropriate Does Not Necessarily Mean the Very Best

The law does not require that your school district provide the very best possible education, but an appropriate education. "Appropriate" is an elusive but tremendously important concept. It is used throughout IDEA and frequently in the IEP process. For one child, an appropriate education may mean a regular class with minor support services, while a hospital placement might be appropriate for another.

The 2004 amendments to IDEA make clear that you have the right to reject special education and related services. As Congress said, you have the "ultimate choice" in these matters; the school district cannot force anything on your child if you don't want it. While it has been very rare for a school district to take a parent to due process to require the provision of special education and related services, it has happened. This change in statutory language will eliminate that possibility.

3. Educational Placement or Program

Your child's educational placement or program, along with related services (discussed in Section 4, below), will take center stage in the IEP process.

a. Least Restrictive Environment

IDEA does not tell you or the school what specific program or class your child should be in; that is a decision for the IEP team. IDEA does require school districts to place disabled children in the least restrictive environment (LRE) that meets their individual needs. What is LRE for a particular child, like what constitutes an "appropriate education," will depend on that child's abilities and disabilities. Although Congress expressed a strong preference for mainstreaming (placing a child in a regular classroom), it used the term LRE to ensure that individual needs would determine each individual placement decision—and that children who really need a more restricted placement (such as a special school) would have one.

Placement vs. Program

The terms placement and program are often used interchangeably, but there are some differences in meaning. As used in IDEA, placement refers to the various classrooms or schools where a child may be. Program has a broader connotation: It includes not only where the program is located, but also the components of that program, including the services, curricula, teaching methods, class makeup, and so on. Placement and program components should both be addressed in your child's IEP.

IDEA states that a child should be in the regular classroom unless the child cannot be educated satisfactorily there, "even with the use of supplementary aides and services." (20 U.S.C. § 1412(a)(5).) LRE further requires that a child should be educated as close to home as possible and in the class he or she would attend if nondisabled. (Current IDEA regulations at 34 C.F.R. §§ 300.550-552.) If a child will not participate with nondisabled children in the regular classroom and in other school activities, the IEP team must explain why. (20 U.S.C. § 1414(d)(1)(A).)

Is Mainstreaming a Requirement?

Court decisions interpreting the least restrictive environment rule have been as varied as the children in special education. Some court opinions have concluded that mainstreaming is a requirement of IDEA; other judges have ruled that it is "a goal subordinate to the requirement that disabled children receive educational benefit." (*Doe v. Arlington*, 882 F.2d 876,878 (4th Cir. 1999).)

A common example of the possible conflict between mainstreaming and an appropriate education setting occurs with a child who needs very specialized curricula, intense services, specialized staff, or a protected environment. The child's unique needs may conflict with the right to be mainstreamed.

What is clear from the court decisions and due process hearing decisions that have dealt with this issue is that there is no absolute right to a mainstreamed or alternative program. Whether the right to be mainstreamed is more powerful than the right to an appropriate education, or vice versa, will depend on the individual facts of each case.

---

b.   Range of Placements

While IDEA expresses a preference for regular education, it recognizes that some children with disabilities should not be in a regular class. Individual need determines the appropriateness of a placement. If regular classroom placement is not appropriate, IDEA requires that the school district provide a range of alternative placements—called a "continuum of placement options"—including the following:

- regular classes for part of the school day
- special classes in regular schools—for example, a special class for children with developmental disabilities
- special public or private schools for children with significant difficulties, such as a school for emotionally troubled students
- charter schools
- residential programs
- home instruction, and
- hospital and institutional placement.

If a child's unique needs dictate an alternative to a regular classroom, the continuum requirement ensures that the school district will make different placement options available. No matter where children are placed, however, IDEA requires every child to have access to the general curriculum taught in the regular classroom. The IEP must specifically address how this requirement will be met. (20 U.S.C. § 1414(d)(1)(A).)

4.   Support or Related Services

Support or related services are the additional help your child needs to meet his or her IEP goals. These services are not educational per se—they are the psychological, occupational, therapeutic, or practical assistance your child needs to succeed. IDEA requires schools to provide related services for two reasons:

- to help your child benefit from special education, and
- to ensure that your child has the chance to "achieve satisfactorily" in a regular classroom.

Under IDEA, related services include the following:

- speech-language pathology and audiology services
- psychological services
- physical and occupational therapy
- recreation, including therapeutic recreation
- social work services
- counseling services, including rehabilitation counseling

- orientation and mobility services
- medical services for diagnostic and evaluation purposes
- interpreting services
- psychotherapy
- one-to-one instructional aide
- transportation
- art therapy
- technological devices, such as FM/AM systems or special computers, and
- school nurse services. (20 U.S.C. § 1401(26).)

IDEA 2004 Amendments to Related Services

When Congress amended IDEA, it made a few changes to the list of related services. Congress added "interpreting services," although it did not specify whether sign language interpreters must be certified, an important issue for deaf and hard of hearing children. Congress also added "school nurse services designed to enable a child with a disability to receive a free appropriate public education." (See "Is a Medical Service a Related Service?" below for more information.)

Congress also specified that a surgically implanted medical device, or the replacement of such a device, is *not* a related service. (20 U.S.C. § 1401(26).) This language refers to cochlear implants.

The latest version of the law also requires that the related services listed in the IEP be "based on peer-reviewed research to the extent practicable." (20 U.S.C. § 1414(d)(1)(A).) See Chapter 10 for more information on this new requirement.

This is not an exhaustive list. Because everything under IDEA is driven by a child's individual needs, the IEP team has the authority to provide any service your child needs, even if it's not listed specifically under IDEA.

Is a Medical Service a Related Service?

The question of what constitutes a related service has been debated since IDEA was enacted in 1975. One particularly difficult issue has been whether a medical service constitutes a related service, if it is needed for a child to benefit from special education. In 1999, the U.S. Supreme Court confirmed that a medical service is a related service if it is limited to "diagnostic and evaluation purposes."

The court also ruled, however, that other medical services might constitute related services under the rules of the IDEA if they can be performed by a nonphysician. In the case heard by the court, the child needed and was granted the services of a nurse to provide, among other things, daily catheterization, suctioning of a tracheotomy, and blood pressure monitoring. (*Cedar Rapids Community Sch. Dist. v. Garret F., by Charlene F.,* 119 S. Ct. 992 (1999).)

Congress codified the *Cedar Rapids* ruling when it amended IDEA in 2004. The law now provides that school nurse services qualify as a related service. (20 U.S.C. § 1401(26).) Parents will always have to show that a particular related service is necessary to their child's education, but there is no longer any dispute that services that can be performed by nurses can be required under IDEA.

5. Assistive Technology

IDEA requires that a child be provided with assistive technology services. These services include:

- evaluating how the child functions in his or her customary environment
- leasing or purchasing assistive technology devices
- fitting, maintaining, and replacing assistive technology devices

- using and coordinating other therapies, interventions, or services in conjunction with such technology, and
- training and technical assistance for the child, the child's family, and the educational staff.

Technological devices are defined as any item, piece of equipment, or system acquired, modified, or customized to maintain, increase, or improve the functional capabilities of a child with a disability. An assistive technology device or service might be an augmentative communication system, a computer, an FM trainer, computer software, pulmonary devices, a touch screen, a calculator, a tape recorder, a spell-checker, books on tape, and even items such as oxygen tanks. (20 U.S.C. §§ 1401(1) and (2).)

6. Transition Services

IDEA requires the IEP team to develop a transition plan to be included in the first IEP in effect when your child turns 16. (Before the 2004 amendments, transition planning had to begin when a child turned 14; check with your state's department of education to find out whether it will follow the new IDEA rule or continue to provide for transition planning beginning at age 14.)

In the transition plan, you and the IEP team must spell out how your child will proceed after high school, whether to college, to work, to a training program, or to develop the skills necessary to live independently as an adult. (20 U.S.C. § 1414(d)(1)(A).) The plan must include "appropriate measurable postsecondary goals," based on appropriate transition assessments focused on training, employment, education, and independent living skills. The IEP must also list the specific transition services that will be required to help your child reach these transition goals.

7. Due Process

In law, "due process" generally refers to the right to a fair procedure for determining individual rights and responsibilities. Under IDEA, and as used in this book, due process means your child's right to be evaluated, receive an appropriate education, be educated in the LRE, have an IEP, and be given notice of any changes in the IEP.

Due process also refers to your specific right to take any dispute you have with your child's school district—whether a disagreement about an evaluation, eligibility, or any part of the IEP, including the specific placement and related services—to a neutral third party to help you resolve your dispute. These rights are unique; children not in special education do not have them.

There are two options for resolving disputes through due process: mediation and a due process hearing. Mediation is a process in which you and the school district meet with a neutral third party who helps you come to an agreement. The mediator has the power of persuasion, but no authority to impose a decision on you.

If you cannot reach an agreement in mediation (or prefer to skip mediation altogether), you can request a fair hearing, in which you and the school district present written and oral testimony about the disputed issues before a neutral administrative judge, who will decide who is right and issue an order imposing a decision. If you or the school district disagree with the decision, you can appeal to a federal or state court, all the way to the U.S. Supreme Court. But before you conjure up images of walking up the marble stairs to the highest court in the land, you should know that most disputes with school districts are resolved before a hearing and certainly before you find yourself in a courtroom.

There are some new rules for due process. When Congress amended IDEA in 2004, it made several important changes:

- Parents must file for due process within two years after they knew, or should have known, of the underlying dispute. If your state has its own deadline, the state rule will apply.
- Once a due process request has been filed, the other party has ten days to respond.
- Within 15 days after receiving a due process request, the school district must convene a meeting to try to resolve the dispute. The school district cannot have an attorney at this meeting unless the parents bring one.
- If parents bring a due process action for any improper purpose, "such as to harass, to cause unnecessary delay, or to needlessly increase the cost of litigation," they may have to pay the school district's attorney's fees. (20 U.S.C. § 1414.)

If you believe that your school has violated a legal rule—for example, by failing to hold an IEP meeting—you should file a complaint (discussed in Chapter 13). The complaint process is quite different from due process (covered in Chapter 12). A due process matter involves a factual dispute between you and the school district. A complaint involves a failure by the district to follow the law.

8. Suspension and Expulsion

Some children with disabilities have trouble behaving themselves in school. Like all other kids, children with disabilities sometimes act out, try to get attention in the wrong ways, or are more interested in their friends than their schoolwork. But sometimes, these children have behavioral problems that are directly related to their disabilities. A child with ADD who can't pay attention in class, a child whose developmental delays lead to immense frustration, or a child whose autism makes it hard to follow a teacher's instructions can create disciplinary

problems. A child who has secondary emotional difficulties because of a disability may be disruptive or even get into fights. How can schools balance their responsibility to maintain order with their duty to provide an appropriate education for children with disabilities?

Most states have laws and procedures about disciplinary action—including suspension and expulsion—quite separate from special education laws and procedures. These disciplinary rules apply to all students within a school district. For special education students, however, these rules must be applied in conjunction with the laws and procedures of IDEA, including specific protections that apply when a child with a disability is subject to suspension or expulsion. Like all children in school, your child must follow the rules; otherwise, he or she may be suspended or expelled. Before the school district can take this type of action, however, IDEA requires a very careful analysis of whether the disability played a role in your child's behavior and, if so, whether suspension or expulsion is really justified.

In 1997, Congress added many new rules to IDEA regarding the suspension and expulsion of special education students. Although these rules provide specific rights and procedures for children in special education who are subject to discipline, Congress clearly intended to allow school districts to remove students who misbehave or are dangerous.

Get some help if your child is in trouble. The IDEA rules and procedures applicable to suspensions and expulsions are pretty complicated—and the stakes for your child in these situations are potentially very high. This section provides an overview of this area of the law, but you'll probably want to contact a parent support group or special education lawyer if your child faces serious disciplinary action. This is one situation in which you shouldn't try to go it alone.

a. IDEA and Disciplinary Action

IDEA provides that a student with an IEP cannot have his or her program, placement, or services changed unless the school district and the child's parents agree to the change. Absent such an agreement, the child is entitled to remain or "stay put" in the current program until either a new IEP is signed or a hearing officer decides that the child's program can be changed. (20 U.S.C. § 1415(j).) The school district cannot remove your child or unilaterally change your child's program— if it tries to do so, you can assert your child's stay-put right to maintain the current placement until a new IEP is in place or a hearing officer approves the change. This very broad rule is intended to prevent a school from moving a child without parental approval.

A proposed suspension or expulsion clearly constitutes a change in placement, and this is where state laws on suspension and expulsion run directly into IDEA requirements. Can a school district suspend or expel (remove the child from school) without violating the stay-put rule? The answer is, as you probably expected, yes and no. The law clearly states that a child with disabilities can be suspended or expelled, but the suspension or expulsion cannot take place unless certain IDEA procedures are followed. (20 U.S.C. § 1415(j) and (k); these rules are further explained in the current IDEA regulations at 34 C.F.R. §§ 300.517-529.)

Congress created different rules depending on the length of the suspension or expulsion. This part of IDEA is fairly complex, but generally, children who are facing more than ten days out of school have more procedural protections under the law.

b. Suspensions or Expulsions for Up to Ten Days

Any special education child removed from school *for up to ten consecutive days* is not entitled to the IDEA procedures and protections. Because such a removal does not constitute a "change in placement," the child cannot claim the right to stay put. Because many suspensions are for fewer than ten consecutive days, most special education students who are suspended do not have the right to contest that removal based either on IDEA's stay-put rule or on IDEA's specific disciplinary procedures. In short, a child with disabilities can be suspended from school for up to 10 days just like any other student.

c. Suspensions and Expulsions Exceeding Ten Days

If a school district intends to suspend or expel a special education student for more than ten consecutive days, that *might* constitute a change in placement. In these situations, additional IDEA procedures kick in before the child can be removed. These procedures might also apply to a child who is removed from school for more than ten nonconsecutive days, if the removal represents a "pattern."

What is meant by a pattern? The law isn't entirely clear, but essentially you have to look at whether the frequency and length of the removals— and the total time the child is out of school— create a change in placement similar to that caused by a removal for more than ten consecutive days. Courts have begun to issue some decisions on what constitutes a pattern, but this is still a vague and uncertain part of the disciplinary process—and one good reason why you will probably want to talk to an expert and/or attorney if your child is in this situation.

Once a special education student is to be removed for more than ten days (whether consecutively or over a longer period of time), specific IDEA procedures kick in to protect the child. Before the removal takes place, an IEP team must hold a "manifestation review" to decide whether the student's behavior was a manifestation of his or her disability. If the IEP team determines that the behavior was a manifestation of the child's disability, then the student's placement cannot be changed except through an agreed-to IEP (signed by the school district and the parents) or a fair hearing decision. The child can remain in the current placement and assert his or her stay-put right. The student cannot be suspended (for more than ten days) or expelled unless the school follows IDEA procedures for a change in placement.

If the IEP team determines that the behavior was not a manifestation of the disability, the child has no stay-put rights and can be removed. To reach this conclusion, however, the team must decide that all three of the following statements are true:

- in relationship to the behavior that led to the disciplinary action, the IEP placement and services were appropriate and behavior intervention strategies were provided consistent with the IEP
- the child's disability did not impair his or her ability to understand the impact and consequences of the behavior, and
- the child's disability did not impair his or her ability to control the behavior subject to the disciplinary action.

(You can find these requirements in the current IDEA regulations at 34 C.F.R. § 300.523.)

d. Dangerous Behavior

IDEA makes an exception to the ten-day rule for disciplinary problems involving weapons or drugs. A special education student who brings a weapon to school or possesses, uses, sells, or solicits the sale of drugs at school or during a school function can be removed for up to 45 days without parental agreement. This means the student cannot assert the right to remain in the current placement pending the conclusion of the required IDEA disciplinary procedures. The student is entitled, however, to an "interim alternative placement" as determined by the IEP team.

e. Related Requirements

As a general rule, IDEA requires the IEP team to develop a "behavioral intervention" plan for students whose behavior "impedes his or her learning or that of others." (Current IDEA regulations at 34 C.F.R. § 300.346(a)(2)(i).) It would not be surprising if a special education student facing suspension or expulsion had such a plan in his or her IEP. If a student is removed for more than ten days, IDEA also requires the IEP team to do a "functional behavioral assessment" and implement a "behavioral intervention plan" if one is not already in place.

For a child whose disability impairs his or her ability to relate to others or behave appropriately, the plan should address those needs and provide strategies for helping that student improve peer relationships and/or school behavior. For example, a child who takes out the frustration of a disability by lashing out at other students might be taught alternative methods to express frustration, such as talking to a counselor, taking a "time out," or expressing anger more constructively ("I don't like it when you interrupt me when I'm speaking in class").

Need more information on discipline? For lots of great ideas on dealing with disciplinary and behavior problems, as well as detailed information on drafting behavioral intervention plans, check out the website of the Center for Effective Collaboration and Practice (a group dedicated to helping students, teachers, and parents address emotional and behavioral concerns) at http://cecp.air.org.

9. Additional IDEA Rights

IDEA provides for many rights, including the following additional mandates.

a. Summer School

Current IDEA regulations require the school district to provide children with summer school or an "extended school year" if necessary to meet their needs or if, without summer school, their skills will be affected by the pause in program and services. (34 C.F.R. § 300.309.)

b. Private School

IDEA gives your child the right to be placed in a nonprofit or private (including parochial) school if your school district cannot provide an appropriate program. (20 U.S.C. § 1412(a)(10).)

There must be an IEP agreement or due process or court ruling that the private school is appropriate before the school district is required to pay for a private school placement. If you place your child in a private school unilaterally—on your own—your school district is not required to pay.

Although the school district does not have to pay tuition costs for children whose parents place them in private school, it must offer special education and related services to these children. The school district need not provide these services at the private school, nor does it have to provide any services different than or in addition to those that would be available if the child were in public school.

Under the 2004 amendments to IDEA, school districts must now consult with private schools about whether and how special education and related services will be provided to children whose parents placed them in private school. The private school can file a complaint with the state educational agency if it feels the district is not complying with this "consultation" requirement in a timely and meaningful manner. (20 U.S.C. §1412(a)(10).) The law remains clear, however, that the school district does not have to provide services at the private school, so this new consultation or "right to talk" requirement doesn't create new or expanded rights for children whose parents place them in private school.

IDEA Notice Requirements and Private School Placements

If you plan to remove your child to a private program, you must notify the school district of your intent either:

- at the most recent IEP meeting you attended prior to removing your child from public school, or
- at least ten business days before the actual removal. (20 U.S.C. § 1412(a)(10)(C).)

If you don't provide this notice, and then pursue due process to seek reimbursement for your child's placement in a private school, reimbursement may be denied, or you may receive only partial payment.

---

c. Special Education in Prison

Imprisoned children between the ages of 18 and 21 who were identified and had an IEP prior to incarceration are also entitled to a free, appropriate public education. (20 U.S.C. § 1414(d)(7).)

B. Individualized Education Program

IEP may seem complicated—it is a meeting, a document, and a description of your child's entire educational program. While the IEP is discussed in detail in Chapters 10 and 11, here are a few introductory concepts:

- By law, you are an equal partner in the IEP process. As a general rule, no part of the IEP can be implemented without your approval.

- Your child's first time in special education will follow an initial eligibility IEP. Thereafter, IEP meetings will be held yearly, focusing on the specifics of your child's current educational program and what next year's IEP will look like. While the procedures for these two kinds of IEPs (called eligibility and program IEPs) are the same, there are some important differences—see Chapters 7, 10, and 11.

- You and the school district must agree to and sign an IEP before your child either begins special education initially or begins a new school year.

- Whenever you or your child's school district wants to change your child's current IEP, the district must schedule a new IEP meeting and develop a new written IEP. You and the school district can agree to hold the meeting via video conference or conference call, or agree to make changes in the written IEP without an IEP meeting. (See "New Rules for IEP Meetings," below.)

- You are entitled to an IEP meeting whenever you feel one is needed—for example, if you have concerns about your child's progress, there are classroom problems, or the related services or placement is not working.

- The IEP, once signed by you and the school district, is binding; the school district must provide everything included in that IEP.

New Rules for IEP Meetings

The 2004 amendments change some of the rules for IEP meetings. Here are some of the new provisions (Chapters 10 and 11 cover IEP meetings in detail):

- Changes to the IEP can now be made without a meeting, if both the parent and the school district agree and the changes are made in writing. If you decide to forgo an IEP meeting, you should make sure you understand the changes and that the written agreement reflects them accurately.

- IEP meetings can now be held by video conference or conference call rather than in person.

- Members of the IEP team can be excused from attending in certain circumstances, if you agree to their absence.

- If a child transfers from one school district to another (in or out of state), the new school district must provide a program "comparable" to the one described in the existing IEP.

- A new pilot program in about 15 locations will experiment with less-frequent IEP meetings. Each pilot can set up a system to develop IEPs that cover a period of up to three years, rather than the current model which requires annual IEPs. Participation will not be required—you and your child still have the right to annual IEPs if you wish— but this new program bears watching as a possible wave of the future.

This section provides details about the written IEP. Every IEP, in every school district in every state, must include the same information (although forms will vary).

1. Current Educational Status

The IEP must include a description of your child's current status in school in the areas of cognitive skills, linguistic ability, emotional behavior, social skills and behavior, and physical ability. (20 U.S.C. § 1414(d)(1)(A)(i).) Current functioning may be reflected in testing data, grades, reports, or anecdotal information, such as teacher observations. IDEA calls this the "present level of educational performance." This part of the IEP must describe how your child's disability affects his or her involvement and progress in the general curriculum. Formal testing or assessments of your child will provide a good deal of information.

 Chapters 6 and 8 cover evaluations and other ways to develop useful evidence of your child's educational status and needs.

2. Measurable Annual Goals

Goals are the nuts and bolts of your child's daily program as detailed in the IEP. They generally refer to academic, linguistic, and other cognitive activities, such as reading or math.

Example:

Goal: John will read a three-paragraph story and answer eight out of ten questions about the story correctly.

While goals are usually academic and cognitive in nature, there is no restriction on what goals may cover or say. They should reflect whatever the IEP team determines is important to your child's education. Goals can relate to physical education, how your child socializes with peers, even how your child will move about the school.

The current language of IDEA (as amended in 2004) refers to "measurable annual goals," including academic and functional goals designed to meet your child's educational and other needs

and enable him or her to be "involved in and make progress in the general curriculum." The law also requires your child's IEP to describe how yearly progress toward meeting these goals will be measured. (20 U.S.C. 1414(d)(1)(A).) This is a change from the former version, which required the IEP team to come up with "benchmarks"—short-term objectives that would help a child achieve these broader goals. It's not yet clear what effect this change will have, but the new language seems broad enough to encompass short-term, specific objectives (although they won't be called by that name) as well as long-term goals.

Whether your child is receiving a free appropriate public education (FAPE) may depend on whether the program offered by the school district can help him or her achieve the goals in the IEP. If you and the school district disagree about whether a specific placement or service is appropriate, one key issue will be whether your child's goals can be met without it.

 Chapter 9 shows you how to write goals that support your child's placement and service needs.

3. Instructional Setting or Placement

The IEP must include information about the appropriate instructional setting or placement for your child. Section A3, above, discussed various placement options; here are a few examples of specific IEP placements:

Examples:

- A child with significant physical disabilities or learning disabilities might be placed in a regular classroom with support services.
- A child with significant language and cognitive delays might be placed in a special class.
- A child who is terrified of large spaces and crowds could be placed in a small, protected nonregular school.

- A child with serious emotional difficulties might be placed in a residential program.

4. Related Services

As mentioned in Section A4, above, related services are developmental, corrective, and other supportive services necessary to facilitate your child's placement in a regular class or to allow your child to benefit from special education. These must be included specifically in the IEP.

Once the IEP team determines the appropriate related support services, the team should specify the nature of each service, including:

- when it begins
- the amount (such as all day, once a day, twice a week, once a week, or once a month)
- the duration (such as 15, 30, 45, or 60 minutes per session)
- the ratio of pupils to related service providers, and
- the qualifications of the service provider.

5. Other Required IEP Components

The IEP must also specifically address:

- how your child's disability affects his or her involvement and progress in the general curriculum used in the regular classroom
- how your child's need to be involved in general curriculum will be met
- how special education and related services will help your child advance toward attaining annual goals; be involved in general curriculum, extracurricular, and nonacademic activities; and participate with children with and without disabilities
- whether any program modifications or supports for school personnel are necessary for your child to benefit from special education
- how you will be regularly informed of your child's progress

- how your child will participate in any district or statewide assessment of student achievement used for the general education population, and whether any modifications or accommodations will be necessary
- how your child's transition services will be provided (once your child is 16 years old), and
- how your child's need for assistive technology will be met.

For blind and visually impaired students, the IEP team must provide for instruction in Braille and the use of Braille, unless the IEP determines that Braille is not appropriate. (20 U.S.C. § 1414 (d)(3)(B)(iii).)

In addition, IDEA requires that the IEP team "consider" the following:

- strategies, including positive behavioral interventions, to address the needs of children with behavior difficulties (20 U.S.C. § 1414(d)(3)(B)(i))
- the language needs of children with limited English proficiency (20 U.S.C. § 1414(d) (3)(B)(ii)), and
- the communication needs of deaf and hard of hearing children, including opportunities for direct communication with peers and staff, and instruction in the child's language and communication mode. (20 U.S.C. § 1414 (d)(3)(B)(iv).)

For more details, contact your school district, your state department of education (Appendix 2), or a disability group (Appendix 3). See Appendix 4 for a sample IEP that includes these provisions.

6. Optional Components

The IEP may include other components, such as specific teaching methods, particular class subjects, or anything else the IEP team agrees should be included. (20 U.S.C. § 1414(d)(1)(A).)

More Information: Special Education and Local Schools

Your school district is required by IDEA to provide you with a copy of federal and state statutes and regulations, and any relevant policies. Be sure to request this information, along with the school's IEP form. Most school districts have some kind of parent guide, as do most states. Contact your school district for a copy.

Examples:

- An autistic child may be instructed in a method called Lovaas.
- A deaf child may be taught in American Sign Language.

C. State Special Education Laws

IDEA is a federal law, binding on all states. The federal government provides financial assistance to the states to implement IDEA; in exchange, states must adopt laws that implement IDEA.

State laws generally parallel IDEA and often use identical language. State law can provide children with more, but not fewer, protections than IDEA does. IDEA is always your starting point, but you should check to see what your state law says about special education—it may provide more rights.

Each state's educational agency is responsible for making sure local school districts comply with the federal law. The federal government allocates billions of dollars a year to the states for special education. The pressure on states to come up with special education funding is significant, particularly given competing interests for education dollars. Moreover, while Congress promised, when IDEA was passed, to provide approximately 40% of its cost to states, it has actually provided only between 8% and 13%, which has created significant shortfalls for states and the local school

districts. The funding process varies from state to state, but it is often complex. No matter how your state funds special education, it is most important that you remember this general rule: Money (and how it gets from Washington to your state to your district to your child) should not determine what is in your child's IEP—but in reality, financial constraints affect almost all school districts.

Budgetary Constraints Are Getting Worse

Cost should not be a factor in determining the appropriate educational program for your child. If a school district says "we can't afford it," you can rightfully respond that the law requires the IEP team to make decisions based on your child's individual needs—not on the school's budget.

However, the sad truth is that state governments are facing rising deficits, which means that funding for schools is on the chopping block. As spending for education decreases, many schools will have to cut back on educational programs and staff. Unfortunately, this means that some districts will make IEP decisions based on budgetary constraints rather than on educational need. While you need not be swayed by arguments about funding, don't be surprised to hear them.

This problem will only get worse until federal and state governments start funding education and special education commensurate with their importance in our society. Even as laws that impose stricter standards for students, teachers, and classroom size go into effect, schools aren't given the funding they need to implement these new requirements. As a result, many educators are leaving the profession. Until parents and professionals unite to address this funding problem, legislators will continue to give education the short end of the fiscal stick.

D. Working With Your School District

Most, if not all, of your dealings will be with your local public school district, which has the legal responsibility for your child's IEP. Sometimes, however, special education programs are the responsibility of a larger educational unit, such as a county office of education. This is often the case when a school district is small or there are not enough children to establish a specific special education class.

The term used to describe the appropriate local educational agency can vary from state to state. Always start with the school district in which you reside. It has the ultimate responsibility for your child, even if there is a larger, area-wide agency involved. As used in this book, the term "local school district" refers to whatever educational unit is involved.

1. Key Players in the IEP Process

The key participants in the IEP process are:
- you
- your child (if appropriate)
- your child's teacher (potentially the best ally or worst enemy you have in the IEP process), whether a regular teacher or a special education teacher
- a school administrator with responsibility for special education—a site principal or special education administrator
- specialists, such as a school psychologist, speech or occupational therapist, communications specialist, or physical education specialist, and
- anyone else you or the school wants to attend, such as your child's physician, your lawyer, the school's evaluator, or an outside independent evaluator you selected.

New Teacher Certification Requirements

When Congress amended IDEA in 2004, it added language to conform the requirements of IDEA with the requirements of No Child Left Behind (NCLB), the education law passed in 2001. (For more on NCLB, see "No Child Left Behind," below.) IDEA now provides that any public elementary or secondary school special education teacher in your state must have obtained "full" state certification as a special education teacher, passed the state special education licensing examination, or completed valid state "alternative" certification requirements and hold a license to teach in your state. (20 U.S.C. §1401(10).) This rule does not apply to special education teachers in private or charter schools.

Chapter 10 covers the IEP participants in detail, including who has the critical roles, who has authority, and who should attend the IEP meetings. Chapter 10 also covers how to prepare yourself and your IEP participants for the IEP meeting.

More Information: State Special Education Laws

State special education laws (statutes) are normally found in the education code of each state. State departments of education often have their own regulations implementing the law.

Appendix 2 includes addresses, phone numbers, and websites of state departments of education. We highly recommend you get a copy of your state laws and any publications explaining your legal rights from your state department of education (many are online). Ask about the state special education advisory commission—IDEA requires that each state have one, composed of educators and parents.

Because laws and policies change, it is important to keep up to date, especially if you are involved in a dispute with your school. For more information on legal research, see Chapter 14.

---

2. The Realities of Schools and Special Education

School districts and their special education administrators are as varied as parents. Their programs, services, and budgets will differ, as will their personalities. All of these factors influence the kind of programs school districts offer and how they deal with children and parents. Depending on the population breakdown in the district, there may be many special education programs or only a few. Philosophical differences may have an impact on programs and services. Some administrators believe very firmly that most, if not all, children with disabilities should be mainstreamed or in regular education. Some administrators believe with equal vigor that special programs are important and children with disabilities, more often than not, belong in special classes.

Finding out what programs are in your district, and what personalities and philosophies you'll face, is important. Ask around. Talk to your child's teacher and other parents; go to a PTA meeting. Many school districts have community advisory committees for special education; the parents involved in that group can be invaluable resources and will likely know the specific programs and approaches in your school district.

Demonizing the "Other" Side

It is not uncommon for parents to view school administrators and other staff as impediments rather than partners in the special education process. Sometimes school personnel return the favor by viewing parents as unreasonable and difficult.

While there are times when such viewpoints are justified, remember that a majority of educators are passionate, hard-working, and caring individuals. They teach in a complicated environment with too much paperwork, too many requirements, and not enough support or pay. Demonizing all teachers or administrators does little more than polarize everyone—and your child is the one who will suffer from these strained relationships. Viewing everyone associated with the school as an enemy is a poor strategy for getting your child's needs met. And in most cases, it's simply not fair.

Of course, you should be vigilant and stick up for your rights, but remember that most folks on the other side of the table are there because they believe in your child. In return, you should expect those hard-working educators to see you as the determined, loving, and concerned parent that you are.

Chapter 8 provides detailed advice on how to explore available school programs. Chapter 15 discusses parent groups.

E. Some Overriding IEP Principles

In any endeavor, the details—particularly technical matters and legal language—can be overwhelming: IEP, due process, least restrictive environment, related services. What do these words really mean, and how do you use them to help your child?

As you go through this book and the IEP process, you will become more familiar and comfortable with IEP terms. Particularly in the early stages of your planning, keep your focus on the following key factors.

1. Your Child's Needs Dictate the Contents of the IEP

IDEA uses the term "unique" to describe your child's needs. As emphasized in this chapter, the IEP must fit the child, not the other way around. Practically speaking, this means that if your child needs a small class (fewer than ten children), a teacher with specific skills, and a variety of support services, then your local school district is required to provide them. Always ask whether a particular goal, service, placement, or other IEP component is providing your child with a free appropriate public education as required by law, and is serving his or her unique needs.

2. Factors Determining Individual Need

Your child's age, disability, and specific needs—academic, social, linguistic, emotional, cognitive, and physical—are key elements in determining the IEP. Of course, other factors may come into play, including necessary educational strategies, methodologies, and curricula.

3. Specific Classroom and Instructional Services

Your child's needs must translate into specific support or related services and a specific class or program. All the discussion in the world about unique needs will be meaningless if you and the IEP team don't eventually discuss (and come to terms on) services and placement.

4. Broad Discretion in Determining the IEP

It is human nature to want specificity. At some level, we may have liked Congress to have said exactly what should be part of a special education program, and what should go into the IEP. But in passing IDEA, Congress knew it could not say specifically what should be in an IEP for child #1 or #999 or #99,999. There are too many variables and too many individual considerations.

That is why IDEA does not say that a child with disabilities will be placed in a particular program with particular services. Instead, the unique needs of each child must determine what specific program and services are required. Thus, the IEP team has broad discretion. This flexibility is good for you, but also requires hard work and preparation on your part.

Section 504 of the Rehabilitation Act of 1973

Separate from any rights under IDEA, your child may also qualify for special services under the Rehabilitation Act of 1973 (29 U.S.C. § 794), more commonly known as Section 504. This is essentially an access law that prohibits a school district from denying your child access to an educational program or educational facilities. For more information on Section 504, see Chapter 7, Section E2.

No Child Left Behind

In 2001, Congress passed education legislation called "No Child Left Behind" (NCLB). When amending IDEA in 2004, Congress added language to align it with the requirements of NCLB, primarily by imposing standards for special education teacher qualifications and emphasizing the teaching of "core academic subjects": English, reading or language arts, math, science, foreign languages, civics and government, economics, arts, history, and geography.

NCLB's stated purpose is to increase "accountability" for schools by requiring rigorous state educational standards in reading and math and by mandating state testing to determine whether children are meeting those standards. Test results must be broken out by race, ethnicity, income, English proficiency, and disability. School districts that don't show yearly progress, as reflected in standards and testing, will be subject to corrective action and possibly even forced restructuring. Children who attend schools that are not making yearly progress will have the opportunity to transfer to other schools, including charter schools, and to obtain supplemental services.

The effects of NCLB remain uncertain because of its complex requirements and the federal government's failure to adequately fund the law. Some states are trying to "opt out" of NCLB's provisions, primarily because the law imposes major new requirements without the funds necessary to implement them. Some advocates worry that the lack of funding provided for NCLB could result in fewer dollars available for all educational programs, including special education. Because of these issues, NCLB is still a work in progress—and it isn't clear exactly how NCLB's mandates will affect special education. Contact your district and your state department of education to find out how the law will be administered locally.

3

Getting Started: Tips for All Parents

If your child has had a disability since birth or from a young age—perhaps he or she is in a wheelchair and needs support to access a regular classroom, is developmentally disabled, has difficulty writing, or has a hearing loss or reduced vision—you've probably known for a while that your child would need special education.

If you've just recently realized that your child is having difficulty in school—from a simple problem with reading or math to a profound problem involving cognitive functioning or emotional difficulties—you may not have given much thought to special education. Perhaps a teacher, pediatrician, neighbor, or friend has pointed something out to you. The recognition may come as surprise or even a shock. What does this mean for your child's immediate educational experience? What does it mean for the future? Will your child now be labeled—as learning disabled, visually impaired, emotionally disturbed?

The process you are about to embark on can be hard and frustrating. There may be times when the school makes life tough. Your child's difficulties may persist or even get worse. At times, the problems may seem insurmountable. There may be a teacher shortage, insufficient school funds, or awful program options. For all your preparation, you may feel like you're getting nowhere. The IEP process can be difficult and frustrating.

There may be times you ask yourself why this happened to your family. But if you plan, organize, and persevere, if you take small, daily steps (rather than try to solve the problem in one fell swoop), you will help your child. You may not make the school experience perfect, or even always tolerable, but your child will benefit from your efforts.

Whether you, your child's teacher, or another professional discovers the difficulty, your school district has a clear legal responsibility under IDEA to ensure that all children with special education needs within the district are identified, located, and evaluated (see Chapter 2, Section A1). Usually, this means (or should mean) that your child's teacher or the school principal, or perhaps the school psychologist, will contact you, indicate the areas of initial concern, and perhaps suggest a meeting to discuss these concerns. The school will then likely recommend an evaluation by a specialist in your child's disability. The evaluation is the first major step toward special education eligibility and the development of an IEP. (Chapter 6 discusses evaluations in detail.)

IDEA regulations are changing. The regulatory citations throughout this book are to the current IDEA regulations—those that will be in effect until the Department of Education issues final regulations interpreting the 2004 amendments to IDEA. The Department expects to release these final regulations at the end of 2005; many of them will be identical or similar to the existing regulations cited in this chapter (although the citations will be different), while others will be new. When you use this book, you should make sure that you have the most current version of the regulations. See "Warning: Special Education Rules Are in Flux," in Chapter 1, for information that will help you stay up to date. You can find the most recent version of IDEA, including the 2004 amendments, starting at 20 U.S.C. § 1400; the most pertinent sections are included in Appendix 1.

Parents of Children Between Three and Five Years Old

If your child is between ages three and five and is not yet enrolled in school, contact the local school district if you believe your child has a disability. Your child may be entitled to services under IDEA even before starting school. To be eligible, your child must be experiencing delays in physical, cognitive, communication, social, emotional, or adaptive development. (20 U.S.C. § 1401(3)(B).) If your child is found eligible, the IDEA rules and IEP procedures outlined in this book will apply.

Even though your school district has the responsibility to start the process, you shouldn't wait for the school to contact you if you have concerns. If you suspect that your child has special education needs and you haven't heard from the school district, get in touch with them. This chapter will help you get things started.

➡️ If your child has already been found eligible for special education or you have had experience with the IEP process, you can skip Section A. Even if you have been through the IEP process, however, be sure to read the discussion on securing your child's records in Section B. Many intelligent and determined parents who have been through numerous IEPs have not taken this important step.

A. First Steps

What's the first thing you should do if you believe your child is eligible for special education? There's no number to look up in the phone book. This section provides some suggestions on how to get started.

1. Recognize Your Child's Special Needs

It is very common for parents to realize that their child has unique needs and simply not know what to do about it. It may be that your child's problems can be isolated and addressed very specifically, or the problems may be more serious. But don't assume the worst; let the information you gather determine how serious the matter is and what you should do about it.

Start by focusing on your child's specific difficulties. Think back and consider whether your child has experienced any of the following:

- academic problems in reading, spelling, or math

- delays in developmental areas, such as language or fine motor skills
- difficulties processing or retaining information, such as understanding simple instructions or problems with short- or long-term memory
- social or emotional problems
- trouble sleeping, eating, or getting along with the family
- sustained difficulties in paying attention or staying focused
- inappropriate or hyperactive behavior, or
- delays in physical milestones or other physiological difficulties, such as hearing loss, sight problems, difficulties with mobility, or handwriting problems.

Write down what you can remember about your child's past behavior or what you've observed recently. Try to think clearly, focusing on specific behavior patterns. You may feel some emotional upheaval or fear; you may even worry that you have done something wrong. These feelings are normal. Almost everyone who has had a child in special education has felt exactly as you do right now.

A child who is having difficulty in school will not automatically qualify for special education. There may be interim steps or nonspecial education solutions for your child. Those steps are discussed below, in Section A3.

At this stage, you may also want to contact the school principal to request information about special education.

📄 A sample letter requesting information on special education is below; a blank, tear-out copy is in Appendix 5.

💡 **Get into the habit of writing.** You can always request information about special education by calling the school principal, who is likely to either provide the information or refer you to the district's special education administrator. But it's better to make your request in writing. A letter is

Request for Information on Special Education

Date: February 20, 20xx

To: Ronald Pearl, Principal

Mesa Verde Elementary School

123 San Pablo Ave.

San Francisco, CA 94110

Re: Amber Jones, student in second-grade class of Cynthia Rodriguez

I am writing to you because my child is experiencing difficulties in school. I understand there is a process for evaluating a child and then determining eligibility for special education programs and services. Please send me any written information you have about that process. Please also send me information about how I can contact other parents and local support groups involved in special education.

Thank you very much for your kind assistance. I look forward to talking with you further about special education.

Sincerely,

Mary Jones

Mary Jones

243 Ocean Ave.

San Francisco, CA 94110

Phones: 555-1234 (home); 555-2678 (work)

more formal, won't be forgotten as easily as a phone call, and creates a record of your contact with your school district. In this book, you will be reminded frequently of the importance of putting things in writing.

2. Make a Formal Request to Start the Special Education Process

At any time, you can formally ask to begin the process of special education evaluation. To start:

- Call your school and ask for the name and phone number of the special education administrator.
- Call the special education administrator and ask about the eligibility process in the district.
- Follow up your phone call with a written request (and keep a copy for your records).

A sample letter making a formal request to start the special education process and conduct an evaluation is below; a blank, tear-out copy is in Appendix 5. Other sample letters in this chapter make slightly different requests. You can combine some or all of these requests into one letter, if you wish.

3. Gather Information

Whether you plan to begin the formal evaluation process right away or wait a bit, you should start gathering information on your child's situation. Here are some good ways to start.

a. Talk to Your Child's Teacher

Find out what your child's teacher thinks is going on and recommends as a possible solution. Here are a few specific questions to ask:

- What are the teacher's observations? What are the most outstanding and obvious

problems, and how serious are they? Is it a problem with math, reading, or broader cognitive issues (processing information or memory lags)? Does the problem have social or emotional manifestations?

- Would some adjustments in the classroom help, such as extra attention from the teacher, after-school tutoring, or measures to address behavioral problems?
- What recommendations might be useful at home? Does the teacher think that you need to spend more time on homework, walking your child through certain subject matters?
- What are the observations, conclusions, and recommendations of other school personnel?
- Are your child's difficulties serious? Do they require more formal special education involvement? If so, what are the next steps?

If you and the school agree to go ahead with interim, nonspecial education steps, be sure to monitor your child's progress closely so you can determine whether they are working. Chapter 8, Section B, provides suggestions about tracking your child's progress.

b. Talk to Your Child's Pediatrician

Your child may have an organic or medical problem. Although most pediatricians are not experts in special education, they can discuss a child's developmental stage; other health-related matters that will affect the educational experience; and cognitive, physical, linguistic, and emotional factors that might impact special education eligibility and possible educational solutions.

c. Talk With Other Parents

The local PTA should have information on parents with special education children, and most school districts have advisory committees of parents with children in special education. Call the school principal to find out about these groups.

Request to Begin Special Education Process and Evaluation

Date: _____ February 20, 20xx _____

To: Ronald Pearl, Principal

      Mesa Verde Elementary School

      123 San Pablo Ave.

      San Francisco, CA 94110

Re: Amber Jones, student in second-grade class of Cynthia Rodriguez

I am writing to you because my child is experiencing difficulties in school.

[Describe specific difficulties your child is exhibiting.] _____

_____

_____

_____

_____

_____ .

I am formally requesting that the school immediately begin its special education process, including initial evaluation for eligibility. I understand that you will send me an evaluation plan that explains the tests that may be given to my child. Because I realize the evaluation can take some time, I would appreciate receiving the evaluation plan within ten days. Once you receive my approval for the evaluation, please let me know when the evaluation will be scheduled.

I would also appreciate any other information you have regarding the evaluation process, how eligibility is determined, and general IEP procedures.

Thank you very much for your kind assistance. I look forward to working with you and your staff.

Sincerely,

Mary Jones

Mary Jones

243 Ocean Ave.

San Francisco, CA 94110

Phones: 555-1234 (home); 555-2678 (work)

Chapter 15 explains how to find or start a parents' group. Appendix 3 has information on various national special education support groups.

d. Do Some Research

Look for written materials on special education and your child's area of difficulty. A wealth of information is available online.

Appendix 3 has information on special education materials and organizations, both general and disability specific.

B. Obtain Your Child's School Records

As a part of your information gathering, it's important to find out what is in your child's school file and what effect it will have on the IEP process. You'll need this information to assess the seriousness of your child's difficulties and the possible need for special education. If your child is found eligible for special education, reviewing the school file will help you determine the services and programs that may be appropriate.

Whether you are new at this or have been through many IEPs, whether you anticipate a major change in your child's educational program or no change at all, and even if you're not sure that you want your child in special education in the first place, it is important to secure copies of your child's school file on a yearly basis. New and important items may be added each year.

While the contents of your child's file may vary, it is likely you will find:

- report cards and other progress reports
- medical data (immunization records, health reports)
- attendance records
- disciplinary reports

- testing data
- assessments and other testing material
- teacher comments and other observations, and
- pictures of your child (it's fun to see the kindergarten picture, the second grade picture with the missing teeth, and so on).

1. Your Right to Access Your Child's School File

You have a legal right to inspect and review any education records relating to your child. If your child is already in the special education system, you have this right under IDEA. (20 U.S.C. § 1415(b)(1).) The rules in this section refer to children already in the special education system.

 Getting records for kids who aren't in special education. If your child has not yet been found eligible for special education, you still have a legal right to his or her file under the Family Educational Rights and Privacy Act (FERPA). (20 U.S.C. § 1232(g).) State law may also provide a right to your child's file, separate from IDEA or FERPA rights. State law can vary, however, and you should find out the specifics—such as how requests should be made and how long the school has to provide you the file. Call your state department of education or your school district for information regarding these rules.

2. How to Get Copies of Your Child's File

When seeking a copy of your child's school file, make a written request for *everything*. The written request should go to the administrator in your school district who is responsible for special education. That may be the school principal or a person in your district's central office. The site principal can refer you to the appropriate person.

A sample letter requesting your child's school file is below; a blank, tear-out copy is in Appendix 5.

IDEA requires that your child's school grant your request without unnecessary delay and before any IEP meeting. The school must send you the file within 45 days, although it can and should send it more quickly. (See 34 C.F.R. § 300.562(a) of the current IDEA regulations.) The Family Educational Rights and Privacy Act includes the same 45-day deadline.

If you have any problem getting a copy of your child's school file in a timely manner:

- Call and write the appropriate administrator, indicating that the law requires the school to provide the records without "unnecessary delay."
- If the principal or administrator does not respond to your request, contact the school district superintendent and your state department of education. Failure to provide you with your child's records is a violation of the law. Chapter 13 covers procedures for handling legal violations by your district.

Some states have tighter deadlines. Your state special education law may give schools a shorter deadline to provide copies of your child's record than the 45-day limit provided by IDEA. California schools, for example, must provide copies of the record within five days of a parent's request. Get a copy of your state's special education laws from your department of education early on so you know your rights—and cite the law when you request your child's file.

3. Cost of Getting Files

Under current IDEA regulations, the school may charge a fee for making copies of your child's records, as long as the fee "does not effectively prevent you from exercising your right to inspect and review those records." (34 C.F.R. § 300.566.) This means that you cannot be charged an excessively high fee—or *any fee at all*, if you can show you cannot afford it. In addition, the school cannot charge a fee for searching and retrieving records.

If your child is not in special education, any fee for records might violate the Rehabilitation Act of 1973 (29 U.S.C. § 794) and the federal Freedom of Information Act. At least one court (*Tallman v. Cheboygan Area School*, 454 N.W. 2d 171 (Mich. Ct. App. 1990)) has said that charging a fee for search and retrieval would violate the Freedom of Information Act.

While some districts can be very uncooperative about providing free copies of your child's file, others provide them as a matter of course. If your district charges you an excessive fee for searching and retrieving the file or charges you when you can't afford to pay a fee, write a letter to your administrator.

Request for Child's School File

Date: <u>March 3, 20xx</u>

To: <u>Ronald Pearl, Principal</u>

<u>Mesa Verde Elementary School</u>

<u>123 San Pablo Ave.</u>

<u>San Francisco, CA 94110</u>

Re: <u>Amber Jones, student in second-grade class of Cynthia Rodriguez</u>

I would like a copy of my child's file, including all tests, reports, evaluations, grades, notes by teachers or other staff members, memoranda, photographs—in short, *everything* in my child's school file. I understand I have a right to these files under <u>IDEA, specifically</u> <u>20 U.S.C. § 1415(b)(1) [or the Family Educational Rights and Privacy Act (FERPA) (20 U.S.C. § 1232 (g)) if your child has not yet been found eligible for special education].</u>

I would greatly appreciate having these files within the next five days. I would be happy to pick them up. I will call you to discuss how and when I will get the copies.

Thank you for your kind assistance.

Sincerely,

Mary Jones

Mary Jones

243 Ocean Ave.

San Francisco, CA 94110

Phones: 555-1234 (home); 555-2678 (work)

Request for Reduction or Waiver of Fee Charged for Child's School File

Date: March 20, 20xx

To: Ronald Pearl, Principal
Mesa Verde Elementary School
123 San Pablo Ave.
San Francisco, CA 94110

Re: Amber Jones, student in second-grade class of Cynthia Rodriguez

On March 3, 20xx, I requested copies of everything in my child's school file. Your secretary called me on March 19, 20xx, and stated that there would be a fee for the copies [*or* an excessive fee, or a fee for searching and retrieving]. IDEA specifically states that you cannot charge a fee if it prevents me from exercising my right to inspect and review my child's file. I am on a fixed income and I cannot afford the fee you are charging.

[*or:* IDEA prohibits you from charging such a high fee. A fee of 15¢ a copy seems fair, not $1 a copy.]

[*or:* IDEA specifically prohibits you from charging a fee for searching for and retrieving the files.]

Therefore, I would appreciate it if you would send me copies, at no cost, at once. Thank you for your kind attention to this matter.

Mary Jones
Mary Jones
243 Ocean Ave.
San Francisco, CA 94110
Phones: 555-1234 (home); 555-2678 (work)

Go for the Copies

IDEA allows you to inspect and review your child's school file as well as receive copies. (Current IDEA regulations at 34 C.F.R. § 300.562.) These are two different rights—and you should exercise them both. You should always get copies of your child's file. If you can, you should also go to the school and review the original file, just to make sure the school district gave you everything.

4. What to Look for in Your Child's School File

Items that you are likely to find in your child's file are listed at the beginning of this section. As you review those documents, look for any information about your child's performance and needs, as well as comments from teachers and other professionals.

 Chapter 4 discusses in greater detail how to organize your child's records.

5. Amending Your Child's File

You have the right to request that any false, inaccurate, or misleading information, or information that violates the privacy or other rights of your child, be amended or removed from your child's school file. You also have the right to an explanation of the records. (34 C.F.R. §§ 300.562(b)(1) and 300.567 of the current IDEA regulations.)

If the school refuses to amend or remove the information, you have the right to a due process hearing on the issue. (See Chapter 12.)

 A sample request to amend the child's school file is below; a blank, tear-out copy is in Appendix 5.

Request to Amend Child's School File

Date: _April 1, 20xx_

To: _Ronald Pearl, Principal_

Mesa Verde Elementary School

123 San Pablo Ave.

San Francisco, CA 94110

Re: _Amber Jones, student in second-grade class of Cynthia Rodriguez_

I recently reviewed a copy of my child's file and would like to have a portion of the file amended, specifically:

The memorandum from the school psychologist, Ms. Taylor, stating that my child had

severe emotional problems, is inaccurate and inappropriate because Ms. Taylor did no

testing and only briefly observed my child. This is insufficient to support the conclusion

she reached.

IDEA gives me the right to request that all information that is "inaccurate or misleading, or violates the privacy of [my] child" be amended. (34 C.F.R. § 300.567.) I feel that this is just such a case and, therefore, request that you rectify the situation immediately.

Please notify me in writing as soon as possible of your decision regarding this matter. Thank you.

Sincerely,

Mary Jones

Mary Jones

243 Ocean Ave.

San Francisco, CA 94110

Phones: 555-1234 (home); 555-2678 (work)

4

Getting Organized

Whether you are entering special education for the first time or preparing for your child's tenth IEP, you will be dealing with many issues and tasks, and vast amounts of written material. This chapter will help you organize the information you'll need throughout the IEP process. It also explains how to most effectively plan your IEP year.

Gathering information, getting organized, and figuring out what should go into your child's program are all related. If you haven't yet read Chapter 3, be sure to review Section B on securing your child's school file before proceeding. And when you get to Chapter 5 on developing an IEP blueprint for your child's ideal program and services, you will use much of the information from this chapter.

Use the Forms in This Book

Nearly two dozen sample forms, checklists, and letters appear throughout this book, with tear-out copies in Appendix 5. You can simply photocopy (make as many copies as necessary) and insert the relevant forms into your IEP binder—either as a separate section or folded into one of the major sections listed below. The IEP blueprint (discussed in Chapter 5) is one key document you should include as a separate section in your binder. Another is the IEP material organizer form (discussed in Chapter 10), which you'll use to highlight key information in your binder and easily access your materials during the IEP meeting. These and other forms have spaces for far more information than you'll be ready to provide right now. That's okay. You're just getting started. It's perfectly fine to leave many of the form sections blank. You can fill them in later, as you read this book and get into the IEP process.

A. Start an IEP Binder

Many parents have found a simple three-ring binder with clearly labeled sections to be an invaluable organizing tool. A binder allows you to keep everything in one convenient location—from report cards to IEP forms.

Include every important document in your IEP binder. What's an important document? Anything containing substantive information about your child or procedural information concerning how and when things happen in the IEP process. While certain items can probably go into a file drawer, if you have any doubt, add them to your binder.

Listed below are some of the most important materials for your binder. Make as many sections as necessary to help you easily locate the information you'll need throughout the IEP process.

1. Your Child's File and Relevant School Materials

Your child's school records will play a key role at the IEP meeting, in developing the IEP itself, and possibly at any due process mediation or hearing. As emphasized in Chapter 3, Section B, you should get copies of *everything* in your child's school file, including report cards, attendance and disciplinary records, evaluations and testing data, and teacher comments. Review the documents carefully and put important items in your binder.

You can put everything in one large section of your binder labeled "school records," or you can divide the material into several sections. You'll probably have an easier time locating the information if you break it down into categories.

In addition to your child's file, your binder should include other relevant school materials, such as:

- evaluations
- samples of your child's work
- notes from your child's teacher and other staff members

- correspondence to and from the school
- past IEPs
- your notes and information on available programs and services, including the qualifications of particular teachers or service providers within the school district (Chapter 8 discusses how to develop information on available school options), and
- forms and informational materials sent to you by the school district, such as the school's IEP form and copies of key statutes and regulations on special education. (As mentioned earlier, the school is required by IDEA to provide you with a copy of federal and state statutes and regulations.)

Always get a copy of your school's IEP form. Whether you're new to the IEP process or you've been through it before, be sure to get a copy of the local IEP form (this varies from district to district) and any school guidelines on the IEP process. Because IDEA was amended in 2004, your school district is likely to change its form, so it's important to make sure you have the most current copy. Keep the form and related materials in your binder. (You can find an example of an IEP form in Appendix 4.)

Binder Versus File Drawer

As your child progresses in school, your binder could quickly become unwieldy. Consider developing a new one each year. You can keep a file drawer or box of dated material—for example, "2004 evaluation" or "2005 report cards." Include in your binder only information that is relevant to the current IEP year.

---

2. Your Child's Health and Medical Records

Your child's school file will probably include some medical information, such as the results of hearing or vision tests done at school. Be sure your binder includes these as well as medical records and important letters from your child's pediatrician and other health professionals.

3. Independent Evaluations

As explained in Chapter 8, an independent evaluation may be the most important document supporting what you want for your child. You'll definitely want to keep a copy of all independent evaluations in your binder.

4. Information on Programs and Services Outside the School District

If you're exploring private programs or service options, such as a specialized school for children with autism, be sure to include details in your binder, such as suggestions made by other parents, school brochures, and notes of your conversations and visits. (Chapter 8 explains how to develop information on programs and services outside of your school district.)

5. Special Education Contacts

You'll want to have a list of the names, mailing addresses, phone and fax numbers, and email addresses of people you will deal with on a regular basis, such as your child's teacher, the district's special education administrator, your child's physician, the school nurse, staff members who provide related services, parents or parent groups, and the like.

Keep this list of contacts in a prominent place in the front of your binder. Also, keep a copy with you, should you need to phone or write any of your contacts when you're away from home.

A sample Special Education Contacts form is below; a blank, tear-out copy is in Appendix 5. Make as many copies as you need.

Special Education Contacts

Name, Address, Phone and Fax Numbers, and Email Address

School Staff

School: Lewis Elementary, 123 Rose St., Chicago, 60611; 555-1234 (main phone), 555-5678 (fax)

David Werner, Principal, 555-9876, DWE@aol.com

Charlene Hanson, District Special Ed. Administrator, 4444 Main, Chicago, 60611; 555-4201 (phone),
555-7451 (fax), chsed @dusd.edu

Thayer Walker, Carrie's teacher, 567 Elm Ave., Chicago, 60611 (home); 555-0111 (classroom),
555-0114 (home)

Dr. Judy Goffy, school psychologist, 555-4333 (phone); 555-7455 (fax), drjg@aol.com

Outside Professionals

Dr. Hugh Maloney, independent evaluator, 780 Spruce Lane, Chicago, 60612; 555-5169 (phone),
555-5170 (fax), drhm @compuserv.com

Martha Brown, tutor, 2229 Franklin, Chicago, 60612; 555-1490

Other Parents

Kevin Jones (son Robert in Carrie's class), 7 Plainview Dr., Chicago, 60614; 555-5115, kj@aol.com

Melaney Harper, District Community Advisory Chair, 764 Rockly, Chicago, 60610; 555-7777 (phone),
555-9299 (fax)

Support Groups

Chicago Learning Disabilities Association (contact: Mark Kelso), 775 Kelly Rd., Chicago, 60610;
555-6226 (phone), 555-7890 (fax), chldas@aol.com

State Department of Education

Special Ed. Office (contact: Dr. Hillary Casper), State Department of Education, 88 Capitol Row,
Springfield, 61614; 217-555-8888 (phone), 217-555-9999 (fax), ilsped@worldnet.att.net

Other

Dr. Joan Landman, Carrie's pediatrician, 32 Ashford Rd., Chicago, 60611; 555-2222 (phone),
555-0987 (fax)

Illinois Special Ed. Advocates (Steve Miller, Esq.), 642 Miller Dr., Chicago, 60611; 555-4511 (phone),
555-8709 (fax), spedatt@netcom.com

6. IEP Journal

The importance of keeping a record of all conversations, visits, and information-gathering activities, whether on the phone or in person, cannot be overemphasized. In particular, you want to note the following in an IEP journal:

- the date and time of the conversation or meeting
- the names and positions of all people who participated in the discussion, such as your child's teacher, other school staff, the special education administrator, your pediatrician, or another parent
- what was said by whom (this is *really* important), and
- any necessary follow-up actions (for example, a person you should call).

You'll want to fill in your IEP journal just as soon as possible after a conversation or meeting has ended. The longer you wait, the more likely you are to forget certain details or confuse dates, times, and statements or promises made. Don't be shy about taking notes when you meet or talk with someone. To establish written verification of what you've been told, you'll want to send a confirming letter soon after your conversation. Confirming letters are covered in the following section.

A sample IEP Journal page is below; a blank, tear-out copy is in Appendix 5. Make several copies and keep a few with you—to use if you make phone calls from work, for example. Use the class visitation checklist in Chapter 8, Section C, to keep detailed notes on visits to school programs.

IEP Journal

Date: _____11/3/04_____   **Time:** _____4:30_____ a.m./p.m.

Action: ☒ Phone Call ____201-555-0105_____   ☐ Meeting _____

☐ Other: _____

Person(s) Contacted: _____Dr. P. Brin (Sp. Ed. Administrator)_____

Notes: ___I explained that Steve is having problems in reading, comp., and spelling, plus some___ social difficulties.

I said Steve needs an aide.

Dr. B: "We can't do that now; wait until the IEP."

I said we need IEP at once.

Dr. B: "We just had one; can't schedule another for at least _two_ months."

IEP Journal

Date: _____11/5/04_____   **Time:** _____2:10_____ a.m./p.m.

Action: ☐ Phone Call _____   ☒ Meeting ____Washington School_____

☐ Other: _____

Person(s) Contacted: _____Met w/ T. Walker (teacher)_____

Notes: ___T. Walker said, "Steve will need at least two hours per day of a 1:1 aide next year."___

I asked if he needs an aide now.

T. Walker: "Probably."

7. Confirming Letters

Confirming what someone has said to you creates some proof of that conversation. A confirming letter can provide useful evidence—of what was said, by whom, and when—for an IEP meeting or a due process hearing.

To be sure the school district receives confirming letters, send them certified mail, return receipt requested.

Example:

Your son needs a good deal of one-to-one help. You believe that a qualified aide should sit with him to work on reading, math, and spelling at least half of the school day. Your child's teacher tells you during a classroom visit that he agrees that your son needs one-to-one help for much of the day. In addition, the special education administrator admits to you that the current amount of aide time your son is receiving is not enough. You note both of these conversations in your IEP journal and send the administrator a confirming letter. Later, at the IEP meeting, the administrator balks at providing your son with more aide time. Your confirming letter will be quite helpful in establishing that both your son's teacher and the school administrator told you your son needs more aide time.

Sample Confirming Letter

> Date: May 14, 20xx
>
> To: Salvador Hale, Special Education Administrator
> Coconut County School District
> 1003 South Dogwood Drive
> Oshkosh, WI 50000
>
> Re: Rodney Brown,
> fourth grader at Woodrow Wilson School
>
> I appreciated the chance to speak with you yesterday regarding Rodney's current problems with reading comprehension. I agree with your comment that he will need at least half of the day with a one-on-one aide. I look forward to our IEP meeting next week and resolving Rodney's current difficulties in school.
>
> Sincerely,
>
> *Martin Brown*
>
> Martin Brown
> 145 Splitleaf Lane
> Oshkosh, WI 50000
> Phones: 555-4545 (home); 555-2500 (work)

8. Calendars

Section B, below, describes the tasks and events that typically take place during the yearly IEP process, and Section D explains how to keep track of these tasks and events on a monthly calendar. To stay organized, keep a copy of your calendar in your binder.

B. The Yearly IEP Cycle

Part of successful organizing is having a clear sense of when things happen in the IEP cycle. Once your child is evaluated and found eligible for special education, the yearly IEP process will involve three broad considerations:

- Review—how are things currently going?
- Reassess—what additional information is needed?
- Rebuild—will the program be the same next year, or does it need changing?

IDEA requires that an IEP be in place before your child begins the school year. (20 U.S.C. § 1414(d)(2)(A).) To develop a complete IEP, you'll need to gather information, deal with evaluations, prove that your child is eligible for special education, prepare for the IEP meeting, attend the IEP meeting, and work out any disagreements you might have with the school. This means you'll have to start planning well in advance to make sure everything gets done in time.

The best way to think about the IEP cycle is to start from your final goal—an IEP in place by the start of the school year—and work backward.

1. Finish Before Summer

To make sure that all special education issues are resolved before the school year begins, you will want an IEP meeting in the spring of the preceding year. This will give you time to resolve any disputes before the next school year starts. Because school personnel are usually gone during the summer, plan for the IEP meeting in May—or better yet, April—in case there is a dispute that has to be resolved through due process.

2. Request Your Meeting During the Winter

To ensure that your child's IEP meeting takes place in the spring, put the school district on notice by submitting a written request in February or March stating that you want the annual IEP meeting in April or May.

3. Begin Planning in the Fall

You'll need to be well prepared for the spring IEP meeting. Don't start collecting information a few weeks or even a month or two in advance. You'll need much more time than that. Start in the fall or early winter of the preceding year.

4. The Cycle Isn't Set in Stone

Let's say you've just discovered that your child's problems in school might require special education. It's October. You didn't participate in the IEP cycle the previous year because it wasn't an issue. You'd prefer not to wait until the spring to have an IEP meeting to develop a plan for the following year, as your child would lose almost a whole year of school. Or, you went through the IEP cycle the previous year, but the current program is not working. It's November, and you don't want to wait until spring for a new program. What do you do?

Speak up. Don't wait until spring to raise issues that need immediate attention. Start gathering information, and request an evaluation and IEP meeting ASAP. The IEP cycle is an ideal, but you should request an immediate IEP meeting if you need one.

Midyear IEP meetings are a bad idea. Many students' IEP meetings take place in December or January. While you can request an IEP meeting at any time (and you should when there is an immediate concern), it is not generally a good idea to have your yearly IEPs after school starts. Otherwise, you'll be making decisions after your child is already in a program. The easiest way to get back on schedule is to indicate at the midyear IEP meeting that you want another one at the end of the school year, preferably in April or May. Follow up your request with a confirming letter.

C. Sample Year in the Life of Your Child's IEP

Let us assume you are planning for the school year that begins in the fall of 2006. Ideally, by starting your preparation a year ahead of time, in the fall of 2005, you will have enough time without rushing or facing last-minute problems.

The sections below follow the general IEP yearly calendar and are intended to give you an introduction to the IEP year. Specific tasks are listed in each section; you'll find the details in Chapters 5 through 11.

1. Information Gathering: Fall (September-December)

No matter how many times you have been through the special education process, the fall months are generally a good time to gather information and develop a sense of what your child's program should be. The specific tasks include the following:

- Talk to teachers, school staff, and other parents (Chapter 3, Section A3).
- Request copies of your child's school records (Chapter 3, Section B).
- Request an evaluation of your child as appropriate (Chapter 6).
- Begin drafting your child's blueprint (Chapter 5).
- Schedule visits to your child's class or other programs you think might be viable (Chapter 8, Section C).
- Gather other information, such as letters from your pediatrician and your child's tutor (Chapter 8, Section F).

2. Evaluation: Winter (January and February)

After the first few months of school, the key issues for your child should begin to crystallize for you. You will know that your child needs to be in special education or, if already eligible for special education, what programmatic components make sense. Now is the time to assess what information you have or need to make a strong case for eligibility. Steps to take include the following:

- Assess the current information in your child's record and decide whether it supports your IEP goals for your child.
- Monitor the progress your child is making under the current program.
- Complete additional evaluations, if you need more supporting information (discussed in Chapters 6 and 8). Depending on who will be doing any additional evaluations and their calendars, you may need to plan for them earlier in the year.
- Continue developing your child's IEP blueprint (Chapter 5).

3. IEP Preparation and IEP Meeting: Spring (March-May)

Spring is when you focus on working toward getting an IEP program in place for your child. This may be the most labor-intensive time of the whole cycle. Tasks include the following:

- Finalize your child's IEP blueprint of program and service needs (Chapter 5).
- Draft goals for your child's IEP program (Chapter 9).
- Prepare for the IEP meeting and invite participants who will speak on your child's behalf (Chapter 10).
- Attend the IEP meeting (Chapter 11).

4. Dispute Resolution: Spring-Summer (June-August)

If you did not reach an agreement with the school administrators on your child's IEP program, then you can, as discussed earlier, go to a due process mediation or hearing. It is important that this process is completed before the beginning of the new year. (See Chapter 12 for information on due process.)

5. School Begins: Fall (September)

You've been through your first (or another) IEP cycle. You'll want to monitor your child's progress in school and see if the IEP program is working. Remember: If it's not, you can request another IEP meeting and try to come up with some changes that make sense.

D. Keep a Monthly Calendar

It is vitally important to keep track of details of IEP tasks (such as drafting goals) and events (such as evaluations, school visits, and the IEP meeting).

Write everything down on a monthly calendar (your own or the form provided here), including dates on which:

- you were told things would happen—for example, "Scott's school file should be mailed today"
- you need to schedule a meeting—for example, "Request IEP meeting no later than today"
- you need to call or meet with someone such as a teacher, a pediatrician, or another parent, or
- you need to start or complete a particular task, such as develop an IEP blueprint.

A sample Monthly IEP Calendar is below; a tear-out copy is in Appendix 5. Make copies for each month of the year.

E. Track Your Child's Progress

Whether your child is just entering special education or already has an IEP in place, it's vitally important that you keep track of his or her progress in school. Gauging how well your child is doing will help you in several ways:

- It will provide you with a basis for comparing one semester or year to the next, and one subject to the next. If you don't keep close tabs on your child's progress, you won't know whether he or she is improving or getting worse, whether certain subjects are posing more difficulty than others as time goes by, or whether a particular classroom, service, or teaching methodology is having a positive effect.
- It will help you make your case for eligibility. If your child is not yet in the special education system, you can use the materials you gather to show that your child's academic achievement is not what it should be, or that certain subjects are posing particular difficulty.
- It will help you draft effective goals. When you sit down with the IEP team to write goals for your child, you will know exactly what subjects give him or her trouble—and where he or she needs to work especially hard to see improvement. This will help

Monthly IEP Calendar

Month and Year: Oct '05

1	2	3	4	5	6	7
		Call Dr. Brin (Request visit)		Follow up evalua-tion request if not received		
8	9	10	11	12	13	14
	Meet w/ Janice re: her son's experiences			Call Dr. Pearl re: recomm. on auditory problem		
15	16	17 Call at 4 p.m. T. Walker to discuss Steve's sign reading problem	18	19 Send school written request for evaluation	20	21
22	23 Call J. Brown of parent group	24	25 4:15 meet w/ T. Walker	26	27	28
29	30	31 Begin Steve's IEP blueprint				

you tailor the goals to your child's particular needs. (See Chapter 9 for more on goals.)

- It will help you argue for a particular placement or service. If your child is not making appropriate progress, you can argue that the current placement or related services need to be changed. Keeping track of how your child is doing in every subject will give you the information you need to evaluate your child's educational program.

- It will help you develop a positive relationship with your child's teacher. Most teachers welcome parents who want to play an active role in their child's education, as long as the parents are respectful of the teacher's time and experience. By keeping in touch with your child's teacher and weighing in on issues of special concern, you'll help the teacher do a better job educating your child. And there's a lot that parents can learn from teachers, too—including which teaching methods might be appropriate, or what exercises or activities you can do at home to reinforce classroom lessons.

Get into the habit of reviewing all of your child's homework, classroom assignments, tests, and teacher reports. (Be sure to keep any that seem to really illustrate your child's difficulties or successes for your IEP binder.) Plan to visit your child's classroom often—volunteer your time, serve as a class parent, or participate in planned activities for parents. This will give you a chance to see how your child does in the classroom environment.

Talk to the teacher to set up a reasonable schedule for a brief update or conversation about your child. Remember, most teachers have more work to do than they have hours to do it in, so don't expect to hear from the teacher every day or every week. Instead, ask for some communication twice a month or so, on a day and time that's convenient. Some teachers find it easiest to send parents a brief email report of their child's progress; others would rather have a phone conversation. (If the teacher prefers a conversation, make sure to take notes.)

Create a section in your IEP binder for documents relating to your child's progress. Save copies of written updates from the teacher and samples of your child's schoolwork here. For more information on keeping track of your child's progress with an existing IEP, see Chapter 8, Section B.

■

5

Developing Your Child's IEP Blueprint

At some point in the IEP process, you'll need to describe in detail what you believe your child's educational program should look like, including the placement and support services your child needs. I call the specifics of this program a blueprint. Despite the fancy name, a blueprint is just a list of items or components that you want in your child's program.

Why create a blueprint? Primarily to help you be an effective advocate for your child. To convince others that your child needs particular services or assistance, you must first be able to articulate exactly what you want for your child and why it's appropriate.

There are a few other reasons for creating a blueprint:

- It forces you to be specific. For example, stating that your child needs help in reading is not as effective as saying your child needs a one-on-one reading specialist one hour per day, four days per week.
- You'll know exactly what documentation you will need to support your request at the IEP meeting. For example, if your blueprint includes a one-on-one reading specialist one hour per day, four days per week, you'll need information from your child's school record or a person at the IEP meeting to support that position.
- IDEA requires that the program fit the child, not the other way around. Just because the school district offers a particular class or program doesn't necessarily mean that it is appropriate for your child. A blueprint helps you determine what may be missing from the program suggested by the school.
- The blueprint serves as a standard against which you can evaluate your child's existing program and options currently available to you.
- The blueprint provides you with a continual reference point as you talk with others about your child's needs and move toward the IEP meeting.

In essence, the blueprint represents your ideal IEP program. It is your starting point—a sort of "druthers" test. That is, if you had your druthers, if you could be the special education administrator for your school district for one day, this is the IEP program you would design for your child.

You may think it's too early to draft a blueprint. Perhaps your child was just evaluated and found eligible for special education, but hasn't been in special education yet. Or maybe your child has been in special education for some time, but is scheduled for a new evaluation in another month. It's possible a new special education administrator will take over in the spring, with promises of new program options about which you know little. In any of these situations, you may think you don't know enough. In truth, there's always more information you can gather. But you have to start sometime, and now is as good a time as any. Don't worry if your blueprint is skeletal at first; it's for your use only.

Even parents new to special education usually have some intuitive sense of what their child needs. Take a moment to think about it. By the time you finish this chapter, you'll have the beginnings of a useful blueprint, not just vague notions of what might help. And as you go through other chapters and gather information on your child's needs, you'll be able to develop a more complete blueprint.

A. Begin at the End: Define Your Child's Needs

It's the first day of school in the upcoming school year. Close your eyes and picture what your child's classroom will look like. Is there a tutor? A sign language interpreter? No more than ten kids in the room? Is it a regular classroom? A special education class in a neighboring school district? A special private school? Don't hold yourself back.

Sit down with a pad of paper and pen or in front of your computer, and write out the ideal program and services for your child. Remember that your blueprint is your wish list for your ideal IEP. Don't dwell on the fact that you fought over the IEP last year or you're expecting a fight again. Don't draft your blueprint to follow the school district's program if you think it's not appropriate.

B. Preparing an IEP Blueprint

This section covers the seven key components of a blueprint, the items you want included in your child's IEP. You can use the blueprint to develop your IEP form, although the two documents won't be identical. (Chapter 11, Section C, explains how to do this.)

Some components are quite general, such as ideal classroom setting; others are very specific, such as a particular class. Some of these seven components may not be relevant to your child's situation and may be ignored. You may not have enough information to complete each section now. As you know more, you can fill in the gaps.

A sample IEP Blueprint is below; Appendix 5 includes a blank tear-out copy. Be sure to put your blueprint draft into your binder, along with supporting information and documents. (See Chapter 4.)

1. Classroom Setting and Peer Needs

In this section, specify the type of classroom you'd like for your child, including the kinds of peers he or she should be with. Specific items to identify (when relevant) include:

- regular versus special education class
- partially or fully mainstreamed
- type of special education class (for example, for autistic students)
- number of children in the classroom
- ages and cognitive ranges of children in class
- kinds of students (with similar or dissimilar disabling conditions) and what behaviors might or might not be appropriate for your child—for example, a child with attention deficit disorder may need a classroom where other children do not act out, and
- language similarities—for example, a deaf child may need a class of children who use the same sign language.

2. Teacher and Staff Needs

Use this section to identify your desires concerning teachers and other classroom staff, such as:

- number of teachers and aides
- teacher-pupil ratio—for example, your child may require a ratio of no more than four students to one teacher
- experience, training, and expertise of the teacher—many special education classes are set up for children with specific disabilities; if your child has communicative disabilities or emotional problems, a class with a teacher for the learning disabled may not be appropriate, and
- training and expertise of aides.

IEP Blueprint

The IEP blueprint represents the ideal IEP for your child. Use it as a guide to make and record the educational desires you have for your child.

Areas of the IEP	Preferred Situation for Your Child
1. Classroom Setting and Peer Needs— issues to consider:	
☐ regular versus special education class	
☐ partially or fully mainstreamed	
☐ type of special education class	
☒ number of children in the classroom	A class of no more than 10 students
☒ ages and cognitive ranges of children in class	Age range 9-10; same cognitive range as Mark
☒ kinds of students and behaviors that might or might not be appropriate for your child, and	No behaviorally troubled students No mixed "disability" class
☐ language similarities.	
2. Teacher and Staff Needs—issues to consider:	
☒ number of teachers and aides	1 teacher; 1 full-time aide or 2 half-time aides
☒ teacher-pupil ratio	10:1 teacher-pupil ratio
☒ experience, training, and expertise of the teacher, and	Teacher with specific learning disability training, experience, credentials
☒ training and expertise of aides.	Aide: previous experience working with L-D students
3. Curricula and Teaching Methodology— be specific. If you don't know what you *do* want, specify what you *don't* want.	Slingerland method Large-print material Teaching strategies that include significant repetition

Areas of the IEP	Ideal Situation for Your Child
4. Related Services—issues to consider: ☒ specific needed services	1:1 aide two hours per day
☒ type of services	Speech and lang. therapy three times/week, 40 min. per session, 1:1
☒ frequency of services, and	
☒ length of services.	30 minutes of psych. counseling once a week with psychologist experienced with children with learning disabilities and emotional overlay
5. Identified Programs—specify known programs that you think would work for your child and the school that offers them.	Special day class (5th grade) for learning disabled at Washington School (Ms. Flanagan)
6. Goals—your child's academic and functional aims.	Improve reading fluency and comprehension: Read three-paragraph story with 80% comprehension; complete reading within 10 minutes. Improve peer relationships: Initiate five positive peer interactions/week.
7. Classroom Environment and Other Features—issues to consider: ☒ distance from home	No more than five miles and less than 30-minute bus ride to neighborhood school
☐ transition plans for mainstreaming	
☐ vocational needs	
☒ extracurricular and social needs, and	Involvement in afterschool recreation and lunchtime sports activities
☒ environmental needs.	Small school (no more than 250 students); quiet classroom; protective environment (school procedures to ensure students do not wander); acoustically treated classroom

Areas of the IEP	Ideal Situation for Your Child

8. Involvement in the General Curriculum/ Other—to what extent will your child be involved in regular programs and curriculum, and what help will your child need to do it?
 	
☐ current academic level in reading, writing, social skills, etc., and
 	
☒ statewide assessment exams: Will your child take them? Will accommodations be necessary?
	Large-type materials
	Repeated review/drill
	1:1 aide to work on reading comprehension
	
	Assessments:
	   Large-print versions
	   Additional time to complete testing
	   Supervised breaks within test sections

3. Curricula and Teaching Methodology

In this section, identify the curricula and teaching method or methods you feel are appropriate for your child. You may have no idea right now. As you gather information, however, you will begin to learn about the various teaching methods, materials, strategies, and curricula used with children with disabilities.

Be as specific as possible. If you don't know what you *do* want, specify what you *don't* want. For example, an autistic child will require very different curricula and teaching methods from a child with hearing and speech impairments. A child in a regular classroom may require only a minor adjustment to the regular classroom curriculum.

Is There a Right to a Specific Methodology?

While IDEA does not specifically require that a methodology or curriculum be included in the IEP and provided to the child, there is no prohibition against it. If a child needs a specific methodology to benefit from special education, then it is required; if you cannot prove that it's necessary, then the school district does not have to provide it.

4. Related Services

Include in your blueprint a list of necessary services, including the type and amount of services (such as number of times per week and length of time per session).

Chapters 2 and 8 provide details on related services, such as speech therapy, aide support, physical therapy, transportation, and psychological services.

5. Identified Programs

In Section 1 of the blueprint, you may have stated whether you want your child in a regular classroom or special education classroom. If you know about a program in a particular school that you think would work best for your child, be it in a regular classroom or a special education classroom, public or private, identify that here.

6. Goals

IDEA used to refer to a child's "goals and objectives" (and some school representatives may continue to use these terms): Goals were long range in nature, while objectives were generally more specific, short-term benchmarks that would help a child achieve the broader goal. When Congress amended IDEA in 2004, however, it took out all references to objectives and benchmarks. The law now refers to measurable annual goals including "academic and functional goals" designed to meet the child's disability-related and other educational needs. (20 U.S.C. § 1414(d)(1)(A).)

If you're wondering what effect this might have on the process of developing an IEP for the coming school year, you're not alone. Because the statutory language is very general, however, it gives the IEP team a lot of latitude when coming up with goals—and nothing in the law prevents the team from using very specific, concrete goals (much like the objectives that used to be required).

Examples of goals include:
- improve reading comprehension or other academic skills, such as math, spelling, or writing
- improve social skills

- resolve a serious emotional difficulty that impedes school work
- improve fine or large motor skills
- develop greater language and speech skills
- develop independent living skills, or
- improve auditory or visual memory.

 Chapter 9 discusses how to prepare goals.

7. Classroom Environment and Other Features

Use your blueprint to identify any other features of the program you want for your child, such as:
- distance from home
- transition plans for mainstreaming
- vocational needs
- extracurricular and social needs, and
- environmental needs—protective environment, small class, small campus, acoustically treated classroom, or the like.

8. Involvement in the General Curriculum

In this section of the blueprint, you should describe the extent to which you want your child to be involved in regular school programs and curriculum. For example, if you want your child placed in a regular classroom using the regular curriculum, but your child will need some one-on-one time with an aide and some modifications to the regular classroom teaching methodologies, you should indicate that here.

You should also jot down any modifications you believe your child will need in order to take statewide assessment tests. As these tests become more common, school districts are having to accommodate children with disabilities—and the 2004 amendments to IDEA state that the IEP should include any modifications a child will need to participate in these tests. There are a variety of possible accomodations, but not all are available and allowed in every state and for every test. (See, for example, the test variations available to California's statewide assessments, as listed in the sample IEP form in Appendix 4.) This is your blueprint, so you should list the accommodations that would best ensure that the assessments measure your child's ability, not the effects of his or her disability. Be warned, however, that this is an area where school districts don't have much flexibility to deviate from the state's rules about what is and is not allowed as an accommodation.

C. Other Sources of Information for the Blueprint

Developing your blueprint is an important part of gathering information and developing a sense of what your child needs. As you learn more about your child's needs from professionals and others, and find out what services and programs are available, add to or change your blueprint as appropriate.

People who are trustworthy and know your child—such as other parents, your pediatrician, the classroom teacher, or a tutor—are excellent sources of information for your blueprint. Pose your question like this: "Terry is having some problems with reading (math, cognitive growth, language development, social issues, emotional conflicts, mobility, fine or gross motor activities, or whatever), and I'm wondering if I should look for a new program (or different related services). Do you have any suggestions of people I might talk to, or programs or services I might consider?"

Chapter 8 contains important information about gathering facts, visiting school programs, and developing supportive material, such as an independent evaluation. This information will help you work on your blueprint.

D. What's Next?

If you are new to special education, the next step is to learn about the evaluation and eligibility processes—how your child is evaluated and qualifies for special education. Review Chapters 6 and 7 carefully.

If you are not new to special education, your next step will depend on your child's situation. Your child may need an evaluation before the IEP meeting—if so, be sure to read Chapter 6. If your child does not need an immediate evaluation and has already been found eligible for special education, move on to Chapter 8. ■

6

Evaluations

Evaluations are important tools that help you and the school district determine what your child's needs are and how they can be met. The school district will rely very heavily on the results of the evaluation to determine whether your child is eligible for special education and, if so, what the IEP will include.

Evaluations are observations, reports, and tests that provide specific information about your child's cognitive, academic, linguistic, social, and emotional status. Evaluations describe your child's current developmental level—how he or she reads, perceives information, processes information, performs physical tasks, calculates, remembers things, relates to other children, and uses language.

Evaluations or assessments? This chapter covers evaluations—the tests and other information-gathering methods used to determine a child's eligibility for, and progress in, special education. Many advocates use the term "evaluations" interchangeably with the term "assessments," but they have different legal meanings. Under IDEA, assessments are the statewide tests that evaluate the progress of all schoolchildren (not just those in special education) towards meeting various academic and other standards. Don't worry if your school district or a teacher refers to eligibility testing as an "assessment"; just make sure you understand how they are using the term.

Special Education Evaluations vs. General Assessments

Most (if not all) states require schools to administer a variety of tests to measure how children are doing in school and whether they are meeting certain state standards. These tests—often called general assessments—measure a child's mastery of specific subject matter, such as American history or algebra. Most children also take tests to graduate from high school and qualify for college. While special education evaluations often measure similar abilities or aptitudes, they are intended to be used for a different purpose: to determine whether a child is eligible for special education and which special education services will be helpful to a particular child.

Since 1997, IDEA has required schools to include children in special education in state- and district-wide assessments, with appropriate accommodations for each child's unique needs. When IDEA was amended in 2004, Congress added language stating that children in special education must be provided with "appropriate accommodations and alternative assessments" if necessary. Any alternative assessments given must be aligned with state content standards—that is, they must be related to any state rules regarding required subject areas for testing. (20 U.S.C. §1412(a)(16).)

Not all of these tests are sensitive to special education test-takers, however. For example, California requires high school seniors to pass an "exit exam" before they graduate, but the State Board of Education has generally ignored the needs of special education students and failed to make appropriate exit exam accommodations or modifications. The state was sued for this inexcusable oversight. You should carefully review any state or district tests in which your child participates to make sure that the test is appropriate and that your child receives any accommodations necessary to take the test.

The evaluation report will be a key factor in decisions made at an IEP meeting about your child's program and services. Ideally, the report will support what you want included in the IEP. For example, if you feel your child needs placement in a specific special education program, your chances of securing that placement are increased, if the evaluation report recommends it.

This chapter covers evaluations done by local public school districts. You also have the right to have your child evaluated by someone outside of the school district, often referred to as a private or independent evaluation. As discussed in Chapter 8, such independent evaluations are very valuable when you disagree with the school district's evaluation or feel that an independent expert will provide an evaluation supportive of your child's blueprint.

IDEA regulations are changing. The regulatory citations throughout this book are to the current IDEA regulations—those that will be in effect until the Department of Education issues final regulations interpreting the 2004 amendments to IDEA. The Department expects to release these final regulations at the end of 2005; many of them will be identical or similar to the existing regulations cited in this chapter (although the citations will be different), while others will be new. When you use this book, you should make sure that you have the most current version of the regulations. See "Warning: Special Education Rules Are in Flux," in Chapter 1, for information that will help you stay up to date. You can find the most recent version of IDEA, including the 2004 amendments, starting at 20 U.S.C. § 1400; the most pertinent sections are included in Appendix 1.

A. When Evaluations Are Done

There are two kinds of evaluations: an initial eligibility evaluation to determine whether you child qualifies for special education, and subsequent or follow-up evaluations to get up-to-date information on your child's status and progress. The initial evaluation must be done *before* your child can be found eligible for special education.

While you can wait for the school district to initiate the evaluation process, you don't want to delay unnecessarily. If you haven't heard from the school, make a formal request for an evaluation.

A sample Request to Begin Special Education Process and Evaluation is in Chapter 3, Section A2; a blank, tear-out copy is in Appendix 5.

The Evaluation Process, Step by Step

Here is how an evaluation process typically proceeds:

1. You request an evaluation, or the school identifies your child as possibly needing special education. (See Chapter 3.)
2. The school presents you with an evaluation plan listing all testing to be done on your child in order to determine eligibility for special education, or to assess your child's current status if already in special education.
3. You approve the plan (or ask that certain tests or evaluation tools be added and/or eliminated).
4. You meet with the evaluator to discuss specific concerns and your own evaluation of your child's problems, based on your personal observations, physician reports, and the like.
5. The school evaluates your child.
6. You receive a copy of the school's report.
7. You schedule independent evaluations if necessary. (See Chapter 8.)
8. You attend the IEP eligibility meeting (or the yearly IEP meeting, if your child is already in special education), where the evaluation results are discussed.

As amended in 2004, IDEA requires the school district to complete your child's first evaluation and determine whether your child is eligible for special education within 60 days of receiving your consent to do the evaluation. And that's 60 calendar days, not business or school days—weekends and holidays count toward the 60-day deadline. If your state has its own time frame for the initial evaluation and determination of eligibility, then that deadline will apply rather than the 60 days specified by IDEA. (20 U.S.C. § 1414(a)(C)(i)(I).) Remember, your school is required to provide you with an explanation of all applicable special education law, whether federal or state.

If you "repeatedly" fail or refuse to "produce" your child for the evaluation, then the school dis-trict will not be required to meet the 60-day deadline. If your child changes school districts before the previous district made an eligibility determination, the new district has a responsibility to make "sufficient progress" in meeting the 60-day deadline, but will not necessarily be bound to it. (20 U.S.C. § 1414(a)(C)(ii)(I)(II).)

Once your child is found eligible for special education, he or she must be evaluated at least every three years, or more frequently if you or a teacher requests it. You have a right to have your child reevaluated at least once a year; if you want more frequent reevaluations, you will need the school district's consent. (20 U.S.C. § 1414(a)(2).) See Section F, below, for more on reevaluations.

B. Evaluation Components

Evaluations almost always include objective tests leading to numerical conclusions about a child. Depending on your child's disability, many tests are available—including ones to evaluate general intelligence, reading comprehension, psychological states, social development, and physical abilities. You may have already heard of some of them, such as the Wechsler Test, Kaufman Assessment, and Draw-a-Person. For each test, the report should include an explanation of the test and the test's results.

An evaluation need not be made up of only formal tests. It can also include supportive material that provides information or recommendations about your child's educational status, such as:

- a general description of your child
- teacher and parent reports
- full-scale evaluations by experts specializing in your child's disability
- letters from a family doctor or counselor
- daily or weekly school reports or diaries, and
- other evidence of school performance, including work samples.

Finally, the report should draw a conclusion about your child's eligibility for special education and make specific recommendations about strategies, curricula, interventions, related services, and programs needed for your child.

Legal Requirements for Evaluations

IDEA guarantees every child certain rights in the evaluation process. An evaluation must:

- use a variety of evaluation tests, tools, and strategies to gather information about your child
- not be racially or culturally discriminatory
- be given in your child's native language or communication mode (such as sign language if your child is deaf or hard of hearing)
- validly determine your child's status—that is, it must include the right test for your child's suspected areas of disability
- be given by trained and knowledgeable personnel, in accordance with the instructions provided by the producer of the tests
- not be used only to determine intelligence
- if your child has impaired speaking or sensory skills, accurately reflect your child's aptitude or achievement level—not just your child's impairment
- evaluate your child in "all areas of suspected disability," including health, vision, hearing, social and emotional status, general intelligence, academic performance, communicative status, motor abilities, behavior, and cognitive, physical, and developmental abilities, and
- provide relevant information that will help determine your child's educational needs. (20 U.S.C. § 1414(b).)

In addition, the process must include other material on your child, such as information you provide (a doctor's letter or a statement of your observations), current classroom assessments and observations (objective tests or subjective teacher reports), and observations by other professionals. (20 U.S.C. § 1414(c)(1).)

C. Evaluation Plans

Before the school district begins the formal evaluation process—either an initial evaluation or a reevaluation—it must send you a written assessment plan and receive your written approval.

The evaluation plan must include:

- specifically named tests
- a section where you can request additional tests or other methods of evaluation, and
- a place for you to provide your written approval or disapproval.

IDEA requires the school district to get your permission before it can evaluate your child. Your consent must be "informed," which means that you must understand fully what you are consenting to. If you don't give permission, the school district can still seek to evaluate your child, but it will have to go to due process and get an order from the hearing judge allowing it to proceed. If the school district doesn't force the issue, however, then it is not obligated to provide special education or hold an IEP meeting. (20 U.S.C. § 1414(a)(1).)

The 2004 amendments to IDEA allow a teacher or specialist to "screen" children to determine appropriate teaching strategies "for curriculum implementation" without parental permission; such screenings are not considered evaluations to which you must consent. While this new rule seems like a sensible way to let teachers do their jobs, it may be hard to tell the difference between a screening and a full-fledged evaluation. You should certainly ask teachers and the special education administrator to give you detailed information on any such screenings they conduct. Then, if the school tries to use screening information during eligibility discussions at an IEP meeting, you can object that this information is not supposed to be part of the eligibility process. (20 U.S.C. § 1414(a)(1)(E).)

If your child is already in special education and you refuse to allow further evaluation, your child retains the right to his or her current program and services, but the district can take you to due process to get approval to reevaluate your child over your objections. (See Chapter 12 for more on due process.)

1. Evaluating the Tests

In almost all cases, a person in your school district who is knowledgeable about special education will determine which tests are to be given to your child. There's a very good chance that this person will also administer the tests or supervise whoever does the testing. How will you know if the proposed tests are appropriate for your child?

The best source of information is people who are familiar with special education testing. Likely candidates include the person who developed the evaluation plan, your child's teacher, other parents, and your pediatrician. Other possibilities include independent special education evaluators you've worked with or school special education personnel you trust. You may also want to talk to organizations that represent the specific disability of your child, such as the Council for Exceptional Children or a state association for learning disabilities.

Chapter 8 discusses independent evaluations. Appendix 3 provides a list of advocacy, parent, and disability organizations you might consider contacting for information on different types of evaluations. Appendix 3 also references books on testing.

Here's what you want to find out:
- whether the proposed tests are appropriate to assess your child's suspected disability
- what the tests generally measure, such as general cognitive skills or language abilities
- whether the tests' results are usually numeric scores or more descriptive statements about your child's performance (or both)
- whether the tests' results will provide a basis for specific recommendations about classroom strategies, teaching methods, and services and programs for your child

- how the tests are administered—for example, are they timed, are they oral or written
- the evaluator's expertise, training, and experience in doing this kind of testing, and
- how the results are evaluated—for example, will your child score in a certain percentile ("Mary is in the 88th percentile") or will your child be given a different type of rating ("Mary scored at the second-grade level").

Testing Children With Limited English Proficiency

The 2004 amendments to IDEA recognize an important change in American demographics: that the "limited English proficient population is the fastest growing in our nation." (20 U.S.C. § 1400(11).) To address this issue, Congress has created rules about the evaluation of children with limited English proficiency. The district must administer evaluations in the child's native language, so that the tests will yield "accurate information on what the child knows and can do academically, developmentally, and functionally." (20 U.S.C. § 1414(b)(3).) Tests and evaluations that don't take this issue into consideration will not be considered "appropriate."

These protections also apply to deaf and hard of hearing children who may also not be proficient in English. Many of these children not only have a different native language—American Sign Language or ASL—but also use an entirely unique communication mode—visual or sign language.

2. Adding to the Plan

If you have concerns about the plan submitted to you, you have every right to ask for changes. IDEA states that the process should include evaluations and information provided by the parents.

(20 U.S.C. § 1414(b).) You can request that specific tests be administered to your child, or that certain information (such as a formal interview with you, a review of your child's school work, a teacher's observations, or a pediatrician's report) be used to evaluate your child and be included as part of the report. Be as specific as possible in your request. For example, if your child has limited fine motor skills and problems with handwriting, ask the evaluator to analyze handwriting samples.

What "other information" should be included in the plan? By this time, you have probably gathered information about your child—secured the school file and talked to teachers, other parents, or experts—and have some sense of the key issues. Be sure to take a look at your blueprint, no matter how incomplete it may be. See Chapter 5.

Many special education evaluators are not comfortable evaluating testing and other data that don't produce a numerical result. The plan you receive may consist primarily of standardized tests. The school district may object if you ask for an evaluation of subjective reports or anecdotal observations. Nevertheless, you have the right to insist that this information be included in your child's evaluation. Subjective reports and anecdotal observations may be key to coming up with the ultimate IEP program.

If the evaluator refuses to make the changes you request, send a letter to the school district's special education administrator. Explain that you are exercising your right under IDEA (20 U.S.C. § 1414(a) and (b)), to request that additional materials be added to your child's plan, and that the evaluator refused to do so. Describe exactly what you want included and the reasons the evaluator gave you for the refusal. As always, keep a copy of your correspondence.

3. Approving or Rejecting the Plan

Ultimately, you must sign the plan, indicating whether you accept or reject it. Signing the plan need not be an all-or-nothing proposition. You can:

- accept the plan
- accept the plan on condition, or
- reject the plan.

a. Accepting the Plan

If you accept the plan as submitted to you, mark the appropriate box—most evaluation plans have approval and disapproval boxes—sign and date it, and return it to the school district. If there is no acceptance box, write "plan accepted," sign and date it, and return it. Be sure to make a photocopy of the plan and add it to your IEP binder.

b. Accepting the Plan on Condition

There are two possible reasons why you might accept the plan with a condition. First, you might accept the tests proposed, but want additional tests administered or additional information considered. In this situation, try to get the evaluator to agree informally, or ask for help from the school district. (See Section C2, above.)

Second, you may not want certain proposed tests administered to your child—perhaps you believe that they aren't reliable or that they test for a problem that your child doesn't have. Whatever the reason, indicate your partial acceptance of the plan on the form as follows:

> I approve only of the following tests:
> _Wrat, Kaufman_____
>
> Date: _March 1, 20xx_____
>
> Signature: _Jan Stevens_____

c. Rejecting the Plan

You have every right to reject the plan and force the evaluator or school district to work with you to find an acceptable plan. Your reasons for rejecting will probably fall into one or more of the following situations:

- the tests are not appropriate
- you want additional tests and materials as part of the evaluation, or
- the evaluator is not qualified.

Evaluating the Evaluator

Your child's evaluation must be administered by trained and knowledgeable personnel in accordance with any instructions provided by the producer of the tests. (20 U.S.C. § 1414(b)(3).) How can you judge the qualifications of the evaluator?

- Ask the special education administrator for the credentials of the evaluator. If the administrator refuses, assert your right to know under IDEA.
- Ask other parents and your child's teacher what they know about the evaluator.
- If you are working with an independent evaluator (see Chapter 8), ask if he or she knows the school's evaluator.
- If possible, meet with the evaluator prior to the testing (see Section D, below).

To reject the plan, check the disapproval box, sign and date the form, and return it to the school district. If there is no box, write "evaluation plan rejected," sign and date the form, and return it. Keep a copy.

If the plan is not clear or does not give you enough room for your objections, you should attach a letter to the plan. A sample letter is below. Use this as a model and adjust it depending on your specific situation.

After you submit your rejection (partial or complete) of the plan, the evaluator or school district will probably attempt to find a plan that meets your approval. If the district feels the evaluation should proceed under the plan you've rejected, it has the right to proceed to mediation or a due process hearing to force this issue, although this is rarely done (see Chapter 12).

D. Meet With the Evaluator

After you accept the plan proposed by the school district, the evaluator will contact you to schedule the testing of your child. Now is the time to think ahead. In a few months, when you are at the IEP meeting planning your child's IEP program, the school district will pay the most attention to the evaluation done by its own evaluator. Therefore, you will want to take some time to establish a positive relationship with the evaluator before testing begins.

A good relationship is one in which the parties don't have preconceived ideas or view each other with hostility. Try to put aside negative comments you've heard from other people (or any bad experiences you've had with the evaluator in the past). Start with the assumption (or new attitude) that the evaluator is there to help your child get an appropriate education. Of course, this may not be an easy task. The evaluator may not be easy to talk to or may be put off by parents who want to play an active role. No matter what attitude the evaluator adopts, you should try to remain rational and pleasant.

Sample Letter Rejecting Evaluation Plan

Date: December 14, 20xx

To: Carolyn Ames, Administrator, Special Education
         Central Valley School District
         456 Main Street
         Centerville, Michigan 47000

Re: Evaluation Plan for Michael Kreeskind

I am in receipt of the November 21, 20xx, evaluation plan for my son Michael. I give my permission for you to administer the Vineland, PPVT-III, and Wechsler tests, but not the rest of the ones on your list. I have investigated them and feel they are too unreliable.

In addition, I am formally requesting that the plan reflect:

- that the evaluator will meet with me and my husband to review Michael's entire history and will include the issues raised during that meeting in the report, and

- that the evaluator will review samples of Michael's work and letters from professionals who have observed Michael.

I have one final concern. I have reviewed the credentials of Brett Forrest, the evaluator selected by the district to evaluate Michael. I am concerned that Mr. Forrest has no prior experience evaluating children with Michael's disability. Specifically, I do not believe he is trained or knowledgeable about the tests to be administered, as required under IDEA (20 U.S.C. § 1414(b)(3)(IV).) Therefore, I do not approve of the assigned evaluator, Brett Forrest. I request that an appropriate one be assigned and that we be provided proof of the evaluator's qualifications.

Thank you very much.

Michelle Kreeskind
Michelle Kreeskind
8 Rock Road
Centerville, Michigan 47000
Phones: 555-9876 (home); 555-5450 (work)

Reality Check: The Evaluator Works for the School District

While you should assume that the evaluator wants to develop a good and appropriate educational plan for your child, don't lose sight of the fact that the evaluator is an employee of the school district. The evaluator probably knows what the school district will offer regarding your child's eligibility for special education or in terms of an IEP program, and the report may very well reflect the school's position. Some evaluators know exactly what a school district can provide and, unfortunately, tailor their reports accordingly, rather than prepare a report based on what a child truly needs.

On the other hand, just because the evaluator's report doesn't support what you want, it doesn't necessarily follow that the evaluator is acting against your child's best interests. The conclusions may be well reasoned and supported by the data. Be objective. Are the recommendations consistent with or contrary to the data? If you conclude that the evaluator is biased against you, request a new one. Remember, you always have the right to an outside or independent evaluation (see Chapter 8).

Your job is to educate the evaluator about your child. The evaluator will have test results to evaluate and reports to read. But he or she doesn't live with your child or stand before your child in a classroom. To the extent possible, help the evaluator see your child from your perspective, particularly as it relates to the academic programs and services you feel are necessary. Ideally, you want the report to recommend eligibility and the specific program components you want for your child, as articulated in your blueprint (in Chapter 5).

So how do you go about getting your points across? If possible, meet with the evaluator before the testing is done. The law doesn't require an evaluator to meet with you, but the law does not prohibit it, either. Call up and ask for an appointment. State that you'd appreciate the chance to talk, are not familiar with all the tests, would like to find out how they are used, and would just feel a lot better if you could meet for 10 to 15 minutes. If the evaluator cannot meet with you, ask for a brief phone consultation or consider sending a letter expressing your concerns.

Whether you meet in person, talk on the phone, or state your concerns in a letter, you'll want to be clear and objective.

Eligibility evaluation. Let the evaluator know the specific problems your child is having in school, the material you have documenting those problems, and why you believe those problems qualify your child for special education.

Example:

"Carl has had a terrible time with reading. He's only in the second grade, but he is way behind. His teacher agrees—I have some notes of my conversation with her from last October. I could provide you with a copy of them if that would help. I'd greatly appreciate it if you could focus on Carl's reading problem in your evaluation."

IEP program evaluation. If your child is already in special education or is likely to be found eligible, let the evaluator know of the IEP program components you believe are important. Here are a few examples.

Examples:

"Billy needs a small class where none of the children exhibit behavioral problems, with classroom strategies and methodology geared for children with his learning disability."

"Howard needs the Lovaas method for autistic children. I would like you to evaluate the reports done by his doctor, his teacher, and the classroom aide, and address their suggestions in your recommendations section."

Letter Requesting Evaluation Report

Date: _____ November 1, 20xx _____

To: Harvey Smith, Evaluation Team

Pine Hills Elementary School

234 Lincoln Road

Boston, MA 02000

Re: Robin Griffin, student in first-grade class of Sean Jordan

I appreciate your involvement in my child's evaluation and look forward to your report. Would you please:

1. Send me a copy of a draft of your report before you finalize it. As you can imagine, the process can be overwhelming for parents. It would be most helpful to me to see your report, because the proposed tests are complicated and I need time to analyze the results.

2. Send me your final report at least four weeks before the IEP meeting.

Again, thank you for your kind assistance.

Sincerely,

Lee Griffin

Lee Griffin

23 Hillcrest Road

Boston, MA 02000

Phones: 555-4321 (home); 555-9876 (work)

Be careful about how specific you get. The evaluator may think you're trying to take over and might not appreciate being told exactly what to include in the report. For example, a straight-out, "Please recommend that Mary have a full-time, one-on-one aide" or "Please write that Tom should be placed in the learning disability program at Center School" may be met with hostility. You may need to be less direct, such as, "The teacher wrote that Mary cannot learn to read without constant one-on-one attention. Please address that need in your report." Remember, your blueprint is a good guide here.

This part of the process is not easy. Don't be disappointed if the evaluator doesn't agree fully or even partially with what you are requesting. The best you can do is be clear about what your child's problem is, what you feel your child needs, and what materials support your conclusions. Ultimately, if the evaluator does not address your questions and you have good evidence to support those concerns, the value of the school's evaluation may be diminished.

E. Reviewing the Report

After your child is evaluated, the evaluator will issue a report. Some issue their reports in two stages: a *draft* report and a *final* report. Ask how and when the evaluator plans to issue the report. Ideally, the evaluator will issue a draft report that you can review before the final report is submitted prior to the IEP meeting.

Even if the evaluator will issue only one version of the report, it is imperative that you see it before the IEP meeting. Under IDEA, the school district must provide you with a copy of the evaluation report and with information documenting eligibility. (20 U.S.C. § 1414(b)(4)(B).)

By asking to see the report (preferably a draft of the report) ahead of time, you convey to the school district your intention to carefully review the evaluator's work. This will help you keep a sense of control over the process and prepare for the IEP meeting. It will also keep you from wasting valuable time at the IEP meeting.

A sample letter requesting the report is included here; a blank, tear-out copy is in Appendix 5.

If you disagree with anything in the draft report or feel something is missing, ask the evaluator to make a change or add the missing information. Be prepared to point to material outside the report that supports your point of view. If the evaluator refuses, put your request in writing, with a copy to the special education administrator.

If the evaluator won't make the changes—or sends you only the final version—what can you do if you disagree with the final report? You can reject it. While you can express your disagreement before the IEP, it might be strategically wise to wait for the meeting and prepare your counterarguments with the evidence you have, including existing material and your independent evaluation (if any).

Don't forget independent evaluations.
You have the right to have your child evaluated by someone outside of the school district, often referred to as a private or independent evaluation. As discussed in Chapter 8, such independent evaluations are of value when you disagree with the school district's evaluation. The independent evaluator can analyze the district's evaluation and perhaps point out its shortcomings.

F. Reevaluations

In addition to the right to an initial eligibility evaluation, IDEA also gives your child the right to periodic reevaluations. Your child must be reevaluated at least once every three years or when the school district determines that there is need for improved academic and functional performance. In addition, you, the school district, or your child's teacher can request a reevaluation once a year—and if you make this request, the school district must grant it.

You do not have a unilateral right to more than one reevaluation per year, however: The school district will have to consent to any additional yearly reevaluations. (20 U.S.C. § 1414(a)(2).) While it is certainly true that a student can be over-evaluated, which can tax both your child's and the school district's stamina, there may simply be times when a second or third evaluation in one year is necessary. For example, if your child isn't progressing as you expected, teachers are raising concerns, IEP goals seem way out of reach, or for any other reason a significant change is necessary, it's probably time for a reevaluation. If you find yourself in this situation, put your request to the school district in writing, noting as specifically as possible why additional information is needed and why the current evaluation is not adequate, complete, or up to date. ∎

7

Who Is Eligible for Special Education?

ligibility is the process the school district uses to determine whether or not your child qualifies for special education. This is a two-step process. First, your child is evaluated. Then, you meet with school administrators at an IEP meeting where the school actually determines whether or not your child is eligible for special education. This IEP eligibility meeting is different from the IEP program meeting, where your child's annual academic program is developed, although they may be combined (see Section D, below).

Eligibility, like evaluations, IEP meetings, and other aspects of the special education process, is bound by the rules of IDEA. And like those other procedures, eligibility is frequently the source of disagreement between parents and a school district.

 If your child has already been found eligible for special education, skip ahead to Chapter 8.

Your child may be found eligible for special education for any number of reasons—for example, because of a learning disability, sensory or physical impairments, or psychological problems. To qualify, your child will have to meet the criteria discussed in Section A, below.

Eligibility rules for children with learning disabilities have changed. When Congress amended IDEA in 2004, it made important changes to the eligibility standards for children with learning disabilities. For detailed information on these new rules, see *Nolo's IEP Guide: Learning Disabilities,* by Lawrence Siegel.

Eligibility Is Not an Annual Event

Once your child is found eligible for special education, he or she won't need to requalify each year. There are only three situations when your child's eligibility might be redetermined:

- Your child dropped out of special education and wants to reenter.
- You or the school district proposes a change from one eligibility category to another.
- There is evidence that your child no longer qualifies for special education. Reevaluation is not required if your child's eligibility status changes because he or she graduates from high school with a regular diploma or exceeds the age of eligibility (22 years old). (20 U.S.C. § 1414(c)(5)(B).)

A. Eligibility Definitions

In order to qualify for special education, your child must meet two eligibility requirements: (1) he or she must have a disabling condition, as defined in IDEA, and (2) that condition must have an adverse impact on your child's education. In other words, it is not enough to show that your child has a disability—you must also show that your child's disability is causing enough problems to warrant special education help.

1. Disabling Condition

IDEA provides a list of disabling conditions that qualify a child between the ages of three and 22 for special education. The list includes:

- hearing impairments, including deafness
- speech or language impairments, such as stuttering or other speech production difficulties

- visual impairments, including blindness
- multiple disabilities, such as deaf-blindness
- orthopedic impairments caused by congenital anomalies, such as a club foot
- orthopedic impairments caused by diseases, such as polio
- orthopedic impairments caused by other conditions, such as cerebral palsy
- learning disabilities
- serious emotional disturbance (see "Emotional Disturbance as a Disabling Condition," below)
- autism
- traumatic brain injury
- mental retardation, and
- other health impairments that affect a child's strength, vitality, or alertness, such as a heart condition, tuberculosis, rheumatic fever, nephritis, asthma, sickle cell anemia, hemophilia, epilepsy, lead poisoning, leukemia, diabetes, Attention Deficit Disorder (ADD), and Attention Deficit Hyperactivity Disorder (ADHD).

 You can find the legal definition of each of the above disabilities at 20 U.S.C. § 1401(3).

 If your child has learning disabilities, see *Nolo's IEP Guide: Learning Disabilities,* by Larry Siegel, which explains in detail the eligibility requirements for children with learning disabilities.

Fitting your child's condition into a disability covered by IDEA and finding data to prove that your child's disability is causing academic problems can be tough—and emotionally trying. But it's a necessary part of qualifying for special education. If you find yourself in a muddle, remember these tips:

- **Take it slowly.** Some of the qualifying conditions have multilayered definitions. Don't try to take it in all at once. Breaking down a definition into manageable parts will help you figure out what evidence you need to show that your child meets all of the eligibility requirements.

- **You're not a doctor and you don't have to become one.** Don't be put off by some of the complicated terminology. For now, you need a basic understanding of your child's condition and how it affects his or her educational experience. Ask your pediatrician, the school nurse, or the evaluator. Contact other parents and local or national support or advocacy organizations. (Chapter 15 discusses parent organizations, and Appendix 3 lists useful resources.)

- **Focus on key portions of each definition.** Pay attention to words such as "severe" or "significant." These are clues that a minor disability may not qualify your child for special education. A child who doesn't fall under one of the delineated conditions may fit into the catchall category, "other health impairment." If your child's strength, vitality, or alertness is limited because of a chronic or acute health problem, he or she may qualify under this category.

- **The IEP team has flexibility in finding eligibility.** The list of qualifying disabilities is long, but not exhaustive. If your child exhibits the characteristics of any of the disability categories, he or she may very well be deemed eligible for special education, even if there hasn't been a formal diagnosis. In addition, the IEP team has some discretion in determining eligibility. If your child has been diagnosed with a mild condition, it's up to the IEP team to decide whether it's serious enough to justify a finding of eligibility.

- **Your input is important.** The IEP team must draw upon information from a variety of sources, including parental input, when determining eligibility. (20 U.S.C. § 1414(d)(3)(A).) You can, and should, use this opportunity to make sure that the IEP team understands and considers every aspect of your child's disability, not just test scores.

A Word About Labels

This list of disability categories asks you to define your child as "this" or "that." Labeling is one of the difficult and unpleasant parts of the IEP process. Many people feel that labels are unnecessary, even harmful—and from a psychological perspective, they may be right. From a legal perspective, however, your child will be eligible for special education only if he or she fits into one of these categories. If you can, focus on the specifics of your child's condition rather than the label. Remember, your goal is to secure an appropriate education for your child; proving that your child qualifies for special education under one of the eligibility categories is part of the process.

There's a fine line, however, between acknowledging the label for the purpose of meeting the eligibility criteria and making sure your child does not become defined by that label. For example, Bill has dyslexia, which causes him some significant problems in school and qualifies him for special education. But Bill is also a terrific center on the basketball team, he hates to clean up his room, at times he frustrates and certainly worries his parents, he has a good heart, and, most important, he is quite determined to make his way in the world. These are the qualities that label him.

Emotional Disturbance as a Disabling Condition

A child who has an "emotional disturbance" (this is the term used by IDEA) qualifies for special education. Although this term can conjure up images of bizarre behavior and institutionalization, children with a wide range of emotional difficulties can qualify for special education in this category. When you look at the actual defining language in IDEA, you'll see that it encompasses issues that might affect most human beings at some point in their lives, and certainly could arise for children who have a disability.

IDEA defines an emotional disturbance as a condition that has existed over a long period of time and adversely affects your child's educational performance (20 U.S.C. § 1401(3)(A)), resulting in:

- inability to learn that is not explained by intellectual, sensory, or health factors
- inability to build or maintain satisfactory interpersonal relationships with peers and teachers
- inappropriate behaviors or feelings under normal circumstances (for example, extreme frustration, anger, or aggression over minor setbacks or disagreements)
- general pervasive mood of unhappiness or depression, or

- tendency to develop physical symptoms or fears associated with personal or school problems (for example, a child might get a stomach ache before tests or oral reports).

A child who is only socially maladjusted will not qualify for special education, although a child who is emotionally disturbed under IDEA can, of course, be socially maladjusted. Like any other disability, emotional disturbance must adversely affect your child's educational performance in order to make him or her eligible for special education. If your child qualifies for special education in another disability category but also shows some signs of emotional disturbance, the IEP team still can (and should) address those emotional difficulties in the IEP by developing goals and objectives and providing services to meet those emotional needs. Rather than label the behaviors as an "emotional disturbance," simply have the IEP team address them as one of many aspects of your child's disability. For example, the IEP might describe how the teacher, teacher's aide, school counselor, and written goals and objectives could address how your child might deal in a concrete and helpful way with peers who make fun of his or her disability.

- **Keep up with legal changes.** To stay on top of current interpretations of the rules, you'll want to stay in touch with advocacy groups for updates on how the eligibility process is evolving. (See Appendix 3 for a list of organizations.) You'll also want to make sure you have the most current version of the IDEA regulations—see "Special Education Rules Are in Flux," in Chapter 1, for more information.

2. Adverse Impact

It is not enough to show that your child has a disabling condition; you must also demonstrate that your child's disability has an adverse impact on his or her educational performance.

IDEA does not say how "adverse impact" is measured, but your child's grades, test scores, and classroom or other behavior will provide important evidence of adverse impact. While grades can most directly show whether a disabling condition is adversely affecting educational performance or achievement, they don't tell the whole eligibility story. A parent can (and should) argue that a child who receives As, Bs, or Cs but cannot read at age level, follow instructions, or relate to peers is not benefiting from his or her education, and therefore that his or her disability is directly affecting educational performance, regardless of grades.

If your child is getting passing grades, you will need to make the connection between your child's disability and school performance in some other way. Factors to consider (other than grades) include:

- limited progress—for example, little or no improvement in reading, math, or spelling even though the teacher does not fail your child; high school students might have significant difficulty in social studies, algebra, or English
- difficulties in cognitive areas, such as mastering basic concepts, memory, or language skills—forgetting to turn in home-

work, trouble with reading comprehension, or difficulty grasping abstract concepts in math or history might demonstrate these problems

- discrepancy between performance and ability—for example, the child is developmentally and chronologically ten years old, but reads at a six-year-old's level; your eighth-grader has an above average IQ but is performing at the sixth-grade level on math and spelling tests
- evidence of emotional, behavioral, or social difficulties, or
- physical difficulties, such as handwriting, hearing, or coordination problems.

The IEP team has a lot of discretion in determining whether your child is eligible for special education. If your child has passing grades, the team may have to exercise that discretion to find that his or her disability has adversely affected educational performance in other ways.

3. What's Not in the Law

Almost as telling as what IDEA requires is what it doesn't. Contrary to what school district representatives may tell you, none of the following is required by IDEA.

a. Requirement of Numeric Proof

IDEA does not require that your child score at a certain level on specific tests to qualify for special education. Numeric information is important and may prove a key element in determining eligibility, but a test score is not the end of the story.

b. One Test as Sole Determinant

Eligibility cannot be determined based on the results of one test. IDEA specifically requires that any evaluation to determine eligibility include information provided by the parents of the child. Furthermore, IDEA requires that the school district draw upon information from a variety of sources, including aptitude and achievement tests, teacher recommendations, and the child's physical condition, social or cultural background, and adaptive behavior.

c. Eligibility Based on Environmental, Cultural, or Economic Status

IDEA specifically states that a child cannot be determined eligible for special education solely because of limited English proficiency or environmental, cultural, or economic disadvantage.

B. Preparing for the IEP Eligibility Meeting

After your child is evaluated, the school district will schedule an IEP meeting to discuss your child's eligibility for special education. Depending on the circumstances of your case, your school district may hold off scheduling the IEP program meeting until after your child is found eligible. But if eligibility seems likely, the school district may be prepared to hold the IEP program meeting immediately after the eligibility meeting; otherwise, it must do so within 30 days of determining that your child is eligible for special education.

The strategies for a successful IEP eligibility meeting are the same as for a successful IEP program meeting. In preparing for the IEP eligibility meeting—or the possibility of a joint IEP eligibility and program meeting—review Chapters 10 and 11.

To prepare for the eligibility meeting, follow these tips:

- **Get a copy of your child's school file.** If you don't already have a copy, see Chapter 3.

- **Get copies of all school evaluations.** Evaluations are covered in Chapter 6. A sample letter requesting the report is in Chapter 6, Section E.

- **Know the school district's position in advance.** If the evaluation report recommends eligibility, call the special education administrator and ask if the district will agree with that recommendation. If the answer is yes, ask if the IEP eligibility meeting will go right into an IEP program meeting. If the evaluation report is not clear about eligibility, call the administrator and ask what the district's position is on your child's eligibility. If the evaluation recommends against eligibility, be prepared to show that your child is eligible. Here are a few suggestions:

  ▲ *Review the school file and evaluation report.* Cull out test results and other information that support your child's eligibility.

  ▲ *Organize all other reports and written material that support your position on eligibility.* Observations from teachers and teacher's aides are especially important. Ask anyone who has observed your child and who agrees that he or she should be in special education to attend the IEP eligibility meeting. If a key person cannot attend, ask for a letter or written observation report.

- **Consider having your child evaluated by an independent evaluator.** An independent evaluator may be necessary if the school district's report concludes that your child is not eligible for special education. Even if your child is found eligible, you may disagree with the school's recommendations regarding services and programs—many times these are spelled out in the school district's report.

- **Get organized.** Get your documents together before the eligibility meeting so you can immediately find what you need.

Chapter 8 provides tips on how to best organize existing material—and develop new information—to make your case at an IEP eligibility or program meeting. Chapter 8 also discusses how to use an independent evaluator.

C. Attending the Eligibility Meeting

Many of the procedures and strategies used at the IEP eligibility meeting are similar to those used at an IEP program meeting. Chapters 10 and 11 explain how to prepare for, and participate in, an IEP meeting. This section highlights some issues that are particularly important for eligibility meetings.

1. Who Should Attend?

Who should attend the eligibility IEP meeting depends a great deal on whether you anticipate a debate about eligibility. If your school district appears ready to find your child eligible for special education, then you probably don't need anyone at the meeting other than you and your child's other parent. If the school district does not agree that your child is eligible, or you don't know the district's position, you may want to ask people who can support your position to attend the meeting. Such people might include:

- an independent evaluator
- your child's current teacher, and
- other professionals who know your child.

Whether you ask any of these people to attend the IEP eligibility meeting may depend on their availability, the strength of their point of view, and cost. Sometimes, a letter from your pediatrician or another professional might be just as effective—and is certainly less expensive—than paying your pediatrician to attend in person. As a general rule, do not pay someone to attend the IEP eligibility meeting unless you are certain that

there will be a disagreement and that you will need that person to support your position. In most cases, an independent evaluator is your most effective advocate.

2. Preparing Your Participants

Make sure your participants are prepared to:
- describe who they are, their training, and how they know your child
- discuss their conclusions about your child's eligibility for special education and the basis for those conclusions—observation, long-term knowledge of your child, or testing, and
- contradict any material concluding that your child is not eligible for special education.

3. Submitting Your Eligibility Material

As you prepare for the IEP eligibility meeting and accumulate material (such as an independent evaluation supporting your child's eligibility), you will have to decide whether to show the material to the school district before the meeting. IDEA does not require you to do so, but consider the kind of relationship you want to establish with the school district. If you ask for the school district's evaluation in advance, it is only fair to offer the district a copy of yours. Granted, you will give the school a chance to prepare a rebuttal. On the other hand, if you submit an independent evaluation or other material at the IEP meeting, the school may ask to reschedule the meeting in order to review your material. In the long run, your best bet is to treat the school district as you want to be treated. If you have favorable material not in the school district's possession, submit it in advance, or at least call the administrator and ask if he or she wants your information ahead of time.

4. Meeting Procedures

An IEP eligibility meeting generally proceeds as
follows:

- general introductions
- review of school material
- review of any material you want to introduce,
  and
- discussion of whether your child qualifies
  for special education and, if so, on what
  basis.

5. Outcome of Meeting

If the school district determines that your child is
eligible for special education, then it will prepare
for the IEP program meeting—to happen immediately after the eligibility meeting (see Section D,
below) or on another date. If the school district
finds that your child is not eligible for special
education, see Section E, below.

D. Joint IEP Eligibility/ Program Meeting

The school district may combine the IEP eligibility and program meetings into one. In such a
situation, your child would be found eligible for
special education, and then the IEP team would
shift gears and immediately begin developing the
IEP program—goals, program, placement, services, and the like. Holding one meeting may
save you time and scheduling headaches, but it
also requires that you do a lot of preparation up
front. If you're not ready to discuss the IEP program at the IEP eligibility meeting, ask for another meeting to give yourself time to prepare.

On the other hand, if you'd like to combine
the meetings (assuming your child is found
eligible), ask the school district to do so. Make
your request well before the scheduled eligibility
meeting so everyone will have enough time to
prepare.

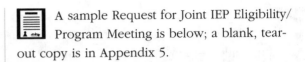 A sample Request for Joint IEP Eligibility/
Program Meeting is below; a blank, tear-
out copy is in Appendix 5.

E. If Your Child Is Not Found Eligible for Special Education

You may attend the IEP eligibility meeting, point
out significant information supporting your child's
eligibility, and argue your point in a manner wor-
thy of Clarence Darrow—all to no avail. What
then? You have two options.

1. Exercise Your Due Process Rights

As explained in Chapter 2, due process is your
right to take any dispute you have with your
child's district—whether a disagreement about an
evaluation, eligibility, or any part of the IEP—to a
neutral third party to help you resolve your dispute. Due process is covered in Chapter 12.

2. Seek Eligibility Under Section 504 of the Rehabilitation Act

Section 504 of the federal Rehabilitation Act (29
U.S.C. § 794) is a disability rights law entirely
separate from IDEA. It requires all agencies that
receive federal financial assistance to provide
"access" to individuals with disabilities. Histori-
cally, Section 504 has been used to require public
agencies to install wheelchair accessible ramps,
accessible rest rooms, and other building features,
and to provide interpreters at meetings. Section
504 also requires school districts to ensure that
children with disabilities are provided access to
educational programs and services through physical modifications (such as ramps, widened door-
ways, and accessible restrooms and other school
facilities) and assistance from interpreters, note
takers, readers, and the like.

Request for Joint IEP Eligibility/Program Meeting

Date: March 10, 20xx

To: Valerie Sheridan

McKinley Unified School District

1345 South Drive

Topeka, KS 00078

Re: Carl Ralston, student in fourth-grade, Eisenhower School

I believe there is sufficient information for us to discuss both my child's eligibility for special education and the specifics of my child's IEP at the same meeting. I would appreciate it if you would plan enough time to discuss both those important items at the April 14, 20xx IEP meeting. I would also like to see any and all reports and other written material that you will be introducing at the IEP meeting, at least two weeks before the meeting.

Thanks in advance for your help. I hope to hear from you soon.

Sincerely,

Albert Ralston

Albert Ralston

78 Elm Drive

Topeka, KS 00078 Elm Drive

Phones: 555-1111 (home); 555-2222 (work)

Your child may be entitled to assistance under Section 504 even if he or she is not eligible under IDEA. The first step in the process is to refer your child for Section 504 services—this simply means asking the school to consider your child's eligibility under Section 504. Some school districts automatically consider children who are found ineligible under IDEA for Section 504 services; if yours does not, request—in writing—that it do so.

Once a child has been referred, the school will evaluate eligibility. It will look at:

- whether the child has a physical or mental impairment
- whether the child's impairment substantially limits the child's "major life activities," including learning, and
- what types of accommodations the child needs in order to receive a free, appropriate public education.

If your child is found eligible for help under Section 504, the school must develop a written plan describing the modifications, accommodations, and services your child will receive. Like an IEP, the Section 504 plan must be individually tailored to meet your child's needs. Many schools have developed a standard form for Section 504 plans; ask your school if it has one.

Because Section 504 tries to achieve the same result as IDEA—to give children the help necessary for academic success—many of the tips and strategies described in this book will be useful to you as you develop a Section 504 plan for your child. The eligibility, procedural, and other requirements of Section 504 are different from IDEA's requirements, however. Because this book focuses on the IEP process, you'll need to get more information on Section 504 if you decide to proceed.

Need more information on Section 504?
Contact the U.S. Department of Education, Office of Civil Rights (contact information is in Appendix 2), your school district, your local community advisory committee, or one of the disability groups listed in Appendix 3. You can find a copy of the Section 504 regulations in Appendix 1.

8

Exploring Your Options and Making Your Case

Once your child is found eligible for special education, the IEP team must decide what type of instruction and assistance your child will receive. This chapter will help you develop material supporting your child's special education needs. By now, you should have a copy of your child's school file and the school district's evaluation report. You should also have developed a rudimentary IEP blueprint for your child. In addition, you may have spoken to other parents, your child's teacher and classroom aide, your child's pediatrician, and others who have recently observed your child. In other words, you may have a mountain of information available—and you may not know exactly how to put it to use.

The key to a successful IEP meeting is developing and using information that supports your position regarding your child's educational needs. This chapter will explain how to:

- review your child's school file and the school district's evaluation report (Section A)
- keep tabs on your child's current progress in school (Section B)
- look into available special education programs and services—both in and out of the school district—that may be appropriate for your child (Sections C and D)
- figure out whether available programs and services fit your child's education needs and whether you need additional information to make your case (Section E), and
- make a list of other materials you might generate to support your position, such as an independent evaluation, a statement from your child's teacher, or a statement from your child's pediatrician or other professional (Sections F and G).

Key Elements for Child's Program

Child: William Smith		
Date: June 1, 20xx		
Desired IEP Components	District Material	District Position
Placement in regular class	4-4-98 Evaluation	Agrees, p. 4
1:1 aide for regular class	4-4-98 Evaluation	No position
	3-12-98 Biweekly Teacher Report	Teacher agrees
Adaptive Physical Ed.	5-2-98 Adaptive P.E. Evaluation	Disagrees (but see comment on p. 5)

Chapter 10 provides a system for organizing all of your materials—positive and negative—to best make your case at your child's IEP meeting.

A. Review the School District's Information

Your first step in preparing for the IEP program meeting is to figure out what position the school will probably take, and whether you can use any of the school district's own documents and statements to show that your child needs a particular program. Start by reviewing all of the information you've received from the school district. As you look over your child's school file, evaluation report, and other school district items, there are several issues to consider.

1. Read Between the Lines

Can you figure out what position the school district will take, simply by reading your child's file and evaluation report? Sometimes it's easy—for example, if the report says "Martha qualifies for special education as a student with specific learning disabilities," or "Henry needs speech therapy twice a week," you'll know exactly where the school district stands. Sometimes it's not so clear. For example, the report might say, "Henry has difficulty in producing the 'th' and 's' sounds" but not mention needed services. Don't be surprised to find more vague statements than definitive ones.

2. Where to Look for the School District's Position

You can find the school district's position in a variety of materials. It is most likely to come up in an evaluation report, but you may also find the school district's position in a letter, teacher report or memo, your child's report cards, or another written item in your child's file. Your child's teacher, the school evaluator, or another district employee may even have stated the school district's position in a conversation.

If the school district employee's statement supports your position, be sure to send a confirming letter (see Chapter 4, Section A7).

3. Sources of the School District's Data

It's important to figure out who is saying what in the school district's material. These speakers are the district's experts, and their opinions will greatly influence the IEP process. Specifically, you'll want to know each person's:

- name and position—for example, a teacher, teacher's aide, or evaluator
- training and expertise, and
- first-hand experience with your child.

4. Keeping Track of the School District's Statements

Once you've reviewed all of the information available from the school district, make a chart like the one shown above to highlight key elements of your child's program (see your blueprint for ideas), whether the school district agrees or disagrees with your position, and where in the school district's materials the issue is addressed. Note where the school district's data supports or opposes your position, and where you have gaps to be filled—little or no information to show that a particular program or service is necessary for your child to receive an appropriate education. Finally, note the source of the information—was it in writing, or did someone say it to you?

5. Changing a Report or Evaluation

If there is something in your child's school file or the evaluation report that is inaccurate and harmful to your child, find out whether the school district is willing to change the statement. Start with a phone call. For example:

"Hello, Mr. Crandel, I'm Vickie Jones's father. I read your evaluation, and I appreciate your help in evaluating Vicki's needs. I did want to ask you a question. You say on page 4 that Vickie does not need help with her reading comprehension. Did you see the teacher's report, which says that she needs one-on-one reading help?"

To make a formal request for a change, see Chapter 3, Section B5 (changing something in a school file) and Chapter 6, Section E (changing a draft evaluation report).

B. Keep Tabs on Your Child's Progress

As you prepare for an IEP program meeting, take some time to learn how your child is currently doing in school—in regular or special education. If your child is doing poorly in school and you're preparing for an IEP eligibility meeting, you'll want to describe at the IEP meeting exactly how your child is floundering. If you are preparing for an IEP program meeting, be ready to explain why the current program is right for your child or why it needs changing.

Here are a few suggestions for getting current information about your child:

- Ask the teacher, teacher's aide, and service provider for periodic reports focusing on key areas of need for your child—reading, behavior, language development, social interaction, spelling, physical mobility, and the like.

- Ask the teacher for samples and reports of your child's work.
- Visit your child's class (see Section C, below).
- Set up periodic meetings with your child's teacher. If your child already has an IEP, ask the teacher whether the current IEP goals are being met.

Example:
One of your child's current IEP goals is to read a three-paragraph story and demonstrate 80% comprehension by answering questions. Ask the teacher if your child can read a three-paragraph story. Then ask about your child's reading comprehension level. If it's not up to 80%, where is it—60%? 40%? 20%?

To easily organize this material, you can create a chart for your child's teacher to complete on a regular (such as monthly) basis, updating your child's progress in key areas such as math, reading, behavior, and motor development, as well as emotional and psychological issues and self-help skills.

A sample Progress Chart is below; a blank, tear-out copy is in Appendix 5. You can tailor this chart to your child's particular goals. This form will help you track your child's general progress, as well as whether your child is meeting the IEP goals. (See Chapter 9 for more details on developing goals.)

C. Explore Available School Programs

To prepare for the IEP program meeting, you will want to gather information about your child's existing program and other possible programs that may be appropriate for your child.

Program possibilities include:

- placement in a regular classroom, perhaps with support services—ask about local

Progress Chart

Student: __Mary Hamilton__

Class: __Ms. Frank's 3rd Grade__

Date: __February 23, 20xx__

Key Goals	Current Status	Comments
Math	Progressing appropriately? ☒ yes ☐ no	On schedule to complete goals.
Reading	Progressing appropriately? ☒ yes ☐ no	On schedule to complete goals. Needs to improve reading fluidity.
Writing	Progressing appropriately? ☒ yes ☐ no	On schedule to complete goals.
Spelling	Progressing appropriately? ☐ yes ☒ no	Reversals continue to be problem.
Social-Behavioral	Progressing appropriately? ☐ yes ☒ no	Still problems with focus; hard time not teasing others.
Language development	Progressing appropriately? ☒ yes ☐ no	On schedule, but some problems going from specific to general.
Motor development	Progressing appropriately? ☐ yes ☒ no	Small motor problems affecting handwriting.
Other	Progressing appropriately? ☐ yes ☒ no	When struggling with spelling and handwriting, seems to feel high level of stress.

options, including your child's neighborhood school

- placement in a program designed specifically for children with learning disabilities, difficulties with communication, or other disabling conditions—ask about special day classes at your neighborhood school, nearby schools, or other schools in the area, or
- placement in a specialized program, such as a private school or residential program—ask about the existence and location of any such programs.

1. Ask About Available Programs

Contact your child's teacher, the school evaluator, the district special education administrator, other parents, your PTA, and your local community advisory committee. Ask about programs generally used for children with similar needs.

The school administrator (or even the classroom teacher) may be reluctant to tell you about programs. You may hear, for example, "It is way too early to be looking at programs for next year, Mr. and Mrs. Smith. We've just started this year." Or "We don't think it is appropriate to discuss programs until the IEP team meets and drafts goals. Then we can talk about programs."

Although school personnel may have reasons for making assertions like these, you have every right to find out about available program options. Emphasize that you are not looking to change programs or force an early IEP decision—you are merely trying to gather information. You might respond, "I appreciate what you are saying, Ms. Casey, but it will really be helpful to me and my child to begin as early as possible, so we can plan ahead. I am not looking for a change in programs or for a commitment on your part. Is there some reason why I shouldn't gather information about programs in the district?"

2. Visit Programs

The best way to find out what a particular school or program has to offer is to spend some time there. However, while school administrators may provide you with some information about existing programs, they may be reluctant for you to actually visit a program before the IEP meeting. Although the IEP team may not know which program will meet your child's needs until after you have the IEP meeting, nothing in IDEA prevents you from visiting potential programs before the meeting, as long as your requests are reasonable.

If the administrator refuses to let you visit programs, put your concerns in writing.

A sample Program Visitation Request letter is below; a blank, tear-out copy is in Appendix 5.

If the administrator still refuses your request, don't give up. Indicate that you understand his or her concerns, but feel that you could not possibly make a decision in the IEP about placement without some basic information about available programs. Make it clear that you are more than willing to visit programs again after the IEP meeting.

If you get nowhere, contact the administrator's superior. If that fails, you can file a complaint with your state department of education or other appropriate educational agency, as discussed in Chapter 13. The complaint might not be processed until after the IEP meeting. If this happens, you'll have to decide whether to postpone the IEP or ask (at the IEP meeting) to see the programs after the meeting. In that case, you may not be ready to sign the IEP. (See Chapter 11, Section E, for information on signing the IEP.)

Obviously, you don't need a school administrator's permission to visit private programs in the area. Simply call and schedule your own appointments.

Program Visitation Request Letter

Date: ___April 6, 20xx___

To: ___Mr. John White, Special Education Administrator___

___Carlson Unified School District___

___8709 Fourth Street___

___Helena, MT 00087___

Re: ___Elizabeth Moore___

I appreciate the concerns you have, and I realize that you can't know what programs are appropriate for my child until after the IEP meeting. Nonetheless, I think it would be very helpful for me to see existing programs so I can be a more effective member of the IEP team. I do not feel I can make an informed IEP decision without seeing, firsthand, all possible options. I want to assure you that I understand that by giving me the names of existing programs, you are not stating an opinion as to their appropriateness for my child.

I assure you that I will abide by all rules and regulations for parental visits. If those rules and regulations are in writing, please send me a copy.

Thanks in advance for your help. I hope to hear from you soon.

Sincerely,

Arnette Moore

Arnette Moore

87 Mission Road

Helena, MT 00087

Phones: 555-3334 (home); 555-4455 (work)

a. When to Visit Programs

Ideally, you will want to visit programs in the fall of the school year. While it may seem logical to visit right before the IEP meeting, checking out possible program options earlier offers these advantages:

- The sooner you see a particular program, the sooner you'll have a sense of whether or not it is appropriate for your child.
- If you can't judge whether a particular program is a good fit for your child, there will be time for others, such as an independent evaluator, to take a look and give you an opinion.
- You'll have time to visit a program more than once, if necessary.

b. Visitation Guidelines

The purpose of your visits is to gather information. As you plan your visits, keep in mind these points:

- Ask to visit *all* program options.
- Follow the policies and rules established by the school district, school site administrator, and teacher.
- If an independent evaluator or other professional will attend the IEP meeting, it is a good idea to have him or her visit with you. Be sure to inform the school district ahead of time.
- Do not ask for any personal information about the students, such as names of individual children. A teacher should *not* give you this information. You can (and should) talk with any parents you know who have children in the programs.
- Secure as much detail as possible about each program or class. Include the same categories of information you use in your blueprint (see Chapter 5):

- ▲ student description (number of students in the program; students' disabilities, age, cognitive range, and language range)
- ▲ staff description (details on teachers and aides)
- ▲ teacher-student instruction (teacher-to-class, small group, or individual)
- ▲ curricula, methodology, and other teaching strategies used
- ▲ classroom environment (behavior problems, noise level, number of teachers and teacher aides, and how much time teacher aides spend in class)
- ▲ related services (how many children leave the class to go to another program and how often; how many children receive related services in the class), and
- ▲ any other comments you have on the program.

IDEA does not require that the teacher provide you with this information, so you should ask in a pleasant, matter-of-fact way. If the teacher balks, indicate that the information you seek is important and noncontroversial, and should be made available.

Write down your observations and the answers to your questions. You can write as you watch the class and talk to the teacher. If you "interview" the teacher with notebook in hand and pencil poised, however, the teacher may be intimidated. By saying, "I have a poor memory; do you mind if I take notes while we talk?" you may put the teacher at ease. If not, try to take notes in an unobtrusive way, or wait until you're outside and write down what you remember as soon as possible.

A sample Class Visitation Checklist is below; a blank, tear-out copy is in Appendix 5. Be sure to keep copies of this important form in your IEP binder.

Class Visitation Checklist

Date: __9/11/04__   Time: __9:00-10:15__   a.m./~~p.m.~~

School: __Jefferson School, Chicago__

Class: __Third-grade Special Day Class for Learning Disabled (Teacher: Sue Avery)__

Student Description:

Total students: __17__   Gender range: __12 boys, 5 girls__

Age range: __7 - 10 (ten kids are nine or younger; seven ten-year olds)__

Cognitive range: __"Wide range, probably from pre-K through 5th-grade skills," says S. Avery__
__(teacher)__

Language/communication range: __Two students with hearing impairment, two other students__
__with delayed communication skills (1st-grade level)__

Disability range: __12 students have specific learning disability, three are borderline retarded,__
__one has emotional disturbance, and one autistic-like behavior__

Behavioral range: __Five students acting out throughout class, four other students constantly__
__demanding of teacher. Two students sent to principal because of behavior. Rest of class__
__generally cooperative, quiet.__

Other observations: __Overall impression was of a class of children with varied needs and behavior,__
__which made it difficult for the teacher to focus on any one group of children for very long.__

Staff Description:

Teachers: __Sue Avery has four years' experience working with learning disabled children. She__
__was generally very patient with students (less so with the behaviorally troubled children), but__
__she seemed easily distracted.__

Aides: __In class two hours per day; worked with all children, no one child more than few__
__minutes. Seemed mostly to check in with students superficially, but not provide any sustained__
__1:1 help. Aide has no specific training working with learning disabled children.__

Other observations: __Neither teacher nor aide seemed fully comfortable with curriculum,__
__particularly given varied needs of students. Both were very nice to students.__

Curricula/Classroom Strategies:

Curricula: "Using Mathematics," (Book 2) for math, teacher-developed materials for spelling, and "Project Explore" for science lessons.

Strategies: Teacher/aide, when working 1:1 in reading, divided words into simple sounds using much repetition; no overall strategy or specific curriculum designed for learning disabled children.

Classroom Environment:

Description: Classroom had tiled floor so sound echoed. Quite loud; no other apparent acoustical treatment to reduce noise; all added to a noisy room. Various work stations and cubicles set up so students can work 1:1 or by themselves. Somewhat effective, but noise was distracting to all students. Classroom situated near playground, so much visual stimulation outside classroom window and noise from outside.

Related Services:

At least four students received their related services in class, one had speech therapy, another had a special aide who worked with her in the corner.

Other Comments:

School site principal (Lee Parsons) is interested in special education but has no training or expertise in the field. She did express reservations about excessive mainstreaming of children with disabilities into regular classrooms. Visited one mainstreamed class; teacher seemed interested, but expressed concern that the school had not provided any support or training for dealing with special education students in her regular class.

How This Program Relates to IEP Blueprint:

Program does not meet Tara's blueprint:

- Cognitive and behavioral range of students too wide
- Teacher unable to provide individual attention
- Aide not trained for working with L-D kids
- Question about curriculum

D. Find Out About Related Services

Classroom programs are only one component of your child's IEP program. Related services, such as occupational, physical, or speech therapy, are also very important (see Chapter 2).

Gathering information about related services will be a little different from gathering information about programs. You'll still want to talk to your child's teacher, the school evaluator, the district special education administrator, other parents, your PTA, and a local parent group for disabled children to find out about related services for children with similar needs. But the similarities end there.

Service providers, such as physical therapists, usually work one-on-one with individual children or in small groups. So visiting these specialists in action may not be possible. Instead, when you talk to people about the services available, ask about the background, training, and experience of the specialists. Candid conversations with other parents should be most helpful.

Keep detailed notes of your conversations and include them in your IEP binder.

E. Compare Your Blueprint With the Existing Programs and Services

Once you have information about your school district's programs and services, compare what's available to what you believe your child needs. Obviously, if the school provides services you feel will meet your child's needs (as described in your blueprint), the IEP process should be relatively simple. On the other hand, if there is a gap between what your child needs and what is available, you face the task of convincing the IEP team that the school options are inappropriate.

You'll need to detail the shortcomings of the programs and services offered by the school district. Be as specific as possible: Is the problem the frequency or location of a service, the pupil-teacher ratio, the qualifications of the teacher or service provider, the specific work to be done with a service provider, the class makeup, the teacher methodology, the curriculum, or other important features?

Make a comprehensive, side-by-side comparison of your blueprint and what you know about the school's options, and put the details on the bottom of the class visitation checklist.

F. Generate Additional Supporting Information

Once you've reviewed your child's school file, developed your blueprint, reviewed the school evaluation, evaluated your child's progress, and gathered information about program and service options, you may need further data to support your goals. This material will be invaluable in preparing for the IEP meeting.

1. Help From School Personnel

Contact any teachers, evaluators, or service providers who are likely to support your position. You can do this by phone or in person. Explain what programs and services you want for your child (your blueprint), and why you feel they are appropriate. Note any discrepancy between what you want and what you believe the school district has available. Explain why you want what you want for your child and ask for their ideas and opinions.

Ask if the teacher, evaluator, or service provider would be willing to write a statement supporting what you want for your child or to state his or her position at the IEP meeting.

If you talk to someone who supports your point of view but doesn't want to put anything in writing, follow up the conversation with a confirming letter (see Chapter 4, Section A), such as, "Thank you for the chance to chat today. I appreciate your frankness and was glad to hear that you agree that Max needs an aide in order to function effectively in the regular class."

Be aware that a confirming letter can put the teacher in an awkward position. If the teacher says one thing to you (and you confirm it in a letter) and then says another thing at the IEP meeting, the letter may be important proof of what was originally said—but this may lead to some friction between you and the teacher. If the teacher will not speak frankly at the IEP meeting, however, the confirming letter will be valuable proof of what was said earlier—and might discourage the teacher from changing his or her tune.

No matter what, be sure to keep notes of what was said, including the date, time, and place of the conversation, in as much detail as possible. This is your record in case the school representative gives a different story later.

2. Help From People Outside the School

Anyone who knows your child or has some expertise in special education or your child's disability may be of value. This includes your child's doctor, tutor, therapist, or other specialist.

Ask each person to write a letter to the IEP team stating:

- how he or she knows your child
- his or her expertise
- any specific comments on your child's condition and educational experience, and
- recommendations for your child in terms of programs, services, or other IEP components.

Example:

"Teresa needs extensive help with small and large motor skills, and should work with an occupational and physical therapist at least three times a week."

G. Independent Evaluations

An independent evaluation may be the most important document supporting what you want for your child. An independent evaluation, like the school district's evaluation, can be as comprehensive or as narrow as your child's needs dictate. In most cases, an independent evaluation will use a variety of tests to evaluate your child's needs.

Chapter 6 discusses evaluations in general, and Chapter 11 covers how to present an independent evaluation at the IEP meeting.

Under IDEA, you have an absolute right to have an independent evaluation of your child. Moreover, your school district is required to provide you with information on where you can get an individual evaluation.

While IDEA requires the school district to consider the results of the independent evaluation in making any decision regarding your child's education, it does not require that your school district agree with the results. While an independent evaluation may include persuasive information, your child's school district can reject the conclusions. (You do have the right to go to due process (mediation session or hearing) to prove the district is wrong. See Chapter 12.)

1. When to Use an Independent Evaluation

You may want an independent evaluation because you need more information about your child or because the school district's evaluation does not support what you want. If the district's position is clear—and you disagree with it—an outside evaluation may very well be needed.

2. Finding Independent Evaluators

Independent evaluators generally work in private practice or are affiliated with hospitals, universities, or other large institutions. How do you find a qualified independent evaluator? Here are a few tips:

- Ask parents of children with similar disabilities. Check with the PTA or your school district's advisory committee of parents with children in special education.
- Get recommendations from the school. A trusted teacher, aide, service provider, or other school employee may be able to give you some names.
- Talk to your child's pediatrician.
- Call a local hospital, particularly a university medical hospital. A department that employs experts in your child's disability may be able to do the evaluation or refer you to someone who can.
- Contact an organization that specializes in your child's particular disability. (See Appendix 3.)
- Call local private schools for disabled children. Private schools often work with credible independent evaluators.

How Not to Find an Independent Evaluator

Evaluators are often psychologists. If you look in the phone book, you will see a long list of psychologists. But choosing randomly from the phone book is a poor method for selecting a reputable and knowledgeable evaluator. The only thing you really know about these people is that they could afford to pay for a listing.

3. Selecting the Right Evaluator

Speak to various independent evaluators, and ask the following questions for each person:

- Does the evaluator have significant expertise, training, and experience in dealing with your child's disability?
- Is the evaluator affiliated with a well-respected institution?
- Were you referred by someone who actually worked with the evaluator ?
- Do you trust the person (or institution) who recommended the evaluator ?
- Will the evaluator give you references?
- Did the evaluator's references like the results of the evaluator's work and find the evaluator easy to work with?
- Is the evaluator impartial? (An evaluator who has previously done work for—and been paid by—your child's school district may not be truly independent.)
- Can the evaluator complete the evaluation and written report well in advance of the IEP meeting?
- Can the evaluator attend the IEP meeting, if necessary?

The answers to these questions, your own impressions, and recommendations from others are key factors in making your decision. It is also important that the independent evaluator be able to clearly articulate his or her position, professionally and vigorously.

4. Getting an Independent Evaluator on Your Side

The reason you are hiring an independent evaluator is to support your educational goals for your child. Be very clear on your plans and perspectives.

Examples:

- You have very specific desires (your blue-print) concerning the related service you believe is best for your child—you know what you want in terms of type, amount, and duration of service; type of service provider; and teacher-pupil setting. Be sure the evaluator makes recommendations that support the program and services you want for your child: "Given Michelle's need to develop expressive speech, she requires speech therapy four times a week, each session of 50 minutes. She also needs one-to-one work with a qualified speech thera-pist experienced in working with children who have an expressive language delay."
- You want your son placed in a school for children with emotional disturbances. Ideally, the evaluator will write, "Philip requires placement in a program with no more than ten children, a full-time aide, a teacher qualified to work with emotionally troubled children, and a class where there are no behavioral problems. The Woodson School in Boston is the only program that can meet Philip's needs."

If the evaluator can't or won't name a specific school or program, then make sure he or she will name the specific components of an appropriate program. Continuing the example above, if the independent assessor won't say Philip needs to be placed in the Woodson School, he or she should say that Philip needs placement in a pro-gram that has the characteristics of the Woodson School.

It is of course possible that your goals may not be supported by the data. Good evaluators will not write something they disagree with or make a recommendation they do not believe in. They will tell you when the evidence—the testing data—does not support what you want.

You want an evaluator who will:

- show you a draft evaluation report
- consider your concerns about the draft report

- make specific recommendations about your child's educational status and appropriate programs and related services to meet your child's needs, and
- provide a written rationale for these recommendations.

5. How an Independent Evaluation Proceeds

Most independent evaluators will meet with you and review your child's school file, the school district's report, and other district material. The evaluator will then explain what testing will be done, secure your approval, do the testing, and prepare a report. Depending on your child's characteristics and needs, the evaluator may also want to observe the child in class.

6. When to Submit the Independent Evaluation

Just as you want to review the school district's evaluations before the IEP meeting, the school district will likely want to see your independent evaluation before the IEP meeting. Of course, the more time the school has to review the independent evaluation, the more time the administration will have to find data to counter its conclusions. Does this mean you should delay giving the school district your evaluation? While such a strategy has its attractions, the bottom line is that the school district is entitled to the same courtesy that you are.

Holding off on giving the district a copy of your evaluation could ultimately prove counter-productive. The district may distrust you and your evaluation. The delay may be grounds for post-poning the IEP meeting. And your relationship with the district may be affected. Because you will likely be working together for many years, you should maintain a positive relationship, if possible. If one party will be nasty, unfair, or un-trustworthy, let it be someone other than you.

While there is no hard-and-fast rule here, providing the independent evaluation (and other key material) a week before the IEP meeting is usually appropriate.

7. Cost of an Independent Evaluation

Independent evaluations can be quite costly, anywhere from several hundred dollars to several thousand dollars.

But you may not have to pay for the evaluation. Under IDEA, a parent has the right to an independent educational evaluation of her child (by someone of your choosing) at public expense if you disagree with an evaluation obtained by the school district. The school district must pay for that independent evaluation unless it exercises its due process rights under IDEA and convinces the hearing officer that the school district evaluation was appropriate. (Current IDEA regulations at 34 C.F.R. § 300.502(b).)

While a school district rarely proceeds to due process on the issue of paying for an independent evaluation, that doesn't mean your school district won't. To win, the district has to show only that its own evaluation was appropriate, the appropriate tests were used, the evaluator was properly trained and knowledgeable, and your child was evaluated in all areas of suspected disability. The district must either pay for the independent evaluation or initiate due process "without unnecessary delay." (Current IDEA regulations at 34 C.F.R. § 300.502(b)(2).)

So the real problem for parents is how to get the district to pay for the evaluation, particularly because IDEA does not require the school district to pay in advance or provide assurances that it will pay. If you want the school district to pay, you will probably have to pay the evaluator yourself and seek reimbursement from the district.

Here are some ideas on getting the district to pay:

- Ask the evaluator to bill the school district directly. Because the evaluator wants to be paid, he or she may not be willing to do this. But there's no harm in asking.
- If the evaluator won't bill the district, pay the bill and submit a copy to the district, with a cover letter explaining that IDEA requires the district to pay unless it pursues due process.
- If the district doesn't go to due process and still won't pay, file a complaint (as discussed in Chapter 13). ■

9

Writing Goals

Goals are the nuts and bolts of your child's education: the academic, cognitive, linguistic, social, and vocational aims you have for your child.

Objectives Are No More

Special education law used to use the term "goals and objectives" to describe the accomplishments a child would aim for during the school year. In 1997, Congress changed the term "objectives" to "benchmarks," but the meaning remained the same: short-term accomplishments that would help a child achieve a broader goal and measure progress towards that goal.

In 2004, Congress eliminated both terms. The statute now refers to "measurable annual goals, including academic and functional goals designed to meet the child's needs." (20 U.S.C. § 1414(d)(1)(A)(i)(II).) It remains to be seen how school districts will interpret this change in language, but the terms certainly remain broad enough to give the IEP team latitude to develop whatever aims are appropriate for your child. This chapter includes examples of broad goals, as well as more detailed, short-term goals.

Examples of IEP Goals:

Tim will improve his reading comprehension.
Tim will read a four-paragraph story and demonstrate 75% comprehension using objective classroom tests.

Ellen will improve her peer relationships.
Ellen will initiate three positive peer interactions each day, per teacher observation.

Juan will master all third-grade math skills.
Juan will identify sets of ones and tens with 90% accuracy, using appropriate textbook tests.

Jane will improve her writing skills.
Jane will write a three-sentence paragraph with subject and predicate sentences, per teacher evaluation.

Mark will improve short-term auditory memory.
Mark will be able to listen to a set of ten related items and list them with 75% accuracy.

IDEA requires that an IEP program include a statement of measurable annual goals (20 U.S.C. § 1414(d)(1)(A)) for two reasons:
- to ensure that the child is involved and progressing in the general curriculum, and
- to meet other educational needs that result from the child's disability.

Because IDEA requires the school district to provide an appropriate education for your child, the question underlying many IEP decisions is, "Can this child's goals be met in a specific program or with a particular related service?" Your child's ability to meet the goals may very well determine whether the school district is providing an appropriate education.

What Goals Are Not

- Goals are not used for students who are in regular education. They are written for special education students—even special education students who are mainstreamed into regular classes.
- Goals are not part of a contract between you and the school district—that is, the school is not legally liable if your child does not meet the goals. Goals are a way to measure your child's progress.
- Goals are not the totality of your child's instructional plan. They are important aims to be accomplished during the school year.

A. Areas Covered by Goals

Goals can cover a wide variety of skill or need areas. If your child is not having difficulties in certain areas, however, the IEP team typically will not develop goals in those areas.

Goals can cover a wide range of areas, including:

- academic skills, such as math computation, reading comprehension, spelling, and writing
- cognitive skills, such as abstract thinking and memory
- emotional and psychological issues, such as overcoming fears or improving self-esteem
- social-behavioral skills, such as relating to peers
- linguistic and communication skills, such as expressing oneself effectively
- self-help and independent living skills, such as using money, dressing, using transportation, or using the toilet
- physical and recreational skills, such as improving fine and large motor skills
- vocational skills, such as work skill development, and
- transition skills, such as exploring work or college options.

B. Developing Goals

IDEA does not specify how to write goals, what subjects to cover, how many to include, or how to implement or measure them. The details are up to the IEP team. This flexibility allows you to develop goals that will be useful in conjunction with the programs and services you want for your child.

This section describes the typical elements of goals.

A sample Goals form appears later in this chapter. Also, see the section on goals in the sample IEP in Appendix 4.

1. Child's Present Level of Performance

The written IEP must include a statement of your child's present levels of "academic achievement and functional performance," including how the child's disability affects his or her involvement and progress in the general curriculum. (20 U.S.C. § 1414(d)(1)(A).) This information will demonstrate how your child is doing and where your child needs to improve, which will in turn help the IEP team develop appropriate goals in each subject and behavioral area.

The IEP program should spell out your child's current level of skill in each particular goal area. For example, for a reading comprehension goal, a child's present level of performance may state, "Beth's current reading comprehension is at the mid–fourth-grade level. She enjoys reading but requires help in maintaining focus."

2. Who Implements Goals

Your child's classroom teacher is usually responsible for implementing your child's goals. Depending on the goal, however, an aide or support professional may also be involved. For example:

- A child's language goals may be the responsibility of a speech therapist.
- Physical education or motor goals, such as handwriting improvement, may be the responsibility of an occupational or physical therapist.
- Emotional goals may be covered by a school counselor or therapist.

3. Completion Dates

Goals are normally written for a one-year period, but this is not set in stone. Some goals may very well be complete in less than a year—and it may be a good idea to set a shorter time frame in the written IEP.

Example:

Lily is in a special day class with no main-streaming in a regular classroom. Her IEP reading goal has a completion time of one year. Lily's parents feel that she could reach her reading goal more quickly if she were in a regular classroom. Establishing a shorter period may help her parents convince the school that Lily should be mainstreamed.

4. Measuring Goals

IDEA requires a child's goals to be "measurable." The IEP must describe how your child's progress toward the annual goals will be measured and when "periodic reports" on that progress will be given to you. (20 U.S.C. § 1414(d)(1)(A).)

There are a number of ways to measure goals, including objective testing, teacher or other staff observation, assessment of work samples, or any other method agreed to by the IEP team. Many IEP goals include a quantifiable accomplishment level, such as "Mia will read a four-paragraph story with 90% reading comprehension as measured by the Woodcock Reading Mastery Test."

Don't Set Your Sights Too Low

Be wary if an IEP team member from the school district suggests setting your child's goals fairly low. The district may want to set low standards so your child can achieve them without too much help from the school. If the school wants to eliminate a particular support service (such as a one-on-one aide) or keep your child in a special day class rather than mainstreaming him or her in a regular class, it might propose goals that your child can meet without this extra help.

IDEA does not require goals to be quantifiable—that is, capable of being measured in numbers. Although numbers can be of value, not everything of value can be reduced to numbers. For example, how does one measure numerically whether goals were met in areas relating to emotions, psychology, self-help, or vocational skills?

Example:

As a part of Sue's IEP program, Sue will explore whether she wants to go to college or begin work right after high school. As goals, these are stated as follows:

Sue will explore at least five areas of vocational interest.

Sue will read about five areas of vocational interest, write a brief explanation of each, and visit local examples of each.

The best ways to "measure" Sue's achievement may be teacher observation or Sue's completion of a personal diary.

C. When to Draft Goals

While specific goals are approved at the IEP meeting and included in the IEP program, it makes sense to draft them ahead of time.

In fact, it is not uncommon for school representatives to write goals in advance. Under IDEA, the school cannot simply present its goals at the IEP meeting, insist that you accept them, and refuse to discuss alternatives. That would violate a basic tenet of IDEA—that the IEP team makes all IEP decisions as a group, at the meeting. Still, you should anticipate that the school district might draft goals in advance. Prepare for the IEP meeting by asking the school district (in writing) for a copy of any predrafted goals at least two weeks in advance.

You, too, should draft goals in advance of the IEP meeting. You do not have to give a copy to the school district before the IEP meeting unless it asks you to, which would be unlikely. However, even if you aren't asked for a copy, you can give your goals to the school district in advance. Some advocates might argue against doing this because it gives the district time to counter your goals. Others argue that if you present your goals for the first time at the IEP meeting, the school district might need time to review them—and have to postpone the meeting.

In general, it is best to be open and provide the school district information in advance, unless the element of surprise is necessary in your particular situation.

D. Writing Effective Goals

Writing goals for the first time may seem as foreign to you as writing a medical prescription or nuclear physics equation. But don't worry—you'll get the hang of it. Like much of the IEP process, writing goals requires information gathering, asking questions, and a little practice.

1. Get Your School's IEP Form

Every school district has its own form on which the IEP program is written. As mentioned earlier in this book, you should get a copy and any guidelines that accompany it. As you begin to draft your child's goals, refer to the school's current IEP form for guidance.

2. Gather Your Information

Your dining room table or desk may be overrun with special education papers. If they are not already organized in a binder (as recommended in Chapter 4), take some time to gather them together. Make sure you have:

- your child's school file
- all evaluation reports
- written reports from professionals, and
- your blueprint.

Start with your blueprint—your desires for your child's education. The goals should support what's in your blueprint. While the blueprint won't show you how to write specific goals, it will help you think about what you ultimately want for your child. The goals you create will be the stepping stones your child uses to achieve these ultimate ends.

3. Talk to Professionals

Talk with your child's teacher, other support staff, your independent evaluator, service providers, and others who know your child. They might be willing to suggest specific goals, or at least to review yours.

If this is your child's first IEP, ask the professionals what areas your goals should cover and how to make them as specific as possible. Be sure to explore with them all the areas that you feel require goals.

If this is not your child's first IEP, ask professionals the following questions:

- What previous goals should be retained?
- If previous goals are carried over, why were they not accomplished before? What can be done to better ensure completion this year? Using the Progress Chart in Chapter 8, Section B, will help you monitor goals throughout the year.
- What new goals should be developed?

By talking with your child's teacher and other staff members about goals, you may learn their opinions about your child's placement and services. You may also develop an informal agreement on goals before the IEP meeting.

4. Talk to Other Parents

If you know other special education families, ask to see their IEPs, particularly if their child's needs are similar to your child's. Even if the needs are not the same, other parents may have very valuable information about how to draft goals; many are probably old pros at writing them.

Also, check with the PTA or school district's local advisory committee on special education for written material on goals, advice, and the names of any local individuals or organizations that provide help to special education parents. (Chapter 15 discusses parent organizations.)

Finally, check Appendix 3 for support organizations you can contact for help.

5. List Your Goals Areas

Your job is to develop goals for each skill area that relates directly to your child's needs. Eight such areas are listed in Section A, above. Be as precise as possible. For example, don't simply state "academic achievement." Specify reading, writing, math, cognitive, spelling, and the rest. Under social-behavioral, you might specify peer goals as well as self-control goals.

A sample Goals Chart is below; Appendix 5 includes a blank, tear-out copy. This chart is intended to give you a feel for what goals look like and provide you with language often used for different types of goals. Also, be sure to see the sample IEP form in Appendix 4.

6. Connect Goals to a Specific Program and Services

The best goals don't only state your immediate expectations for your child's performance, but also provide support for the program and services you want for your child. In fact, the goals in our sample form do just this. In the case of Leah, the sample is very descriptive—a "small and protected educational environment" and "a quiet and safe school environment." While not all goals are written this way—schools often argue that goals are not the place to mention programs or services—IDEA does not prevent such added language. You should argue for it and, at a minimum, include it in your draft goals.

When referring to a specific program or service, be as precise as you can. If you can mention the name of a special school or the details of the service, so much the better. If you don't have the exact information, then add something that will support your broad IEP program goals.

The key is to write the goals so that an objective person will conclude that your child will need the particular program or service to meet them. Even if the school district doesn't include the language in the final goals, you can use your draft as a reminder of what you want.

Write a variety of goals for each skill area, incorporating specific language and referring to the desired program and services. Then write a second set, omitting references to the program and services, but describing the programs and services you want. For example, assume you want your child in a regular classroom with a one-to-one aide in order to improve her reading comprehension. The ideal goal would be, "Mary, in Ms. Jones's regular third-grade class at Spencer School, will improve her reading comprehension, using her full-time one-to-one aide." The alternative would be, "With the assistance of her one-to-one aide, and by modeling her regular peers, Mary will improve her reading comprehension." If the school district disagrees that Mary should be mainstreamed, suggest implicit, instead of explicit, language, such as "modeling her regular peers."

Goals Chart

Skill Area	Annual Goal	Present Performance Level	How Progress Measured	Date of Completion
Reading	Ted, in his sophomore English class, will improve reading comprehension. He will demonstrate 90% comprehension of the assigned novel in his 10th-grade English class	Ted demonstrates 50% comprehension of the assigned novel.	Essays assigned for homework, tests, and teacher observation	June 20xx
Math	Bob, in his mainstreamed class, will master fourth-grade math skills. He will subtract a one-digit number from a two-digit number with 90% accuracy.	Bob subtracts a one-digit number from a two-digit number with 25% accuracy.	Teacher material	June 20xx
Emotional and psychological	Leah, in a class of no more than 12 students in a small and protected educational environment, will reduce her outward anger.	Leah averages five daily angry outbursts as observed.	Teacher and therapist observation and recording	June 20xx

Skill Area	Annual Goal	Present Performance Level	How Progress Measured	Date of Completion
Social-behavioral	Sara will improve her peer relationships. With the support of her aide and in a class of no more than ten students, Sara will initiate three positive peer interactions per day.	Sara is unable to initiate positive peer interactions.	Teacher-aide observation and recording	June 20xx
Linguistic and communication	Adam, in his tri-weekly, 45-minute, one-to-one speech therapy sessions, will improve articulation.	Adam produces the s, sh, and c sounds irregularly.	Speech therapist observation and recording	June 20xx
Self-help and independent living skills (transition services)	Nina will meet with the school guidance counselor each month, identify three fields of work that interest her, and arrange, with the counselor's help, to visit a workplace in each field by the end of the year.	Nina doesn't know what she wants to do when she graduates high school.	Parent and guidance counselor observation	June 20xx

10

Preparing for the IEP Meeting

Now that you've gathered information and figured out what kinds of help your child will need, it's time to get ready for the IEP meeting, where you and the school district will hammer out the details of your child's special education program. Preparing for the IEP meeting will make you a better advocate for your child, allow you to influence the IEP meeting agenda effectively, and reduce your own anxieties. In short, preparation increases your chances of success.

If you are attending your first IEP meeting, be sure to read this entire chapter. If you've done IEPs before, you'll want to at least skim this chapter. You might find some new ideas that you can put to use, and you'll learn some new rules from the 2004 amendments to IDEA.

While this chapter will help you prepare for the IEP meeting, everything that you've done to this point—gathering your child's school records, having your child evaluated, drafting a blueprint, and so on—will be crucial to the success of the meeting. If you've skipped any earlier chapters, you should go back and read them before reading this chapter.

IDEA regulations are changing. The regulatory citations throughout this book are to the current IDEA regulations—those that will be in effect until the Department of Education issues final regulations interpreting the 2004 amendments to IDEA. The Department expects to release these final regulations at the end of 2005; many of them will be identical or similar to the existing regulations cited in this chapter (although the citations will be different), while others will be new. When you use this book, you should make sure that you have the most current version of the regulations. See "Warning: Special Education Rules Are in Flux," in Chapter 1, for information that will help you stay up to date. You can find the most recent version of IDEA, including the 2004 amendments, starting at 20 U.S.C. § 1400; the most pertinent sections are included in Appendix 1.

A. Schedule the IEP Meeting

IDEA sets out rules about scheduling the IEP meeting. (20 U.S.C. § 1414(d).)

- It must be held at a time and location convenient for all parties, especially the parents. The school district cannot simply schedule a meeting on a morning when you must be at work or pick a time without your input.
- It must be held at least once a year.
- It must be long enough to cover all issues.

Do You Need an Interpreter?

The school district must take necessary steps to ensure that you understand the IEP proceedings, including hiring an interpreter if you are deaf or hard of hearing, or if your first language is not English. Be sure to let the school district know in advance if you need an interpreter at the IEP meeting.

1. Date of the IEP Meeting

As discussed in Chapter 4, the best time for the IEP meeting is in the spring preceding the school year for which you are developing the IEP plan. Before you choose a date, you may have to make several calls to the district administrator and your attendees to make sure everyone can attend. Make sure to give yourself at least a month to prepare for the meeting.

2. Length of the IEP Meeting

IDEA does not require that the IEP meeting last for a specific length of time. Before the meeting, ask the school administrator to find out how much time has been put aside. Two or three hours is common. If the administrator has allotted less time than you think is necessary, explain why you think a longer meeting is needed, particularly if it may eliminate the need for a second meeting. If the administrator insists that the time allotted is enough, put your concerns in writing and send a copy to the superintendent of schools. If you're really concerned, you can file a complaint (see Chapter 13), but there is no legal rule setting a minimum length for the IEP meeting.

Sample Letter Requesting More Time for IEP Meeting

Date: September 28, 20xx

To: Ms. Julia Warner
Director of Special Education
Monroe School District
892 South 4th Street
Salem, OR 97307

Re: Karen Jamison, student in first-grade class of Drew Bergman

You indicated that we had one hour for my daughter Karen's October 14th IEP meeting. As I mentioned on September 27, I believe the issues we have to discuss will require at least two hours. It would be a hardship on our family to attend two meetings.

I will be calling you within the next few days to discuss this. I appreciate your understanding in this matter.

Sincerely,
Denise Jamison
Denise Jamison
909 Hanson St.
Salem, OR 97307
Phones: 555-3090 (home); 555-5000 (work)

cc: School Superintendent Phyllis Bander

3. Forgoing the IEP Meeting

Once you have your child's yearly IEP meeting, you and the school district can agree to make changes to the IEP without having another meeting. Instead, you can agree on a written document that changes the IEP. This is a new procedure created by the 2004 amendments to IDEA. (20 U.S.C. § 1414(d)(3)(D).) Both you and the school district must consent to make changes this way.

IEP meetings can be taxing and often require parents to take time off work, so this can be a good alternative—unless you feel that you need the kind of discussion that typically takes place in an IEP meeting. If you choose to skip the meeting, be sure that your written agreement to change the IEP is clear and precise. You should also ask the school district to give you a new IEP document showing those changes, as required by 20 U.S.C. § 1414(d)(3)(F).

4. Meeting by Conference Call or Video Conference

The IEP meeting can be held via phone or video conference. (20 U.S.C. § 1414(f).) (If you are deaf or hard of hearing, the school district will need to set up the meeting so you can use a relay system or TTY.) Both you and the school district must agree to use one of these alternate procedures; the school district cannot set this up without your approval.

While these options offer some advantages, especially if your schedule makes it difficult to leave your home or work to attend a meeting, there are also some potential drawbacks. In a phone conference, it can be difficult to identify who is talking and to clearly hear what is being said. These procedures can also inhibit the kind of free-wheeling discussion that can be very important in an IEP meeting.

When a Child With an IEP Transfers to Another School District

The 2004 amendments to IDEA create new rules that apply when a child transfers from one school district to another. If the child is transferring within the same state, then the new school district must provide, in consultation with the parents, a free, appropriate public education "comparable" to that in the child's existing IEP. This comparable program will be in effect until a new IEP is developed. (20 U.S.C. § 1414(d)(2)(C)(i)(I).) If the child transfers to a different state, the same rules apply, except the comparable program will remain in effect until the new school district conducts an evaluation of the child. (20 U.S.C. § 1414(d)(2)(C)(i)(II).)

The term "comparable" doesn't necessarily mean "identical," but it certainly suggests something close. While you can't insist that your child be provided exactly the same program in all of its particulars, you shouldn't settle for a less-effective alternative. For example, if your child had a placement in a regular classroom with a 1:1 aide two hours a week, a comparable program would be a regular classroom with the same aide time, but the new classroom may be different in terms of curricula, teaching materials, and so on.

The new school district must also take reasonable steps to "promptly" obtain your child's records, including the written IEP and supporting documents, from the previous school district. The previous school district must take reasonable steps to respond to the request promptly. (20 U.S.C. § 1414(d)(2)(C)(ii).)

B. The IEP Meeting Agenda

Knowing the IEP meeting agenda in advance will help you tremendously as you prepare for the meetings. Although IDEA does not require the district to provide you with an agenda, it does require that you be given the opportunity to participate in and understand the proceedings. (Current IDEA regulations at 34 C.F.R. § 300.345(a)(e).) It would not be unreasonable, therefore, to know what issues will be discussed.

Most IEP meetings cover the following issues:

- your child's current status—how he or she is doing, whether or not previous goals were fulfilled, and what the current evaluations state
- specific goals
- specific support or related services, and
- specific program, including the type, make-up, and location of the class.

Ask the school district special education administrator for an agenda or a description of the specific issues that will be discussed at the meeting. After you receive it, check it against your blueprint to make sure that the issues you've flagged will be covered at the meeting. If a crucial item is not on the agenda, let the administrator know, preferably in writing.

C. Organize Your Materials

Having access to key material is vitally important in an IEP meeting. You don't want to be fumbling about, looking for that one report or quote that could really help. Following these steps will help you organize the mountain of material.

1. Review Your Blueprint and All Written Material

Your starting point in getting organized is your blueprint. You should also gather all written material, such as evaluations, previous IEPs, notes and reports from your child's teacher and other staff members, work samples, and letters to and from your child's school district. These should all be in your IEP binder, clearly labeled and organized for easy reference.

Review all of these documents. Plan to bring to the meeting everything that supports your blueprint. Also bring any materials that counter the negative points school district representatives might raise.

2. Highlight Supportive Material

Go through your binder and highlight or underline every important positive and negative statement. You may want to tab certain key statements for easy reference. How do you know what statements to highlight? Focus on the following:

- Test results, staff observations, reports, and other information on your child's current educational status. Highlight descriptive statements, such as "Tom scored at the first-grade level on the Brigance Test, Counting Subtest" or "Sheila has difficulty staying focused in class; any activity beyond three to five minutes can be quite taxing for her."
- Recommendations regarding program placement, related services, goals, and methodology. Look for statements such as "Carla would benefit from 30 minutes of speech therapy a week" or "Jim needs to be in a small classroom in which there are minimal disturbances or acting out behavior."
- The consequences of providing or not providing specific placements, services, methodology, and other program components—for example, "Teri has significant fears about large groups and open space; placing her in a large class on a big campus will increase those fears and put her at risk for serious emotional difficulties."

As you go through all your IEP-related information, you will probably highlight a lot of what you read, making the task of organizing the material seem overwhelming. To make it manageable, use different colored highlighters or tabs to differentiate the important from the less important

statements or items—such as yellow for very important, green for somewhat important, and blue for less important. You can also make second copies of all significant items and keep them in a separate section in your IEP binder.

3. Use an IEP Material Organizer Form

Once your material is highlighted, you should take the time to create an additional document that will help you organize and access important information. I call it, for want of a more creative term, an IEP Material Organizer Form.

A sample IEP material organizer is below; Appendix 5 includes a blank, tear-out copy. Use one page for each major issue.

An IEP material organizer divides your written information, notes, and reports into important topics (such as related services or methodologies), keyed to your blueprint. As you can see from the sample, the IEP material organizer form allows you to find specific information—such as an evaluation report, a pediatrician letter, or key statements made by a teacher or other potential witnesses—that support or dispute your blueprint items.

You can divide the IEP material organizer into subtopics that track your child's specific needs. For example, under "placement," you might have subtopics like class size, peer needs, type of class, location of class, and the like. Under the related service of a one-to-one aide, you might add the length and number of sessions, the qualifications of the aide, and what the aide will do. Under a curricula/methodology issue such as a reading program, you might include when the reading work is done or at what pace.

Feel free to use the IEP Material Organizer Form to subdivide issues in whatever way works for you.

IEP Material Organizer Form

Use this form to track documents and people that provide support for or opposition to your goals.

Issue: _____ Related Service: 1:1 Aide

Document or Witness* Name(s):	Binder Location (if applicable)	Helps You	Hurts You	Key Supportive or Oppositional Information	Rebuttal Document or Witness Name(s) (if hurts) (If none, what will you say at meeting?)
Lee Portaro (District) 3/1/xx evaluation	1C		✓	Recomm. #s 3, 6, 8, 10 (p. 8)	Brown Evaluation
Suzanne Brown 2/4/xx evaluation (independent)	1B	✓		Narrative (p. 3, ¶s 4, 5). Recomm. #s 1-7, p. 12	
Weekly Teacher Reports	1F	✓	✓	9/6/xx, 10/4/xx, 1/17/xx Support 10/14/xx, 11/5/xx, 2/2/xx Against	Portaro Report: No IEP Agreement on Aide
5/2/xx IEP	1A	✓	✓	Narrative (¶s 7, 8) Against Narrative (¶s 2, 5) Support	Portaro p. 3 (¶ 2)
Dr. Baker (Pediatrician) 1/22/xx letter	1G	✓		P. 2, Concerns for psychological impact if no aide	
Phil Anderson (tutor) 12/6/xx letter	1H	✓		Reports positive results with direct work, 1:1 work	
Karla Jones (District Psychologist)	1M		✓	Sees Steve once/month Reports no adverse psych. impact	Brown, p. 3, ¶s 6, 9
Student Work	1P	✓		Steve on 10/5 assignment writes "Don't understand, who cares."	

* A "witness" is someone (teacher, doctor, evaluator, tutor, psychologist) who gives an oral or written opinion regarding your child's needs at the IEP meeting.

4. Identify Negative Material and Prepare Rebuttals

Keeping in mind your blueprint and goals for your child, what materials hurt your position? Do test results, staff observations, or evaluator recommendations state that your child doesn't need what you want for him or her? Do lines such as "Ben does not need any special education services now" or "Leo should be provided one hour of aide time a week" (when you believe he needs one hour per day) or "Nicole cannot function in a regular classroom at this time" (when you're in favor of mainstreaming) appear in the written materials?

Some negative material is less direct. For example, a test result may not reflect the difficulties your child is actually experiencing. If an evaluation concludes that "Sandy is at age level for reading," you might face an uphill climb in convincing the school district she needs additional help. Or, a teacher's observation may undermine a placement or service you want. A teacher's statement that "Steven frequently acts out and disrupts classroom activities" may make it very hard for you to have Steven mainstreamed.

Here are some ways to counter negative material:

- Look for anything that directly or indirectly contradicts a troublesome statement or report. For example, an aide's statement that "Steven's behavior is erratic, but with help he can control his behavior and focus effectively and quietly on his work" might help you convince the school that Steven can be mainstreamed.
- Look for professional opinions contrary to the school's position. Usually, statements in an independent evaluation can counter school data.
- Are the qualifications of the person who wrote the unfavorable statement appropriate? If a psychologist completed the school evaluation, find out if he or she has expertise in the specific areas to which the negative comments refer.

- Is the negative statement crystal clear? For example, what exactly does this observation mean: "While Jane does not need a small class, there is some indication that she has a difficult time in a large school environment"? The reference to a large school environment may indirectly support a small class placement.
- Is the unfavorable statement supported by data, testing results, or anecdotal information? If not, be prepared to point that out.

Use the IEP material organizer form to identify negative statements and rebuttal information. While you should be prepared to address or rebut a troublesome statement, conclusion, or recommendation, this may simply not be possible. As a general rule, don't bring up negative statements unless the school district raises them first.

5. Provide Documents Before the IEP Meeting

In preparation for the IEP meeting, have everything in your binder marked, tabbed, highlighted, and referenced in your IEP material organizer. Also, make copies of material you want to show to school district representatives at the IEP meeting. This includes anything that supports your blueprint or rebuts negative information. The material can be in any form—a letter, report, independent evaluation, teacher's report, or work sample. You may want to make a copy for each person who will attend the meeting.

Provide the school district with a copy of all material you've generated, such as an independent evaluation. Give these to the district a week before the meeting. This way, school representatives can't argue that they need more time to review your material and must postpone the meeting.

As mentioned earlier, there may be a reason to surprise the district at the IEP meeting by introducing a particular item for the first time. As a general rule, however, it is best to play it straight and provide material ahead of time.

D. Draft Your Child's IEP Program

IDEA requires you and the school district to develop the IEP program together. This does not mean, however, that you cannot—or should not—draft key portions of what you want to see in the IEP program beforehand. Drafting some language ahead of time can help you organize your arguments and recognize any potential roadblocks to getting what you want for your child.

Can Your School District Write the IEP Before the Meeting?

All IEP members, including you, must have a full opportunity to discuss all aspects of your child's IEP. This means that the district can't just present you with a completed IEP at the start of the IEP meeting and tell you to take it or leave it. Like you, however, the district can prepare draft statements ahead of time. School district representatives will probably have discussed the IEP agenda and their thoughts on your child's needs before the meeting as well—and they have every right to do so.

The key portions of the IEP program are:

- goals
- specific programs and placement
- related services, and
- other items, including curricula, methodology, and a description of the placement.

Writing out your IEP program will not only help you learn your material, but it will also force you to think again about how to make your case for the key issues. When you prepare your program you can either fill out a blank school district IEP form—you should get a copy early in the process—or write out your statements so you're ready to discuss them at the IEP meeting. As the IEP team proceeds, bring up the specific components you want in the IEP program.

Your blueprint and IEP Material Organizer Form will help you draft an IEP and participate effectively in the IEP meeting. Chapter 11 explains how the IEP form and blueprint work together and how to get as much of your blueprint as possible included on the IEP form.

1. Goals

Goals refer to the things you want your child to achieve—usually involving reading, math, and language skills, social development, motor skills, behavioral issues, and other cognitive areas of need. Chapter 9 covers goals in detail.

2. Specific Programs and Placement

Program and placement refer to the exact school, class, and classroom characteristics you want for your child.

> Examples:
> - Placement in the special day class for learning disabled students at Hawthorne School.
> - Placement in a special day class for children with developmental delays, no more than 12 students, and a qualified teacher; SDC at Laurel or Martin Schools is appropriate.
> - Placement in Tina's home school, the regular third-grade class.

3. Related Services

Related services are developmental, corrective, and other supportive services (such as transportation) that your child needs to benefit from special education or to be placed in a regular class.

Examples:
- Jason needs three speech therapy sessions per week, each session for 30 minutes, one-on-one with a qualified speech therapist.
- Maria needs a full-time one-on-one aide in order to be mainstreamed in a regular fifth-grade class, the aide to be qualified to assist Maria specifically in the areas of reading comprehension, spelling, fifth-grade math, and developing positive peer relationships.

The 2004 amendments to IDEA require the provision of related services to be based on peer-reviewed research, "to the extent practicable." This means that the IEP team should decide which services are appropriate based on well-established data, gathered according to prevailing methods in the field—not simply on what you or the school district "feel" might work or on what the school district has to offer. Of course, there may not be peer-reviewed research on every potential related service, and there doesn't have to be. If your child needs a related service to benefit from his or her education, that service is required by IDEA—the "to the extent practicable" language protects your right to a necessary related service even if there isn't peer-reviewed research to back it up.

4. Other Components

Other components of the IEP program include:
- curricula, including how your child will be involved and progress in the general curriculum found in the regular classroom, and whether specific related services or special education are needed to ensure your child's involvement and progress
- teacher methodology
- program modifications or supports required for your child; a program modification might be allowing your child to sit at the front of the classroom or providing a classroom that is acoustically designed to minimize distracting noise.
- transition plans, including vocational needs, and
- extracurricular activities such as after-school clubs, lunchtime activities, and sports.

 Chapter 2 provides details on each of these components of the IEP.

Child Profile

The school district might balk if you present them with a fully drafted IEP program or a blueprint. As an alternative, you might prepare a statement for the IEP meeting that incorporates important information without necessarily triggering school district opposition. Instead of emphasizing goals, placement, and services, emphasize your child's personality and needs.

Example:

Sally has a learning disability with specific difficulties with auditory memory, spelling, and reading comprehension. She has some emotional difficulties because of her learning disability, which appear in the forms of anxiety, fear of other children, and concern with safety. She has on a few occasions run off campus. When placed in a large classroom her fears can be increased.

Sally needs a program in which the environment is not overly active, with no behavioral problems; she should not be on a large campus, which might overwhelm her. She needs to be in a classroom of no more than 15 children; she benefits from the Slingerland method and requires instruction in simple, small steps. She needs one-on-one help with reading for at least two hours a day, and does best when this help is provided in continuous segments that are at least 30 minutes long.

This child profile combines parts of the blueprint with a description of your child and her needs. It is not unlike a school district's evaluation, which normally includes a narrative section describing your child. Although you will want to draft the child profile for the meeting, do not give it to the school district in advance. Focus on:

- describing your child (quiet, kind, determined, afraid)
- your child's areas of need, including academic, social, and environmental, and
- weaving in references to specific service and placement needs.

E. Establish Who Will Attend the IEP Meeting

Under IDEA, any person with knowledge or expertise about your child may attend the IEP meeting. This includes the following people:

- you and your child's other parent
- your child, if appropriate (see Section 2, below)
- a representative of the school district who is qualified to provide or supervise your child's special education and is knowledgeable about the general curriculum
- your child's special education teacher
- your child's regular classroom teacher if your child is, or may be, in a regular class
- a person who can interpret the evaluations and their impact on instructional strategies
- at your discretion or the discretion of the school district, other people who have knowledge or expertise regarding your child or her needs
- if your child is 16 or older, someone who knows about transitional services, and
- if your child received early childhood services (called Part C services in IDEA), a representative of those Part C services can be invited to the meeting at your request. (20 U.S.C. § 1414(d)(1)(B) and (C).)

New Rules on Meeting Attendance

Under the 2004 amendments to IDEA, certain IEP members can be excused from the meeting. If the member's area of curriculum or related services will not be modified or discussed, that person does not have to attend—but only if you and the school district both agree, in writing, to excuse that person. For example, if your child receives physical therapy and that service is not going to be discussed or changed, then the physical therapist need not attend. (20 U.S.C. 1414(d)(1)(C)(i).) Of course, if you think the service should be discussed or changed, you should insist that the member attend.

Even if someone's area of curriculum or services will be discussed or modified, that person may still be excused, but only if you and the school district consent and the absentee submits written "input into the development of the IEP" to the team before the meeting. In this situation, you should be very sure that the excused member's written report is sufficient before you agree. Because IEP meetings are fluid, you cannot always know which issues may come up, what direction the discussion will take, or when a response or comment from a particular team member might be helpful. Proceed with caution when considering excusing an IEP attendee.

Representatives From Noneducational Public Agencies

Sometimes, representatives from other public agencies may attend an IEP meeting, particularly if responsibility for certain IEP services is entrusted to an agency other than the school district. In California, for example, mental health services are provided by the county mental health department, and therefore a representative from that agency will often be present. In Vermont, a representative of an agency other than the school district will attend to discuss transition services. If the child has been involved with the juvenile authorities, a probation officer may attend, depending on the laws in your state.

Prior to the IEP meeting, talk with any of these additional folks and find out why they are attending the meeting, what they will do there (such as report on your child), and what position (if any) they plan to take on your child's needs.

1. Representing the School District

Knowing who will attend the IEP meeting on behalf of the school district will help you prepare. The school district should give you a written list of attendees, but if you are not told at least two weeks before the meeting, write the district and ask for the following information for each person who will attend:

- name
- reasons for attending
- qualifications and specific title, and
- whether he or she knows your child and, if so, in what capacity.

Prepare a list of all participants, including the positions they are likely to take on your child's needs.

A sample IEP Meeting Participants form is below; Appendix 5 includes a blank, tear-out copy.

IEP Meeting Participants

Name	Position/Employer	Purpose for Attending	Point of View
Fred Brown	Third-grade teacher, Kentington School District	Gene's teacher	Supports Gene's placement in regular class; does not think Gene needs aide
Diana Hunt	Psychologist, Kentington School District	Did evaluation	Recommends placement in special day class
Violet King	Psychologist, independent evaluator	Did independent evaluation	Supports regular class and aide
Jane Gough	Speech therapist, Kentington School District	Representative of school district	Agrees with need for speech therapy, but not on amount
Phil Chase	Administrator, Kentington School District	Representative of school district	No stated position

a. Your Child's Teacher

If your child is in a regular class, then his or her current teacher must attend the IEP meeting. Your child's teacher has the most information about your child's education and the most experience with your child. The teacher may write reports about your child's progress, help write goals, be responsible for seeing that these goals are met, and make recommendations for the next school year.

The teacher can be your best ally or your worst enemy in the IEP process. Either way, the teacher is often the most convincing team member. The teacher's opinion may carry the most weight and influence how far your school district will pursue a dispute. If the teacher supports your position, you have a better chance of success. If the teacher does not, the school district may feel it would win any due process dispute and, therefore, may decide to stand its ground at the IEP meeting.

Making sure the teacher understands your concerns and is prepared to speak frankly about them is crucial, but not always easy to achieve. Teachers work for their school districts, and may face subtle or not-so-subtle pressure to make recommendations that fit within the school's budgetary or other constraints. A teacher who speaks frankly regardless of what a school administrator thinks is invaluable—but not always easy to find. It is therefore vital that you keep in contact with the teacher, ask his or her opinion, and indicate your specific concerns. Be specific, direct, fair, and always conscious of the teacher's time.

Chapter 8, Section B, discusses the importance of keeping in regular contact with your child's teacher and talking with teachers and other school personnel before the IEP meeting.

b. School Administrator

In most cases, someone representing the school district will attend the IEP meeting. This may be the district special education coordinator, student services director, county or regional office of education administrator, or school principal. There are all kinds of administrators, just like there are all kinds of parents. The administrator may be a kind, cooperative, and terrific advocate for your child—or may be burned-out, unpleasant, and remarkably bureaucratic.

You will be working with the administrator a good deal and will want to know where he or she stands on your child's IEP. Your inclination might be to ask the administrator in advance of the meeting what his or her position is regarding the key issues for your child. Is it a good idea to do so? Many a wise administrator will let you know when he or she agrees with you, but will not let you know in advance about disagreements. That doesn't mean you can't ask, but it does mean you should consider the pros and cons of asking the administrator's position prior to the IEP meeting.

Pros
- You will find out if the administrator agrees with you.
- If you get an honest answer, you'll know what the administrator thinks and how strong his or her feelings are.
- If you disagree with the answer, you may convince the administrator to change his mind, or you will better know how to prepare for the IEP meeting.
- You may learn about options you like.

Cons
- The administrator will learn your goals and be able to counter them.
- You may put the administrator on guard, making it difficult for you to communicate with staff, visit programs, and the like.

If you decide to ask and the administrator opposes your goals for your child, consider the following:

- If the administrator will not support you on a particular item, he or she may have violated IDEA—that is, made a decision before the IEP meeting. This may be the basis of a formal complaint against the school district (see Chapter 13). This doesn't mean you should trap the administrator into making a decision outside of the IEP meeting. But if it happens, be aware of your rights.
- If the administrator has not made a decision, you may want to share the materials you have that support your position. You might give the administrator some ideas as to why the district can agree with you. On the other hand, you may help the administrator prepare to rebut you at the IEP meeting. You'll have to judge the chance of making the administrator into an ally rather than a well-prepared adversary.

c. School Psychologist and Other Specialists

Depending on your child's condition and needs, other professionals may be involved in the IEP meeting, such as a school psychologist, speech therapist, occupational therapist, physical therapist, adaptive physical education specialist, or resource specialist. They may provide evaluation reports and other information regarding your child, and are likely to have opinions about goals, services, and placement. Like your child's teacher, these specialists may be great allies or formidable foes.

As with the teacher or administrator, speak with the specialists ahead of time to find out their positions on key issues.

d. Limits on School Representatives

Are there limits to who can attend the meeting? Federal policy states that a school may not invite so many people as to make the IEP intimidating. State laws and policies may also cover who may attend IEP meetings. California, for example, requires that the IEP meeting be "nonadversarial"— and having ten district employees may make the IEP meeting feel very adversarial indeed.

IDEA requires that people who attend the IEP meeting at the invitation of a parent or the school district must have knowledge or special expertise about the child. If it seems inappropriate for a particular person to attend based on this standard, notify the school in writing (even if you initially call) of your concern. State why the individual is not qualified to attend, or why his or her attendance is not necessary or helpful. If the school insists that the person attend, see Chapter 13 on filing a complaint. And at the IEP meeting, state for the record, without being personal, that you feel so-and-so should not be there. When it's time to sign the IEP plan, reiterate your objection.

Sample IEP Meeting Attendance Objection Letter

Date: _May 15, 20xx_

To: _Dr. Sean Gough_

Hamilton School District

1456 Howard Ave.

Little Rock, AR 72212

Re: _Amy Crane, student in third-grade class of Carol Smith_

I understand that _Joan Green, the district's psychologist,_
will be at _Amy's_ IEP meeting. _Joan Green_
knows nothing about _Amy_ and appears to have no knowledge that
might be of use to the IEP team. I am formally requesting that _Ms. Green_
not attend, unless there is some clear reason that makes _Ms. Green's_
attendance appropriate and necessary for the development of _Amy's_
IEP plan. As you know, IEP meetings can be particularly difficult for parents. We are already
anxious about ours and would prefer that you not take action that will heighten our stress
level.

If you insist on _Ms. Green_ attending without any reason, then we
will file a complaint with the state and federal departments of education.

I will call you in a few days to find out your decision on this issue. Thank you for considering
my request.

Sincerely,

Eva Crane

Eva Crane

88 2nd Street

Little Rock, AR 72212

Phones: 555-1998 (home); 555-8876 (work)

A sample letter objecting to a particular person attending the IEP meeting is above; a blank, tear-out copy is in Appendix 5.

One Teacher Too Many

I once represented a child at an IEP meeting where there were a dozen school representatives, including several administrators, the school nurse, and Bruce, the "teacher of the day." I asked Bruce if he knew my client, Laura. The answer was no—he had neither met her nor knew anything about her. I asked him why he was there. Without hesitation he said he was there to "represent the teachers of the area." The involvement of someone like Bruce—or anybody else with no knowledge of your child or the relevant educational issues—would be contrary to federal policy and the underlying purpose of the IEP meeting.

2. Representing the Parents

While some of the people representing the school district may support your goals for your child, you may want some or all of the following people to attend the IEP meeting on your behalf:

- your spouse or partner
- your child
- others who know your child, such as a relative or close family friend
- independent evaluators or other professionals who have worked with your child, and
- an attorney.

Contact these people well in advance to let them know the date, time, location, and likely duration of the meeting. Make sure they understand the key topics that will arise during the IEP meeting, and the issues and solutions they are there to discuss. Let them know the positions of the various school representatives on the key issues, and be sure to show them copies of materials that both support and are contrary to your goals.

Remind your attendees that the IEP meeting is informal and that points of view should be stated in a positive but firm way. Disagreements can be spirited, but should remain professional and respectful.

Some of the people you ask to attend—such as an independent evaluator, a pediatrician, another specialist, or a lawyer—might charge you a fee. Find out the cost ahead of time. If you can't afford to have the person stay for the entire meeting, let the school administrator know in advance that you will have someone attending who needs to make a statement and leave. Before the meeting, ask the administrator to set aside a specific time for that person to speak.

Some people you want to attend might not be able to, or you might not be able to afford to pay them to attend. In either situation, ask the person to prepare a written statement for you to read at the meeting. Some people's testimony may actually be better in writing than it would be in person—for example, someone who is timid or reluctant to strongly state a position in person might come across better in writing.

Chapter 8, Section F, discusses items to include in a written statement from your child's doctor or other people from outside the school.

a. Parents

While work schedules or living arrangements may make attending the IEP meeting difficult, it is generally best if both parents attend, even if you are divorced or separated. If you have differences of opinion, resolve them before the IEP meeting. If you argue with each other during the IEP meeting, you could damage your credibility and chances of success.

If one of you cannot attend, prepare a strong and emotional statement for the other to read.

Can an IEP Meeting Be Held Without You?

Your school district has a duty to ensure that you are present at the IEP meeting. It can hold an IEP meeting without your involvement only in unusual situations, and only after following very specific procedures, including:

- notifying you early enough of the meeting to ensure you have the opportunity to attend
- scheduling the meeting at a mutually convenient time and place, and
- finding ways of including you—including individual or conference telephone calls—if you cannot attend.

The district can proceed without you only if it can prove that it took specific steps to convince the parent to attend, by showing records of attempts to arrange a mutually agreeable time and place, detailed phone records, correspondence, and even visits to the parent's home or workplace. (Current IDEA regulations at 34 C.F.R. § 300.345.)

Sample Statement to IEP Team

To: Marilyn Haversham's IEP Team

From: Claudine Haversham (Marilyn's mom)

Date: March 1, 20xx

I cannot attend the March 15th IEP meeting, but I wanted you to know that I am very concerned that Marilyn might be removed from her regular program. She is such a happy child now that she is mainstreamed. As her mother, I see the joy in her eyes when she gets up in the morning to get ready for school. A placement in a more restrictive environment would be devastating to my daughter. I must be frank and tell you that we will vigorously oppose any efforts to remove Marilyn from her current program.

I greatly appreciate your sensitivity to Marilyn's needs and your past assistance in making her educational experience a positive one.

Sincerely,

Claudine Haversham

Claudine Haversham

b. Your Child

A student may attend the IEP meeting if it is appropriate or if the IEP team is considering transition services for a child. (20 U.S.C. § 1414(d)(1).) (See Chapter 2, Section A, for a discussion of transition services.)

When is it considered appropriate for a child to attend? A child who can speak about his or her hopes and needs may be a compelling self-advocate. But be careful—if your child is unpredictable or unsure of the importance of the meeting, you may not want to risk the possibility of a "wrong" answer. For example, you want your son to remain in his mainstreamed program. A school district representative says, "Tell me, Tommy, do you want to stay in your class?" You're not going to be happy if Tommy responds, "Nope."

If your child does attend, focus on his or her feelings and hopes. You probably want to avoid referring to the written materials, unless your child is older—perhaps a teenager. In that case, you can ask something like, "Carl, the school evaluator says you had a hard time in Ms. Shaver's class, particularly with other students. Why do you think that was so?" Be sure you know what his answer will be.

c. Relatives, Friends, and Child Care Workers

It is important to limit the number of people who attend the IEP meetings—the more people in attendance, the longer the meeting can drag on. Therefore, you'd normally not bring a relative, friend, or child care worker to the meeting. But if someone can present a view of your child that wouldn't otherwise be told, you might want that person to come. For example, if your daughter's regular babysitter can describe how your otherwise shy and reserved child talks for the first 30 minutes after she gets home about how she loves being in a regular class, it may be powerful testimony.

Generally, a sibling or peer of your child, particularly a young one, should not attend unless he or she is the only person who can speak to an issue or has a really powerful presence. Preparing young attendees will be very important, with focus on the sibling or peer's "feelings" about your child, rather than more formal information.

Bring Someone to Take Notes

Ask a friend or relative to attend the IEP meeting and take notes for you—paying careful attention to who says what regarding important items. A notetaker can be invaluable, particularly if you anticipate a controversial meeting.

d. Independent Evaluators and Other Professionals

Because the conclusions reached by any independent evaluator who tested your child will probably be instrumental in helping you secure the right services and placement, it is crucial that the evaluator attend the IEP meeting. The evaluator must be able to clearly articulate his or her professional opinion on the key blueprint items and on all evaluation data. The evaluator must also be prepared to rebut contradictory information presented by the school district.

Other professionals, such as a pediatrician, private tutor, therapist, or psychological counselor, can be important witnesses on your behalf if they know your child and can speak to key issues affecting the IEP plan. Prepare these individuals as you would prepare an independent evaluator.

e. An Attorney

If you hire or consult an attorney during the IEP process, that person can attend the IEP meeting. You can also hire a lawyer just for the IEP meeting. (See Chapter 14 for information on working with lawyers.) As a general rule, you may want an attorney at the IEP meeting if your relationship with the school district has deteriorated and you anticipate a complicated and difficult IEP meeting.

If you bring an attorney to the IEP meeting, school representatives are more likely to be on guard and less likely to speak frankly. On the other hand, if the school administrators haven't been cooperative and you feel the plan that will emerge from the IEP meeting will be harmful to your child, bringing an attorney shows you mean business. You're much better off not using an attorney—it does change the entire experience—but if you must, then find one who is reasonable and cooperative.

If you plan to have an attorney at the IEP meeting, you should notify the school district reasonably in advance. Except in unusual situations, you will be responsible for paying your attorney, with little chance of reimbursement. (See Chapter 14, Section D, for information on when you might be reimbursed for lawyer's expenses.)

F. Final Preparation Concerns

As you finish your IEP preparation, consider these additional recommendations.

1. Taping the IEP Meeting

You (and the school district) have the right to tape record the meeting. While a tape recording may be the best proof of what was said, it may have an inhibiting effect. People don't always want to make a particular statement "on the record." In addition, tape recordings are not always of great quality; participants are not always audible, and it can be hard to discern what was said and who said it.

If you decide to tape record, bring a good-quality recorder. Bring extra tapes and batteries in case an outlet is not accessible. The school district can tape record even if you object—just as you can tape over the objections of school representatives. If the school district tapes the meeting, you

are entitled to a copy of the tape, and it becomes part of your child's file—just as the district can ask for a copy of your tape.

You should notify the district in advance that you want to tape record the meeting.

School Resistance to Tape Recording

The U.S. Department of Education, Office of Special Education Programs, has issued several statements reinforcing the right of parents to tape record IEP meetings. If, once you get to the meeting, the special education administrator says you cannot tape record, ask to reschedule the meeting. You can also state that this affects your ability to function at the IEP meeting, that it is against the law, and that you will file a complaint. (After the meeting, follow up with a letter to the school administrator; see Chapter 13 for advice on filing a complaint.)

2. Reducing Your Anxiety

It is a given that you will be nervous at the meeting, so don't worry about being anxious. But do give some thought to what you might do before the IEP meeting to relax. It may be taking a walk or jogging, soaking in the bathtub, going out for breakfast, or any other activity that helps you settle your nerves. If you need to get a babysitter or take time off from work, set it up well in advance, so you're not scrambling the day before the meeting.

By preparing—knowing your material, completing your IEP blueprint, drafting your IEP plan, and talking to your IEP participants ahead of time—you will do much to reduce your anxiety.

IEP Preparation List

Things to do before the IEP meeting:
- Find out the date, time, and location.
- Get a copy of the school's agenda.
- Make your own agenda.
- Prepare your IEP material organizer.
- Draft IEP plan.
- Find out who is attending on behalf of school district.
- Invite and prepare your own IEP participants.
- Give the school a copy of the following:
  - independent evaluations
  - documents such as formal reports and work samples
  - names and titles of people attending IEP, and
  - notice of intent to tape record IEP meeting (if applicable).
- Create meeting reminder list of items you want to be sure to remember:
  - "Make sure we read statements of Dr. Wilson and Rona (babysitter), who can't attend."
  - "Make sure Dr. Ramirez covers Lydia's physical therapy needs."
  - "We don't have to sign all of the IEP— we can object."

11

Attending the IEP Meeting

Your IEP meeting is soon. You'll enter the room, sit down, put your binder on the table, take a deep breath, and do just fine. You'll do fine because being nervous is natural, the school administrator probably feels the same way and, most important, you are prepared for this meeting. You've developed your child's blueprint and drafted an ideal IEP, supported by various documents. You're familiar with the school's IEP form, policies, programs, and services. You know who will attend the meeting and where each person stands on key issues. You have people with you who are prepared to help you make your case.

Chapter 10 provides valuable advice on preparing for the IEP meeting. Chapter 7 provides tips on preparing for and attending an IEP eligibility meeting.

IEP meetings are not always required. Once the annual IEP meeting takes place, the 2004 amendments to IDEA allow you and the school district to agree to make written changes to the IEP without holding another meeting. This can save time, but there may be some risks to proceeding without a meeting. See Chapter 10, Section E, for more information.

A. Getting Started

IEP meetings can take a lot of time, so it's very important that you be punctual. In fact, you'll want to be at least ten to 15 minutes early so you can get the lay of the land, see the meeting room, and perhaps say a few words to the teacher or school administrator. More important, being early will give you the chance to talk to your participants and make sure everyone is clear about their roles at the meeting.

1. What to Bring

Bring your IEP binder and the written material you've gathered, including evaluations, letters, reports, and your IEP material organizer form. Make sure you have extra copies of key documents, such as an independent evaluation.

2. Get the Notetaker Organized

It's a good idea to bring someone to take notes, particularly if you anticipate a controversial meeting. Make sure you provide your notetaker with paper and pens (or a laptop computer). Remind your notetaker to take detailed notes regarding important items, particularly those that relate to your blueprint—what was said and who said it are especially important. These notes, particularly for items that you and the school district dispute, will be extremely important should you end up filing for due process (see Chapter 12) or making a formal complaint (see Chapter 13). If you do not have a notetaker, make sure you give yourself time to jot down important statements.

3. Set Up the Tape Recorder

If you're planning to tape record the meeting, set up the equipment and check that it's working.

Chapter 10, Section F, explains how to notify the school district in advance of your intent to tape record the IEP meeting and how to deal with any dispute that arises about taping the meeting.

4. How the Meeting Will Begin

The IEP meeting is typically led by the school administrator responsible for special education programs, although it may be led by the school site principal, the school district evaluator, or even a teacher.

Most IEP meetings begin with introductions. School representatives will explain their roles at the meeting. You should do the same with your participants. If, for example, a friend will take notes or an outside evaluator will present a report, make that clear.

After introductions, the administrator will probably discuss the agenda and then explain how the meeting will run and how decisions will be made.

 Obtaining the agenda in advance is discussed in Chapter 10, Section B.

If the agenda is different from what you anticipated or omits issues you want to cover, bring up your concerns at the beginning of the meeting. You have the right to raise any issue you want at the IEP meeting. Also, if the agenda appears too long for the allotted time, explain that you don't think there will be enough time to cover everything, and ask that certain items be discussed first. If your request is denied, do your best to keep the meeting moving forward.

While most IEP meetings follow a certain pattern (discussed in Section D, below), don't be surprised if yours seems to have a life of its own, going in directions you did not anticipate. Just make sure your key issues are covered before the meeting ends.

IEP Meeting Basic Dos and Don'ts

Is there an etiquette to the IEP meeting? There should be. As in any potentially difficult encounter, try to proceed in a positive way.

Dos
- Do respect other opinions.
- Do try to include all IEP team members in the process.
- Do ask questions in a fair and direct way.
- Do state your position firmly, but fairly.
- Do explore ways of reaching consensus.

Don'ts
- Don't interrupt.
- Don't accuse.
- Don't make personal attacks.
- Don't raise your voice.
- Don't question another's motives.

You might begin by saying that you appreciate everyone's attendance, the time and energy they're giving to your child, and their professional dedication. Emphasize that you are determined to discuss all issues in a fair and thorough way, and that you are looking forward to a challenging but ultimately positive meeting in which everyone's point of view is respected.

B. Simple Rules for a Successful IEP Meeting

Several simple rules can help you get the most out of the IEP meeting.

1. Know Your Rights

IDEA was created for your child and provides for:
- a free appropriate public education (FAPE) in the
- least restrictive environment (LRE), based on an
- individualized education program (IEP).

Parents are coequal decision makers—just as important as everyone else at the IEP meeting.

 Chapter 2 explains your child's legal rights under IDEA.

2. Don't Be Intimidated

You have special knowledge of your child's needs. School personnel are not the only experts. If you have documents to support each item you want in the IEP plan, you may be even better prepared than school representatives.

At the same time, don't automatically assume that teachers or other school officials are wrong. There are many dedicated teachers and school administrators who want to provide the best education for your child, have expertise in educating children with disabilities, and have been through this process numerous times before. This doesn't mean you won't encounter opposing opinions or

---

How to Deal With Intimidating or Nasty Comments

For many parents, dealing with teachers and school administrators in an IEP meeting can be intimidating. You don't want to (but may) hear:
- *I'm sorry, Mr. Walker, but you're wrong.*
- *I'm sorry, Ms. Richards, the law doesn't say that.*
- *Your evaluation report is incorrect.*
- *Our policy precludes that.*
- *Maybe they do that in another school district, but we don't.*
- *I will not agree to that!*
- *That's enough on that subject!*

In most cases, you can ignore these kinds of comments or make a simple response. (Section B5, below, discusses how to challenge blanket assertions.) Try to determine whether the comment is anything more than just an impolite or negative remark. If it is unimportant, say your piece and move on.

"I don't appreciate your tone of voice, Ms. Hanson. I have treated you with respect and expect the same from you. Even if we disagree, we can do it in a civil way. More important, your statement is not correct (or reasonable or produc-

tive or conducive) to a positive IEP meeting."

If the comment seems important, you may need to be more assertive.

"Ms. Hanson, I resent your comment and believe you are undermining this IEP meeting. Please understand, I will do what is necessary to ensure my child receives the program she needs and bring your behavior to the attention of the appropriate individuals."

If you don't feel calm and your voice is shaky, that's okay, too. Just don't yell or get overly aggressive. If necessary, you may want to raise the possibility of filing a formal complaint regarding something that seems illegal—for example, if the district won't allow you to discuss your independent evaluation. (Chapter 13 covers complaints.) But don't make a threat without first thinking it through. Do you really have grounds to file a formal complaint? Is there any validity to the school representative's comment? Is it worth alienating the school district and changing the atmosphere of the IEP meeting? In most cases, you can make your point without threatening to file a formal complaint.

perhaps even run up against someone who is just plain nasty or incorrect. But as a general rule, most folks are in special education because they want to help.

3. Focus on Your Child's Needs—Not Cost or Administrative Constraints

IDEA recognizes that each child's needs are unique and, therefore, that each individual program will be different. If you can show that your child needs a specific service, such as a one-to-one aide or two hours of occupational therapy each week, then the law requires it.

If the school district does not have the staff to provide the related service your child needs, such as a speech therapist, then the school should pay for a private therapist.

A child's needs—not cost—should dictate all IEP decisions. For example, the school administrator cannot refuse to discuss or provide a service or placement because it "costs too much." An administrator may try to get the point across indirectly, by saying something like "If we provide that service for your child, another child will not get services she needs." Don't argue the issue; simply respond with something like this:

> *Mr. Keystone, it is wrong for you to make my child responsible for your budgetary difficulties. I won't be put in the position of making a choice between my child's needs and the needs of other children. The law is clear that we should be discussing an appropriate education for my child, not the cost.*

If you can't reach agreement, and the school district representatives continue to admit that there is an administrative or budget problem, be sure you (or your notetaker) has written this down in case you end up in due process.

This is not to say that cost is never an issue. Let's say you want your child in Program X and the school offers to put your child in Program Y, which is less costly for the district. You're unable to reach an agreement and decide to resolve the matter through due process. If the district can prove Program Y is appropriate for your child, it will likely prevail at the due process hearing.

Remember: IDEA does not require the best education for your child, but an appropriate one. You won't win a fight for the ideal program when an appropriate one is available.

 Don't describe the program you want as "the best," "optimum," or "maximum." The school district might use these descriptions as evidence that you want more than the "appropriate" education to which your child is entitled under IDEA. If you feel that a program or service offered by the school isn't right, characterize it as "inappropriate"—this will signal that you don't think the school district is meeting its legal obligations.

4. Know When to Fight— and When Not To

It is important to realize when you don't have a case. Understanding the IEP process and having a clear step-by-step strategy does not mean that all problems will always be resolved in a manner you think best. You may be fully prepared, do a superb job in the IEP meeting, and still not have enough evidence to support your position. Knowing the strength of your case will help you know when to fight and when to concede.

Fight for the crucial issues and be more flexible on others. For instance, goals and test protocol may be important, but, ultimately, the related services, placement, and methodology are what matter in your child's education. Fighting for 30 minutes over the wording of one goal is probably a waste of time; spending 90 minutes on a major issue like placement is probably worth it.

5. Ask Questions

You should always feel comfortable asking questions—and there will undoubtedly be times during the IEP meeting when you need more information or clarification. There are several very good reasons to ask questions: to obtain basic information, to persuade someone of your position, or to question a blanket assertion.

a. Obtain Basic Information

During the IEP meeting, many technical terms will be used. If you don't understand something, ask what it means. It's better to ask—even for the tenth time—than to proceed without understanding.

Most important, find out what these terms mean for your child. Knowing that your child scores at the 42nd percentile on the Wechsler is useless unless it tells you something about your child's abilities and opportunities for improvement.

b. Persuade

Asking questions can be an effective way of persuading others that your position is right and theirs may be wrong. State your questions positively, such as "Do you [IEP team members] agree with the recommendations on page eight of Dr. Calderon's report?" or "Ms. Porter, do you agree that Amy should be placed in a regular eighth-grade class with a one-to-one aide?"

Sometimes you may need to establish agreement on preliminary matters before asking these kinds of big questions.

Example:
You want a particular IEP member to agree with you on placement. You realize that you must first establish agreement on the evaluation supporting that placement. You first ask, "You read Dr. Harper's report. She states that

Carolyn needs, and I am quoting, 'a quiet environment in which there are no behavioral problems or acting out by other students.' Do you agree with Dr. Harper?" The IEP member agrees and you follow up by asking, "Given Dr. Harper's report and our desire that Carolyn be placed in the special day class at the Manning School, do you agree with that placement?"

Someone may chafe at being asked such a pointed question and may feel cross-examined. One good way to respond would be to say, "I certainly don't mean to cross-examine you and appreciate you reminding me of that. Please understand that I am not a lawyer but a parent. What is important to Carolyn is not the nature of the question but the answer. I will certainly try not to be too formal; would you like me to try to put it another way?"

c. Challenge Blanket Assertions

Nothing is more frustrating for a parent than hearing lines like the following:
- *"Unfortunately, we are not allowed to discuss that issue."*
- *"We don't provide that service."*
- *"That's not our policy."*
- *"Sorry, but you can't do that."*
- *"That's not the law."*

If an assertion seems illegal or illogical, ask what it's based on. If the administrator says something vague like "It's our policy," "It's the law," "It's our best judgment," or "It's the way things are," keep asking why. Request a copy of the law or policy.

If possible, refer to your documentation. For example, the district administrator says that as a general rule, the district doesn't provide more than two hours of a related service per week. An evaluation states that your child needs three hours. Point that out and ask how the district's rule complies with IDEA, which requires that the specifics of a service be determined by the IEP team.

The administrator may say something like "Mrs. Wasserman, that is just the way it is and I won't respond any further to that question." You'll want to follow up with something like "I'm sorry you won't answer my question; it is a fair question, and I plan to ask your superintendent or the school board to answer it." If the issue is key, you may want to file a complaint, as discussed in Chapter 13.

Or the school district may not agree with you on an important IEP component. For example, you feel there is clear support for a specific placement, but the administrator disagrees. Ask for a detailed explanation of the school district's reasoning, supported by appropriate material.

6. Pay Attention to What's Written on the IEP Form

Make sure you know what statements are entered onto the IEP document, and voice any objections immediately—whether it's about a particular goal, or a general statement made on the narrative page of the IEP form. (Section D, below, discusses the narrative page.)

7. Keep Your Eye on the Clock

Whether the school has allotted two hours or five hours for the IEP meeting, keep track of time. If you are 45 minutes into a 90-minute meeting and the IEP team is still talking in generalities, you should say, "We need to move on to a specific discussion of Cora's goals, placement, and related services."

A good school administrator will keep the meeting on schedule. If the administrator is not doing so, take the lead. Be ready to suggest moving on to the next issue when the discussion on a particular topic has gone on long enough.

8. Don't Limit Your Options to All or Nothing

At some point during the IEP meeting, you may realize that you will not reach agreement on all issues. For example, you feel your child needs at least two sessions of speech therapy a week, 30 minutes per session. The district offers one 30-minute session. You've done your best to persuade them, to no avail. What do you do?

The school district cannot present you with a "take-it-or-leave-it" position—for example, "We've offered speech therapy once a week. You want it twice a week. You can either agree with us and sign the IEP or disagree and go to a hearing." Furthermore, the school district cannot insist that you give up your right to due process—for instance, "We've offered speech therapy once a week and that's all we'll offer. We'd advise you to sign the IEP form and not make waves."

Your best bet is to make sure the IEP document specifically states that you agree that a specific service is needed—or that a particular placement is appropriate—and that your child will receive at least what the school district has offered. Then make sure your opinions are reflected on the parent addendum page.

You can agree to the lesser amount of a service such as speech therapy and indicate on the IEP form that you believe your child needs two sessions of speech therapy, but will accept the one session so he or she will have something while you pursue due process. Or you agree on placement and related services, but not certain goals (or vice versa).

Section F, below, discusses how to prepare and use a parent addendum page, which is a very important IEP tool for any disputed items.

9. Don't Be Rushed Into Making a Decision

If you're on the fence about a particular issue, don't be rushed into making a decision. Ask for a break and go outside for a few minutes to think about what the school has offered. If you are concerned that pausing on some issues may mean delay on others, ask for a day or two to make up your mind on a particular issue so that the IEP team can proceed with other items. This may require a second IEP meeting, unless you eventually agree with the rest of the IEP team on the issue. If an item is that important, however, then a second meeting is worth the time.

C. Become Familiar With Your School's IEP Form

You should get a copy of your school district's IEP form before the IEP meeting. While forms vary, they will almost always have sections on the following:

- present level of educational performance
- goals (and evaluation procedures)
- related services
- placement/program
- effective dates of the IEP
- attending summer school or an extended school year, and
- a narrative page or pages for recording various important statements, such as comments on evaluations, or keeping a running account of the meeting discussion. This important part of the IEP is described in Section D, below.

In addition, IEP forms typically include the following types of information:

- identifying information, such as your child's name, gender, date of birth, grade, school district, and parents' names and addresses
- the type of IEP (eligibility or annual review) and date of the IEP meeting

- your child's eligibility status and category of disability
- the amount of time your child will spend in a regular or mainstreamed program, if applicable
- your child's English proficiency, and
- signatures of IEP team members and parents.

The IEP team may include other important information in the IEP, such as a specific curricula or teaching methodology, a specific classroom setting, peer needs, or a child profile.

 You can find a sample IEP form in Appendix 4.

The IEP Form and Your IEP Blueprint

The IEP form and your blueprint (your list of desired program components) will have similar categories but will not be identical.

Most of your blueprint items, such as related services and placement, have a corresponding section in the IEP. But in some cases, you may find that the IEP form does not have space for all the details you included on your blueprint. For example, the IEP form will allow you to specify the kind of program or placement— such as a regular class or special day class—but might not provide space for the details of the placement—such as peer numbers and makeup, the classroom environment, and the school environment. Other blueprint items, such as methodology and curricula, may not have a corresponding section on the IEP form. And the school administrator may not be familiar with a blueprint like yours.

As you prepare for the IEP meeting, keep in mind that while the IEP form may not reference all of your blueprint items, IDEA allows the IEP team to discuss and agree on any element it feels is necessary for your child. These types of details can go on the IEP narrative page (see Section D, below) or, if the school disagrees, a parent addendum page (see Section F, below).

D. Writing the IEP Plan

Usually, someone from the school district will write the IEP plan as the meeting progresses, by filling in specific sections, checking off boxes on the IEP, and completing the narrative or descriptive page.

You should ask frequently to see what has been written, to make sure it accurately reflects what was discussed or agreed upon. You may want to check every 30 minutes or so, with a simple "Excuse me, but can we break for just a few minutes? I want to see what the IEP looks like so far." If these breaks seem forced, ask to review the form each time you complete a section. Pay special attention to the narrative page—this will be more subjective than other parts of the IEP.

How does the IEP team make an actual decision on IEP components? IDEA establishes no set method for reaching agreement. The school administrator may not even raise the question of how agreement is reached. You can request voting, but, in most IEP meetings, the team tries to reach consensus through discussion. No matter how the administrator proceeds, make sure your objections are heard and no one assumes consensus when there isn't any.

How items are recorded on the IEP plan is equally important. From the beginning to the end of the IEP meeting, you want to be sure that the IEP's narrative page, goals, placement, and related services reflect your point of view.

Under IDEA, the written IEP must include:

- your child's current levels of academic and functional performance
- how your child's disability affects his or her involvement and progress in the general curriculum
- measurable annual goals, including academic and functional goals designed to meet your child's needs
- a statement of the special education, related services, and supplementary aids and services your child will receive, as well as program modifications necessary for your child to meet annual goals and be involved and progress in the general curriculum
- a description of how your child's progress towards those goals will be measured, and when and how that progress will be reported to you
- a statement of any accommodations your child will need when taking state or other systemwide assessments and tests
- if your child is 16 or older, a transition plan
- if your child will not be in a regular classroom or program, an explanation of the reasons for this placement, and
- a description of the program where your child will be placed.

1. Child's Current Educational Status

If your child is presently enrolled in school, the IEP team will review your child's current IEP goals, program, and related services. Your child's current status may be reflected in testing data, grades, and teacher reports or observations. If this is an eligibility IEP meeting, the team will review evaluation data; it will do the same every three years (or more frequently) when your child is reevaluated. Discussion of your child's current status may be broad or specific. It may occur at the beginning of the IEP meeting or as you review specific items, such as goals, for the upcoming year.

Watch what you—and others—say about your child's current situation. For example, if you are concerned about the current program, you won't want the IEP narrative page to state that "Sam's placement has been highly successful this past year." If such a statement is made and entered onto the IEP document—perhaps on the narrative page—be sure to object, with something like "I'm sorry, but I don't think that statement is accurate, and I certainly cannot agree with it. It should not be on the IEP as reflecting our consensus."

2. Evaluations

A school district representative (most likely the evaluator) will either read or summarize the school district's evaluation. If the evaluator starts reading the report, ask him or her to synthesize the salient points, rather than spend precious time reading the report verbatim—especially if you reviewed a copy before the meeting.

This may be the time to use your IEP material organizer (see Chapter 10) to point to other documents—such as previous IEP plans, an independent evaluation, other reports, teacher notes, and the like—to support or contradict the school evaluation.

If you haven't already introduced the independent evaluation, you will do so once the district has finished presenting its evaluation. You or your evaluator should provide a synopsis of the report, focusing on:

- the evaluator's credentials
- the reason for the evaluation
- the tests used
- the key conclusions regarding the testing, and
- the specific recommendations.

Be sure to highlight the test results and recommendations not covered in the school evaluation. This is also the time to introduce any other supporting material, including letters, work samples, and other professional opinions.

On most IEP forms, the narrative page refers to the evaluations. The IEP plan might specify the sections, results, or statements in the reports on which you all agree. Even if there is only one statement you all agree on, be sure it gets into the IEP document if it is essential to your child's needs. If the person drafting the IEP plan includes something from an evaluation with which you disagree, make sure your objections are noted.

Sometimes, the evaluation reports are attached to the IEP document. This can work in your favor if you agree with the report.

If an evaluation is not attached, or there is some disagreement over the evaluation, the narra-

tive page should specify what parts of the evaluation are included or excluded.

> **Examples:**
> - The IEP team agrees with Sections 1, 2, 4, 6, and 8 of the school evaluation and Sections 3, 5, 9, 10, and 12 of the independent evaluation, and incorporates them into the IEP.
> - The IEP team disagrees with the rest of both evaluations and does not incorporate them into the IEP.

You can use the parent addendum page to state the reasons for your disagreement (see Section F, below).

3. Goals

If this is not your child's first IEP, the IEP team will next review the previous year's goals. This discussion is likely to lead to one of four different outcomes:

- You and the school district agree that the goals were met.
- You and the school district agree that certain goals were met, but others were not.
- You and the school district agree that the goals were not met.
- You and the school district disagree on whether the goals were met.

Although you won't be working on placement and services during this part of the meeting, keep in mind that your child's success or failure in meeting the goals will likely affect whether the placement and services are changed. If your child met the goals, perhaps it means the placement is correct and should continue. Or maybe it means your child is ready to be mainstreamed. If the goals weren't met, your child may need a smaller class. Or maybe the placement is fine, but more tutoring (a related service) is necessary.

Once you finish reviewing the previous goals— or if this is your child's first time in special education—it's time to write goals for the coming year. Chapter 9 explains how to draft goals—and recommends that you do so in advance. It's possible the school representatives have also prepared some ahead of time.

Remember, you want the IEP team agree on goals that support the placement and related services you want for your child.

What if you disagree with each other's goals?

- Do your best to convince school members of the IEP team that your goals are consistent with the recommendations made by others, such as the evaluator, the classroom teacher, or your child's aide.
- Ask school members what they specifically disagree with in your goals.
- If you can't agree on all goals, try to reach consensus on some—half a loaf is better than none.
- If attempts to compromise fail, suggest dropping all predrafted goals and coming up with something new.

If you and the school representatives disagree about past or future goals, be sure the IEP document clearly states that. At the very least, record your concerns on your parent addendum (see Section F, below).

4. Transition Services

If your child is 16 or older, the IEP team must discuss transition services, including advanced courses and vocational classes.

The IEP team should consider strategies to assist your child in assessing, securing information about, and taking steps regarding vocational, employment, independent living, and post–high school educational plans. Your child can look into transition in a variety of ways, including looking at potential jobs, learning how to function in the community, accessing other agencies that will provide support for adults with disabilities, and researching college opportunities.

Once your child reaches the age of 16, the IEP must include a statement about his or her transition needs, as those needs relate to your child's courses of study. This means that the team must indicate what advanced placement or vocational courses or classes are necessary to meet your child's unique educational and career needs. For example, if your child wants to go to college, do clerical work, or look into computer jobs, then his or her studies must provide for ways to explore these possibilities.

The IEP must also include a statement about necessary transition services. This means that the IEP must provide for services that will help your child develop the skills necessary to meet his or her vocational, academic, or independent living plans for the future (after high school ends). Such transition services might include help in developing the skills to create a resume, perform certain jobs, access and use community services (such as public transportation), and find out about job training or college programs. The IEP must also indicate whether there are noneducational agencies that might provide additional support to your child (such as the department of health or job training agencies), and how your child can access the services these agencies provide.

As you prepare for the IEP meeting, talk to your child's teacher and other professionals about his or her vocational, college, and independent living skill needs. If your child wants to go to college, what skills will that require, and what institutions or agencies might be available to help your child develop those skills? If you child plans to look for work after high school, what are his or her vocational interests, and how can your child get the training and experience necessary to get into those fields? If your child needs help developing independent living skills, such as using transportation, balancing a checkbook, or keeping house, what kinds of school activities will help?

5. Related Services

Your discussions regarding related services (and placement, covered in the next section) are likely to generate the most debate. You and the school district may have very different notions of the type and amount of related services that are appropriate for your child.

Under IDEA, related services are developmental, corrective, and other supportive services, including transportation, that a child with disabilities needs to benefit from special education. They also include the services your child needs to be educated in a regular classroom. Remember, the burden is on the school district to show that your child cannot achieve satisfactorily in a regular classroom, even with the use of some related services (see Chapter 2, Section A).

Independent evaluators and others supporting your position should be prepared to state their opinions in detail—for example, "Given Gavin's severe difficulties in articulation, he needs a minimum of three 30-minute sessions each week, one-to-one with a speech therapist who has a lot of experience in articulation work." If someone is not there to make this statement, be prepared to point to written materials that show your child's need for the particular related service.

The related services section of the IEP document requires more detail than any other. It's not enough to say, "Gavin will receive speech therapy." The IEP team should specify how often (three sessions per week), how long (30-minute sessions), the ratio of pupils to related service provider (one-to-one), and the qualifications of the service provider.

The more vague the description, the more flexibility the school district has to give your child something less than (or different from) what he or she needs. Speech therapy two to three times a week is very different from speech therapy three times per week. Try to avoid terminology such as "or," "about," "to be determined," or "as needed." When in doubt, be specific; it's that simple.

As amended in 2004, IDEA now requires the provision of related services to be based on peer-reviewed research "to the extent practicable." (20 U.S.C. § 1414(d)(1)(A)(iv).) Of course, most parents want their children to receive services that are based on sound research. On the other hand, the school district cannot refuse to provide a necessary service just because there is no such research available. The phrase "to the extent practicable" creates a way around the research requirement.

Some advocates worry that this new language may create a rationale for school districts to avoid providing related services: "Sorry, we'd like to provide it, but there is no peer-based research." While this fear is real, the bottom line is that IDEA requires the school district to provide a related service if your child needs it, whether there is peer-reviewed research available or not.

Some Related Services May Be the Responsibility of Other Agencies

In some states, certain related services, such as mental health services, are the responsibility of a noneducational public agency. Still, these services should be discussed at the IEP meeting, and the school district is responsible for making sure representatives of those other agencies attend the meeting. Those noneducational agencies have the same responsibilities as the school district—and therefore the same role to play at the meeting—regarding the services they must provide.

6. Placement or Program

Placement or program refers to both the kind of class (such as a regular class, special day class, or residential placement) and the specific location of the program (such as a regular fifth-grade class at

Abraham Lincoln School). Placement or program, sometimes referred to on the IEP form as the instructional setting, is central to a successful IEP and an effective educational experience. Placement or program is most often some kind of public program, but IDEA requires placement in a private school if there is no appropriate public option. Placement or program is generally the last item discussed at the IEP meeting.

As explained in Chapter 2, IDEA requires that your child be educated in the least restrictive environment. This means that to the maximum extent appropriate, children with disabilities are to be educated with children who are nondisabled. Special classes, separate schooling, or other removal of children with disabilities from a regular class should happen only if the nature or severity of the disability is such that your child cannot receive a satisfactory education in a regular class, even with the use of supplementary aids and services.

Despite the LRE guideline, there is no absolute rule that your child must be mainstreamed. IDEA prefers a mainstreamed placement, but many courts have ruled that a child's individual needs determine the appropriateness of a placement.

If you don't want your child mainstreamed, point out that although the law favors regular classroom placement, individual need determines whether a particular placement is appropriate for a particular child. Courts have clearly stated that there is no prohibition to placing a child in a nonregular class. In fact, if a child needs such a placement, it is by definition the least restrictive environment. (See *Geis v. Board of Education*, 774 F.2d 575 (3d Cir. 1985) and *Stockton by Stockton v. Barbour County Bd. of Educ.*, 25 IDELR 1076 (4th Cir. 1997).) (For more on court cases and legal research, see Chapter 14.)

If you want your child mainstreamed, emphasize your child's basic right to the least restrictive environment. You should also emphasize your child's right to be educated as close to home as possible, in the school the child would attend if not disabled. Ultimately, the burden is on the school district to prove that your child should be removed from a regular classroom.

School representatives may be prepared to discuss a specific program in a named school. Or, they may propose a kind of class, such as a special day class, but want to leave the specific location up to the school administration. If the school representatives suggest this latter option, object. The IEP team should decide both the kind of class (such as a special day class for language-delayed children) and the specific location (such as a regular class at King School).

You and the school administrator will probably know before the meeting where each of you stands on placement. Still, an open-minded IEP team should fully discuss your child's placement needs. The school administrator will probably state that the IEP team has reviewed your child's record, agreed on goals, resolved related services, and decided that a particular placement is called for.

If you disagree with the administrator's conclusion, state your preference and refer to supportive materials—particularly items that are very persuasive about placement. Then ask (or have your independent evaluator ask) pointed questions, such as:

> *Ms. Parton, you said Betsy should be placed at Johnson School in the special day class. We believe Betsy should be placed in the regular class at Thompson School with a one-to-one aide. The evaluation by Dr. Jones is specific about that, and Betsy's current teacher agrees. Can you explain why you disagree?*

If the school administrator is not persuaded or does not answer your question adequately, be direct and frank:

> *With all due respect, I think your answer is vague and does not address the specifics in Dr. Jones's report and your own teacher's comment about Betsy's readiness for a regular classroom. I feel very strongly about this, and we will go to due process on the issue of place-*

ment if we have to. I also think that with the documentation and the law on mainstreaming, we will be successful in due process. I really feel that going in that direction is a bad use of school resources and will only make the ultimate move that much more expensive for you. I just don't understand—given the evidence—why you want to put me and my wife, your district personnel, and, most important, our child through that.

7. Narrative Page

The narrative page is the place to record information that can't be conveyed by checking a box or won't fit in the space provided on the form. The narrative page can include information on any other topic covered, whether covered by the IEP document or not. Here are some examples of narrative page statements.

Examples:

- The IEP team agrees that the school district and outside evaluations are complete and appropriate, and are incorporated into the IEP.
- The IEP team incorporates the child profile provided by Steven's parents into the IEP.
- The IEP team agrees that Melissa needs a school environment in which there are no behavioral problems.
- The IEP team agrees that Henry is beginning to show signs of emotional distress; the classroom teacher will report on a weekly basis to the family about any signs of such distress. The district psychologist will observe Henry in class. The IEP team agrees to meet in three months to review this matter and to discuss the possible need for more formal evaluation or the need for additional related services.

- The IEP team agrees with the recommendations made by Dr. Jones on page 4 of her report.
- Ms. Brown, Steve's teacher, is concerned about Steve's lack of focus.
- The IEP team agrees with recommendations 1, 2, 5, 7, and 9 made by Dr. Jones on page 4 of her report.
- Carolyn's parents expressed concern about class size.

Sometimes, the person recording the IEP document may write something that you and the school district don't agree on. Make sure the narrative is changed to reflect your disagreement or to indicate that the statement reflects only the point of view of the school personnel. Basically, you don't want the narrative to imply agreement when there is none.

Include a Child Profile in the IEP Plan

In Chapter 10, Section D, I suggested that you create a child profile to give school officials a perspective on your child beyond numbers and test results. The school administrator may question whether law or policy allows a child profile to be included in the IEP document. IDEA does not prohibit it, so nothing prevents the IEP team from discussing and including a child profile.

Emphasize that your statement about your child will help the school staff implement the goals, and for that reason it should be included in the IEP document. If the school administrator disagrees, ask why. Try to convince the team of the importance of the profile. If the administrator continues to refuse, use the parent addendum to include it.

E. Signing the IEP Document

At the end of the IEP meeting, the school administrator will ask you to sign the IEP document. School officials will be signing the form as well. You don't have to sign the IEP document on the spot. You may want to take it home and return it the next day. This will give you time to decide whether you agree or disagree with each aspect of the plan. It will also give you time to record your disagreements coherently on a parent addendum (discussed in Section F, below).

Of course, if you agree with the school representatives on all issues and don't need time to mull anything over, then go ahead and sign. Read the document carefully, however, to make sure the statements and information are correct and reflect the IEP team's intentions. Also, make sure that everything on your agenda was covered and that all important issues have been resolved.

If you do take the IEP document home, be sure that all other participants have signed off on each item to which they agreed.

Every IEP form has a signature page with a variety of checkboxes, including:

- a box to indicate you attended
- a box to indicate that you were provided your legal rights
- a box to indicate your approval of the IEP document, and
- a box to indicate your disapproval.

There may also be boxes to indicate partial approval and whether or not you want to initiate due process.

Take care in checking the appropriate boxes. If you partially agree, check the partial agreement box or, if there is no partial agreement box, check the approval box—*but* carefully and clearly write next to it: "Approval in part only; see parent addendum." (Section F, below, discusses the parent addendum.)

You must state your position clearly on the IEP. There are no legally required phrases to use—plain and direct English will do fine.

1. Full Agreement

Congratulations! Check the correct box and sign the form.

2. Nearly Full Agreement

It's possible that the IEP team will agree on all important items concerning related services, methodology, and program or placement, but disagree on some secondary issues, such as goals or statements in an evaluation. In this situation, you have two choices:

- You can check the box to indicate your approval and sign your name. This might make sense if the issues on which you disagree are minor and you want to foster a good relationship with the school district.
- You can check the box to indicate partial approval, list the items you dispute (on the signature page if there's room or on the parent addendum), and sign your name.

Sample

Date: April 24, 20xx

Signature: *Lucinda Crenshaw*

I agree with all of the IEP except for:

- items 3, 4, and 6 on the district's evaluation
- goals numbers 2 and 5.

You Don't Have to Accept "All or Nothing"

The school district cannot present you with an "all or nothing" choice. For example: "We're offering two sessions of occupational therapy. Either agree with the two sessions or there will be no occupational therapy for your child." You can agree to the two sessions without giving up your right to seek more. See Sections B8 and F for examples.

---

3. Partial Agreement

In this situation, you agree on some, but not all, of the big issues (related services, methodology, and program or placement). You can check the box to indicate partial approval, state that your disagreements are on the parent addendum, spell out your disagreements on the parent addendum, and sign your name.

Sample

Date: April 24, 20xx

Signature: *Lucinda Crenshaw*

I agree with all of the IEP except for those items listed on the parent addendum page, designated as "Attachment A" and attached to the IEP.

4. Nearly Total Disagreement

In this case, you don't agree on any of the major items concerning related services, methodology, and program or placement, but do agree on certain goals, parts of the evaluation, and minor items. Again, you can check the box to indicate partial approval, state that your disagreements are on the parent addendum, spell out your disagree-ments on the parent addendum (see Section F, below), and sign your name.

5. Total Disagreement

In some instances, there is total disagreement. If so, sign your name after checking both the box acknowledging that you attended the meeting and the disapproval box. You could also refer to the parent addendum page.

At this stage, your options are informal negotia-tions, mediation, or a due process hearing.

 See Chapter 12 for information on due process, including your child's status when there is no IEP agreement.

F. Parent Addendum Page

When you disagree with the school personnel and cannot reach a compromise, make sure to state your position clearly. You or your notetaker should keep a list of all issues you dispute on a separate piece of paper.

A parent addendum page is an attachment to the IEP where you can record these disagree-ments and give your point of view. There is no IDEA requirement for an addendum page, although your district's IEP form may have one. The addendum page need not be a formal docu-ment—a blank piece of paper will do.

You will most likely complete the addendum page at or near the end of the meeting. The content of the addendum page is vastly more important than its format. Your statement should:

- relate to issues concerning your child's education—don't use the addendum to state general complaints
- be in plain English, and
- state your point of view on all key items of dispute.

As shown in Section E, above, you should indicate on the signature page that you disagree with part of the IEP document and refer to the attached addendum page for the detail of the disagreement.

Date: _____

Parent Signature**: _____

** See Addendum page (designated as "A") for a statement regarding what we are agreeing to and not agreeing to. My signature above is to be read only in conjunction with the statement on "A."

If your school's IEP form includes an addendum page, use it; otherwise, mark "Attachment A" at the top of a blank piece of paper and write something like the following:

Parent Addendum Page of Carol and Steven Stack
IEP for Beatrice Stack
March 12, 20xx

You have an absolute right to state your position, but if, for some reason, the school district does not allow you to attach an addendum, indicate on the signature page that you do not agree with everything in the IEP document, that you want to attach an addendum, and that the school administration will not let you. Then file a complaint (see Chapter 13).

Example Addendum Statements:

- The district does not agree with the recommendations of Dr. Jones's independent evaluation but has refused to state why. We believe that her evaluation is valid and should be fully incorporated into the IEP as representing useful and valid information about Tonya.
- We do not agree with recommendations 3, 6, 9, and 14 of Dr. Lee's evaluation of January 21, 20xx. We do agree with the rest of her report.
- The IEP team agrees with sections 3, 7, 8, and 9 of the school's report and all of Dr. Friedman's evaluation, but the school will not put this agreement into the IEP. We believe those agreed-to sections should be incorporated into the IEP.
- Dr. Pentan of the school district stated that we have no right to include a child profile in the IEP. IDEA does not say that, and if the IEP team agrees, the profile can be part of the IEP. We believe the profile provides valid and important information regarding Fernando.
- While the teacher reported that Stanley increased his reading comprehension (this relates to goal #4 on page 2), we have observed at home, over a long period of time, that his reading comprehension seems substantially below the test results.
- We don't agree that Sandy's goals were met because the evaluation of the goals was inaccurate.
- The district offered speech therapy one time a week, 20 minutes per session. Moira needs three 40-minute sessions per week, each session to be conducted one-to-one with a licensed speech therapist. This is supported by the May 2, 20xx report of Dr. Shawn Waters. We accept the one session and give permission for that to begin, but this acceptance is not to be construed as agreement about the amount of the related services, only agreement as to the need.
- The IEP agrees that Nick be placed in the regular fifth-grade class at Kennedy School. We agree with placement in the regular fifth-grade class at Kennedy School, but we believe Nick needs an aide to allow him to achieve satisfactorily in that regular class.

- We believe that the regular seventh-grade class at Roosevelt School is the only appropriate placement for Tony. We believe placement in the special day class at Roosevelt as offered by the school district is inappropriate. We agree to placement in the regular classroom at Roosevelt for three periods a day, although such agreement is not to be construed as agreement on partial mainstreaming. We will proceed to due process on the issue of full-time mainstreaming in the regular seventh-grade class at Roosevelt.

Less Frequent IEP Meetings: A New Model

As both parents and educators know, IEP meetings can be tiring, difficult, and sometimes contentious, and can involve a lot of paperwork. They take up a lot of time for teachers, administrators, and you. Congress has received complaints about this, and has decided to establish a pilot program to find out what happens when IEP meetings are held less than once a year. The program calls for participating districts to establish comprehensive, multiyear IEPs to last for up to three years.

Here are some details on the new program:
- The Secretary of Education can approve up to 15 proposals to establish pilot programs across the country.
- Participation is **optional.** If your state or school district is chosen for the pilot program, you can opt out if you wish.
- In 2006, the Secretary of Education will submit a report to the House of Representatives' Committee on Education and the Workforce, describing how effective the multiyear IEP program has been and making recommendations as to whether it should be implemented more broadly.

If your state or district establishes a program, you should participate only if you are absolutely confident that this kind of procedure makes sense for your child. Ask your district for details about how the pilot program will work.

Should Congress ultimately decide to expand this program, there will almost certainly be a long and heated debate before the law is changed to do away with annual IEP meetings. While this need not be at the top of your priority list, all of us should keep an eye on this development.

12

Resolving IEP Disputes Through Due Process

The purpose of this book is to help you successfully develop an IEP plan for your child, and thereby make this chapter irrelevant. But the nature of the IEP process is such that disagreements arise, and some cannot be resolved informally.

Under IDEA, you have the right to resolve these disputes with your school district through "due process." (20 U.S.C. § 1415.) There are two ways to resolve disputes through due process: mediation and a hearing.

In mediation, you and representatives of the school district meet with a neutral third party who tries to help you reach a compromise. The mediator has no authority to impose a decision on you. You are not required to mediate, but it can be a very good way to resolve your dispute—and avoid the time, expense, and anxiety of a due process hearing.

If you cannot reach an agreement in mediation, or if you prefer to skip mediation altogether, you can request a due process hearing where you and school district personnel present written evidence and have witnesses testify about the disputed issues before a neutral third party, called a hearing officer. Much like a judge, the hearing officer considers the evidence, makes a decision, and issues a binding order. Either you or the school district can appeal the decision to a state or federal court.

Due process is available to resolve factual disputes—that is, when you and your child's school district cannot agree on eligibility or some part of the IEP plan. If the school district has ignored a legal rule—by failing to hold an IEP meeting, do an evaluation, meet a time limit, or provide an agreed-to part of the IEP—you must file a complaint rather than pursuing due process. (Complaints are covered in Chapter 13.)

Don't Delay Filing for Due Process— You May Lose Your Rights

The 2004 amendments to IDEA now require you to formally file for due process within two years after you knew or should have known of the dispute. (20 U.S.C. §§ 1415(b)(6) and (f)(1)(C), (D).) Time limits like these are known in the legal world as "statutes of limitations." If you do not file within the two-year limit, you lose your right to file for due process.

There are two exceptions to this two-year limit:

- If your state has a different statute of limitations, the state's statute will apply. Check with your school district, state department of education, and/or a parent support organization in your state to find out about time limits. (See Appendixes 2 and 3 for contact information.)

- If the school district misrepresents to you that it has resolved the dispute, or withholds information from you that is required by law, the two-year time limit will not apply. For example, you ask for a specific related service and the school district tells you at the IEP meeting that its evaluator believed such a service would harm your child. If the evaluator, in fact, said no such thing, and you didn't learn of the misstatement for a while, the two-year limit might not apply.

It would be fairly unusual to have a dispute with the school district that you weren't aware of for a lengthy period of time. After all, most due process matters involve a disagreement over services or placement, and these disputes are usually evident right from the start—and certainly by the IEP meeting. The school either agrees to mainstream your child, provide a 1:1 aide, or meet your child's other needs, or it doesn't. It's generally a good idea to start considering a due process proceeding as soon as you know you have a disagreement that can't be resolved with another IEP meeting.

⚠️ **IDEA regulations are changing.** The regulatory citations throughout this book are to the current IDEA regulations—those that will be in effect until the Department of Education issues final regulations interpreting the 2004 amendments to IDEA. The Department expects to release these final regulations at the end of 2005; many of them will be identical or similar to the existing regulations cited in this chapter (although the citations will be different), while others will be new. When you use this book, you should make sure that you have the most current version of the regulations. See "Warning: Special Education Rules Are in Flux," in Chapter 1, for information that will help you stay up to date. You can find the most recent version of IDEA, including the 2004 amendments, starting at 20 U.S.C. § 1400; the most pertinent sections are included in Appendix 1.

Alternatives to Informal Negotiations and Formal Due Process

Informal discussions with the school district and formal due process aren't the only ways to resolve disputes. Other methods, such as building parent coalitions and becoming involved in the local political process, can also be effective. These options are discussed in Chapter 15.

In addition, IDEA provides that a state or local school district can establish alternative dispute resolution (ADR) procedures for parents who choose not to use due process.

In ADR, you and a district representative meet with a neutral third party who is under contract with a parent training center or community parent resource center, or who is from an appropriate alternative dispute resolution entity. The purpose of the meeting is for you to explore alternative ways to resolve your dispute and for the third party to explain the benefits of mediation. This ADR meeting is intended to be nonadversarial, while mediation is the first step in formal due process. Be aware, however, that using ADR may delay resolution of the dispute— so if you need immediate action or the time limit for pursuing due process is coming up, you might want to skip this step.

If you're interested in ADR, call your school district or state department of education (see Appendix 2) to find out if ADR is available.

A. Before Due Process: Informal Negotiations

Before invoking due process, you may want to try to resolve your dispute through informal discussions or negotiations with the school. While resolving some problems might require formal action, many issues can be settled informally.

In addition, some disputes may not even qualify for due process. (See Section B, below.) For example, you and the school principal may disagree over when you can visit the classroom or why the evaluator had to reschedule your child's testing. Because you can't take these issues to due process, you'll have to hash them out informally or not at all.

After the 2004 amendments to IDEA, the school district must set up a negotiating meeting after you file for due process. (See Section 4, below, for more information.) Although this meeting occurs only after a hearing request is filed, you may still be able to resolve the dispute before moving on to mediation or a hearing.

1. Pros and Cons of Informal Negotiation

Informal negotiation is useful for several reasons. Ultimately, it may save you stress, preparation time, and money. It will also help you maintain a more positive relationship with the school district, and will keep problems from escalating. Finally, informal negotiation is easier to pursue than due process.

Even if you eventually pursue your due process rights, it might be a good idea to start with informal negotiation. This will show that you are reasonable and fair-minded and don't immediately look to an adversarial method of settlement. Informal negotiations will also help you understand the school district's position, which will be valuable if you end up in mediation or at a due process hearing.

In limited situations, however, there may be reasons to go immediately to due process. For example, you should skip the informal negotiations if:

- You need an immediate resolution because the issue affects your child's well-being, safety, or health. For example, if you think that your child needs psychological counseling for depression, but the district disagreed, you may not have time for informal meetings.

- The school administrator is so unpleasant or inflexible that you just don't want to deal with him or her.
- The IEP meeting made it clear that it would be a waste of time to try to resolve things informally.

2. Basics of Informal Negotiation

To begin informal negotiations, call or write your child's teacher, school principal, or special education administrator and ask for a meeting to discuss your concerns. You can raise the issues in your phone conversation or letter, but ideally you'll want an appointment to discuss the problem face to face.

Before the meeting, prepare a brief and clear written description of the problem and a recommended solution. Also, find out if any school personnel support you. If so, ask them to attend the meeting or ask for permission to present their opinions at the meeting.

During the meeting, emphasize problem solving, not winning. Try to structure the negotiation as a mutual attempt to solve a problem. Avoid personal attacks on school personnel. Respect the school's point of view even if you disagree. Acknowledge the school representatives' concerns. Even if you strongly disagree, you don't lose anything by saying, "I understand your concerns, but I think we can address those by doing...."

Finally, be respectful, but firm—for example, you can say, "It is clear we disagreed at the IEP meeting. I am not averse to trying to solve this informally, but I will not hesitate to pursue my due process rights if we cannot."

Good Books on Negotiation

Getting to Yes: Negotiating Agreement Without Giving In, by Roger Fisher and William Ury (Penguin Books). This classic book offers a strategy for coming to mutually acceptable agreements in all kinds of situations.

Getting Past No: Negotiating Your Way From Confrontation to Cooperation, by William Ury (Bantam Books). This sequel to *Getting to Yes* suggests techniques for negotiating with difficult people.

3. After Meeting Informally

If you do not resolve your dispute informally, send a letter briefly stating the problem, the solution you think makes sense, and what you are considering next, such as contacting an attorney, pursuing mediation or a due process hearing, or filing a complaint with your school board or the state department of education.

If you resolve your problem informally, it is very important to follow up the meeting with a confirming letter.

A sample letter confirming the results of your informal negotiation is below; a blank, tear-out copy of this form is in Appendix 5.

Use the Law to Make Your Case

As you try to persuade your school district—in writing or in person—that you are correct, cite the legal authority for your position, if possible. Referring to a section in IDEA or even a court decision may help you convince the school district. See Chapter 14, Section F, for tips on legal research.

If the meeting does not resolve the problem to your satisfaction, then you may proceed to due process (either mediation or a hearing) or file a complaint.

4. Resolution Session

Once you or the school district files for due process, the school district must schedule a meeting, formally called a "resolution session," to try to resolve the dispute before mediation or a hearing. (20 U.S.C. § 1415(f).) The rules for this session are as follows:

- You have the right to attend.
- Members of the IEP team who have knowledge about the dispute must attend.
- Someone who has the authority to make a decision on the school district's behalf must attend.
- The meeting must be held within 15 days after the school district receives notice of your due process request.
- The school district may not bring an attorney to the meeting unless you bring an attorney.
- If you resolve the dispute at the meeting, it must be put in writing and signed by both you and the school district representative. The written agreement can be enforced by any state or federal court.
- Either party can void the written agreement within three business days (weekends and holidays don't count) of signing it. The party who voids the agreement doesn't have to give a reason, and the other side doesn't have to approve the decision.
- If you don't reach a resolution within 30 days of filing your due process request, you can waive the resolution meeting and go straight to mediation or a hearing, but only if the school district agrees. You cannot decide, on your own, to forgo the meeting.

Sample Letter Confirming Informal Negotiation

Date: <u>June 1, 20xx</u>

To: <u>Michael Chan, Principal</u>

     <u>Truman Elementary School</u>

     <u>903 Dogwood Drive</u>

     <u>Paterson, NJ 07506</u>

Re: <u>Tasha Kincaid, student in second-grade class of Marlene Walker, Truman School</u>

I appreciated the chance to meet on <u>May 28, 20xx</u> and discuss <u>Tasha's placement</u>. I also appreciated your point of view and the manner in which we solved the problem.

I want to confirm our agreement that <u>Tasha will be placed in the regular third-grade class at Truman School for the upcoming school year. [If you have already requested due process, add: Once you have confirmed this in writing to me, I will formally withdraw my due process request.]</u>.

I greatly appreciate the manner in which you helped solve this problem. <u>Please tell the third-grade teacher, Ms. Solarz, that I would be delighted to meet with her before school starts to discuss effective ways to work with Tasha.</u>

<u> </u>.

Thank you.

Sincerely,

<u>*André Kincaid*</u>

<u>André Kincaid</u>

<u>4500 Fair Street</u>

<u>Paterson, NJ 07506</u>

<u>Phones: 555-3889 (home); 555-2330 (work)</u>

B. Typical Due Process Disputes

Remember, due process is used to resolve only factual disputes, not disagreements over what the law requires or allows. Here are some due process disputes:

- eligibility for special education
- results of an evaluation
- goals
- specific placement or program
- related services
- proposed changes to your child's current IEP program, and
- suspension or expulsion of your child.

Several kinds of disputes are *not* eligible for due process, including:

- requesting a specific teacher or service provider by name for your child
- hiring or firing school staff
- assigning a different school administrator to your case, or
- requesting a specific person to represent the school district in the IEP process.

These concerns may be addressed through non-IDEA activities, such as parent organizing (see Chapter 15) or informal negotiations with the school.

C. When to Pursue Due Process

Due process is hard; it takes time, energy, and sometimes money, and it can be quite stressful. When you consider whether to go forward, think about these factors:

- **The precise nature of the problem.** You will have to pinpoint exactly what your dispute is, and make sure it is a factual dispute. For example, if you feel your child's education is generally not working (and you have not yet gone to an IEP meeting), or you object to the attitude of the school administrator, your concern is not yet ready for due process. If, however, your child has fallen behind in a regular class, you feel he or she

should be in a special class, and the IEP team did not agree, you have a problem that qualifies for due process resolution.

Don't File for Due Process Until After the IEP Meeting

Many parents make the mistake of requesting a due process hearing before the issue is considered at an IEP meeting. Unless there are very unusual circumstances—for example, your child's health or well-being is threatened—you must go to an IEP meeting and reach an impasse there before you can request due process. However, if your school district has been dragging its feet about holding the IEP meeting or otherwise failing to address your child's needs, filing for due process before the IEP meeting can get things moving.

- **The importance of the issue to your child.** Placement or related-service disputes are often central to your child's educational well-being. On the other hand, a dispute over goals or evaluation conclusions may not be significant enough to go to due process, because it does not directly impact your child's placement and related services.

- **The strength of your case.** Can you win? What evidence do you have to support your position? What evidence exists against it? What are the qualifications of the people making supportive or contrary statements? Remember that the district is required to provide your child with an appropriate education, not the best possible one. After the IEP meeting, review and update your IEP material organizer form (discussed in Chapter 10) to evaluate the evidence for and against you. If you want other opinions on the strength of your case, consider these sources:

▲ Nonschool employees, your independent evaluator, an outside tutor, or an attorney. Describe the disputed issue, your evidence, and the evidence against you, and ask whether you have a good chance of winning.

▲ Other parents, particularly those who have been through due process with your school district. How does the school district react? Is the school likely to take a hard-line position, or might it offer a compromise after you show you are determined to go forward?

▲ Local parent and disability organizations. (Chapter 15 discusses how to find and work with a parents group.) If you need help finding a local group, start by contacting a national organization (see the list in Appendix 3).

- **The bottom line concerns for the school district.** For any disputed issue, the school district will have some bottom-line concerns—notably the cost and administrative difficulty of providing what you want. For example, the school administrator may be willing to compromise on a dispute between two public school program options, rather than pay for costly private school placement. The school's bottom line may affect your bottom line—and how far you'll go to get it.

- **The cost of going forward.** Due process witnesses (including independent evaluators) and attorneys will charge for their time. If you prevail at a due process hearing, you are likely to be reimbursed for those costs, but not if you lose. (See Chapter 14 for information on using an attorney and attorney's fees.)

- **Time considerations.** Remember, you must file for due process within two years of learning of the dispute or within your state's statute of limitations, if it has one. (See "Don't Delay Filing for Due Process— You May Lose Your Rights," above.) Don't

take too long to weigh your decision or spend too much time trying to reach an informal resolution.

D. Your Child's Status During Due Process

While you are in dispute with the school district, your child is entitled to remain in the current placement until you reach an agreement with the school, settle the matter through mediation, receive a due process hearing decision rendered that neither you nor the school district appeal, or get a final court decision. This is called the "stay put" provision. (20 U.S.C. § 1415(j).) "Stay put" can be a complicated legal right. If you are concerned about whether your particular situation involves a "stay put" issue, see an attorney at once or contact a nonprofit disability rights organization.

Example:

Your child is in a regular sixth-grade class with a one-to-one aide, two hours a day. At the IEP meeting, the school district offers a special day class, not a regular class, for seventh grade. You want your child to continue in a regular class. You are unable to reach an agreement at the IEP meeting. You initiate due process, during which time your child is entitled to remain in a regular classroom with the aide until the matter is resolved.

Exceptions to the Stay Put Rule

IDEA entitles your child to remain in his or her current placement pending due process unless your child carries a weapon to school or a school function, or knowingly possesses, uses, sells, or solicits illegal drugs while at school or a school function. In situations involving weapons or drugs, the school district can change your child's placement to an appropriate interim alternative educational setting for up to 45 days, or suspend your child for up to ten school days. See Chapter 2, Section A for more information on discipline for students in special education.

E. Using a Lawyer During Due Process

Using an attorney in due process certainly escalates the adversarial nature of the dispute, but by the time you've reached due process, that is probably not your primary concern. Using an attorney may also speed things along and increase your chances of success.

In mediation, an attorney will present your case and counter the school district's arguments. In a due process hearing, an attorney should prepare witnesses, submit exhibits, make the opening statement, and direct the proceeding. An attorney can also play a less active role, such as providing advice and helping you organize your case material, without attending the proceeding. Your attorney will contact the district to let them know that he or she is involved in the case.

Not surprisingly, legal costs can be considerable. To prepare for and attend a one-day mediation session, an attorney will likely charge from $500 to $1,000—sometimes less, sometimes more. The cost for a two- to three-day hearing may range from $1,500 to $7,500 or more. It is not unusual for an attorney to use ten to 25 hours to prepare

for a three-day hearing. If you use an attorney for advice only—for example, to help organize your case—your legal costs will be lower.

 See Chapter 14 for a thorough discussion of attorneys and legal fees.

Check Out Free or Low-Cost Legal Services

The school district must provide you with a list of free or low-cost legal services available in your area. See Chapter 14, Section C, for advice on finding and working with an attorney.

1. Attorney Fees in Mediation

During mediation, you should ask the school district, as part of your proposed settlement, to pay your attorney fees. Your legal fees are one of many bargaining chips you can use to negotiate a settlement in mediation. However, the school district doesn't have to pay your fees, just as it doesn't have to agree to any other particular settlement term. Because mediation (and any settlement you reach as a result of it) is voluntary, the school district may or may not agree to pay your fees. Remember, a mediation is usually a settlement in which neither party gets everything it wants; attorney fees may be one of those things you are willing to forgo in order to get something more important.

The school district's decision will depend largely on how strong your case is and how motivated the school district is to settle. The school district may try to avoid having to reimburse you by agreeing to provide the education you want, if you agree to drop your demand for attorney fees. You will have to assess the strength of your case to decide whether you are willing to forgo your legal fees. If your case is very strong, the school district may decide that they are better off paying your fees now rather than later, when you will have run up a higher legal bill. Your attorney can advise you of the pros and cons in this situation.

2. Attorney Fees in a Due Process Hearing

If your case goes to hearing and you win, you will be entitled to reimbursement of your attorney's fees. If you lose the hearing, you're responsible for your own attorney's fees, but you will not have to pay the school district's attorney's fees, absent unusual circumstances (see below).

If you win on some issues but not on others, you will be reimbursed for the time your lawyer spent on the winning issues (but not on the losers).

a. Liability for the School District's Legal Fees

The 2004 amendments to IDEA create a new risk for parents: You may have to pay the school district's legal fees if you file for due process for "any improper purpose," defined as an intent to harass, cause unnecessary delay, or needlessly increase the cost of litigation. In addition, your attorney may have to pay the district's fees if he or she filed for due process or filed a lawsuit and the action was "frivolous, unreasonable, or without foundation." (20 U.S.C. § 1415(i)(3)(B).)

These new rules are intended to discourage parents from filing unfounded or frivolous actions. Congress believed that some parents (and their lawyers) were filing actions even if they knew their claims weren't valid, in order to try to force a settlement. If the school district's potential legal costs to fight the claim were higher than the cost of giving in, the district might decide to settle rather than paying a lawyer to fight it out, even if the parents' claim was unfounded.

These provisions are controversial. Of course, parents should always think very carefully before filing for due process, and shouldn't file just to harass or delay. On the other hand, plenty of

parents have had to fight their school districts at every turn just to get the services to which their children are legally entitled, and these parents shouldn't have to worry about having to foot the school district's legal bills.

Even with these new rules, however, there remains a big difference between filing a difficult or even losing case and filing one that is frivolous or lacks foundation. I believe that courts will be very reluctant to dampen the rights of children and their families, and so will require very compelling evidence of parental misconduct before ordering a family to pay the district's fees.

Of course, you don't want to have to respond to the school district's request for fees, defend your intentions to a judge, and possibly even face a separate hearing on the issue before you are vindicated. With that in mind, here are some examples of filings that may cross the new line:

- **Harassment.** You request IEP meetings every two months, request reevaluations numerous times each year, come to the school daily to complain, and file for due process several times a year.
- **Unnecessary delay.** You stall IEP and/or due process procedures without any legitimate reason.
- **Increasing costs.** You and your lawyer file unnecessary motions and otherwise take steps that prolong the litigation, without any legitimate purpose.
- **Frivolous actions.** Your attorney files for violation of a right that doesn't exist under IDEA or is patently beyond the scope of the law. For example, your child has a very mild speech impairment and all of the experts (including your own) recommend a regular classroom placement with two-hour pullout sessions with an aide once a week. You request that your child be placed in a private, residential program in another state and refuse to budge from your position
- **Unreasonable actions.** You seek a placement or service that is obviously outside the scope of IDEA—for example, that the

teacher remain after school for three hours every day to help your child with home-work.

- **Actions without foundation.** You have no evidence or support for what you are seek-ing. For example, you want a private psychotherapist for your child, but there is no evidence from your witnesses or the school that your child has any psychologi-cal difficulties.

While well-meaning parents who act in good faith should not run into trouble under these rules, you should proceed very carefully. Talk to a special education attorney to make sure you are nowhere near violating these provisions. And check the final new regulations to find out whether there are any elaborations of these rules. (See "Warning: Special Education Rules Are in Flux," in Chapter 1, for information on regula-tions.)

b. Reduced Attorney's Fees

If you prevail and are entitled to have your attorney's fees paid by the school district, a judge can order that you receive a reduced amount if your attorney unreasonably extended the contro-versy, your attorney's hourly rate exceeds the prevailing rate in your community (what other attorneys with similar experience and expertise would charge), your attorney spent excessive time and resources on the case, or your attorney did not properly inform the school district about the nature of the dispute. (See Section F, below.)

These failings would typically be committed by your attorney (not you), so you should not be responsible for paying any amount the court dis-allows. You should discuss this possibility ahead of time, before you hire a lawyer. If the attorney doesn't know about this rule, it suggests a lack of knowledge about special education law in general. (See Chapter 14 for pointers on hiring an attorney.)

3. Other Legal Advocates

There are nonattorney advocates who can be quite skilled in due process. Their fees are usually lower than a lawyer's fees, but you are not entitled to reimbursement of an advocate's fees if you settle in mediation, prevail in a fair hearing, or prevail after representing yourself.

Special education attorneys, nonprofit law centers, and disability and parent support groups may know the names of special education advocates in your area.

F. How to Begin Due Process

You must formally request due process in order for a mediation or hearing to be scheduled. Due process requests are sometimes referred to as due process complaints, the term used in IDEA. Note, however, that a due process complaint (filed when you and the school district have a factual dispute) is different from a complaint regarding a legal violation (covered in Chapter 13). Either you or the school district can file for due process.

1. Filing a Written Request

You must provide specific written information about the dispute to initiate due process. There can be no hearing or mediation until you com-plete this first step. (20 U.S.C. § 1415(b)(7).) You must provide this written notice to the school dis-trict **and** send a copy to the state department of education branch responsible for special educa-tion. (See Appendix 2 for contact information.)

Your written request must include the follow-ing information:

- your name and address
- your child's name and address
- the name of your child's school
- a description of the disputed issues
- your desired resolution—not only what you want for your child's education, but also

that you want to be reimbursed for your due process costs, such as attorney's fees, witness fees, and independent evaluation costs, and

- whether you want to mediate or go directly to a hearing.

Most due process matters involve a disagreement between you and the school district over a particular disputed item—for example, you want a particular placement or service, but the school district won't provide it. You may also believe the school district has violated procedural rules under IDEA. For example, if the school district does not hold a yearly IEP meeting, does not process your request for an initial evaluation, or does not allow you to bring anyone with you to the IEP meeting, you should raise those issues in your due process request.

When putting together the required information, it's best to be precise. You can use a short list to describe the existing problem and your proposed solution. The 2004 amendments to IDEA require each state to develop a model form to assist parents in filing for due process. Ask your school district or state department of education for a copy.

Keep a copy of your due process request for your records. It's best to send this request "certified mail, return receipt requested," so you'll have proof of the date it was received.

A sample Letter Requesting Due Process is below; a blank, tear-out copy is in Appendix 5.

2. Other Notice Requirements

The party that receives a due process request (which may be you or the school district, depending on who files for due process) can object that it does not meet the requirements discussed in Section 1, above. The objecting party has 15 days after receiving the request to send the other party

and the hearing officer a written statement explaining why the request is insufficient.

Within five days of receiving this written statement, the hearing officer must decide whether the initial request is adequate. If it is not, the filing party can amend the request, but only if the other party agrees **and** has an opportunity to have a resolution session (see Section A4, above) or if the hearing officer consents. If the filing party needs time to file an amended request, the timeline for the due process decision will be extended as well.

Of course, you can avoid all of these rules by simply filing a clear, sufficient request in the first place (see Section 1, above). IDEA requires your school district to provide you with written information about your due process rights, procedures, and requirements.

G. Preparing for Due Process

While a mediation session and a due process hearing are different, preparing for the former will help as you get ready for the latter. In addition, the preparation you did for the IEP meeting will be of enormous help as you go through due process. The recommendations in this section apply to both mediation and the due process hearing.

1. Organize Your Evidence

First, pull out your child's file, the reports, evaluations, and other documents in your IEP binder (see Chapter 4), your blueprint (see Chapter 5), and your IEP material organizer form (see Chapter 10).

Make a list of the disputed issues. Using a blank IEP material organizer form, write next to each disputed issue the witnesses, documents, or facts that support your point of view—and those that oppose it. You should make a separate list of your potential witnesses and people who might testify for the district.

Letter Requesting Due Process

Date: _March 1, 20xx_

To: _Philip Jones_   **Sent Certified Mail**

Due Process Unit

Wisconsin Department of Education

8987 Franklin Ave., La Crosse, WI 54601

Re: _Steven Howard_

Our son, Steven Howard, is a fourth-grader at Clinton School in La Crosse. His school district is the Central La Crosse Elementary School District, 562 5th Ave., La Crosse, WI.

We are formally requesting due process, beginning with mediation. We believe _Steven requires a full-time, one-on-one aide in order to be fully mainstreamed in next year's regular fifth-grade class at Clinton School. The school district has refused to provide that aide_.

We believe an appropriate solution would include, but should not be limited to, the following:

- _a qualified full-time academic aide, to work one-on-one with Steven in the regular fifth-grade class at Clinton School for the coming school year, and_

- _reimbursement for all attorney's fees, witnesses, independent assessments, and other such costs as accrued by us for the February 14, 20xx IEP meeting and subsequent due process_.

Please contact us at once to schedule the mediation.

Sincerely,

William Howard   Kate Howard

William and Kate Howard

1983 Smiley Lane

La Crosse, WI 54601

Phones: 555-5569 (home); 555-2000 (work)

Now find every piece of evidence you have to support your position. Review your binder, original material organizer forms, and notes from the IEP meeting. Focus not only on reports and evaluations, but also on comments made at the meeting. Gather all your supportive evidence together, or tab it in your binder and highlight key statements. Make photocopies of all written materials that support your point of view to have available during the mediation or hearing.

Now work on the school district's case—that is, figure out what evidence contradicts your point of view. Think about any evidence you can use to rebut the district's likely arguments.

2. Make a List of Expenses

Once you've gathered evidence, make a list of expenses you've incurred throughout the IEP process, such as the costs of:

- independent evaluations
- tutors
- lost wages for attending IEPs
- private school or private related-service costs
- personal transportation costs, such as those incurred driving your child to a private school
- attorney's fees
- costs for other professionals (such as a private speech therapist or counselor), and
- photocopying.

Note the date a payment was made or cost incurred, the name of the payee, and purpose of the expense. Attach all receipts.

There are no rules on how you must prepare or present these expenses. At mediation or the hearing, you will want to request payment for the expenses; if the district agrees to pay some or all of them, or if the hearing officer rules in your favor, the receipts will be your proof that you really spent this money.

3. Prepare an Opening Statement

At the beginning of a mediation session or hearing, you will need to make an opening statement explaining why you're there and what you want. Some people are comfortable making notes and then talking extemporaneously; others write out a complete statement and read it. Do what's easiest for you. The opening statement should include the following:

Description of your child. Briefly describe your child, including his or her age, current educational program, general areas of educational concern, and disabling conditions. Give a short explanation of your child's educational history.

Description of items in dispute. Briefly describe the specific items in dispute—for example, the amount of a related service or the placement.

Description of what you want and why. Summarize what your child needs—for example, speech therapy three times a week, in a one-to-one setting with a therapist qualified to work with students with language delays, placement in the Smith School, or the use of the Lindamood-Bell program or the Orton-Gillingham method.

Description of your evidence. Often, you'll close with a strong statement briefly summarizing the evidence you have for your position. In some mediations, however, you may decide not to reveal all of your evidence right away. You will have to judge the best approach considering the situation, the personalities involved, and even your intuition. (See "How Much Evidence Do You Reveal in Mediation?," below.)

H. Mediation Specifics

Mediation is the first official step in due process. It is less confrontational than a hearing, and is intended to explore ways to compromise and settle your dispute.

The mediator is a neutral third party, usually hired by the state department of education, who is knowledgeable about IDEA and special education matters. The mediator has no authority to force a settlement on you. If you reach settlement, however, your agreement will be put into writing and will be made binding on you and the district— you both must abide by and follow the written settlement.

While mediation is fairly similar from one place to another, the way sessions proceed will vary depending on the style of the mediator and the rules established by your state.

Contact your state department of education to find out the details of your state's laws on mediation. See Appendix 2.

Mediation must be made available to you at no cost. Mediation is completely voluntary. If you don't want to mediate, you don't have to. If you prefer, you can go straight to a hearing and skip mediation.

If mediation is not successful, any settlement offers and other comments made during the mediation cannot be used as evidence at the fair hearing or any subsequent legal proceedings. This rule allows you to discuss matters in a frank manner without fear that your statements will later be used against you.

1. Pros and Cons of Mediation

You may be asking yourself why you would try mediation, particularly because it ends in compromise, rather than a clear victory for one side or the other. There are some compelling reasons to go to mediation:

- **Know thine enemy.** Mediation gives you a chance to understand more fully the school district's arguments. Of course, the school district gets the same opportunity to hear about your case, but sharing information in this way may bring you closer to a solution.

- **The school district may be motivated to compromise.** Mediation takes the school district one step closer to a hearing and the possibility of a ruling against the school, with all the attendant costs, including possible attorney's fees. The school administrator may be far more flexible in mediation than at the IEP meeting, feeling that a compromise now is better than an expensive loss later.

- **Mediation is constructive.** Mediation encourages the parties to work out disagreements. Thus, you may retain a more positive relationship with your school district by mediating the dispute. You also keep control over the outcome—you must agree with any mediated solution. When you go to hearing, the decision-making power is out of your hands.

- **Mediation is cheap.** As a general rule, you will have few or even no costs at mediation; hearings can be expensive, particularly if you use an attorney.

- **Mediation can provide a reality check.** Even if you don't settle the case, mediation gives you a chance to have a neutral party assess your case and point out its strengths and weaknesses.

- **You get two bites of the apple.** By going to mediation, you give yourself two chances at success. If the mediation is unsuccessful, you can move on to a hearing.

There are also downsides to mediation:

- **Half a loaf can be disappointing.** Ideally, you can settle in mediation and get everything your child needs. In reality, however, mediation usually involves compromise, meaning you will probably settle for less than what you would have received if you had won at hearing.

- **Mediation may delay resolution of your dispute.** IDEA requires that a due process hearing decision be issued within 45 days after the date you request due process, whether you go through mediation or go straight to a hearing. In reality, however, extensions of that 45-day rule can be granted if you spend time in mediation. Unless you have a real time problem—your child must be placed in a specific program by a certain date or will suffer dire consequences—most cases can stand the delay.

- **You do things twice.** If you go to mediation and then a hearing, you will have been involved in two procedures, doubling the time, inconvenience, stress, and some costs.

Try mediation. Although there are some downsides to mediation, they are almost always outweighed by the benefits. Unless there is a compelling reason to go straight to a hearing—like a serious time crunch or a truly entrenched opponent—you should give mediation a try.

2. Mediators

The mediator's job is to help you and the school district reach a settlement. The mediator will not decide who is right and who is wrong.
A good mediator will:

- put you and school representatives at ease
- try to establish an atmosphere in which compromise is possible
- be objective
- give you and the school district a frank assessment of the strengths and weaknesses of your positions, and
- go beyond your stated positions to explore possible settlements that may not be initially apparent.

Some mediators play a more limited role—they simply present everyone's positions and hope that the weight of the evidence and formality of the process will lead to a settlement.

3. Mediation Logistics

Mediation sessions must be held at a time and place convenient for you. They are often held at the school district's main office, but they can be held elsewhere. Some people are concerned that having the mediation at a school office gives the district an advantage, but I have found it usually does not matter.

The length of the mediation can vary, but sessions generally take many hours and often a full day. Expect the mediation session to take more time than you would think.

While districts vary, most will send the special education administrator and perhaps another person who has direct knowledge of your child to the mediation. While you can bring outside evaluators, aides, tutors, and any other individuals you want, including a lawyer, you will usually want to save them for the hearing.

Bringing in experts might make mediation more expensive and difficult to schedule. Whether you include experts will depend on:

- how forceful the experts can be
- whether there is any chance of changing the district's mind, and
- the risks of revealing some of your evidence prior to the fair hearing.

If you expect a hearing and don't want to put all your cards on the table at mediation, don't bring the experts. On the other hand, if you want to settle quickly and your experts can aid in that process, bring them along.

4. The Mediation Session

You, the mediator, and the school representatives will gather in a conference or meeting room. After brief introductions, the mediator will explain how the mediation process works, stressing that mediation is a voluntary attempt to resolve your disagreement.

a. Your Opening Statement

You begin by briefly explaining your side of the dispute. (Section G, above, shows how to prepare an opening statement.) Do not hesitate to express your feelings. Your child has important needs, and his or her well-being is at stake. Say that. Express how worried you are. Explain why you feel the school district has not effectively served your child by failing to provide an appropriate education. It's important to show the mediator how imperative the matter is to you and your child. This does not mean tirades or irrational, unfocused monologues. Give your opinion, but don't question the honesty, professionalism, or decency of the school representatives.

Your opening statement should not go on and on or discuss every possible problem. It should be clear and succinct, and run from five to 20 minutes.

If the school has committed any legal violations, you can raise these in your opening statement. While legal violations are subject to the complaint procedure (see Chapter 13), evidence of a legal violation may be a powerful addition to your case, showing the school district's disregard or lack of understanding of the law, and possibly the district's lack of reliability. Nothing in IDEA prevents you from raising legal issues in the mediation. While the mediator cannot remedy legal violations, the mediator can say to district personnel, "You are in trouble because you clearly violated the law; you might want to think about settling this case now."

How Much Evidence Do You Reveal in Mediation?

Section G, above, suggests that you describe your evidence as a part of your opening statement. But you may not want to reveal all your supporting evidence at mediation. By telling all, you may help the school prepare for the hearing. On the other hand, if your evidence is very strong, revealing it may lead to a settlement in your favor. If you're not sure what to do, ask the mediator's opinion in your private meeting. If the mediator feels that the school realizes its case is weak or for some other reason is close to settling, then it may be wise to share everything. On the other hand, if the mediator feels the school is rigid and unlikely to settle, then it may be better not to reveal all of your evidence.

In either case, you'll want to provide at least a synopsis of your evidence, noting where a professional (teacher, related-service provider, administrator, doctor, outside evaluator, or private tutor) has made a clear statement about the disputed issue. Also note the credentials of the person, particularly if he or she is well-known, is loaded with degrees, and has a lot of experience. Highlight all documents or statements by school district representatives that support your position.

b. School District's Opening Statement

After you make your opening statement, the school district's representative presents the district's point of view, perhaps responding to what you have said. Don't interrupt or respond, even though the school's version of the dispute may be very different from yours. Take notes of their main points.

After the school representative finishes, the mediator may invite you to add anything you forgot or to respond to the school's statement. If you respond, make it brief and to the point, focusing on why you disagree with the school's position.

c. Private Sessions With the Mediator

After you and the school representatives make your opening statements, the mediator will meet privately with you, then with the school representatives, then back with you, then back with the school representatives, continuing back and forth as necessary. When you meet privately with the mediator, speak frankly. The mediator cannot disclose anything you say to the school representatives, unless you give the mediator permission. Be sure of this by clearly telling the mediator what you want conveyed to the school district and what you want kept between you and the mediator.

In your first meeting, the mediator may want to clarify issues and begin exploring whether you're willing to compromise.

As the mediator shuttles back and forth, specific evidence may come up related to a disputed issue. For example, you and the school district may have very different views on the validity of the district's evaluation versus your independent evaluation. You can say to the mediator something like "Please convey to Mr. Roberts that my evaluator is a recognized expert and is clear in her recommendations; the district's expert has limited knowledge of my child's disability."

After a few of these private sessions, the mediator should be able to tell you how far the school will go to settle the dispute. At this point, you will have to think about your bottom line. Hopefully, you thought about this before the meeting. Think about what is essential, what you can give up, how strong your case is, and how hard a line the school is taking. Make use of the mediator by asking direct questions, such as:

- What do you think the school will do on the placement issue?
- Do they understand that Dr. Parnell said Victor needs placement in the private school?

- What is their bottom line?
- Do you think we have a case if we go to a hearing?

The strength of the evidence and the work of the mediator will convince the district to settle (or not). If the district has moved from the position it held at the IEP meeting, but some issues remain unresolved, you'll have to decide what to do. You'll have to weigh the importance of the outstanding, nonresolved issues, your willingness to go to a hearing, and the likelihood of ultimate victory.

Tips on Bargaining in Mediation

Bargaining is part of mediation. When presenting what you want, make your list as strong and inclusive as possible. Put in everything you could possibly want, including your expenses and even minor items. But know your priorities, including what you can live without and can therefore use as bargaining chips.

Example:
You feel your child should be in a private school, which costs $15,000 per year. You also want the school district to pay for your private evaluation, which was $1,000. You also have some reimbursement costs, including a tutor, totaling several hundred dollars. Your case is strong enough to go after all of these items. But to compromise, you may have to forego the evaluation and other costs.

---

d. Wrapping Up the Mediation Session

After various private meetings with the mediator, there will be four possible outcomes:

- full settlement of all issues
- partial settlement—you agree on some issues and disagree on others
- no settlement, but you agree to try again with the mediator at a later date, or

• no settlement and no further mediation sessions scheduled.

A mediation settlement can contain anything you and the school district agree to—including that the school will provide all or part of what you want for your child and, if you have an attorney at mediation, pay your attorney fees.

Whatever the outcome, you will all return to the meeting room, and the mediator will complete a mediation form. The mediator will write down what the parties agreed to (if anything), what issues are unresolved (if any), and what the next steps will be if full agreement was not reached.

If you don't reach a settlement on all or some issues, you have three options:

• go to a hearing
• drop the matter—this may make sense if only minor issues remain unresolved, or
• go directly to court—this highly unusual approach requires you to prove that the problem is so serious you can't spend time at a hearing and need a judge to look at the matter immediately; you will need a lawyer's help (see Chapter 14).

Once you and the school district sign the mediation form, both of you are bound by whatever agreement you reached.

I. Due Process Hearing

A hearing is like a court trial, although it won't be held in a courtroom. You and the school district submit evidence in the form of written documents and sworn testimony from witnesses. A neutral third party, called a hearing officer, reviews the evidence and decides who is right and who is wrong. That decision is binding on you and the district. The hearing officer has the authority to act independently of you and the school district—in essence, as a judge. The hearing officer cannot be an employee of the school district or the state educational agency if either agency is involved in the education of your child. (20 U.S.C. § 1415(f)(3)(A).)

Although IDEA establishes specific rules for hearings, states can vary some of the procedural details. For example, Ohio provides that attorneys will act as hearing officers; other states specify qualifications, rather than require that officers be members of particular professions. In most states, the department of education provides a list of hearing officers or contracts with a qualified agency to do so. For instance, in California, the state department of education has contracted with a law school, which in turn hires the hearing officers.

Hearing Officer Qualifications

IDEA imposes several rules on hearing officers. An officer may not be an employee of the state department of education or the school district, and may not have any personal or professional interest that might conflict with the officer's objectivity in the hearing. The officer must have the knowledge and ability to understand IDEA, must conduct the hearing in accordance with appropriate legal standards, and must make and write a decision that complies with the law and standard legal practice. (20 U.S.C. § 1415(f)(3)(A).)

Contact your state department of education to find out the details of your state's laws on hearings. See Appendix 2.

A hearing is used to resolve factual disputes between you and your child's school district, including disagreements about placement, a related service, curricula, or methodology. Section B, above, lists typical IEP due process disputes.

Often, a factual dispute contains a legal dispute. For example, you want your child in a private school, and the school district offers a special day class in the public school. The factual dispute involves which placement is appropriate for your child. The legal issue is whether IDEA allows a private school placement when supported by the facts (it does).

Or, the school district wants to place your child in a special school 15 miles from your home; you want your child placed in a regular class at the local school. Again, the factual dispute involves finding the appropriate placement. The legal issue is IDEA's requirement that your child be placed in the least restrictive environment.

You may be thinking at this point, "I thought legal problems were subject only to the complaint process." Here's how it works: In a hearing, there may be legal issues that shape the factual analysis and outcome. In a complaint, you are only claiming that the school district broke the law—there is no factual dispute regarding an IEP issue.

You can file a complaint and file for due process. In some cases, you may simultaneously file a complaint and due process, as discussed at the end of Chapter 13.

A witness may testify about a legal issue, or you or the school district may raise a legal issue in your opening statements. In most cases, however, legal issues are addressed in a post-hearing brief (see Section 6, below). Discussing legal issues at the hearing or in a brief may seem quite daunting. If you anticipate major legal disputes, see Chapter 14 on lawyers and legal research, or contact an attorney for help on this part of the process.

Fear of Hearings

It's natural to be afraid of a due process hearing—after all, it's like a trial and can be difficult and complicated. But many parents conduct hearings. So how do you get through one with your nerves intact?

- Be organized.
- Take some time to think through the issues and your evidence.
- Know that everybody else is nervous, too.

Never doubt that you can do it. Lots of parents have had these same fears—and done just fine. In preparing for the IEP meeting (and perhaps mediation), you already did a good deal of the hard work.

1. Your Due Process Hearing Rights and Responsibilities

IDEA sets out many rights and responsibilities you and the school district have during the hearing process. (20 U.S.C. § 1415(f)(2)(3)):

- You have the right to be advised and accompanied by an attorney or another person with special knowledge or training.
- At least five business days before the hearing, you and the school district are required to give each other all evaluations and any recommendations based on those evaluations. If you don't, the hearing officer can exclude all evidence about the evaluations. This five-day requirement is usually also applied to exchanging witness lists—the names, qualifications, and topics of testimony of everyone you and the school district will call to testify at the hearing.
- The party who requested due process cannot raise any issues at the hearing that were not included in the written request unless the other side agrees. (See Section F1, above.)

- Before the hearing, you can subpoena witnesses to ensure that they will attend. (Most state educational agencies have subpoena forms.)
- Before the hearing, you have the right to declare the fair hearing closed or open to the public. An open hearing gives access to the public, including the press, which you may want. But an open meeting may also increase the stress and invite district employees to come and go.
- At the hearing, you can present written evidence in the form of exhibits and ask witnesses to answer questions.
- After the hearing, you are entitled to a verbatim record of the hearing (in a written or electronic format). This means that the hearing officer will tape the proceedings.
- After the hearing, you're entitled to a written decision, including findings of fact.
- You have the right to appeal a hearing decision to a state or federal court.

Check your state laws and regulations for any different or additional rules. For example, California requires each party to a hearing to submit a statement of issues and proposed resolutions at least ten days before the hearing. (Cal. Educ. Code § 56505(e)(6).)

2. Pros and Cons of a Due Process Hearing

There are several good reasons to request a hearing:

- If you win, your child will receive the education he or she needs.
- If you win, it's unlikely you will have to fight the battle again.
- If you win, your attorney's fees and other costs will be reimbursed for every issue you prevail on.
- Whether or not you win, you buy time. If your child is currently in a placement you want to maintain, your child is entitled to

remain there until the issue is finally resolved —either through the hearing decision or a final court decision, if you appeal. (Section D, above, discusses this "stay put" provision.)

There are also disadvantages to going to a hearing:

- Hearings are difficult, time consuming, emotionally draining, and contentious.
- You might lose.
- Your relationship with your school district will likely be strained and formal. Future IEPs may be hard. If you lose, the school district may feel invincible.
- If you lose, you won't be entitled to reimbursement for your costs and attorney's fees.

3. Hearing Logistics

The due process hearing must be held at a time and place convenient to you. Normally, hearings are held at the school district office and last anywhere from one to several days.

Once you request a hearing, you will be sent a notice of the date and location of the hearing, as well as the name of the hearing officer. You will also be given the name, address, and phone number of the school district representative. This information is important—you must send your exhibits and witness lists to this representative, as well as to the hearing officer.

4. Preparing for the Hearing

If you go to mediation first, much of your preparation will be done by the time you go to a hearing. But you still have some very important and time-consuming work to do. Give yourself several weeks to prepare, more if you skip mediation and go straight to a hearing.

a. Know Your Case

Review your child's file (see Chapter 3), your binder (see Chapter 4), and your IEP blueprint (see Chapter 5). Be clear on the disputed issues—what you want, what the school district is offering, and how you disagree. Don't confuse personality conflicts with disputes over your child's needs.

b. Determine Your Strategy

At the hearing, you must clearly state your position on each disputed issue and offer evidence to support it, in the form of witnesses and documents.

> **Example:**
> You want your daughter mainstreamed with a one-to-one aide, but your school district offers a special class. At the hearing, you will have to show that:
> - the school district failed to offer mainstreaming placement
> - an aide will help your daughter function in the classroom
> - your daughter will do well socially because her friends are in the class, and
> - a special class will be detrimental to your daughter because it will not address her unique needs and is contrary to IDEA's least restrictive environment requirement.

c. Prepare Exhibits of Written Material

You can submit any written document that contains supportive evidence or provides information that the hearing officer will need to make a decision as an exhibit. But be choosy—you don't necessarily want to turn over your entire IEP binder. The issues in dispute will guide you. Review all of your documents, looking for every-thing that supports your position, such as an evaluation or teacher's report. Note the specific place in each document where the supportive statement is made—that is, the page number and paragraph. You have probably done much of this work with the material organizer form you developed for the IEP meeting.

 Do not submit material that damages your case or reveals private information you don't want known. The school district may submit evidence that harms your case or points out the gaps in your evidence; obviously, you should not. Remember that the school district and hearing officer will get to examine the exhibits you submit—if they contain personal or confidential information that you don't want to reveal, you should try to find a different way to make your point.

Examples of exhibits typically presented at hearings include:
- IEP documents
- evaluations
- letters or reports from your child's teacher or physician
- articles about your child's disability, appropriate teaching methods, or any other issues in your case
- witnesses' résumés and articles they've written that relate to the issues in dispute, and
- your child's classroom work or artwork.

If in doubt, include the item. You never know when you might want to refer to something during the hearing. If you don't include the item when you prepare your exhibit exchange (at least five days before the hearing), you will probably be barred from using it at the hearing.

Arrange your exhibits in an order that makes sense to you, such as the order in which you think you'll introduce them or alphabetical order. Place them in a folder or binder with tabs and a table of contents. Be sure to page number each individual exhibit, too, so you can find specific statements easily.

You'll refer to these exhibits in your own testimony and when you question witnesses. At this stage, it is unlikely that you will have to develop new evidence. But if you do not yet have support for a disputed item, you may need new material—for example, a supportive letter or even an independent evaluation.

d. Choose and Prepare Witnesses

Witnesses are crucial to the outcome of the hearing. Choose and prepare your witnesses with care.

Choosing Witnesses

Double check your list of all potential witnesses, both people who support you and people who might testify for the school district (including participants at the IEP meeting). Try to anticipate what each witness can testify about. One witness may be able to testify about several issues, while others may focus on only one disputed matter. In choosing your witnesses, look for the following:

- the strength of the witness's testimony
- the witness's experience, training, education, and direct knowledge of your child, and
- the witness's willingness to testify under oath. You must make sure a person is willing to testify at the hearing before you put him or her on your witness list. A favorable or supportive report won't help if the witness equivocates at the hearing. In that case, submit the person's written material and have other witnesses refer to that report.

In some cases, you may need to subpoena a reluctant witness to testify at the hearing. A subpoena is an order that requires the witness to appear. Ask your state's education agency where to get subpoena forms.

Preparing Witness Questions

Write out a list of questions for each witness. The following is a general outline:

- Ask the witness to identify him- or herself—for example, "Please state your name, occupation, and place of employment."

- Ask about the witness's experience, education, training, and specific expertise in the area of dispute—you can refer the witness to the résumé or written articles that you included in your exhibits.
- Establish the witness's knowledge of your child—for example:
  - ▲ *"Have you met my son, Philip Jones?"*
  - ▲ *"Please tell us when, for how long, and for what purpose."*
  - ▲ *"Did you also observe him in school?"*
  - ▲ *"Please tell us when that was and for how long."*
- Ask questions to elicit your witness's opinion about the issues in dispute, for example:
  - ▲ *"You stated that you tested Philip. What tests did you administer?"*
  - ▲ *"What were the results?"*
  - ▲ *"What do those results mean?"*
  - ▲ *"What conclusions did you draw regarding Philip's reading difficulties?"*
  - ▲ *"How severe are his difficulties?"*
  - ▲ *"In your professional opinion, what is the appropriate way to help Philip improve his reading?"*
  - ▲ *"Do you have any specific recommendations regarding Philip's reading needs?"*
  - ▲ *"What is your professional opinion regarding Philip's prognosis as a successful reader if he is not provided the help you recommend?"*

Keys to preparing your witnesses. As a general rule, witnesses must be able to clearly state what your child needs and why, the consequences if those needs are met, and the detriment to your child if they are not.

Preparing Your Witnesses

Before the hearing, meet with your witnesses and go over your questions. Their answers may lead to new questions you'll want to ask, trigger a new strategy or approach, and help you and your witnesses prepare for the hearing. Explain that after you're done asking questions, the school district representative will cross-examine the witness by asking additional questions.

Some witnesses, particularly any school employees who agree to testify for your child, may be unwilling to meet during school hours. You may have to arrange to meet them at their home. Others may not want to meet at all. What should you do about witnesses who can help your case but won't talk to you ahead of time? If you can't discuss the case before the hearing, you won't know exactly how the witness will testify. Taking this kind of risk may backfire. One strategy is to leave the person off your witness list and hope the district calls him or her so you can cross-examine. Of course, if the witness is the only person who can testify about a certain element of your case, then you'll probably need to take a chance and use the witness, even though you didn't talk in advance of the hearing.

Another strategy is to include the person on your witness list but don't ask him or her to testify during your presentation. Then, either cross-examine if the school calls the witness, or use him or her as a rebuttal witness to counter something said by a school district witness.

Just before the hearing date, get back in touch with your witnesses to tell them:

- the date, time, and location of the hearing
- what time you need them to arrive to be ready to testify—be sure to let them know that they might not be called on time if an earlier witness took longer than expected or the hearing officer breaks early, and
- how long you expect their testimony to take.

Preparing Yourself as a Witness

You will most likely be a witness at the hearing. You have valuable information about your child's history, previous programs, and needs, as well as your worries, your frustrations, and what teachers have said to you about your child.

Your testimony must cover only matters that you know firsthand. At the same time, your testi-mony doesn't have to cover all aspects of the case. For example, you can testify about the evaluation done on your child and what the evaluator told you. On the other hand, the evaluator is in a better position to give this testimony. In general, then, your testimony should cover the areas in which you are the expert, particularly if no one else will testify on the issue.

You can present your testimony in one of two ways: You can respond to questions (just like you will be asking questions of your witnesses) asked by your spouse, a relative, or close friend, or you can make a statement covering all issues of importance. You can either read your statement or give it from notes. After you're done answering questions or making your statement, the school district representative will cross-examine you.

You want your testimony to be clear, specific, and objective. Break down your points into the following areas, using your mediation statement as a guideline:

- a general description of your child, including age, strengths, and weaknesses (your child profile, discussed in Chapter 10, Section D, can help here)
- your child's disability and the effect of that disability
- any secondary difficulties due to the disability —such as emotional problems
- your child's educational history—that is, the current program and class, and previous placements
- the particular issues in dispute and your desired resolution
- your observations at class visits, meetings with teachers and other professionals, and the IEP meeting (for example, "On February 12, 20xx, I visited the second-grade class at Tower School and I observed....")
- statements others have made to you that support your point of view, including your reaction to those statements—for instance, "On November 3, 20xx, Mr. Mastin of the school district told me there was no room for my child in the second-grade class at

Tower School; I confirmed this conversation in a letter, my Exhibit F, to which Mr. Mastin did not respond."

- your child's specific educational needs and the consequences if they are not met—for example, "Given the assessment by Dr. Pollack, I believe a placement in a program other than the second-grade class at Tower School will have serious emotional and cognitive consequences for my child."

e.   Prepare Questions for School Witnesses

Preparing questions for school witnesses is more difficult than preparing for your own witnesses because you don't know exactly what they'll say. Still, you can develop questions. You can probably guess what many witnesses will say, because you heard their opinions at the IEP meeting.

Start by reviewing your files, the transcript or your notes of the IEP meeting, and the school district's exhibits (you'll get them five days before the hearing). Then make a list of questions to strengthen your case or at least undermine what the school district's witnesses might say.

Example:

Your child's teacher said something very important to you when you visited your child's class. You sent a letter confirming what was said ("Thanks for talking to me today. I was glad to hear that you agreed Jake should remain in a regular class with the help of an aide"). The teacher never objected to your confirming letter, but you now believe she will say the opposite at the hearing. Be ready to point out the discrepancy—for instance, "Ms. Jenkins, you testified this morning that you feel Jake should be placed in a special education class. Do you recall when we met on October 15th, and you told me that Jake was doing well in the regular class but needed an aide to keep up? You don't recall that meeting? Please look at Exhibit B, my November 1st letter to you."

Rules of Evidence

You may have heard of something called the "rules of evidence." These formal rules, which are very specific and sometimes quite arcane, are used in courts to guide judges in deciding what evidence can be included and what must be excluded. These rules don't have to be followed at due process hearings, but the hearing officer can use them as appropriate.

For example, some rules relate to hearsay evidence—information that a witness did not hear or receive directly. "I saw Jack hit Frank" is not hearsay; "Jack told me that Frank hit Bill" is. Hearsay evidence can be excluded at a due process hearing.

Don't worry too much about formal rules of evidence. If the other side objects to a question you ask because it violates a rule of evidence, ask the hearing officer to explain the rule, and then rephrase your question or move on.

f.   Exchange Witness Lists and Evidence

Remember, you should submit a list of your witnesses and must submit copies of written exhibits at least five days before the hearing begins. (20 U.S.C. § 1415(f)(2).) Once you have your exhibits (organized in binders) and your list of witnesses, make two copies. Keep the originals for yourself, send one copy to the hearing officer, and send the other copy to the school district representative. To have proof that the others received the items at least five days before the hearing, send them "certified mail, return receipt requested."

5.   The Due Process Hearing

The hearing normally proceeds as follows:

1. The hearing officer opens the hearing and explains the process. The hearing officer

will usually identify and confirm the written testimony or exhibits that you and the school district submitted. Finally, the officer will set up the tape recorder and make sure the parties are ready.

2. The parties introduce themselves.

3. The hearing officer turns on the tape recorder, and the formal hearing begins.

4. You make your opening statement.

5. The school district makes its opening statement.

6. You question (direct examine) your witnesses.

7. The school representative questions (cross-examines) your witnesses.

8. You ask more questions of your witnesses (re-direct) if you want, the school representative cross-examines again (called re-cross) and so on.

9. The school district calls its witnesses with the same pattern of direct examination, cross-examination, re-direct, and re-cross.

10. You call witnesses after the school finishes, if you want. These are called rebuttal witnesses and are used to clarify or contradict testimony raised by the other side. The school district has the same right.

11. You give a closing statement, if you want.

12. The school district gives a closing statement, if it wants.

13. You and the school district submit written briefs discussing the facts presented at the hearing and any applicable law (see Section 6, below).

14. The hearing officer issues a decision.

Keeping Track During the Hearing

You want to have an ongoing record of the testimony during the hearing, because you may need to refer back to previous testimony. For example, the district calls a witness who testifies for 45 minutes on various issues. When you cross-examine this witness, you want to refer back to a specific statement he or she made that contradicted other testimony. You need to be able to refer to the earlier statements.

Taking notes is the logical way to keep track; however, it will be difficult for you to do so while also conducting the hearing. Instead, have someone else take notes for you, recording the statements of each witness, while you also take notes on key statements. (You can do this on paper or a laptop computer.) If you had a notetaker at the IEP meeting, consider using the same person, who is probably very familiar with the issues by now. You can tape the hearing, but you won't have time to review taped testimony while the hearing is going on. Also, it is more difficult to try to find an exact statement on a tape than to simply refer to written notes.

How do you use the notes? During your cross-examination, you'd say something like "Mr. Adams, you testified that, let me see [look at your notes], and I quote, 'I don't think James needs an aide in class.' Is that correct?" If he concurs, then point out evidence that contradicts him, such as "In her testimony yesterday, Dr. Markham stated that you told her on April 29, 20xx, that James needed an aide. Which statement should we believe?"

---

a. Make an Opening Statement

You can use the opening statement you prepared for mediation as a starting point, but you will need to modify it for a hearing. At mediation, you can say anything. Your aim is to reach a compromise. At a hearing, however, your aim is to prove your case. Your opening statement, therefore, should emphasize what you want for your child and how that is supported by evidence. This doesn't mean you shouldn't include items for which your evidence is weak, but it does mean you should carefully think about what you're requesting—and how likely you are to get it. The hearing officer will consider not only your evidence, but your credibility. If you ask for something unsupported by any evidence, your credibility may be affected.

Be sure to include these details in your opening statement:

- basic facts about your child, including age, disability, and current educational program
- a clear statement of your child's needs and the dispute that brought you to the hearing, and
- a brief statement that what you want is supported by evidence, such as "Cheryl needs a full-time aide, as we will clearly show with evidence, including the testimony of several different professionals and exhibits B, D, and M."

Opening statements can be any length, but five to 15 minutes is typical. If you can, don't read a verbatim statement—instead, use notes to guide you in making your points. If you're very nervous, however, it's okay to read the statement. It is important to express your feelings and bring the human element into the hearing. Be careful not to go off on an unfocused monologue or make your argument a personal attack on school district representatives.

b. Questioning Your Witnesses

After opening statements, your witnesses will testify. Think carefully about the order in which you want to present their testimony. You are telling a story, and you need to present the details of the story in an order that will make sense to someone who has little or no prior knowledge of

the situation. It's often best to begin with someone (possibly you) who can give general background information about your child. Next, you might want a witness who can present the evaluation data, such as your independent evaluator.

After that, you want to go to the core of the dispute and make your case. For example, you and the school district disagree on placement and a related service. During the past year, your child was in a regular class, with no assistance. You want your child to stay in that class with an aide; the school district has offered placement in a special day class. Your first witness can give the details of the regular class. The second can talk about why your child needs that class. The third can describe the services offered by the aide. The fourth can explain why your child needs that aide.

Of course, you may have to modify the presentation and go out of order if a witness is available only on a certain day or at a certain time. Or, you may choose a different order to maximize impact. In some instances, the witness who will give the most dramatic and effective testimony should go last, so the hearing officer is left with that impression. Or that person might go first, to set a tone for the rest of the hearing. Only you can decide which strategy will be most effective in your situation.

c. Questioning Reluctant Witnesses

Question reluctant witnesses with care. You first want to ask the hearing officer to note that the witness is not cooperative. To ensure the person's attendance at the hearing, you should have issued a subpoena. At the hearing, ask something like "Mr. Jones, are you testifying voluntarily?" The response will be something like "No. As you know, I was subpoenaed by you."

Another possibility is to begin your questioning with a statement such as "This witness, Mr. Hobson, the fourth-grade teacher, would not talk to me prior to the hearing. I am calling him as a hostile witness."

Further Suggestions on Questioning Witnesses

No matter how much you prepare, you won't be able to plan exactly how the questioning will go. Be ready to depart from your planned questions. For example, a witness might answer in a way slightly different from what you expected, requiring you to ask follow-up questions. Or the witness may say the opposite of what you expect.

Here are some tips to help you deal with surprises when questioning witnesses:

- Ask for a brief break if you need to gather yourself or consider new questions.
- Keep track of your questions. If you veer off on a line of questioning you had not planned, mark where you are on your list of questions so you can come back to it later.
- Don't ask a question to which you don't know the answer, particularly of a school witness.
- Don't overwhelm the hearing officer with a ton of facts. Parents often try to get everything into the record at the hearing. Know the difference between important facts and minutiae.
- Know when to stop. Stop asking questions when something powerful has been stated. Further questioning will only dilute the impact.
- Don't badger a witness. Ask questions in a firm way, and repeat them if necessary. But don't become hostile, belligerent, or belittling.
- Don't play lawyer. You'll do fine with your own style and language.

d. How to Use Your Exhibits

Have your exhibits available so you can use them when you question witnesses. For example, "Tell me Dr. Whitland, you said Monroe does not need psychotherapy. Would you please look at Exhibit B, page 4? You reported last year that Monroe had severe emotional difficulties that were interfering with his education. Aren't severe emotional difficulties usually addressed in some kind of psychological therapy?"

e. Closing Statements

After all the evidence has been presented and all witnesses have testified, the hearing officer will likely ask if you want to make closing arguments or submit a written brief.

A closing statement is a summary of each party's key evidence as it relates to the disputed issues. For example, you might say, "Every witness called by us agreed that Michele needs four sessions of speech therapy; not one of the school district's witnesses contradicted that. This is fully consistent with Dr. Hanover's written report, Exhibit L." Your closing statement might also note that the recommended education is consistent with IDEA.

6. Post-Hearing Briefs

If you agree to submit briefs, the parties, with the help of the hearing officer, will set a short time frame (usually no more than one week) to submit the briefs. The purposes of the briefs are to highlight the evidence that supports your case and expand on any legal issues pertinent to your dispute.

To develop your brief, first review your notes, your memory, and the evidence. The written brief should precisely point out the evidence that supports your case and the evidence that contradicts the school district's point of view. If there are legal issues, you should review IDEA and any court cases that support your analysis of the law. (See Chapter 14 for advice on legal research.) You may also want to contact a lawyer or support organization for help.

J. Hearing Decision and Appeals

After the hearing, you're entitled to a written decision, including findings of fact. The hearing officer must have "substantive grounds" for the decision, which must include a finding of whether the child received a free, appropriate public education (FAPE). (20 U.S.C. § 1415(f)(3)(E).) Many courts have found that a school district's violation of IDEA procedures constitutes a denial of FAPE.

Both you and the school district have the right to appeal the decision to state or federal court, theoretically all the way to the U.S. Supreme Court. If you lost, several factors will help you decide whether or not to appeal:

- **Strength of your case.** You should already have considered this as part of your decision to pursue due process. For an appeal, you must look at your situation with a more critical eye. Many reviewing courts will defer to the administrative decision and won't want to rehear the evidence anew. Even if you court takes a fresh look at the evidence, remember that a neutral third party has already ruled against you, which suggests that your case has some problems.

- **Costs of an appeal.** There are various costs in appealing a hearing decision to court, including filing fees, fees for serving papers on the school district, witness fees, and other trial costs (such as copying exhibits). There's one more cost: potential attorney's fees. While nonattorneys can represent themselves in court, I strongly recommend hiring an attorney for the appeal. At the very least, have an attorney who specializes in IDEA review your case and advise you of your chances on appeal.

- **Time.** If you or the school district want to appeal the due process hearing decision, you must do so within 90 days after the decision is issued (not the date you actually receive it), unless your state law establishes a different time limit for such appeals. (20 U.S.C. § 1415(i)(2)(B).) Contact your state department of education or a parental support group to find out about your state's timelines. (See Appendixes 2 and 3 for contact information.) ■

13

Filing a Complaint for a Legal Violation

As mentioned in Chapter 12, informal negotiation and due process are typically used to resolve factual disputes between you and the school district. But what if your concern isn't over a program, service, or other factual matter—that is, who is right and who is wrong—but, rather, that the school district has violated a legal requirement under IDEA? For legal disputes, IDEA provides a complaint process.

⚠ **IDEA regulations are changing.** The regulatory citations throughout this book are to the current IDEA regulations—those that will be in effect until the Department of Education issues final regulations interpreting the 2004 amendments to IDEA. The Department expects to release these final regulations at the end of 2005; many of them will be identical or similar to the existing regulations cited in this chapter (although the citations will be different), while others will be new. When you use this book, you should make sure that you have the most current version of the regulations. See "Warning: Special Education Rules Are in Flux," in Chapter 1, for information that will help you stay up to date. You can find the most recent version of IDEA, including the 2004 amendments, starting at 20 U.S.C. § 1400; the most pertinent sections are included in Appendix 1. (When final regulations are issued, the sections on filing a complaint—which currently appear at 34 C.F.R. § 660-662—will be found in 34 C.F.R. § 151-153.)

A. When to File a Complaint

IDEA statutes and regulations set out the school district's legal obligations. Excerpts of key sections of IDEA are contained in Appendix 1. Here are some common school district actions (or inactions) that violate IDEA:

- failing to provide a child's records
- failing to do evaluations
- failing to meet evaluation and IEP timelines

- failing to hold an IEP meeting
- failing to allow parents to effectively represent their child in the IEP meeting—for example, by limiting who can attend or by intimidating the parent
- failing to follow required procedures before suspending or expelling a special education student (see Chapter 2, Section A)
- failing to discuss all elements in an IEP meeting—goals, placement, related services, transition plans
- failing to implement an agreed-to IEP—for example, if your child's IEP calls for three sessions of speech therapy and the school district provides only one session, and
- failing to give notice before changing, or refusing to change, a child's IEP. Your district cannot change your child's IEP without giving you notice of that change and holding an IEP meeting, nor can it refuse you the right to have an IEP meeting if you want a change.

You should file your complaint within a year after the violation occurs. You should also send a copy of your complaint to the school district. To be safe, send this copy—and the complaint you file with a state or federal agency (see Section B, below)—by certified mail, return receipt requested.

Collective Complaints: There's Strength in Numbers

If your school district is violating the law in a way that affects a group of children, consider filing a complaint together. A complaint filed by more than one family can be more effective. Your state department of education has a legal duty under IDEA to monitor all school districts to make sure they are following the law—and to take any necessary steps to force a recalcitrant district to shape up. States are usually more sensitive to what may be a pattern of IDEA violations rather than a one-time incident. If you are able to show that many children are being hurt by the district's failure to follow the law, your state department of education may be quicker to step in and take action. And it's much less costly for a group of parents to hire one attorney to draft and submit a complaint than for each family to hire its own lawyer.

B. Where to File a Complaint

Section A, above, lists common violations of IDEA, but it is not an exhaustive list. If you believe your school district has violated IDEA or any state special education law, contact your state department of education (or a locally designated agency), or the U.S. Department of Education, Office for Civil Rights (OCR). Contact information for both is in Appendix 2.

You can file a complaint with either the state or federal education agency. Both handle violations of IDEA, state law, or Section 504 of the Rehabilitation Act of 1973.

See Chapter 7, Section E, for a brief description of Section 504, which prohibits schools from denying access to children with disabilities.

State departments of education are primarily geared toward investigating IDEA violations, but they will also look into complaints regarding Section 504. In contrast, the federal OCR is primarily concerned with Section 504 or discrimination violations, but will also investigate IDEA complaints.

Before deciding where to file a complaint, contact your state department of education and the regional office of the OCR and ask the following questions:

- What kinds of complaints do they investigate?
- What is the deadline for filing a complaint? Section 504 complaints must be filed within 180 days of the last alleged act of discrimination against your child. IDEA complaints must be filed within the time established in your state statute of limitations (discussed in Chapter 12, Section A).
- How do they handle complaints? In some states, an IDEA or Section 504 complaint is investigated initially by the school district. If you have a choice, opt for an investigator who is not associated with your school district.
- What are their timelines for investigating complaints?
- What remedies are available, such as reimbursement for attorney's fees or the cost of related services?

Notifying the U.S. Department of Education, Office of Special Education and Rehabilitation Services

In addition to filing a complaint, you can notify the U.S. Department of Education, Office of Special Education and Rehabilitation Services, Office of Special Education Programs (OSEP). OSEP will neither investigate the problem nor issue a decision. But OSEP has overall responsibility for monitoring how states implement IDEA and might consider your comments when conducting its annual review of the programs in your state. Contact information is in Appendix 2.

C. What to Include in a Complaint

Your state department of education may have a complaint form for you to use. OCR has one, but you aren't required to use it. Whether you use a form or simply write a letter, include the following information:

- Your name and address (a telephone number where you may be reached during business hours is helpful, but not required).
- Your child's name and school district.
- As precise a description as possible of the violation, including the date, time, and location. If you cite more than one violation or you have very broad concerns, be as specific as possible, describing each violation separately.
- The applicable section of IDEA or any state law, if you know it. Key sections of IDEA are cited throughout this book, and Appendix 1 includes excerpts of IDEA. Contact your state department of education (Appendix 2) for state special education laws and regulations.
- The remedy you want, including reimbursement for costs incurred due to the district's violations.

A sample complaint letter is shown below.

Sample Complaint Letter

February 5, 20xx

John Harrington, Director
Compliance Unit
Special Education Division
Department of Education
721 Capitol Mall
Sacramento, CA 95814

Dear Mr. Harrington:

I am formally requesting that you investigate legal violations by the Valley Unified School District, 458 4th Street, Visalia, California. I am making this request pursuant to IDEA and state law, which gives me the right to file a complaint if I believe the school district has violated IDEA.

The facts in this matter are as follows:

I requested an IEP meeting on October 14, 20xx, just after my child was determined eligible for special education. The school district did not contact us to schedule an IEP meeting until February 2, 20xx, at which time I was told that the meeting would be March 5, 20xx. This violates IDEA, which provides that an IEP will be held within 30 days of a determination that a child needs special education and related services. I request that an IEP meeting be held within 15 days of the conclusion of your investigation. I also request reimbursement for the cost we incurred to hire a private physical therapist because of the school district's failure to address my child's needs.

Please contact me to confirm receipt of this request, set up times for me to meet with your investigator, and establish timelines for completing the investigation.

Sincerely,

Becky Masteron

Becky Masteron
6004 Green St.
Visalia, CA 95800

D. What Happens When You File a Complaint

After you file your complaint, the investigating agency will most likely meet with you to discuss the case, review evidence and records, meet with the school district, and then issue a decision. IDEA requires that the state issue a decision within 60 days after the complaint is filed. If the district is found to have violated IDEA, the agency will make recommendations that the school district must follow to comply with the law. The decision can be appealed to the U.S. Secretary of Education (contact information is in Appendix 2).

Due Process and Complaints

You can simultaneously go through due process and file a complaint alleging a legal violation. If the district is found to have violated the law, you would certainly want the due process hearing officer to know. Indeed, if timing permits, you may want to file your complaint first so you can submit the decision as an exhibit at the due process hearing. Note, however, that the portion of your complaint alleging a factual dispute can be set aside to be resolved through due process.

■

14

Lawyers and Legal Research

Lawyers can play an important role in special education. While the purpose of this book is to guide you through the IEP process without an attorney, there may be times when you might need to hire or at least consult a lawyer.

This chapter covers:

- how a lawyer can help with the IEP and other special education procedures
- what to consider when using an attorney in special education
- finding an effective attorney
- how lawyers are paid
- resolving problems with your lawyer, and
- doing your own legal research.

A. How a Lawyer Can Help

Generally speaking, an attorney can help you in one of two ways. A lawyer can provide advice and assistance as needed throughout the IEP process while you do most of the work, or a lawyer can be directly involved as your formal representative.

Here are some of the specific tasks a lawyer can help you with:

- securing your child's school files
- requesting an evaluation or an IEP meeting
- preparing for the IEP eligibility meeting
- preparing for the IEP program meeting— including drafting goals, your child's profile, and program and service descriptions; reviewing supportive evidence and materials; suggesting who should attend and what material will be most effective; and providing pointers about the IEP meeting
- attending an IEP meeting (remember to notify your school district before the meeting if your lawyer will attend)
- reviewing evaluations and IEP forms before you sign them
- researching a specific legal issue that applies to your situation
- helping you informally resolve a dispute with the school district

- assessing the strength of your case, if you're considering filing a complaint or pursuing due process
- preparing for and attending mediation and the due process hearing
- writing a post-hearing brief
- preparing a complaint for you to file with the appropriate educational agency, and
- representing you in court.

You may choose to have a lawyer do everything from beginning to end in the IEP process or handle only certain tasks. For example, you might want to attend the IEP meeting yourself, but have an attorney review the IEP document before you sign it.

B. Do You Need an Attorney?

Because lawyers can be expensive—and because hiring a lawyer definitely makes the IEP process more adversarial—you'll want to think carefully before bringing in an attorney. Here are some factors to consider:

- **Complexity of the case.** The more complicated your case is, the more likely it is that you could benefit from some legal advice. A dispute involving complicated placement and service issues, for example, might require the special knowledge and experience of an attorney.
- **Strength of your case.** If you really don't know whether you have a good case against the school district, consider talking to a lawyer. A good attorney should tell you how strong your case looks and, therefore, whether or not your situation justifies hiring him or her.
- **Your time and energy.** If you work full time, are a single parent, or have a difficult schedule, you may want someone else to take charge. On the other hand, if you have the time and energy to represent yourself and your child, hiring an attorney may not be necessary.

- **Your budget.** Attorneys aren't cheap. Can you afford the help? Are you entitled to reimbursement for your legal costs? (See Section D, below.)
- **Your self-confidence.** The purpose of this book is not only to help you advocate for your child, but also to give you the confidence to be an effective advocate. Still, you may prefer to hire a lawyer rather than wage the fight on your own.
- **Who represents the school district.** If the school district has an attorney, you may want the same protection and leverage.
- **Your relationship with the district.** Hiring a lawyer may change your relationship with the school district. When you involve attorneys, the atmosphere becomes more formal and potentially combative. School personnel will likely be more guarded and may view you as the troublemaker or squeaky wheel. Of course, if you are at the point where you may need an attorney, your relationship with the school district has already changed. Your child's welfare is more important than a cordial relationship with the school district.

C. Finding an Attorney

Special education attorneys are not as numerous as personal injury or business lawyers. It is also unlikely that attorneys working in more standard areas of law—such as wills and estates, criminal law, family matters, or corporation law—will know anything about special education law.

You may be tempted to hire the attorney who did your will, your sister-in-law who just graduated from law school, or the attorney whose ad in the phone book promises the lowest rates. But special education law is highly specialized. Hiring an attorney who does not know the law or have experience in special education will significantly increase your chance of failure, and could ultimately cost you more rather than less. When you

pay an attorney, you are paying for all the time spent on your case, including time spent doing research. You don't want to pay an attorney for on-the-job training.

1. Compile a List of Potential Attorneys

To find the "right" lawyer, compile a list of potential candidates. Here's how:

- Ask other parents in the school district.
- Ask your pediatrician or other health care professionals.
- Ask school district personnel—the district is required to maintain a list of attorneys and other advocacy resources for parents.
- Contact your state special education advisory commission and ask for referrals. IDEA requires each state to have a special education commission, composed of educators and parents, which advises the state about special education. The commissioners should have plenty of special education contacts.
- Contact your state department of education and ask for referrals (see Appendix 2).
- Contact a nearby Parent Training and Information Center (PTI) (see Appendix 3).
- Contact a local disability rights advocacy organization (see Appendix 3).
- Contact a low-cost or free legal clinic, such as legal aid—while most offices focus on common civil issues (such as domestic disputes or evictions), some offices do special education work for low-income people.
- Use your personal network—friends, colleagues, neighbors, or coworkers who know special education lawyers or who know lawyers who can recommend good special education lawyers.

Nonprofit Legal Clinics

There are nonprofit organizations that provide legal assistance in special education, disability rights, or what is generally called "public interest law." Your school district should have a list of disability-specific or special education nonprofit legal clinics in your area. Also see the organizations listed in Appendix 3.

There are advantages and disadvantages to using a nonprofit legal clinic rather than a private attorney. Advantages to using a nonprofit include:

- the attorneys have likely worked in special education and have handled many cases
- nonprofits often do not charge for their services or have significantly reduced rates, and
- nonprofits, particularly disability-focused offices, have special knowledge and often a strong passion about the issues.

But there are disadvantages to using a nonprofit:

- demand is often greater than supply; you may have to wait some time for an appointment, even just to have someone assess your case, and
- nonprofit organizations often have limited resources—some focus on either precedent-setting cases (unusual disputes) or cases that will have an impact on a large number of children—and may not handle individual cases.

How Not to Find a Special Education Lawyer

There are several bad ways to find a special education lawyer. Avoid these traps for the unwary:

- **Heavily advertised legal clinics.** While they may offer low flat rates for routine services such as drafting a will, most make their money on personal injury cases. I am not aware of any such clinics offering special education help.
- **Referral panels set up by local bar associations.** Bar association panels usually do minimal screening before qualifying lawyers as experts in certain areas. While you might get a good referral from these panels, it is highly unlikely that you'll find a special education lawyer listed.
- **Private referral services.** When it comes to services that advertise on TV and billboards, forget it. It is highly unlikely they offer any special education help.

2. Call the Attorneys on Your List

Once you have a list of recommended attorneys, you can either narrow it down to one or two individuals who were enthusiastically recommended or make initial contact with everyone on your list.

Try to have a brief phone conversation or ask for a short meeting. Some attorneys will chat with you briefly over the phone to determine the nature of your case and whether or not you need an attorney. Other attorneys may have you speak with an assistant, complete a form describing your case, or make an appointment to come in and talk about the case. Before making an appointment, find out the following information:

- the attorney's fee
- how the attorney will review the case and decide whether or not you should proceed, and
- how much the initial review costs.

3. Meet With the Best Candidates

Make an appointment with those candidates who seem like the best prospects. Naturally, if there is a fee for the initial intake, you may want to see only a few attorneys. Be sure to ask what records the attorney needs to evaluate your case.

When you meet with an attorney, you should ask about your specific case, of course. You also want to ask about the attorney's:

- years of experience
- specific special education experience
- experience with your particular legal issue (such as a due process hearing)
- knowledge of special education law and the IEP process
- experience with your school district
- general style—is the attorney confrontational or cooperative (for example, does he or she like mediation or think it's a waste of time and normally go directly to a due process hearing?)
- references, and
- fees.

Pay attention to the answers. Does the attorney clearly answer your questions about fees, experience, and your specific legal issues? Does the attorney try to assess your chances in due

process? If the lawyer makes you uncomfortable, think carefully about whether his or her expertise and success rate is worth putting up with a difficult style.

Will the attorney provide the type of help you want? Is the attorney willing to advise you now, but hold off on full participation unless and until you need it? If the attorney wants to take over the case but you want only a consultant, you have the wrong attorney.

Will the attorney be accessible? This is important—the most common complaint about lawyers is that they don't return phone calls, respond to faxes or email, or make themselves available when a client calls. Discuss the attorney's response time. While no attorney should be expected to respond instantly, you shouldn't have to wait more than a day or two, except in rare circumstances.

Your Responsibility in Working With an Attorney

Your attorney should be responsive and courteous, and keep you informed. But the client-attorney relationship is a two-way street. Keep the following in mind:

- Vague questions are likely to receive vague responses; be clear and specific when you discuss matters or ask questions.
- No matter how good an attorney is, the quality of the case—that is, the strength of the evidence—is the key to success. Your attorney cannot transform a bad case into a good one.
- You have some of the responsibility for controlling your legal bill. Be especially aware of time. If you talk to your lawyer for 30 minutes, you will be billed for 30 minutes, even if you feel you were "just chatting."
- You cannot call up an attorney, chat for five minutes, and have your problem resolved. I frequently receive phone calls that go something like this:

"Hello. I have a question about special education. Do you know special education law?"

"Yes."

"My daughter has an IEP on Thursday. She is learning disabled, and I want her placed in a private school. The school district has offered a special day class. What do you recommend?"

If I tried to answer that question, I would be doing a disservice to myself and the caller. And the caller is being unfair. Many lawyers will try to answer simple questions over the phone from first-time callers—such as, "Can you tell me if a school has to do an evaluation of a child before the child enters special education?"—but most questions are more complicated than that. It is unfair to assume that an attorney can either provide a simple answer to a complex question or provide free advice.

4. Ask for a Case Evaluation

A good attorney will evaluate the evidence before giving you any advice. After reviewing your case materials, a good attorney should be able to:

- tell you the strength of your case
- explain the process
- evaluate your documents and potential witnesses
- tell you if additional supportive material is needed
- estimate the cost of hiring an attorney for due process or beyond
- estimate how long your case may take
- provide insights into school district personnel, particularly if the attorney has worked with the district before, and
- provide a cost-benefit analysis of hiring the attorney to represent you versus using the attorney as an advisor only.

5. A Word on an Attorney's Style

Some attorneys are pleasant, patient, and good listeners. Others are unpleasant, impatient, and bad listeners. Although you may want the former, you may get the latter. Whatever the style of your attorney, make it clear that you know the attorney is busy, but you expect the attorney to treat you courteously, explain matters, keep you fully posted about what is happening, and include you as an active partner in the process. An effective professional relationship must be based on mutual respect.

Furthermore, the attorney should contact you regarding any decision to be made, whether scheduling a meeting, deciding on tactics, reviewing a key issue, or considering a possible resolution of the dispute.

If at any time you don't understand what your attorney has said, requested, or planned, ask for clarification. If the answer isn't clear, ask again. Although you hired the attorney because of his or her professional expertise and knowledge—and therefore have relinquished a certain amount of control—it does not mean you should be kept in the dark.

D. How Attorneys Are Paid

How you pay your lawyer depends on the type of legal services you need and the amount of legal work involved. Once you choose a lawyer, ask for a written agreement explaining how fees and costs will be billed and paid. In some states, a written agreement is required by law; even if it isn't, always ask for one. A good attorney will provide you with a written contract (whether you ask or not). Be sure to tell the lawyer how much you are able (and willing) to spend—if you and the lawyer agree on a cap or limit on legal fees, that should also be in your fee agreement.

As your case progresses, you'll want to make sure you receive a bill or statement at least once a month. A lawyer's time adds up quickly. If your lawyer will be delegating some of the work to a less experienced associate, paralegal, or secretary, the delegated work should be billed at a lower hourly rate. Make sure this is stated in your written fee agreement.

1. Lawyers' Billing Methods

Lawyers charge for their services in three different ways:

Hourly rate. Most special education attorneys charge by the hour. In most parts of the U.S., you can secure competent representation for $100 to $250 an hour. Many clients prefer an hourly rate to a flat fee (discussed next) because you pay only for the attorney's actual time spent on your case. Comparison shopping among lawyers can help you avoid overpaying, but only if you compare lawyers with similar expertise. A highly experienced special education attorney (who has a higher hourly rate) may be cheaper in the long run than a general practitioner (at a lower rate).

The special education attorney won't have to research routine questions and should be able to evaluate your case quickly.

Legal Time

How much time your attorney will spend on your case depends on the nature of your dispute. The following can serve as a general guideline for the amount of time required for common legal tasks:

- initial review of your records and interview with you .... 2-3 hours
- help you with the IEP process—developing a blueprint, contacting evaluators and school personnel; drafting goals and objectives .... 2-5 hours
- attend the IEP meeting .... 2-4 hours (per meeting)
- prepare for and attend mediation session .... 3-8 hours
- prepare for and attend hearing .... 10-35 hours

---

Flat rate. A flat rate is a single fee that will cover all the work the lawyer has agreed to do—for example, the amount the attorney will charge you to prepare for and attend the IEP meeting or prepare for and conduct the fair hearing. You are obligated to pay the flat fee no matter how many hours the lawyer spends on your case. A flat fee can be quite economical if the fee is reasonable and you anticipate a lot of work. On the other hand, if the case is resolved early in the process, you may end up paying much more than you would have paid in hourly fees. Most special education attorneys charge by the hour and may be unwilling to work on a flat fee.

Contingency fee. Contingency fee arrangements are rarely used in special education cases. A contingency fee is a percentage of whatever money the party wins; if you don't win anything, the attorney doesn't earn anything. Because almost all successful special education cases involve providing a program or service rather than an award of money, don't expect a special education attorney to work on contingency.

Legal Costs

In addition to the fees they charge for their time, lawyers bill for a variety of items. These costs can add up quickly and may include charges for:

- photocopies
- faxes
- postage
- overnight mail
- messenger services
- expert witness fees
- court filing fees
- long-distance phone calls
- process servers
- work by investigators
- work by legal assistants or paralegals
- deposition transcripts
- online legal research, and
- travel.

Some lawyers absorb the cost of photocopies, faxes, and local phone calls as normal office overhead, but that's not always the case. When working out the fee arrangement, ask for a list of costs you'll be expected to pay. If the lawyer seems intent on nickel-and-diming you or hitting you with a $3-per-page fax charge, you should talk about it. While this may not reflect the attorney's skills or ability to win a case, it may raise red flags about how he or she does business.

2. Reimbursement for Legal Fees and Costs

If you hire an attorney and pay for his or her services, **and** you prevail at mediation or the fair hearing, you are entitled to be reimbursed by your school district for your attorney's fees and other due process costs. (20 U.S.C. § 1415(i)(3).)

But your right to reimbursement can be limited. First, you are not entitled to reimbursement for the fees you paid an attorney to attend the IEP meeting, unless the meeting was required as part of due process. This might happen if the due process hearing officer orders a second IEP meeting to discuss matters that were improperly omitted in the first meeting.

Second, you are not entitled to reimbursement if the school district makes a settlement offer ten days before the due process hearing, you reject the offer, **and** the hearing officer finds that what you actually won in due process is no better than the school district's settlement offer. If the hearing officer finds that you were substantially justified in rejecting the settlement offer, however, you are entitled to full reimbursement. What constitutes "substantially justified" is not defined in IDEA.

Third, the hearing officer can reduce the amount of attorney's fees to which you are entitled if the officer finds that any of the following are true:

- you unreasonably protracted or extended the final resolution of the controversy
- the attorney's fees unreasonably exceed hourly rates that others in the community charge for similar services
- the time and services provided by the attorney were excessive, or
- the attorney failed to provide certain information required by law. (20 U.S.C. § 1415(i).)

You should discuss these reimbursement issues carefully with your attorney before you evaluate any settlement offers or decide whether to request a fair hearing.

⚠ You may have to pay the school district's attorney fees. The 2004 amendments to IDEA add provisions that make parents liable for the school district's attorney fees, in certain limited situations. See Chapter 12, Section E, for more information.

3. Reducing Legal Fees

There are several ways to control legal fees.

Be organized. Especially when you are paying by the hour, it's important to gather important documents, write a short chronology of events, and explain a problem concisely to your lawyer. Keep a copy of everything you give to your lawyer.

Be prepared before you meet your lawyer. Whenever possible, put your questions in writing and mail, fax, or deliver them to your lawyer before all meetings or phone conversations. Early preparation also helps focus the meeting so there is less chance of digressing (at your expense) into unrelated topics.

Carefully review lawyer bills. Like everyone else, lawyers make mistakes. For example, .1 of an hour (six minutes) may be transposed into a 1. (one hour) when the data is entered into the billing system. That's $200 instead of $20 if your lawyer charges $200 per hour. Don't hesitate to question your bill. You have the right to a clear explanation of costs.

Ask your lawyer what work you can do. There are some things you can do to save time. For example, you could go through the school's record and highlight key statements. Or you could talk with important witnesses to find out their attitudes about key issues in the case. Some attorneys may be comfortable with you doing substantial work; others will not be. Be sure to discuss this ahead of time.

E. Resolving Problems With a Lawyer

If you see a problem emerging with your lawyer, don't just sit back and fume. Call or write your lawyer. Whatever it is that rankles—a too-high bill, a missed deadline, or a strategic move you don't understand—have an honest discussion about your feelings.

If you can't discuss these matters frankly with your lawyer or you are unsatisfied with the outcome of any discussion, it's time to consider finding another attorney. If you don't, you may waste money on unnecessary legal fees and risk having matters turn out badly.

If you decide to change lawyers, be sure to end the first professional relationship before you hire a new attorney. If you don't, you could find yourself being billed by two lawyers at the same time. Also, be sure all important legal documents are returned to you. Tell your new lawyer what your old one has done to date and pass on the file.

Here are some tips on resolving specific problems:

- If you have a dispute over fees, the local bar association may be able to mediate it for you.
- If a lawyer has violated legal ethics—for example, had a conflict of interest, overbilled you, or didn't represent you zealously—the state agency that licenses lawyers may discipline the lawyer.
- Where a major mistake has been made—for example, a lawyer missed the fair hearing deadline for submitting the witness list and exhibits—you might even consider suing for malpractice. Many lawyers carry malpractice insurance.

Remember, while there will be times when you question your attorney's tactics, you have hired someone because of his or her expertise and experience. Before confronting the attorney, ask yourself whether the attorney misfired or you are overreacting.

Your Rights as a Client

As a client, you have the right to expect the following:

- courteous treatment by your lawyer and staff members
- an itemized statement of services rendered and a full advance explanation of billing practices
- charges for agreed-upon fees and nothing more
- prompt responses to phone calls and letters
- confidential legal conferences, free from unwarranted interruptions
- up-to-date information on the status of your case
- diligent and competent legal representation, and
- clear answers to all questions.

A final word on attorneys: We live in a time when public attitudes about attorneys are negative, to some degree rightfully so. There are, of course, many conscientious attorneys, particularly in special education, where you will actually find a high percentage of compassionate, able, and decent professionals.

F. Doing Your Own Legal Research

Using this book is a good way to educate yourself about the laws that affect your rights as a parent of a special education child. Chapter 2 has already provided you with much of the key legal language of IDEA. But because the laws and court decisions of 50 states are involved, no one book can give you all the information you need.

There's a lot you can do on your own, once you understand a few basics about law libraries, statute books, court opinions, and the general reference books that lawyers use to learn about issues. Some basic legal research skills can help you determine how strong your case is and the best and most effective way to go forward. Whether the issue is private school placement, the type or amount of a related service, an evaluation question, or an eligibility issue, IDEA and judicial decisions can help you judge the strength of your case.

Using the Library

Look for a law library that is open to the public—there may be one in your main county or city courthouse or state capitol. Law librarians, who often have experience working with nonlawyers, can help you find the appropriate resources. Publicly funded law schools generally permit the public to use their libraries, and some private law schools also grant access to the public, sometimes for a modest fee.

If you can't find an accessible law library, don't overlook the public library. Many large public libraries have sizable legal reference collections, including state and federal statutes. If you are working with a lawyer, you might also ask about using the research materials at the lawyer's office.

Examples:

- You want your child in a private school that has an identical program to the one available in your school district. Legal research should lead you to the conclusion that your position isn't a winning one. The law is clear—there is no right to a private school in this situation.
- Your daughter is deaf and you want her to have an American Sign Language (ASL) interpreter in her mainstreamed class. You do some research and find that IDEA does not require a specific

language or methodology in the class. You realize that you will have to prove that your child cannot benefit from her education without ASL.

- You want your child who has some autistic behaviors to be mainstreamed with an aide. You visit a law library and discover that in the case of *Board of Education v. Holland,* 4F.3d 1398 (9th Circuit, 1994), the court established guidelines for determining when a child is entitled to be mainstreamed, including an analysis of:
  - ▲ the academic and nonacademic benefits to the child
  - ▲ the effect of the placement on the teacher and other students, and
  - ▲ the cost of the aids and services needed to mainstream.

The materials you can research include the following:

- IDEA statutes and regulations (excerpts are in Appendix 1)
- state statutes
- court cases interpreting IDEA and other relevant statutes
- explanatory documents, such as the U.S. Department of Education policy guidelines and correspondence (these documents do not have the authority of a statute or court case, but they reflect the Department's analysis of the law)
- due process hearing decisions (available through your state department of education and the *Individuals with Disabilities Education Law Reporter,* discussed below)—although these are binding only on the parties to that specific hearing, they may be of value to you in showing how hearing officers make decisions in your state, and
- law review and other articles about IDEA and special education issues.

1. Individuals With Disabilities Education Act (IDEA): Where to Find It

Like all federal laws, IDEA is found in a multi-volume series of books called the United States Code (U.S.C.), which is available in most libraries and online. The U.S.C. consists of separate numbered titles, each covering a specific subject matter. IDEA is found in Title 20, beginning with Section 1400. Appendix 1 includes a copy of key sections of the IDEA statute.

You can find annotated versions of the U.S.C., which include not only the text of IDEA, but also summaries of cases that interpret IDEA and a reference to where each case can be found. Annotated codes also list articles that discuss IDEA. Annotated codes have comprehensive indexes by topic, and are kept up to date with paperback supplements (called pocket parts) found inside the back cover of each volume or in a separate paperback volume. Supplements include changes to IDEA and recent cases.

Your school district is required to provide you with copies of federal law—that is, the statutes and regulations of IDEA. Your school district, however, is not required to inform you of any changes to IDEA made by Congress or of any legal decisions on IDEA. One source of up-to-date information, including policy guidelines on the IDEA, is the U.S. Department of Education (see Appendix 2). But that's not the only source.

Special newsletters provide extensive detail about most fields of law. Special education has one such publication called the *Individuals with Disabilities Education Law Reporter* (IDELR), published by LRP Publications (contact information is in Appendix 3). IDELR issues a bimonthly highlights newsletter, along with the written decisions of IDEA court rulings, fair hearing decisions, Department of Education policy, and other publications. IDELR has a subject index, making it easy to locate the specific cases you want to review. At a current cost of $890 per year, IDELR is aimed at special education lawyers and school districts.

Some law libraries subscribe to IDELR—call the nearest law libraries and ask. Some school districts also subscribe. If this fails, contact a local nonprofit special education or disability organization in your area and ask if they receive IDELR.

2. State Statutes

As noted in Chapter 2, each state has passed a law that parallels IDEA. States are allowed to develop laws that provide students with greater rights than those provided in IDEA. You should take a look at your state's special education laws, which are available in many public libraries and all law libraries.

Many states also make their statutes available online (see Section G, below). In some states, statutes are organized by subject matter, with each title, chapter, or code covering a particular legal area—for example, the vehicle code or the corporations code. Most states have some kind of education code. In some states, statutes are simply numbered sequentially without regard to subject matter, meaning you'll have to use the index to find what you need. State codes are like the federal U.S.C., with annotated volumes, indexes, and pocket parts.

Some states have their own regulations implementing special education laws; check your state department of education for information about these regulations.

 Appendix 2 includes addresses, phone numbers, and websites of state departments of education.

3. Court Decisions

When Congress passes a law, it cannot address every possible situation or clarify what each section of the law means. It is the job of a court—federal or state—to interpret the applicable laws and apply them to particular facts. The court will often explain, clarify, and even expand or limit what actually appears in a statute. These court decisions are often referred to as "case law."

Court decisions are published in state or federal reporters. Each decision has a name and a citation, indicating the volume, name, and page of the reporter in which it appears, the court that issued the decision, and the year of the decision. With the citation, you can locate the printed decision.

> **Example:**
> The first special education case to reach the U.S. Supreme Court was *Rowley v. Board of Education*. It concerned a deaf child who wanted a sign language interpreter in her regular classroom. The U.S. Supreme Court said she didn't need one.
>
> The case was first decided by a federal trial court: The case citation is 483 F. Supp. 536 (S.D.N.Y. 1980). This means that the case can be found in Volume 483 of a reporter called the Federal Supplement, starting at page 536. The court that issued the decision was the federal court for the Southern District of New York. The case was decided in 1980.
>
> That decision was appealed, and the case citation of the appeal court's decision is 623 F.2d 945 (2d Cir. 1980). This means that the

decision can be found in Volume 623 of the Federal Reporter (2d Series), starting at page 945. The court that ruled on the appeal was the Second Circuit Court of Appeals. The appeal was decided in 1980.

The citation of the U.S. Supreme Court decision is 102 S.Ct 3034 (1982). The decision can be found in Volume 102 of the Supreme Court Reports, starting at page 3034. The court decided the case in 1982.

Most cases involving a federal law such as IDEA are decided by the federal courts. IDEA also gives you or the school district the option of appealing the due process decision to a state court, however. Each state has a unique reporting system, but decisions are usually found in regional reporters. For example, in the case of *State of Connecticut v. Bruno*, 673 A.2d 1117 (Conn. 1996), the decision was published in Volume 673 of the regional law reporter called the Atlantic Second Series and begins on page 1117. The case comes from the state of Connecticut (not surprising given the name of the case) and was decided in 1996.

4. Finding Cases on Special Education

Every decision that a court issues is specific to the facts of that case. Even though a case addresses the same underlying legal concepts as yours, it might be very different, factually, from your child's situation. A court case decides whether IDEA procedures and rules were followed in the context of one particular factual situation, for one particular child.

Every once in a while, a court will issue a broader decision that applies more generally. For example, in a famous case in 1986, a federal court ruled that IQ tests were not valid for determining whether African-American students have learning disabilities. (*Larry P. v. Riles*, 793 F.2d 969 (9th Cir. 1984).) It is very unusual, however, for a court to make this kind of blanket ruling.

You can find cases that interpret every aspect of IDEA, including evaluation, educational methodology, eligibility, placement, services, suspension, and expulsion. One great way to find cases is through IDELR (see Section 1, above). IDELR has a set of books called *Topical Index/Current Decisions*. Each book covers cases reprinted in particular volumes of IDELR. The topics are arranged alphabetically. You can use the index to look up topics that apply to your situation.

IDELR reprints not only court decisions, but also decisions made by hearing officers (usually referred to as SEA, or state educational agency, decisions) and the Office of Civil Rights (which investigations Section 504 complaints). IDELR also includes IDEA policy analysis by the U.S. Department of Education, Office of Special Education Programs (OSEP). These materials can be of real value to your child, because they indicate how these departments and agencies interpret IDEA's legal requirements.

 Further reading on legal research. *Legal Research: How to Find & Understand the Law*, by Stephen Elias and Susan Levinkind (Nolo), gives easy-to-use, step-by-step instructions that will help you find legal information.

When you research cases, be sure the case you find has not been overturned or replaced by a more recent court decision. You can do this with a set of books known as Shepard's. A friendly law librarian might have the time and patience to guide you, but if not, Nolo's book *Legal Research* has an easy-to-follow explanation of how to use the Shepard's system to expand and update your research.

When you find a court decision, there will be a short synopsis of the decision at the beginning. This synopsis not only will help you determine whether the case is relevant to your situation, but also will tell you what the court decided. After the case synopsis, there will be a list of numbered items, each item followed by a short summary. The numbers (1, 2, 3, and so on) refer to the location in the written decision where that legal issue is discussed.

Keep in mind that your situation may or may not relate exactly to a particular court decision. It will depend on the similarity of the facts and whether your situation and the legal decision involve the same sections of IDEA. The more alike the facts and pertinent parts of IDEA, the more you can use the decision to your advantage. But the existence of a case that supports your position does not mean that the school district has to apply or even abide by that decision. It is certainly a very persuasive precedent, but it is just an example of how one court has ruled in a similar situation.

If the decision was reached by the U.S. Supreme Court, the federal court of appeals covering your state, your federal district court, or your state supreme court, the case represents the law in your area. Decisions in other federal circuits can be useful as long as there is not a different legal standard in your circuit.

If you find a case that is similar to yours and the decision is a good one, think about writing to your school district, explaining why you think you'll prevail in due process.

⚠ Do legal research with care. Analyzing case law and the meaning and reach of legal statutes can be complicated. Make sure you know what you're talking about before you cite the law. While you can learn a good deal, becoming expert at legal research requires care, time, and training. Proceed carefully, and use what you learn with real caution.

Letter Encouraging School Board Settlement

Date: April 20, 20xx

To: Howard Yankolon, Superintendent
     Eugene School District
     15578 South Main
     Eugene, OR 97412

Re: Clara Centler, student in Westside School, fifth-grade

I appreciated your efforts at the April 14, 20xx, IEP meeting; as you know, we are in disagreement about Clara's need for a one-to-one aide so she can be mainstreamed.

I have requested a due process hearing. I have also done some research on this matter and determined that the facts and the law in the U.S. Supreme Court's decision in *Board of Education v. Holland* are almost identical to our dispute. I strongly believe that with the Supreme Court's direction in that case, it would be a real waste of time and district money to go to due process.

I am therefore requesting that you consider this and meet with me to discuss a possible settlement of our differences.

Sincerely,

Stuart Centler

Stuart Centler
78 Pine Ave.
Eugene, OR 97412
Phones: 555-5543 (home); 555-0933 (work)

G. Online Legal Research

Every day, a growing number of basic legal resources are available online through the Internet. There are a number of different ways to use the Internet to search for material, but by far the most important and common tool for doing research on the Internet is the World Wide Web. The Web provides links among documents and makes it easy to jump from one resource to another. Each resource is organized graphically like a book, allowing you to skip from topic to topic.

In addition, a wide variety of secondary sources intended for both lawyers and the general public have been posted on the Internet by law schools and firms. If you are on the Web, for example, a good way to find these sources is to visit any of the following websites, each of which provides links to legal information by specific subject:

- **www.nolo.com.** Nolo's Internet site contains helpful articles, information about new legislation, and a legal research page you can use to find state and federal statutes.

- **www.law.cornell.edu.** This site is maintained by Cornell Law School. You can find the text of the U.S. Code, federal court decisions, and some state court decisions. You can also search for material by topic.

- **www.law.indiana.edu/v-lib.** This site is maintained by Indiana University's School of Law at Bloomington. You can search by organization, including the U.S. government, state governments, and law journals, or by topic.

- **www.access.gpo.gov/nara/cfr/.** This site provides the entire Federal Code of Regulations.

- **www.statelocalgov.net.** This comprehensive site provides links to state and local government websites. Look here to find a link to your state's department of education, your county government's website, and perhaps even a website for your city or town.

In addition, Appendix 3 includes a section entitled "Legal Resources on Special Education." These resources include websites that offer a wealth of legal and practical materials on special education. ■

15

Parent Organizations and Special Education

The first word in IDEA is "Individuals." Special education law, philosophy, and approach is based on the individual child, which makes it somewhat difficult to approach special education from a collective or group perspective. Each IEP is different, which is why this book has focused on strategies and procedures for parents acting alone.

There are, however, situations in which a group of parents working together can have a tremendous impact on a school district and the programs available for children with disabilities. When a group of parents approaches a school to recommend changes, the school is more likely to take notice. A parent group can also serve as an invaluable resource for information and support as you go through the special education process.

A. Join a Parent Organization

There are many ways to find an existing parent group. You can start by getting in touch with the local PTA. In addition, most school districts have a parent advisory committee (sometimes called community advisory committees, or CACs) specifically formed for special education matters. If you haven't already done so, contact your school district to find out about that committee. It is likely composed of special education professionals and other parents. If you can't find information on a local group, try the state level. Appendix 3 contains a state-by-state list of Parent Training and Information Centers (PTIs). PTIs are parent-to-parent organizations that can provide advice, training, and even advocacy help.

A parent organization can help you in several ways:

- There is strength in numbers. School districts often pay more attention to two parents than one, four parents than two, ten parents than five.
- A parent group can provide you with all kinds of important information about the school administrator, staff (including teach-ers who are not afraid to be frank), existing classes, the local IEP process, and outside support professionals, such as independent evaluators, private service providers, private schools, and attorneys.
- A parent group can suggest successful educational strategies, methodologies geared for your child, and even sophisticated knowledge about IDEA and its legal mandates.
- A parent group can provide the emotional support and advice you will need to navigate the special education process and reinforce the important feeling that you are not alone.

 Community advisory committees may include school district representatives. School personnel regularly attend meetings of these committees, so parents may find it difficult to speak frankly. This is not to say that you shouldn't trust or include school personnel, but you should recognize that there may be times when the presence of school personnel inhibits honest discussion of certain issues. If this is the only organization in your area, consider forming an independent parent organization.

B. Form a Parent Organization

If your community doesn't have a parent organization, the existing group is too tied to or influenced by the school district, or the existing group doesn't meet your needs, you can organize a new group. How do you begin?

First, consider how wide or narrow you want your focus to be. If your numbers can support such a group, you may want to form an organization of parents whose children have similar disabling conditions. You don't need a lot of people. Three or four parents can be quite effective. There is certainly nothing wrong with forming a cross-disability group, and the parents in your area may prefer it. The strength that comes from a large group can often offset the challenges that come with a diversity of concerns.

Sometimes a few simple phone calls will lead to very useful recommendations. Here's how to get started and prepare for your first meeting:

- Invite all possible parents who fit within your chosen scope.
- Ask them for agenda ideas, focusing on common issues and concerns.
- Ask them for the names of other parents to invite.
- Ask your child's teacher or pediatrician to mention the meeting to other parents who might be interested.
- Ask the PTA and your school district to announce the meeting or to include information on it in any mailings.
- Place an announcement in your local newspaper.
- Contact local disability organizations. They may be able to connect you with other parent support groups in your state. They may also be able to advise you if you encounter problems.

At your first meeting, you can decide how formal you want to be and what issues you want to focus on. If you take the formal route, you'll need to select a name, elect officers, decide whether to charge dues (and if so, how much), collect those dues, and establish regular meetings.

No matter how formal or informal you are, you need to spend some time discussing your purpose and what you hope to accomplish. Do you simply want to establish better ties with the school administration? Do you want to address specific concerns, such as the quality of a particular class, intimidation by school personnel during the IEP process, or certain procedures that you find unfair? Once you decide which issues you want to tackle, you can figure out how to formally contact the district and raise your concerns.

At later meetings, consider inviting guests, such as representatives of the school district or a local special education attorney. The attorney will probably charge for his or her time. Your dues or an additional contribution from each family can cover the cost. Also, consider developing a newsletter (online is easiest) to maintain communication with other parents in your area.

Get Involved With the School District

Whether you work alone or with a group, there are many ways to improve your child's educational program through direct involvement with the school district. Volunteer at school or in the administrative office, run for school board, or assist in school fundraisers. Generally, this kind of activity gets you involved, opens doors, and allows you to meet the people in charge. This often can foster a good relationship with school personnel, making it easier for you to pick up the phone and call about—and resolve—a problem.

The same advice goes for your parent group. You should meet with the district on a somewhat regular basis, to find out how you can help the school. Build a relationship between your group and the school. Ultimately, you and the school district really do have the same goal (if, unfortunately, not the necessary budget or time): to help your child grow into an effective, productive, and happy adult.

Appendix 1

Special Education Law and Regulations

Individuals With Disabilities Education Act (Key Sections)

Sec. 1401. Definitions

Except as otherwise provided, as used in this chapter:

(1) Assistive Technology Device

(A) *In general.* The term "assistive technology device" means any item, piece of equipment, or product system, whether acquired commercially off the shelf, modified, or customized, that is used to increase, maintain, or improve functional capabilities of a child with a disability.

(B) *Exception.* The term does not include a medical device that is surgically implanted, or the replacement of such device.

(2) Assistive technology service. The term "assistive technology service" means any service that directly assists a child with a disability in the selection, acquisition, or use of an assistive technology device. Such term includes:

(A) the evaluation of the needs of such child, including a functional evaluation of the child in the child's customary environment;

(B) purchasing, leasing, or otherwise providing for the acquisition of assistive technology devices by such child;

(C) selecting, designing, fitting, customizing, adapting, applying, maintaining, repairing, or replacing assistive technology devices;

(D) coordinating and using other therapies, interventions, or services with assistive technology devices, such as those associated with existing education and rehabilitation plans and programs;

(E) training or technical assistance for such child, or, where appropriate, the family of such child; and

(F) training or technical assistance for professionals (including individuals providing education and rehabilitation services), employers, or other individuals who provide services to, employ, or are otherwise substantially involved in the major life functions of such child.

(3) Child with a disability

(A) *In general.* The term "child with a disability" means a child:

(i) with mental retardation, hearing impairments (including deafness), speech or language impairments, visual impairments (including blindness), serious emotional disturbance (referred to in this chapter as "emotional disturbance"), orthopedic impairments, autism, traumatic brain injury, other health impairments, or specific learning disabilities; and

(ii) who, by reason thereof, needs special education and related services.

(B) *Child aged 3 through 9.* The term "child with a disability" for a child aged 3 through 9 (or any subset of that age range, including ages 3 through 5), may, at the discretion of the State and the local educational agency, include a child:

(i) experiencing developmental delays, as defined by the State and as measured by appropriate diagnostic instruments and procedures, in one or more of the following areas: physical development, cognitive development, communication development, social or emotional development, or adaptive development; and

(ii) who, by reason thereof, needs special education and related services.

(4) Core Academic Subjects. The term "core academic subjects" has the meaning given the term in section 9101 of the Elementary and Secondary Education Act of 1965.

(5) Educational service agency. The term "educational service agency":

(A) means a regional public multiservice agency:

(i) authorized by State law to develop, manage, and provide services or programs to local educational agencies; and

(ii) recognized as an administrative agency for purposes of the provision of special education and related services provided within public elementary and secondary schools of the State; and

(B) includes any other public institution or agency having administrative control and direction over a public elementary or secondary school.

(6) Elementary school. The term "elementary school" means a nonprofit institutional day or residential school, including a public elementary charter school, that provides elementary education, as determined under State law.

(7) Equipment. The term "equipment" includes:

(A) machinery, utilities, and built-in equipment and any necessary enclosures or structures to house such machinery, utilities, or equipment; and

(B) all other items necessary for the functioning of a particular facility as a facility for the provision of educational services, including items such as instructional equipment and necessary furniture; printed, published, and audio-visual instructional materials; telecommunications, sensory, and other technological aids and devices; and books, periodicals, documents, and other related materials.

(8) Excess costs. The term "excess costs" means those costs that are in excess of the average annual per-student expenditure in a local educational agency during the preceding school year for an elementary or secondary school student, as may be appropriate, and which shall be computed after deducting:

(A) amounts received:

(i) under part B [subchapter II of this chapter];

(ii) under part A of title I of the Elementary and Secondary Education Act of 1965 (20 U.S.C. 6311 et seq.); and

(iii) under parts A and B of title III of that Act (20 U.S.C. 6811 et seq. and 20 U.S.C. 6891 et seq.); and

(B) any State or local funds expended for programs that would qualify for assistance under any of those parts.

(9) Free appropriate public education. The term "free appropriate public education" means special education and related services that:

(A) have been provided at public expense, under public supervision and direction, and without charge;

(B) meet the standards of the State educational agency;

(C) include an appropriate preschool, elementary, or secondary school education in the State involved; and

(D) are provided in conformity with the individualized education program required under section 1414(d) of this title.

(10) Highly Qualified

(A) *In general.* For any special education teacher, the term "highly qualified" has the meaning given the term in section 9101 of the Elementary and Secondary Education Act of 1965, except that such term also:

(i) includes the requirements described in subparagraph (B); and

(ii) includes the option for teachers to meet the requirements of section 9101 of such Act by meeting the requirements of subparagraph (C) or (D).

(B) *Requirements for special education teachers.* When used with respect to any public elementary school or secondary school special education teacher teaching in a State, such term means that:

(i) the teacher has obtained full State certification as a special education teacher (including certification obtained through alternative routes to certification), or passed the State special education teacher licensing examination, and holds a license to teach in the State as a special education teacher, except that when used with respect to any teacher teaching in a public charter school, the term means that the teacher meets the requirements set forth in the State's public charter school law;

(ii) the teacher has not had special education certification or licensure requirements waived on an emergency, temporary, or provisional basis; and

(iii) the teacher holds at least a bachelor's degree.

(C) *Special education teachers teaching to alternate achievement standards.* When used with respect to a special education teacher who teaches core academic subjects exclusively to children who are assessed against alternate achievement standards established under the regulations promulgated under section 1111(b)(1) of the Elementary and Secondary Education Act of 1965, such term means the teacher, whether new or not new to the profession, may either:

(i) meet the applicable requirements of section 9101 of such Act for any elementary, middle, or secondary school teacher who is new or not new to the profession; or

(ii) meet the requirements of subparagraph (B) or (C) of section 9101(23) of such Act as applied to an elementary school teacher, or, in the case of instruction above the elementary level, has subject matter knowledge appropriate to the level of instruction being provided, as determined by the State, needed to effectively teach to those standards.

(D) *Special education teachers teaching multiple subjects.* When used with respect to a special education teacher who teaches 2 or more core academic subjects exclusively to children with disabilities, such term means that the teacher may either:

(i) meet the applicable requirements of section 9101 of the Elementary and Secondary Education Act of 1965 for any elementary, middle, or secondary school teacher who is new or not new to the profession;

(ii) in the case of a teacher who is not new to the profession, demonstrate competence in all the core academic subjects in which the teacher teaches in the same manner as is required for an elementary, middle, or secondary school teacher who is

not new to the profession under section 9101(23)(C)(ii) of such Act, which may include a single, high objective uniform State standard of evaluation covering multiple subjects; or

(iii) in the case of a new special education teacher who teaches multiple subjects and who is highly qualified in mathematics, language arts, or science, demonstrate competence in the other core academic subjects in which the teacher teaches in the same manner as is required for an elementary, middle, or secondary school teacher under section 9101(23)(C)(ii) of such Act, which may include a single, high objective uniform State standard of evaluation covering multiple subjects, not later than 2 years after the date of employment.

(E) *Rule of construction.* Notwithstanding any other individual right of action that a parent or student may maintain under this part, nothing in this section or part shall be construed to create a right of action on behalf of an individual student or class of students for the failure of a particular State educational agency or local educational agency employee to be highly qualified.

(F) *Definition for purposes of the ESEA.* A teacher who is highly qualified under this paragraph shall be considered highly qualified for purposes of the Elementary and Secondary Education Act of 1965.

(11) Homeless Children. The term "homeless children" has the meaning given the term "homeless children and youths" in section 725 of the McKinney-Vento Homeless Assistance Act (42 U.S.C. 11434a).

(12) Indian. The term "Indian" means an individual who is a member of an Indian tribe.

(13) Indian tribe. The term "Indian tribe" means any Federal or State Indian tribe, band, rancheria, pueblo, colony, or community, including any Alaska Native village or regional village corporation (as defined in or established under the Alaska Native Claims Settlement Act (43 U.S.C. 1601 et seq.)).

(14) Individualized education program; IEP. The term "individualized education program" or "IEP" means a written statement for each child with a disability that is developed, reviewed, and revised in accordance with section 1414(d) of this title.

(15) Individualized family service plan. The term "individualized family service plan" has the meaning given such term in section 1436 of this title.

(16) Infant or toddler with a disability. The term "infant or toddler with a disability" has the meaning given such term in section 1432 of this title.

(17) Institution of higher education. The term "institution of higher education":

(A) has the meaning given that term in section 1001 of this title; and

(B) also includes any community college receiving funding from the Secretary of the Interior under the Tribally Controlled Community College Assistance Act of 1978 (25 U.S.C. 1801 et seq.).

(18) Limited English Proficient. The term "limited English proficient" has the meaning given the term in section 9101 of the Elementary and Secondary Education Act of 1965.

(19) Local Educational Agency

(A) *In general.* The term "local educational agency" means a public board of education or other public authority legally constituted within a State for either administrative control or direction of, or to perform a service function for, public elementary schools or secondary schools in a city, county, township, school district, or other political subdivision of a State, or for such combination of school districts or counties as are recognized in a State as an administrative agency for its public elementary schools or secondary schools.

(B) *Educational service agencies and other public institutions or agencies.* The term includes:

(i) an educational service agency; and

(ii) any other public institution or agency having administrative control and direction of a public elementary school or secondary school.

(C) *BIA funded schools.* The term includes an elementary school or secondary school funded by the Bureau of Indian Affairs, but only to the extent that such inclusion makes the school eligible for programs for which specific eligibility is not provided to the school in another provision of law and the school does not have a student population that is smaller than the student population of the local educational agency receiving assistance under this title with the smallest student population, except that the school shall not be subject to the jurisdiction of any State educational agency other than the Bureau of Indian Affairs.

(20) Native language. The term "native language," when used with respect to an individual who is limited English proficienct, means the language normally used by the individual, or, in the case of a child, the language normally used by the parents of the child.

(21) Nonprofit. The term "nonprofit," as applied to a school, agency, organization, or institution, means a school, agency, organization, or institution owned and operated by one or more nonprofit corporations or associations no part of the net earnings of which inures, or may lawfully inure, to the benefit of any private shareholder or individual.

(22) Outlying area. The term "outlying area" means the United States Virgin Islands, Guam, American Samoa, and the Commonwealth of the Northern Mariana Islands.

(23) Parent. The term "parent" means:

(A) a natural, adoptive, or foster parent of a child (unless a foster parent is prohibited by State law from serving as a parent);

(B) a guardian (but not the State if the child is a ward of the State);

(C) an individual acting in the place of a natural or adoptive parent (including a grandparent, stepparent, or other relative) with whom the child lives, or an individual who is legally responsible for the child's welfare; or

(D) except as used in sections 615(b)(2) and 639(a)(5), an individual assigned under either of those sections to be a surrogate parent.

(24) Parent organization. The term "parent organization" has the meaning given that term in section 1471(g) of this title.

(25) Parent training and information center. The term "parent training and information center" means a center assisted under section 1471 or 1472 of this title.

(26) Related Services

(A) *In general.* The term "related services" means transportation, and such developmental, corrective, and other supportive services (including speech-language pathology and audiology services, interpreting services, psychological services, physical and occupational therapy, recreation, including therapeutic recreation, social work services, school nurse services designed to enable a child with a disability to receive a free appropriate public education as described in the individualized education program of the child, counseling services, including rehabilitation counseling, orientation and mobility services, and medical services, except that such medical services shall be for diagnostic and evaluation purposes only) as may be required to assist a child with a disability to benefit from special education, and includes the early identification and assessment of disabling conditions in children.

(B) *Exception.* The term does not include a medical device that is surgically implanted, or the replacement of such device.

(27) Secondary school. The term "secondary school" means a nonprofit institutional day or residential school, including a public secondary charter school, that provides secondary education, as determined under State law, except that it does not include any education beyond grade 12.

(28) Secretary. The term "Secretary" means the Secretary of Education.

(29) Special education. The term "special education" means specially designed instruction, at no cost to parents, to meet the unique needs of a child with a disability, including:

(A) instruction conducted in the classroom, in the home, in hospitals and institutions, and in other settings; and

(B) instruction in physical education.

(30) Specific learning disability

(A) *In general.* The term "specific learning disability" means a disorder in one or more of the basic psychological processes involved in understanding or in using language, spoken or written, which disorder may manifest itself in imperfect ability to listen, think, speak, read, write, spell, or do mathematical calculations.

(B) *Disorders included.* Such term includes such conditions as perceptual disabilities, brain injury, minimal brain dysfunction, dyslexia, and developmental aphasia.

(C) *Disorders not included.* Such term does not include a learning problem that is primarily the result of visual, hearing, or motor disabilities, of mental retardation, of emotional disturbance, or of environmental, cultural, or economic disadvantage.

(31) State. The term "State" means each of the 50 States, the District of Columbia, the Commonwealth of Puerto Rico, and each of the outlying areas.

(32) State educational agency. The term "State educational agency" means the State board of education or other agency or officer primarily responsible for the State supervision of public elementary schools and secondary schools, or, if there is no such officer or agency, an officer or agency designated by the Governor or by State law.

(33) Supplementary aids and services. The term "supplementary aids and services" means aids, services, and other supports that are provided in regular education classes or other education-related settings to enable children with disabilities to be educated with nondisabled children to the maximum extent appropriate in accordance with section 1412(a)(5) of this title.

(34) Transition services. The term "transition services" means a coordinated set of activities for a student with a disability that:

(A) is designed to be within a results-oriented process, that is focused on improving the academic and functional achievement of the child with a disability to facilitate the child's movement from school to post-school activities, including post-secondary education, vocational education, integrated employment (including supported employment), continuing and adult education, adult services, independent living, or community participation;

(B) is based on the individual child's needs, taking into account the child's strengths, preferences, and interests; and

(C) includes instruction, related services, community experiences, the development of employment and other post-school adult living objectives, and, when appropriate, acquisition of daily living skills and functional vocational evaluation.

Sec. 1412. State eligibility

(a) In general. A State is eligible for assistance under this subchapter for a fiscal year if the State submits a plan that provides assurances to the Secretary that the State has in effect policies and procedures to ensure that the State meets each of the following conditions:

(1) *Free appropriate public education*

(A) *In general.* A free appropriate public education is available to all children with disabilities residing in the State between the ages of 3 and 21, inclusive, including children with disabilities who have been suspended or expelled from school.

(B) *Limitation.* The obligation to make a free appropriate public education available to all children with disabilities does not apply with respect to children:

(i) aged 3 through 5 and 18 through 21 in a State to the extent that its application to those children would be inconsistent with State law or practice, or the order of any court, respecting the provision of public education to children in those age ranges; and

(ii) aged 18 through 21 to the extent that State law does not require that special education and related services under this subchapter be provided to children with disabilities who, in the educational placement prior to their incarceration in an adult correctional facility:

(I) were not actually identified as being a child with a disability under section 1401 of this title; or

(II) did not have an individualized education program under this subchapter.

(C) *State flexiblity.* A State that provides early intervention services in accordance with subchapter III of this chapter to a child who is eligible for services under Section 1419 of this title, is not required to provide such child with a free appropriate public education.

(2) *Full educational opportunity goal.* The State has established a goal of providing full educational opportunity to all children with disabilities and a detailed timetable for accomplishing that goal.

(3) *Child find*

(A) *In general.* All children with disabilities residing in the State, including children with disabilities who are homeless children or are wards of the State and children with disabilities attending private schools, regardless of the severity of their disabilities, and who are in need of special education and related services, are identified, located, and evaluated and a practical method is developed and implemented to determine which children with disabilities are currently receiving needed special education and related services.

(B) *Construction.* Nothing in this chapter requires that children be classified by their disability so long as each child who has a disability listed in section 1401 of this title and who, by reason of that disability, needs special education and related services is regarded as a child with a disability under this subchapter.

(4) *Individualized education program.* An individualized education program, or an individualized family service plan that meets the requirements of section 1436(d) of this title, is developed, reviewed, and revised for each child with a disability in accordance with section 1414(d) of this title.

(5) *Least restrictive environment*

(A) *In general.* To the maximum extent appropriate, children with disabilities, including children in public or private institutions or other care facilities, are educated with children who are not disabled, and special classes, separate schooling, or other removal of children with disabilities from the regular educational environment occurs only when the nature or severity of the disability of a child is such that education in regular classes with the use of supplementary aids and services cannot be achieved satisfactorily.

(B) *Additional requirement*

(i) *In general.* A State funding mechanism shall not result in placements that violate the requirements of subparagraph (A), and a State shall not use a funding mechanism by which the State distributes funds on the basis of the type of setting in which a child is served that will result in the failure to provide a child with a disability a free appropriate public education according to the unique needs of the child as described in the child's IEP.

(ii) *Assurance.* If the State does not have policies and procedures to ensure compliance with clause (i), the State shall provide the Secretary an assurance that the State will revise the funding mechanism as soon as feasible to ensure that such mechanism does not result in such placements.

(6) *Procedural safeguards*

(A) *In general.* Children with disabilities and their parents are afforded the procedural safeguards required by section 1415 of this title.

(B) *Additional procedural safeguards.* Procedures to ensure that testing and evaluation materials and procedures utilized for the purposes of evaluation and placement of children with disabilities for services under this chapter will be selected and administered so as not to be racially or culturally discriminatory. Such materials or procedures shall be provided and administered in the child's native language or mode of communication, unless it clearly is not feasible to do so, and no single procedure shall be the sole criterion for determining an appropriate educational program for a child.

(7) *Evaluation.* Children with disabilities are evaluated in accordance with subsections (a) through (c) of section 1414 of this title.

(8) *Confidentiality.* Agencies in the State comply with section 1417(c) of this title (relating to the confidentiality of records and information).

(9) *Transition from subchapter III to preschool programs.* Children participating in early-intervention programs assisted under subchapter III of this chapter, and who will participate in preschool programs assisted under this subchapter, experience a smooth and effective transition to those preschool programs in a manner consistent with section 1437(a)(9) of this title. By the third birthday of such a child, an individualized education program or, if consistent with sections 1414(d)(2)(B) and 1436(d) of this title, an individualized family service plan, has been developed and is being implemented for the child. The local educational agency will participate in transition planning conferences arranged by the designated lead agency under section 1435(a)(10) of this title.

(10) *Children in private schools*

(A) *Children enrolled in private schools by their parents*

(i) *In general.* To the extent consistent with the number and location of children with disabilities in the State who are enrolled by their parents in private elementary schools and secondary schools in the school district served by a local educational agency, provision is made for the participation of those children in the program assisted or carried out under this part by providing for such children special education and related services in accordance with the following requirements, unless the Secretary has arranged for services to those children under subsection (f):

(I) Amounts to be expended for the provision of those services (including direct services to parentally placed private school children) by the local educational agency shall be equal to a proportionate amount of Federal funds made available under this part.

(II) In calculating the proportionate amount of Federal funds, the local educational agency, after timely and meaningful consultation with representatives of private schools as described in clause (iii), shall conduct a thorough and complete child find process to determine the number of parentally placed children with disabilities attending private schools located in the local educational agency.

(III) Such services to parentally placed private school children with disabilities may be provided to the children on the premises of private, including religious, schools, to the extent consistent with law.

(IV) State and local funds may supplement and in no case shall supplant the proportionate amount of Federal funds required to be expended under this subparagraph.

(V) Each local educational agency shall maintain in its records and provide to the State educational agency the number of children evaluated under this subparagraph, the number of children determined to be children with disabilities under this paragraph, and the number of children served under this paragraph.

(ii) *Child find requirement*

(I) *In general.* The requirements of paragraph (3) (relating to child find) shall apply with respect to children with disabilities in the State who are enrolled in private, including religious, elementary schools and secondary schools.

(II) *Equitable participation.* The child find process shall be designed to ensure the equitable participation of parentally placed private school children with disabilities and an accurate count of such children.

(III) *Activities.* In carrying out this clause, the local educational agency, or where applicable, the State educational agency, shall undertake activities similar to those activities undertaken for the agency's public school children.

(IV) *Cost.* The cost of carrying out this clause, including individual evaluations, may not be considered in determining whether a local educational agency has met its obligations under clause (i).

(V) *Completion period.* Such child find process shall be completed in a time period comparable to that for other students attending public schools in the local educational agency.

(iii) *Consultation.* To ensure timely and meaningful consultation, a local educational agency, or where appropriate, a State educational agency, shall consult with private school representatives and representatives of parents of parentally placed private school children with disabilities during the design and development of special education and related services for the children, including regarding:

(I) the child find process and how parentally placed private school children suspected of having a disability can participate equitably, including how parents, teachers, and private school officials will be informed of the process;

(II) the determination of the proportionate amount of Federal funds available to serve parentally placed private school children with disabilities under this subparagraph, including the determination of how the amount was calculated;

(III) the consultation process among the local educational agency, private school officials, and representatives of parents of parentally placed private school children with disabilities, including how such process will operate throughout the school year to ensure that parentally placed private school children with disabilities identified through the child find process can meaningfully participate in special education and related services;

(IV) how, where, and by whom special education and related services will be provided for parentally placed private school children with disabilities, including a discussion of types of services, including direct services and alternate service delivery mechanisms, how such services will be apportioned if funds are insufficient to serve all children, and how and when these decisions will be made; and

(V) how, if the local educational agency disagrees with the views of the private school officials on the provision of services or the types of services, whether provided directly or through a contract, the local educational agency shall provide to the private school officials a written explanation of the reasons why the local educational agency chose not to provide services directly or through a contract.

(iv) *Written affirmation*. When timely and meaningful consultation as required by clause (iii) has occurred, the local educational agency shall obtain a written affirmation signed by the representatives of participating private schools, and if such representatives do not provide such affirmation within a reasonable period of time, the local educational agency shall forward the documentation of the consultation process to the State educational agency.

(v) *Compliance*

(I) *In general*. A private school official shall have the right to submit a complaint to the State educational agency that the local educational agency did not engage in consultation that was meaningful and timely, or did not give due consideration to the views of the private school official.

(II) *Procedure*. If the private school official wishes to submit a complaint, the official shall provide the basis of the noncompliance with this subparagraph by the local educational agency to the State educational agency, and the local educational agency shall forward the appropriate documentation to the State educational agency. If the private school official is dissatisfied with the decision of the State educational agency, such official may submit a complaint to the Secretary by providing the basis of the noncompliance with this subparagraph by the local educational agency to the Secretary, and the State educational agency shall forward the appropriate documentation to the Secretary.

(vi) *Provision of equitable services*

(I) *Directly or through contracts*. The provision of services pursuant to this subparagraph shall be provided:

(aa) by employees of a public agency; or

(bb) through contract by the public agency with an individual, association, agency, organization, or other entity.

(II) *Secular, neutral, nonideological*. Special education and related services provided to parentally placed private school children with disabilities, including materials and equipment, shall be secular, neutral, and nonideological.

(vii) *Public control of funds*. The control of funds used to provide special education and related services under this subparagraph, and title to materials, equipment, and property purchased with those funds, shall be in a public agency for the uses and purposes provided in this title, and a public agency shall administer the funds and property.

(B) *Children placed in, or referred to, private schools by public agencies*

(i) *In general*. Children with disabilities in private schools and facilities are provided special education and related services, in accordance with an individualized education program, at

no cost to their parents, if such children are placed in, or referred to, such schools or facilities by the State or appropriate local educational agency as the means of carrying out the requirements of this subchapter or any other applicable law requiring the provision of special education and related services to all children with disabilities within such State.

(ii) *Standards*. In all cases described in clause (i), the State educational agency shall determine whether such schools and facilities meet standards that apply to State educational agencies and local educational agencies and that children so served have all the rights the children would have if served by such agencies.

(C) *Payment for education of children enrolled in private schools without consent of or referral by the public agency*

(i) *In general*. Subject to subparagraph (A), this subchapter does not require a local educational agency to pay for the cost of education, including special education and related services, of a child with a disability at a private school or facility if that agency made a free appropriate public education available to the child and the parents elected to place the child in such private school or facility.

(ii) *Reimbursement for private school placement*. If the parents of a child with a disability, who previously received special education and related services under the authority of a public agency, enroll the child in a private elementary or secondary school without the consent of or referral by the public agency, a court or a hearing officer may require the agency to reimburse the parents for the cost of that enrollment if the court or hearing officer finds that the agency had not made a free appropriate public education available to the child in a timely manner prior to that enrollment.

(iii) *Limitation on reimbursement*. The cost of reimbursement described in clause (ii) may be reduced or denied:

(I) if:

(aa) at the most recent IEP meeting that the parents attended prior to removal of the child from the public school, the parents did not inform the IEP Team that they were rejecting the placement proposed by the public agency to provide a free appropriate public education to their child, including stating their concerns and their intent to enroll their child in a private school at public expense; or

(bb) 10 business days (including any holidays that occur on a business day) prior to the removal of the child from the public school, the parents did not give written notice to the public agency of the information described in division (aa);

(II) if, prior to the parents' removal of the child from the public school, the public agency informed the parents, through the notice requirements described in section 1415(b)(3) of this title, of its intent to evaluate the child (including a statement of the purpose of the evaluation that was appropriate and reasonable), but the parents did not make the child available for such evaluation; or

(III) upon a judicial finding of unreasonableness with respect to actions taken by the parents.

(iv) *Exception*. Notwithstanding the notice requirement in clause (iii)(I), the cost of reimbursement:

(I) shall not be reduced or denied for failure to provide such notice if:

(aa) the school prevented the parent from providing such notice;

(bb) the parents had not received notice, pursuant to section 615, of the notice requirement in clause (iii)(I); or

(cc) compliance with clause (iii)(I) would likely result in physical harm to the child; and

(II) may, in the discretion of a court or hearing officer, not be reduced or denied for failure to provide such notice if:

(aa) the parent is illiterate or cannot write in English; or

(bb) compliance with clause (iii)(I) would likely result in serious emotional harm to the child.

(11) *State educational agency responsible for general supervision*

(A) *In general.* The State educational agency is responsible for ensuring that:

(i) the requirements of this subchapter are met;

(ii) all educational programs for children with disabilities in the State, including all such programs administered by any other State or local agency:

(I) are under the general supervision of individuals in the State who are responsible for educational programs for children with disabilities; and

(II) meet the educational standards of the State educational agency; and

(iii) in carrying out this subchapter with respect to homeless children, the requirements of subtitle B of title VII of the McKinney-Vento Homeless Assistance Act are met.

(B) *Limitation.* Subparagraph (A) shall not limit the responsibility of agencies in the State other than the State educational agency to provide, or pay for some or all of the costs of, a free appropriate public education for any child with a disability in the State.

(C) *Exception.* Notwithstanding subparagraphs (A) and (B), the Governor (or another individual pursuant to State law), consistent with State law, may assign to any public agency in the State the responsibility of ensuring that the requirements of this subchapter are met with respect to children with disabilities who are convicted as adults under State law and incarcerated in adult prisons.

(12) *Obligations related to and methods of ensuring services*

(A) *Establishing responsibility for services.* The Chief Executive Officer of a State or designee of the officer shall ensure that an interagency agreement or other mechanism for interagency coordination is in effect between each public agency described in subparagraph (B) and the State educational agency, in order to ensure that all services described in subparagraph (B)(i) that are needed to ensure a free appropriate public education are provided, including the provision of such services during the pendency of any dispute under clause (iii). Such agreement or mechanism shall include the following:

(i) *Agency financial responsibility.* An identification of, or a method for defining, the financial responsibility of each agency for providing services described in subparagraph (B)(i) to ensure a free appropriate public education to children with disabilities, provided that the financial responsibility of each public agency described in subparagraph (B), including the State Medicaid agency and other public insurers of children with disabilities, shall precede the financial responsibility of the local educational agency (or the State agency responsible for developing the child's IEP).

(ii) *Conditions and terms of reimbursement.* The conditions, terms, and procedures under which a local educational agency shall be reimbursed by other agencies.

(iii) *Interagency disputes.* Procedures for resolving interagency disputes (including procedures under which local educational agencies may initiate proceedings) under the agreement or other mechanism to secure reimbursement from other agencies or otherwise implement the provisions of the agreement or mechanism.

(iv) *Coordination of services procedures.* Policies and procedures for agencies to determine and identify the interagency coordination responsibilities of each agency to promote the coordination and timely and appropriate delivery of services described in subparagraph (B)(i).

(B) *Obligation of public agency*

(i) *In general.* If any public agency other than an educational agency is otherwise obligated under Federal or State law, or assigned responsibility under State policy pursuant to subparagraph (A), to provide or pay for any services that are also considered special education or related services (such as, but not limited to, services described in sections 1401(1) relating to assistive technology devices, 1401(2) relating to assistive technology services, 1401(26) relating to related services, 1401(33) relating to supplementary aids and services, and 1401(34) of this title relating to transition services) that are necessary for ensuring a free appropriate public education to children with disabilities within the State, such public agency shall fulfill that obligation or responsibility, either directly or through contract or other arrangement pursuant to subparagraph (A) or an agreement pursuant to subparagraph (C).

(ii) *Reimbursement for services by public agency.* If a public agency other than an educational agency fails to provide or pay for the special education and related services described in clause (i), the local educational agency (or State agency responsible for developing the child's IEP) shall provide or pay for such services to the child. Such local educational agency or State agency is authorized to claim reimbursement for the services from the public agency that failed to provide or pay for such services and such public agency shall reimburse the local educational agency or State agency pursuant to the terms of the interagency agreement or other mechanism described in subparagraph (A)(i) according to the procedures established in such agreement pursuant to subparagraph (A)(ii).

(C) *Special rule.* The requirements of subparagraph (A) may be met through:

(i) State statute or regulation;

(ii) signed agreements between respective agency officials that clearly identify the responsibilities of each agency relating to the provision of services; or

(iii) other appropriate written methods as determined by the Chief Executive Officer of the State or designee of the officer and approved by the Secretary.

(13) *Procedural requirements relating to local educational agency eligibility.* The State educational agency will not make a final determination that a local educational agency is not eligible for assistance under this subchapter without first

affording that agency reasonable notice and an opportunity for a hearing.

(14) *Personnel qualifications*

(A) *In general.* The State educational agency has established and maintains qualifications to ensure that personnel necessary to carry out this part are appropriately and adequately prepared and trained, including that those personnel have the content knowledge and skills to serve children with disabilities.

(B) *Related services personnel and paraprofessionals.* The qualifications under subparagraph (A) include qualifications for related services personnel and paraprofessionals that:

(i) are consistent with any State-approved or State-recognized certification, licensing, registration, or other comparable requirements that apply to the professional discipline in which those personnel are providing special education or related services;

(ii) ensure that related services personnel who deliver services in their discipline or profession meet the requirements of clause (i) and have not had certification or licensure requirements waived on an emergency, temporary, or provisional basis; and

(iii) allow paraprofessionals and assistants who are appropriately trained and supervised, in accordance with State law, regulation, or written policy, in meeting the requirements of this part to be used to assist in the provision of special education and related services under this part to children with disabilities.

(C) *Qualifications for special education teachers.* The qualifications described in subparagraph (A) shall ensure that each person employed as a special education teacher in the State who teaches elementary school, middle school, or secondary school is highly qualified by the deadline established in section 1119(a)(2) of the Elementary and Secondary Education Act of 1965.

(D) *Policy.* In implementing this section, a State shall adopt a policy that includes a requirement that local educational agencies in the State take measurable steps to recruit, hire, train, and retain highly qualified personnel to provide special education and related services under this part to children with disabilities.

(E) *Rule of construction.* Notwithstanding any other individual right of action that a parent or student may maintain under this part, nothing in this paragraph shall be construed to create a right of action on behalf of an individual student for the failure of a particular State educational agency or local educational agency staff person to be highly qualified, or to prevent a parent from filing a complaint about staff qualifications with the State educational agency as provided for under this part.

(15) *Performance goals and indicators.* The State:

(A) has established goals for the performance of children with disabilities in the State that:

(i) promote the purposes of this title, as stated in section 601(d);

(ii) are the same as the State's definition of adequate yearly progress, including the State's objectives for progress by chil-dren with disabilities, under section 1111(b)(2)(C) of the Elementary and Secondary Education Act of 1965;

(iii) address graduation rates and dropout rates, as well as such other factors as the State may determine; and

(iv) are consistent, to the extent appropriate, with any other goals and standards for children established by the State;

(B) has established performance indicators the State will use to assess progress toward achieving the goals described in subparagraph (A), including measurable annual objectives for progress by children with disabilities under section 1111(b)(2)(C)(v)(II)(cc) of the Elementary and Secondary Education Act of 1965; and

(C) will annually report to the Secretary and the public on the progress of the State, and of children with disabilities in the State, toward meeting the goals established under subparagraph (A), which may include elements of the reports required under section 1111(h) of the Elementary and Secondary Education Act of 1965.

(16) *Participation in assessments*

(A) *In general.* All children with disabilities are included in all general State and districtwide assessment programs, including assessments described under section 1111 of the Elementary and Secondary Education Act of 1965, with appropriate accommodations and alternate assessments where necessary and as indicated in their respective individualized education programs.

(B) *Accommodation guidelines.* The State (or, in the case of a districtwide assessment, the local educational agency) has developed guidelines for the provision of appropriate accommodations.

(C) *Alternative assessments*

(i) *In general.* The State (or, in the case of a districtwide assessment, the local educational agency) has developed and implemented guidelines for the participation of children with disabilities in alternate assessments for those children who cannot participate in regular assessments under subparagraph (A) with accommodations as indicated in their respective individualized education programs.

(ii) *Requirements for alternate assessments.* The guidelines under clause (i) shall provide for alternate assessments that:

(I) are aligned with the State's challenging academic content standards and challenging student academic achievement standards; and

(II) if the State has adopted alternate academic achievement standards permitted under the regulations promulgated to carry out section 1111(b)(1) of the Elementary and Secondary Education Act of 1965, measure the achievement of children with disabilities against those standards.

(iii) *Conduct of alternate assessments.* The State conducts the alternate assessments described in this subparagraph.

(D) *Reports.* The State educational agency (or, in the case of a districtwide assessment, the local educational agency) makes available to the public, and reports to the public with the same frequency and in the same detail as it reports on the assessment of nondisabled children, the following:

(i) The number of children with disabilities participating in regular assessments, and the number of those children who were provided accommodations in order to participate in those assessments.

(ii) The number of children with disabilities participating in alternate assessments described in subparagraph (C)(ii)(I).

(iii) The number of children with disabilities participating in alternate assessments described in subparagraph (C)(ii)(II).

(iv) The performance of children with disabilities on regular assessments and on alternate assessments (if the number of children with disabilities participating in those assessments is sufficient to yield statistically reliable information and reporting that information will not reveal personally identifiable information about an individual student), compared with the achievement of all children, including children with disabilities, on those assessments.

(E) *Universal design.* The State educational agency (or, in the case of a districtwide assessment, the local educational agency) shall, to the extent feasible, use universal design principles in developing and administering any assessments under this paragraph.

(17) *Supplementation of State, local, and other Federal funds*

(A) *Expenditures.* Funds paid to a State under this subchapter will be expended in accordance with all the provisions of this subchapter.

(B) *Prohibition against commingling.* Funds paid to a State under this subchapter will not be commingled with State funds.

(C) *Prohibition against supplantation and conditions for waiver by Secretary.* Except as provided in section 1413 of this title, funds paid to a State under this subchapter will be used to supplement the level of Federal, State, and local funds (including funds that are not under the direct control of State or local educational agencies) expended for special education and related services provided to children with disabilities under this subchapter and in no case to supplant such Federal, State, and local funds, except that, where the State provides clear and convincing evidence that all children with disabilities have available to them a free appropriate public education, the Secretary may waive, in whole or in part, the requirements of this subparagraph if the Secretary concurs with the evidence provided by the State.

(18) *Maintenance of State financial support*

(A) *In general.* The State does not reduce the amount of State financial support for special education and related services for children with disabilities, or otherwise made available because of the excess costs of educating those children, below the amount of that support for the preceding fiscal year.

(B) *Reduction of funds for failure to maintain support.* The Secretary shall reduce the allocation of funds under section 1411 of this title for any fiscal year following the fiscal year in which the State fails to comply with the requirement of subparagraph (A) by the same amount by which the State fails to meet the requirement.

(C) *Waivers for exceptional or uncontrollable circumstances.* The Secretary may waive the requirement of subparagraph (A) for a State, for one fiscal year at a time, if the Secretary determines that:

(i) granting a waiver would be equitable due to exceptional or uncontrollable circumstances such as a natural disaster or a precipitous and unforeseen decline in the financial resources of the State; or

(ii) the State meets the standard in paragraph (17)(C) for a waiver of the requirement to supplement, and not to supplant, funds received under this subchapter.

(D) *Subsequent years.* If, for any year, a State fails to meet the requirement of subparagraph (A), including any year for which the State is granted a waiver under subparagraph (C), the financial support required of the State in future years under subparagraph (A) shall be the amount that would have been required in the absence of that failure and not the reduced level of the State's support.

(19) *Public participation.* Prior to the adoption of any policies and procedures needed to comply with this section (including any amendments to such policies and procedures), the State ensures that there are public hearings, adequate notice of the hearings, and an opportunity for comment available to the general public, including individuals with disabilities and parents of children with disabilities.

(20) *Rule of construction.* In complying with paragraphs (17) and (18), a State may not use funds paid to it under this part to satisfy State-law mandated funding obligations to local educational agencies, including funding based on student attendance or enrollment, or inflation.

(21) *State advisory panel*

(A) *In general.* The State has established and maintains an advisory panel for the purpose of providing policy guidance with respect to special education and related services for children with disabilities in the State.

(B) *Membership.* Such advisory panel shall consist of members appointed by the Governor, or any other official authorized under State law to make such appointments, be representative of the State population, and be composed of individuals involved in, or concerned with, the education of children with disabilities, including:

(i) parents of children with disabilities (ages birth through 26);

(ii) individuals with disabilities;

(iii) teachers;

(iv) representatives of institutions of higher education that prepare special education and related services personnel;

(v) State and local education officials, including officials who carry out activities under subtitle B of title VII of the McKinney-Vento Homeless Assistance Act (42 U.S.C. 11431 et seq.);

(vi) administrators of programs for children with disabilities;

(vii) representatives of other State agencies involved in the financing or delivery of related services to children with disabilities;

(viii) representatives of private schools and public charter schools;

(ix) not less than 1 representative of a vocational, community, or business organization concerned with the provision of transition services to children with disabilities;

(x) a representative from the State child welfare agency responsible for foster care; and

(xi) representatives from the State juvenile and adult corrections agencies.

(C) *Special rule.* A majority of the members of the panel shall be individuals with disabilities or parents of children with disabilities (ages birth through 26).

(D) *Duties.* The advisory panel shall—

(i) advise the State educational agency of unmet needs within the State in the education of children with disabilities;

(ii) comment publicly on any rules or regulations proposed by the State regarding the education of children with disabilities;

(iii) advise the State educational agency in developing evaluations and reporting on data to the Secretary under section 618;

(iv) advise the State educational agency in developing corrective action plans to address findings identified in Federal monitoring reports under this part; and

(v) advise the State educational agency in developing and implementing policies relating to the coordination of services for children with disabilities.

(22) *Suspension and expulsion rates*

(A) *In general.* The State educational agency examines data, to determine if significant discrepancies are occurring in the rate of long-term suspensions and expulsions of children with disabilities:

(i) among local educational agencies in the State; or

(ii) compared to such rates for nondisabled children within such agencies.

(B) *Review and revision of policies.* If such discrepancies are occurring, the State educational agency reviews and, if appropriate, revises (or requires the affected State or local educational agency to revise) its policies, procedures, and practices relating to the development and implementation of IEPs, the use of positive behavioral interventions and supports, and procedural safeguards, to ensure that such policies, procedures, and practices comply with this chapter.

(23) *Access to Instructional Materials*

(A) *In general.* The State adopts the National Instructional Materials Accessibility Standard for the purposes of providing instructional materials to blind persons or other persons with print disabilities, in a timely manner after the publication of the National Instructional Materials Accessibility Standard in the Federal Register.

(B) *Rights of State Educational Agency.* Nothing in this paragraph shall be construed to require any State educational agency to coordinate with the National Instructional Materials Access Center. If a State educational agency chooses not to coordinate with the National Instructional Materials Access Center, such agency shall provide an assurance to the Secretary that the agency will provide instructional materials to blind persons or other persons with print disabilities in a timely manner.

(C) *Preparation and delivery of files.* If a State educational agency chooses to coordinate with the National Instructional Materials Access Center, not later than 2 years after the date of enactment of the Individuals with Disabilities Education Improvement Act of 2004, the agency, as part of any print instructional materials adoption process, procurement contract, or other practice or instrument used for purchase of print instructional materials, shall enter into a written contract with the publisher of the print instructional materials to:

(i) require the publisher to prepare and, on or before delivery of the print instructional materials, provide to the National Instructional Materials Access Center electronic files containing the contents of the print instructional materials using the National Instructional Materials Accessibility Standard; or

(ii) purchase instructional materials from the publisher that are produced in, or may be rendered in, specialized formats.

(D) *Assistive technology.* In carrying out this paragraph, the State educational agency, to the maximum extent possible, shall work collaboratively with the State agency responsible for assistive technology programs.

(E) *Definitions.* In this paragraph:

(i) *National instructional materials access center.* The term "National Instructional Materials Access Center" means the center established pursuant to section 674(e).

(ii) *National instructional materials accessibility standard.* The term "National Instructional Materials Accessibility Standard" has the meaning given the term in section 674(e)(3)(A).

(iii) *Specialized formats.* The term "specialized formats" has the meaning given the term in section 674(e)(3)(D).

(24) *Overidentification and disproportionality.* The State has in effect, consistent with the purposes of this title and with section 618(d), policies and procedures designed to prevent the inappropriate overidentification or disproportionate representation by race and ethnicity of children as children with disabilities, including children with disabilities with a particular impairment described in section 602.

(25) *Prohibition on mandatory medication*

(A) *In general.* The State educational agency shall prohibit State and local educational agency personnel from requiring a child to obtain a prescription for a substance covered by the Controlled Substances Act (21 U.S.C. 801 et seq.) as a condition of attending school, receiving an evaluation under subsection (a) or (c) of section 614, or receiving services under this title.

(B) *Rule of construction.* Nothing in subparagraph (A) shall be construed to create a Federal prohibition against teachers and other school personnel consulting or sharing classroom-based observations with parents or guardians regarding a student's academic and functional performance, or behavior in the classroom or school, or regarding the need for evaluation for special education or related services under paragraph (3).

(b) State educational agency as provider of free appropriate public education or direct services. If the State educational agency provides free appropriate public education to children with disabilities, or provides direct services to such children, such agency:

(1) shall comply with any additional requirements of section 1413(a) of this title, as if such agency were a local educational agency; and

(2) may use amounts that are otherwise available to such agency under this subchapter to serve those children without

regard to section 1413(a)(2)(A)(i) of this title (relating to excess costs).

(c) Exception for prior State plans

(1) *In general.* If a State has on file with the Secretary policies and procedures that demonstrate that such State meets any requirement of subsection (a) of this section, including any policies and procedures filed under this subchapter as in effect before the effective date of the Individuals with Disabilities Education Improvement Act of 2004, the Secretary shall consider such State to have met such requirement for purposes of receiving a grant under this subchapter.

(2) *Modifications made by State.* Subject to paragraph (3), an application submitted by a State in accordance with this section shall remain in effect until the State submits to the Secretary such modifications as the State determines necessary. This section shall apply to a modification to an application to the same extent and in the same manner as this section applies to the original plan.

(3) *Modifications required by the Secretary.* If, after the effective date of the Individuals with Disabilities Education Improvement Act of 2004, the provisions of this chapter are amended (or the regulations developed to carry out this chapter are amended), there is a new interpretation of this chapter by a Federal court or a State's highest court, or there is an official finding of noncompliance with Federal law or regulations, then the Secretary may require a State to modify its application only to the extent necessary to ensure the State's compliance with this subchapter.

(d) Approval by the Secretary

(1) *In general.* If the Secretary determines that a State is eligible to receive a grant under this subchapter, the Secretary shall notify the State of that determination.

(2) *Notice and hearing.* The Secretary shall not make a final determination that a State is not eligible to receive a grant under this subchapter until after providing the State:

(A) with reasonable notice; and

(B) with an opportunity for a hearing.

(e) Assistance under other Federal programs. Nothing in this chapter permits a State to reduce medical and other assistance available, or to alter eligibility, under titles V and XIX of the Social Security Act (42 U.S.C. 701 et seq. and 1396 et seq.) with respect to the provision of a free appropriate public education for children with disabilities in the State.

(f) By-pass for children in private schools

(1) *In general.* If, on the date of enactment of the Education of the Handicapped Act Amendments of 1983, a State educational agency was prohibited by law from providing for the equitable participation in special programs of children with disabilities enrolled in private elementary schools and secondary schools as required by subsection (a)(10)(A), or if the Secretary determines that a State educational agency, local educational agency, or other entity has substantially failed or is unwilling to provide for such equitable participation, then the Secretary shall, notwithstanding such provision of law, arrange for the provision of services to such children through arrangements that shall be subject to the requirements of such subsection.

(2) *Payments*

(A) *Determination of amounts.* If the Secretary arranges for services pursuant to this subsection, the Secretary, after consultation with the appropriate public and private school officials, shall pay to the provider of such services for a fiscal year an amount per child that does not exceed the amount determined by dividing:

(i) the total amount received by the State under this subchapter for such fiscal year; by

(ii) the number of children with disabilities served in the prior year, as reported to the Secretary by the State under section 1418 of this title.

(B) *Withholding of certain amounts.* Pending final resolution of any investigation or complaint that may result in a determination under this subsection, the Secretary may withhold from the allocation of the affected State educational agency the amount the Secretary estimates will be necessary to pay the cost of services described in subparagraph (A).

(C) *Period of payments.* The period under which payments are made under subparagraph (A) shall continue until the Secretary determines that there will no longer be any failure or inability on the part of the State educational agency to meet the requirements of subsection (a)(10)(A) of this section.

(3) *Notice and hearing*

(A) *In general.* The Secretary shall not take any final action under this subsection until the State educational agency affected by such action has had an opportunity, for at least 45 days after receiving written notice thereof, to submit written objections and to appear before the Secretary or the Secretary's designee to show cause why such action should not be taken.

(B) *Review of action.* If a State educational agency is dissatisfied with the Secretary's final action after a proceeding under subparagraph (A), such agency may, not later than 60 days after notice of such action, file with the United States court of appeals for the circuit in which such State is located a petition for review of that action. A copy of the petition shall be forthwith transmitted by the clerk of the court to the Secretary. The Secretary thereupon shall file in the court the record of the proceedings on which the Secretary based the Secretary's action, as provided in section 2112 of title 28.

(C) *Review of findings of fact.* The findings of fact by the Secretary, if supported by substantial evidence, shall be conclusive, but the court, for good cause shown, may remand the case to the Secretary to take further evidence, and the Secretary may thereupon make new or modified findings of fact and may modify the Secretary's previous action, and shall file in the court the record of the further proceedings. Such new or modified findings of fact shall likewise be conclusive if supported by substantial evidence.

(D) *Jurisdiction of court of appeals; review by United States Supreme Court.* Upon the filing of a petition under subparagraph (B), the United States court of appeals shall have jurisdiction to affirm the action of the Secretary or to set it aside, in whole or in part. The judgment of the court shall be subject to review by the Supreme Court of the United States upon certiorari or certification as provided in section 1254 of title 28.

Sec. 1414. Evaluations, eligibility determinations, individualized education programs, and educational placements

(a) Evaluations, parental consent, and reevaluations

(1) *Initial evaluations*

(A) *In general.* A State educational agency, other State agency, or local educational agency shall conduct a full and individual initial evaluation in accordance with this paragraph and subsection (b), before the initial provision of special education and related services to a child with a disability under this part.

(B) *Request for initial evaluation.* Consistent with subparagraph (D), either a parent of a child, or a State educational agency, other State agency, or local educational agency may initiate a request for an initial evaluation to determine if the child is a child with a disability.

(C) *Procedures*

(i) *In general.* Such initial evaluation shall consist of procedures:

(I) to determine whether a child is a child with a disability (as defined in section 602) within 60 days of receiving parental consent for the evaluation, or, if the State establishes a timeframe within which the evaluation must be conducted, within such timeframe; and

(II) to determine the educational needs of such child.

(ii) *Exception.* The relevant timeframe in clause (i)(I) shall not apply to a local educational agency if:

(I) a child enrolls in a school served by the local educational agency after the relevant timeframe in clause (i)(I) has begun and prior to a determination by the child's previous local educational agency as to whether the child is a child with a disability (as defined in section 602), but only if the subsequent local educational agency is making sufficient progress to ensure a prompt completion of the evaluation, and the parent and subsequent local educational agency agree to a specific time when the evaluation will be completed; or

(II) the parent of a child repeatedly fails or refuses to produce the child for the evaluation.

(D) *Parental consent*

(i) *In general*

(I) *Consent for initial evaluation.* The agency proposing to conduct an initial evaluation to determine if the child qualifies as a child with a disability as defined in section 602 shall obtain informed consent from the parent of such child before conducting the evaluation. Parental consent for evaluation shall not be construed as consent for placement for receipt of special education and related services.

(II) *Consent for services.* An agency that is responsible for making a free appropriate public education available to a child with a disability under this part shall seek to obtain informed consent from the parent of such child before providing special education and related services to the child.

(ii) *Absence of consent*

(I) *For initial evaluation.* If the parent of such child does not provide consent for an initial evaluation under clause (i)(I), or the parent fails to respond to a request to provide the consent, the local educational agency may pursue the initial evaluation of the child by utilizing the procedures described in section

615, except to the extent inconsistent with State law relating to such parental consent.

(II) *For services.* If the parent of such child refuses to consent to services under clause (i)(II), the local educational agency shall not provide special education and related services to the child by utilizing the procedures described in section 615.

(III) *Effect on agency obligations.* If the parent of such child refuses to consent to the receipt of special education and related services, or the parent fails to respond to a request to provide such consent:

(aa) the local educational agency shall not be considered to be in violation of the requirement to make available a free appropriate public education to the child for the failure to provide such child with the special education and related services for which the local educational agency requests such consent; and

(bb) the local educational agency shall not be required to convene an IEP meeting or develop an IEP under this section for the child for the special education and related services for which the local educational agency requests such consent.

(iii) *Consent for wards of the state*

(I) *In general.* If the child is a ward of the State and is not residing with the child's parent, the agency shall make reasonable efforts to obtain the informed consent from the parent (as defined in section 602) of the child for an initial evaluation to determine whether the child is a child with a disability.

(II) *Exceptions.* The agency shall not be required to obtain informed consent from the parent of a child for an initial evaluation to determine whether the child is a child with a disability if:

(aa) despite reasonable efforts to do so, the agency cannot discover the whereabouts of the parent of the child;

(bb) the rights of the parents of the child have been terminated in accordance with State law; or

(cc) the rights of the parent to make educational decisions have been subrogated by a judge in accordance with State law and consent for an initial evaluation has been given by an individual appointed by the judge to represent the child.

(E) *Rule of construction.* The screening of a student by a teacher or specialist to determine appropriate instructional strategies for curriculum implementation shall not be considered to be an evaluation for eligibility for special education and related services.

(2) *Reevaluations*

(A) *In general.* A local educational agency shall ensure that a reevaluation of each child with a disability is conducted in accordance with subsections (b) and (c):

(i) if the local educational agency determines that the educational or related services needs, including improved academic achievement and functional performance, of the child warrant a reevaluation; or

(ii) if the child's parents or teacher requests a reevaluation.

(B) *Limitation.* A reevaluation conducted under subparagraph (A) shall occur:

(i) not more frequently than once a year, unless the parent and the local educational agency agree otherwise; and

(ii) at least once every 3 years, unless the parent and the local educational agency agree that a reevaluation is unnecessary.

(b) Evaluation procedures

(1) *Notice.* The local educational agency shall provide notice to the parents of a child with a disability, in accordance with subsections (b)(3), (b)(4), and (c) of section 1415 of this title, that describes any evaluation procedures such agency proposes to conduct.

(2) *Conduct of evaluation.* In conducting the evaluation, the local educational agency shall:

(A) use a variety of assessment tools and strategies to gather relevant functional and developmental information, including information provided by the parent, that may assist in determining

(i) whether the child is a child with a disability; and

(ii) the content of the child's individualized education program, including information related to enabling the child to be involved in and progress in the general education curriculum, or, for preschool children, to participate in appropriate activities;

(B) not use any single measure or assessment as the sole criterion for determining whether a child is a child with a disability or determining an appropriate educational program for the child; and

(C) use technically sound instruments that may assess the relative contribution of cognitive and behavioral factors, in addition to physical or developmental factors.

(3) *Additional requirements.* Each local educational agency shall ensure that:

(A) tests and other evaluation materials used to assess a child under this section:

(i) are selected and administered so as not to be discriminatory on a racial or cultural basis;

(ii) are provided and administered in the language and form most likely to yield accurate information on what the child knows and can do academically, developmentally, and functionally, unless it is not feasible to so provide or administer;

(iii) are used for purposes for which the assessments or measures are valid and reliable;

(iv) are administered by trained and knowledgeable personnel; and

(v) are administered in accordance with any instructions provided by the producer of such assessments;

(B) the child is assessed in all areas of suspected disability; and

(C) assessment tools and strategies that provide relevant information that directly assists persons in determining the educational needs of the child are provided; and

(4) *Determination of eligibility and educational need.* Upon completion of the administration of tests and other evaluation measures:

(A) the determination of whether the child is a child with a disability as defined in section 602(3) and the educational needs of the child shall be made by a team of qualified professionals and the parent of the child in accordance with paragraph (5); and

(B) a copy of the evaluation report and the documentation of determination of eligibility will be given to the parent.

(5) *Special rule for eligibility determination.* In making a determination of eligibility under paragraph (4)(A), a child shall not be determined to be a child with a disability if the determinant factor for such determination is:

(A) lack of appropriate instruction in reading, including in the essential components of reading instruction (as defined in section 1208(3) of the Elementary and Secondary Education Act of 1965);

(B) lack of instruction in math; or

(C) limited English proficiency.

(6) *Specific learning disabilities*

(A) *In general.* Notwithstanding section 607(b), when determining whether a child has a specific learning disability as defined in section 602, a local educational agency shall not be required to take into consideration whether a child has a severe discrepancy between achievement and intellectual ability in oral expression, listening comprehension, written expression, basic reading skill, reading comprehension, mathematical calculation, or mathematical reasoning.

(B) *Additional authority.* In determining whether a child has a specific learning disability, a local educational agency may use a process that determines if the child responds to scientific, research-based intervention as a part of the evaluation procedures described in paragraphs (2) and (3).

(c) Additional requirements for evaluation and reevaluations

(1) *Review of existing evaluation data.* As part of an initial evaluation (if appropriate) and as part of any reevaluation under this section, the IEP Team and other qualified professionals, as appropriate, shall:

(A) review existing evaluation data on the child, including:

(i) evaluations and information provided by the parents of the child;

(ii) current classroom-based, local, or State assessments, and classroom-based observations; and

(iii) observations by teachers and related services providers; and

(B) on the basis of that review, and input from the child's parents, identify what additional data, if any, are needed to determine:

(i) whether the child is a child with a disability as defined in section 602(3), and the educational needs of the child, or, in case of a reevaluation of a child, whether the child continues to have such a disability and such educational needs;

(ii) the present levels of academic achievement and related developmental needs of the child;

(iii) whether the child needs special education and related services, or in the case of a reevaluation of a child, whether the child continues to need special education and related services; and

(iv) whether any additions or modifications to the special education and related services are needed to enable the child to meet the measurable annual goals set out in the individualized education program of the child and to participate, as appropriate, in the general curriculum.

(2) *Source of data.* The local educational agency shall administer such assessments and other evaluation measures as may be needed to produce the data identified by the IEP Team under paragraph (1)(B).

(3) *Parental consent.* Each local educational agency shall obtain informed parental consent, in accordance with subsection (a)(1)(D) of this section, prior to conducting any re-evaluation of a child with a disability, except that such informed parental consent need not be obtained if the local educational agency can demonstrate that it had taken reasonable measures to obtain such consent and the child's parent has failed to respond.

(4) *Requirements if additional data are not needed.* If the IEP Team and other qualified professionals, as appropriate, determine that no additional data are needed to determine whether the child continues to be a child with a disability, the local educational agency:

(A) shall notify the child's parents of:

(i) that determination and the reasons for the determination; and

(ii) the right of such parents to request an assessment to determine whether the child continues to be a child with a disability and to determine the child's educational needs; and

(B) shall not be required to conduct such an assessment unless requested to by the child's parents.

(5) *Evaluations before change in eligibility*

(A) *In general.* Except as provided in subparagraph (B), a local educational agency shall evaluate a child with a disability in accordance with this section before determining that the child is no longer a child with a disability.

(B) *Exception*

(i) *In general.* The evaluation described in subparagraph (A) shall not be required before the termination of a child's eligibility under this part due to graduation from secondary school with a regular diploma, or due to exceeding the age eligibility for a free appropriate public education under State law.

(ii) *Summary of performance.* For a child whose eligibility under this part terminates under circumstances described in clause (i), a local educational agency shall provide the child with a summary of the child's academic achievement and functional performance, which shall include recommendations on how to assist the child in meeting the child's postsecondary goals.

(d) Individualized education programs.

(1) *Definitions*

In this title:

(A) *Individualized education program*

(i) *In general.* The term "individualized education program" or "IEP" means a written statement for each child with a disability that is developed, reviewed, and revised in accordance with this section and that includes:

(I) a statement of the child's present levels of academic achievement and functional performance, including:

(aa) how the child's disability affects the child's involvement and progress in the general education curriculum;

(bb) for preschool children, as appropriate, how the disability affects the child's participation in appropriate activities; and

(cc) for children with disabilities who take alternate assessments aligned to alternate achievement standards, a description of benchmarks or short-term objectives;

(II) a statement of measurable annual goals, including academic and functional goals, designed to:

(aa) meet the child's needs that result from the child's disability to enable the child to be involved in and make progress in the general education curriculum; and

(bb) meet each of the child's other educational needs that result from the child's disability;

(III) a description of how the child's progress toward meeting the annual goals described in subclause (II) will be measured and when periodic reports on the progress the child is making toward meeting the annual goals (such as through the use of quarterly or other periodic reports, concurrent with the issuance of report cards) will be provided;

(IV) a statement of the special education and related services and supplementary aids and services, based on peer-reviewed research to the extent practicable, to be provided to the child, or on behalf of the child, and a statement of the program modifications or supports for school personnel that will be provided for the child:

(aa) to advance appropriately toward attaining the annual goals;

(bb) to be involved in and make progress in the general education curriculum in accordance with subclause (I) and to participate in extracurricular and other nonacademic activities; and

(cc) to be educated and participate with other children with disabilities and nondisabled children in the activities described in this subparagraph;

(V) an explanation of the extent, if any, to which the child will not participate with nondisabled children in the regular class and in the activities described in subclause (IV)(cc);

(VI)(aa) a statement of any individual appropriate accommodations that are necessary to measure the academic achievement and functional performance of the child on State and districtwide assessments consistent with section 612(a)(16)(A); and

(bb) if the IEP Team determines that the child shall take an alternate assessment on a particular State or districtwide assessment of student achievement, a statement of why:

(AA) the child cannot participate in the regular assessment; and

(BB) the particular alternate assessment selected is appropriate for the child;

(VII) the projected date for the beginning of the services and modifications described in subclause (IV), and the anticipated frequency, location, and duration of those services and modifications; and

(VIII) beginning not later than the first IEP to be in effect when the child is 16, and updated annually thereafter:

(aa) appropriate measurable postsecondary goals based upon age appropriate transition assessments related to training, education, employment, and, where appropriate, independent living skills;

(bb) the transition services (including courses of study) needed to assist the child in reaching those goals; and (cc) beginning not later than 1 year before the child reaches the age of majority under State law, a statement that the child has been informed of the child's rights under this title, if any, that will transfer to the child on reaching the age of majority under section 615(m).

(ii) *Rule of construction.* Nothing in this section shall be construed to require:

(I) that additional information be included in a child's IEP beyond what is explicitly required in this section; and

(II) the IEP Team to include information under 1 component of a child's IEP that is already contained under another component of such IEP.

(B) *Individualized education program team.* The term "individualized education program team" or "IEP Team" means a group of individuals composed of:

(i) the parents of a child with a disability;

(ii) not less than one regular education teacher of such child (if the child is, or may be, participating in the regular education environment);

(iii) not less than one special education teacher, or where appropriate, at least one special education provider of such child;

(iv) a representative of the local educational agency who:

(I) is qualified to provide, or supervise the provision of, specially designed instruction to meet the unique needs of children with disabilities;

(II) is knowledgeable about the general curriculum; and

(III) is knowledgeable about the availability of resources of the local educational agency;

(v) an individual who can interpret the instructional implications of evaluation results, who may be a member of the team described in clauses (ii) through (vi);

(vi) at the discretion of the parent or the agency, other individuals who have knowledge or special expertise regarding the child, including related services personnel as appropriate; and

(vii) whenever appropriate, the child with a disability.

(C) *IEP Team attendance*

(i) *Attendance not necessary.* A member of the IEP Team shall not be required to attend an IEP meeting, in whole or in part, if the parent of a child with a disability and the local educational agency agree that the attendance of such member is not necessary because the member's area of the curriculum or related services is not being modified or discussed in the meeting.

(ii) *Excusal.* A member of the IEP Team may be excused from attending an IEP meeting, in whole or in part, when the meeting involves a modification to or discussion of the member's area of the curriculum or related services, if:

(I) the parent and the local educational agency consent to the excusal; and

(II) the member submits, in writing to the parent and the IEP Team, input into the development of the IEP prior to the meeting.

(iii) *Written agreement and consent required.* A parent's agreement under clause (i) and consent under clause (ii) shall be in writing.

(D) *IEP team transition.* In the case of a child who was previously served under part C, an invitation to the initial IEP meeting shall, at the request of the parent, be sent to the part C service coordinator or other representatives of the part C system to assist with the smooth transition of services.

(2) *Requirement that program be in effect*

(A) *In general.* At the beginning of each school year, each local educational agency, State educational agency, or other State agency, as the case may be, shall have in effect, for each child with a disability in the agency's jurisdiction, an individualized education program, as defined in paragraph (1)(A).

(B) *Program for child aged 3 through 5.* In the case of a child with a disability aged 3 through 5 (or, at the discretion of the State educational agency, a 2-year-old child with a disability who will turn age 3 during the school year), the IEP Team shall consider the individualized family service plan that contains the material described in section 636, and that is developed in accordance with this section, and the individualized family service plan may serve as the IEP of the child if using that plan as the IEP is:

(i) consistent with State policy; and

(ii) agreed to by the agency and the child's parents.

(C) *Program for children who transfer school districts*

(i) *In general*

(I) *Transfer within the same state.* In the case of a child with a disability who transfers school districts within the same academic year, who enrolls in a new school, and who had an IEP that was in effect in the same State, the local educational agency shall provide such child with a free appropriate public education, including services comparable to those described in the previously held IEP, in consultation with the parents until such time as the local educational agency adopts the previously held IEP or develops, adopts, and implements a new IEP that is consistent with Federal and State law.

(II) *Transfer outside state.* In the case of a child with a disability who transfers school districts within the same academic year, who enrolls in a new school, and who had an IEP that was in effect in another State, the local educational agency shall provide such child with a free appropriate public education, including services comparable to those described in the previously held IEP, in consultation with the parents until such time as the local educational agency conducts an evaluation pursuant to subsection (a)(1), if determined to be necessary by such agency, and develops a new IEP, if appropriate, that is consistent with Federal and State law.

(ii) *Transmittal of records.* To facilitate the transition for a child described in clause (i):

(I) the new school in which the child enrolls shall take reasonable steps to promptly obtain the child's records, including the IEP and supporting documents and any other records relating to the provision of special education or related services to the child, from the previous school in which the child was enrolled, pursuant to section 99.31(a)(2) of title 34, Code of Federal Regulations; and

(II) the previous school in which the child was enrolled shall take reasonable steps to promptly respond to such request from the new school.

(3) *Development of IEP*

(A) *In general.* In developing each child's IEP, the IEP Team, subject to subparagraph (C), shall consider:

(i) the strengths of the child;

(ii) the concerns of the parents for enhancing the education of their child;

(iii) the results of the initial evaluation or most recent evaluation of the child; and

(iv) the academic, developmental, and functional needs of the child.

(B) *Consideration of special factors.* The IEP Team shall:

(i) in the case of a child whose behavior impedes the child's learning or that of others, consider the use of positive behavioral interventions and supports, and other strategies, to address that behavior;

(ii) in the case of a child with limited English proficiency, consider the language needs of the child as such needs relate to the child's IEP;

(iii) in the case of a child who is blind or visually impaired, provide for instruction in Braille and the use of Braille unless the IEP Team determines, after an evaluation of the child's reading and writing skills, needs, and appropriate reading and writing media (including an evaluation of the child's future needs for instruction in Braille or the use of Braille), that instruction in Braille or the use of Braille is not appropriate for the child;

(iv) consider the communication needs of the child, and in the case of a child who is deaf or hard of hearing, consider the child's language and communication needs, opportunities for direct communications with peers and professional personnel in the child's language and communication mode, academic level, and full range of needs, including opportunities for direct instruction in the child's language and communication mode; and

(v) consider whether the child requires assistive technology devices and services.

(C) *Requirement with respect to regular education teacher.* The regular education teacher of the child, as a member of the IEP Team, shall, to the extent appropriate, participate in the development of the IEP of the child, including the determination of appropriate positive behavioral interventions and supports, and other strategies and the determination of supplementary aids and services, program modifications, and support for school personnel consistent with paragraph (1)(A)(i)(IV).

(D) *Agreement.* In making changes to a child's IEP after the annual IEP meeting for a school year, the parent of a child with a disability and the local educational agency may agree not to convene an IEP meeting for the purposes of making such changes, and instead may develop a written document to amend or modify the child's current IEP.

(E) *Consolidation of IEP Team meetings.* To the extent possible, the local educational agency shall encourage the consolidation of reevaluation meetings for the child and other IEP Team meetings for the child.

(F) *Amendments.* Changes to the IEP may be made either by the entire IEP Team or, as provided in subparagraph (D), by amending the IEP rather than by redrafting the entire IEP. Upon request, a parent shall be provided with a revised copy of the IEP with the amendments incorporated.

(4) *Review and revision of IEP*

(A) *In general.* The local educational agency shall ensure that, subject to subparagraph (B), the IEP Team:

(i) reviews the child's IEP periodically, but not less frequently than annually, to determine whether the annual goals for the child are being achieved; and

(ii) revises the IEP as appropriate to address:

(I) any lack of expected progress toward the annual goals and in the general education curriculum, where appropriate;

(II) the results of any reevaluation conducted under this section;

(III) information about the child provided to, or by, the parents, as described in subsection (c)(1)(B) of this section;

(IV) the child's anticipated needs; or

(V) other matters.

(B) *Requirement with respect to regular education teacher.* A regular education teacher of the child, as a member of the IEP Team, shall, consistent with paragraph (1)(C), participate in the review and revision of the IEP of the child.

(5) *Multi-year IEP demonstration*

(A) *Pilot program*

(i) *Purpose.* The purpose of this paragraph is to provide an opportunity for States to allow parents and local educational agencies the opportunity for long-term planning by offering the option of developing a comprehensive multi-year IEP, not to exceed 3 years, that is designed to coincide with the natural transition points for the child.

(ii) *Authorization.* In order to carry out the purpose of this paragraph, the Secretary is authorized to approve not more than 15 proposals from States to carry out the activity described in clause (i).

(iii) *Proposal*

(I) *In general.* A State desiring to participate in the program under this paragraph shall submit a proposal to the Secretary at such time and in such manner as the Secretary may reasonably require.

(II) *Content.* The proposal shall include:

(aa) assurances that the development of a multi-year IEP under this paragraph is optional for parents;

(bb) assurances that the parent is required to provide informed consent before a comprehensive multi-year IEP is developed;

(cc) a list of required elements for each multi-year IEP, including:

(AA) measurable goals pursuant to paragraph (1)(A)(i)(II), coinciding with natural transition points for the child, that will enable the child to be involved in and make progress in the general education curriculum and that will meet the child's other needs that result from the child's disability; and

(BB) measurable annual goals for determining progress toward meeting the goals described in subitem (AA); and

(dd) a description of the process for the review and revision of each multi-year IEP, including:

(AA) a review by the IEP Team of the child's multi-year IEP at each of the child's natural transition points;

(BB) in years other than a child's natural transition points, an annual review of the child's IEP to determine the child's current levels of progress and whether the annual goals for the child are being achieved, and a requirement to amend the IEP, as appropriate, to enable the child to continue to meet the measurable goals set out in the IEP;

(CC) if the IEP Team determines on the basis of a review that the child is not making sufficient progress toward the goals described in the multi-year IEP, a requirement that the local educational agency shall ensure that the IEP Team carries out a more thorough review of the IEP in accordance with paragraph (4) within 30 calendar days; and

(DD) at the request of the parent, a requirement that the IEP Team shall conduct a review of the child's multi-year IEP rather than or subsequent to an annual review.

(B) *Report.* Beginning 2 years after the date of enactment of the Individuals with Disabilities Education Improvement Act of 2004, the Secretary shall submit an annual report to the Committee on Education and the Workforce of the House of Representatives and the Committee on Health, Education, Labor, and Pensions of the Senate regarding the effectiveness of the program under this paragraph and any specific recommendations for broader implementation of such program, including:

(i) reducing:

(I) the paperwork burden on teachers, principals, administrators, and related service providers; and

(II) noninstructional time spent by teachers in complying with this part;

(ii) enhancing longer-term educational planning;

(iii) improving positive outcomes for children with disabilities;

(iv) promoting collaboration between IEP Team members; and

(v) ensuring satisfaction of family members.

(C) *Definition.* In this paragraph, the term "natural transition points" means those periods that are close in time to the transition of a child with a disability from preschool to elementary grades, from elementary grades to middle or junior high school grades, from middle or junior high school grades to secondary school grades, and from secondary school grades to post-secondary activities, but in no case a period longer than 3 years.

(6) *Failure to meet transition objectives.* If a participating agency, other than the local educational agency, fails to provide the transition services described in the IEP in accordance with paragraph (1)(A)(i)(VIII), the local educational agency shall reconvene the IEP Team to identify alternative strategies to meet the transition objectives for the child set out in the IEP.

(7) *Children with disabilities in adult prisons*

(A) *In general.* The following requirements shall not apply to children with disabilities who are convicted as adults under State law and incarcerated in adult prisons:

(i) The requirements contained in section 612(a)(16) and paragraph (1)(A)(i)(VI) (relating to participation of children with disabilities in general assessments).

(ii) The requirements of items (aa) and (bb) of paragraph (1)(A)(i)(VIII) (relating to transition planning and transition services), do not apply with respect to such children whose

eligibility under this part will end, because of such children's age, before such children will be released from prison.

(B) *Additional requirement.* If a child with a disability is convicted as an adult under State law and incarcerated in an adult prison, the child's IEP Team may modify the child's IEP or placement notwithstanding the requirements of sections 612(a)(5)(A) and paragraph (1)(A) if the State has demonstrated a bona fide security or compelling penological interest that cannot otherwise be accommodated.

(e) *Educational placements.* Each local educational agency or State educational agency shall ensure that the parents of each child with a disability are members of any group that makes decisions on the educational placement of their child.

(f) *Alternative means of meeting participation.* When conducting IEP team meetings and placement meetings pursuant to this section, section 615(e), and section 615(f)(1)(B), and carrying out administrative matters under section 615 (such as scheduling, exchange of witness lists, and status conferences), the parent of a child with a disability and a local educational agency may agree to use alternative means of meeting participation, such as video conferences and conference calls.

Sec. 1415. Procedural safeguards

(a) **Establishment of procedures.** Any State educational agency, State agency, or local educational agency that receives assistance under this subchapter shall establish and maintain procedures in accordance with this section to ensure that children with disabilities and their parents are guaranteed procedural safeguards with respect to the provision of free appropriate public education by such agencies.

(b) **Types of procedures.** The procedures required by this section shall include the following:

(1) An opportunity for the parents of a child with a disability to examine all records relating to such child and to participate in meetings with respect to the identification, evaluation, and educational placement of the child, and the provision of a free appropriate public education to such child, and to obtain an independent educational evaluation of the child.

(2) Procedures to protect the rights of the child whenever the parents of the child are not known, the agency cannot, after reasonable efforts, locate the parents, or the child is a ward of the State, including the assignment of an individual to act as a surrogate for the parents, which surrogate shall not be an employee of the State educational agency, the local educational agency, or any other agency that is involved in the education or care of the child. In the case of:

(i) a child who is a ward of the State, such surrogate may alternatively be appointed by the judge overseeing the child's care provided that the surrogate meets the requirements of this paragraph; and

(ii) an unaccompanied homeless youth as defined in section 725(6) of the McKinney-Vento Homeless Assistance Act (42 U.S.C. 11434a(6)), the local educational agency shall appoint a surrogate in accordance with this paragraph.

(B) The State shall make reasonable efforts to ensure the assignment of a surrogate not more than 30 days after there is a determination by the agency that the child needs a surrogate.

(3) Written prior notice to the parents of the child, in accordance with subsection (c)(1) of this section, whenever such agency:

(A) proposes to initiate or change; or

(B) refuses to initiate or change; the identification, evaluation, or educational placement of the child, in accordance with subsection (c) of this section, or the provision of a free appropriate public education to the child;

(4) Procedures designed to ensure that the notice required by paragraph (3) is in the native language of the parents, unless it clearly is not feasible to do so.

(5) An opportunity for mediation, in accordance with subsection (e).

(6) An opportunity for any party to present a complaint:

(A) with respect to any matter relating to the identification, evaluation, or educational placement of the child, or the provision of a free appropriate public education to such child; and

(B) which sets forth an alleged violation that occurred not more than 2 years before the date the parent or public agency knew or should have known about the alleged action that forms the basis of the complaint, or, if the State has an explicit time limitation for presenting such a complaint under this part, in such time as the State law allows, except that the exceptions to the timeline described in subsection (f)(3)(D) shall apply to the timeline described in this subparagraph.

(7)(A) Procedures that require either party, or the attorney representing a party, to provide due process complaint notice in accordance with subsection (c)(2) (which shall remain confidential):

(i) to the other party, in the complaint filed under paragraph (6), and forward a copy of such notice to the State educational agency; and

(ii) that shall include:

(I) the name of the child, the address of the residence of the child (or available contact information in the case of a homeless child), and the name of the school the child is attending;

(II) in the case of a homeless child or youth (within the meaning of section 725(2) of the McKinney-Vento Homeless Assistance Act (42 U.S.C. 11434a(2)), available contact information for the child and the name of the school the child is attending;

(III) a description of the nature of the problem of the child relating to such proposed initiation or change, including facts relating to such problem; and

(IV) a proposed resolution of the problem to the extent known and available to the party at the time.

(B) A requirement that a party may not have a due process hearing until the party, or the attorney representing the party, files a notice that meets the requirements of subparagraph (A)(ii).

(8) Procedures that require the State educational agency to develop a model form to assist parents in filing a complaint and due process complaint notice in accordance with paragraphs (6) and (7), respectively.

(c) Notification requirements

(1) *Content of prior written notice.* The notice required by subsection (b)(3) shall include:

(A) a description of the action proposed or refused by the agency;

(B) an explanation of why the agency proposes or refuses to take the action and a description of each evaluation procedure, assessment, record, or report the agency used as a basis for the proposed or refused action;

(C) a statement that the parents of a child with a disability have protection under the procedural safeguards of this part and, if this notice is not an initial referral for evaluation, the means by which a copy of a description of the procedural safeguards can be obtained;

(D) sources for parents to contact to obtain assistance in understanding the provisions of this part;

(E) a description of other options considered by the IEP Team and the reason why those options were rejected; and

(F) a description of the factors that are relevant to the agency's proposal or refusal.

(2) Due process complaint notice

(A) *Complaint.* The due process complaint notice required under subsection (b)(7)(A) shall be deemed to be sufficient unless the party receiving the notice notifies the hearing officer and the other party in writing that the receiving party believes the notice has not met the requirements of subsection (b)(7)(A).

(B) *Response to complaint*

(i) *Local educational agency response*

(I) *In general.* If the local educational agency has not sent a prior written notice to the parent regarding the subject matter contained in the parent's due process complaint notice, such local educational agency shall, within 10 days of receiving the complaint, send to the parent a response that shall include:

(aa) an explanation of why the agency proposed or refused to take the action raised in the complaint;

(bb) a description of other options that the IEP Team considered and the reasons why those options were rejected;

(cc) a description of each evaluation procedure, assessment, record, or report the agency used as the basis for the proposed or refused action; and

(dd) a description of the factors that are relevant to the agency's proposal or refusal.

(II) *Sufficiency.* A response filed by a local educational agency pursuant to subclause (I) shall not be construed to preclude such local educational agency from asserting that the parent's due process complaint notice was insufficient where appropriate.

(ii) *Other party notice.* Except as provided in clause (i), the non-complaining party shall, within 10 days of receiving the complaint, send to the complaint a response that specifically addresses the issues raised in the complaint.

(C) *Timing.* The party providing a hearing officer notification under subparagraph (A) shall provide the notification within 15 days of receiving the complaint.

(D) *Determination.* Within 5 days of receipt of the notification provided under subparagraph (C), the hearing officer shall make a determination on the face of the notice of whether the notification meets the requirements of subsection (b)(7)(A), and shall immediately notify the parties in writing of such determination.

(E) *Amended complaint notice*

(i) *In general.* A party may amend its due process complaint notice only if:

(I) the other party consents in writing to such amendment and is given the opportunity to resolve the complaint through a meeting held pursuant to subsection (f)(1)(B); or

(II) the hearing officer grants permission, except that the hearing officer may only grant such permission at any time not later than 5 days before a due process hearing occurs.

(ii) *Applicable timeline.* The applicable timeline for a due process hearing under this part shall recommence at the time the party files an amended notice, including the timeline under subsection (f)(1)(B).

(d) Procedural safeguards notice

(1) *In general*

(A) *Copy to parents.* A copy of the procedural safeguards available to the parents of a child with a disability shall be given to the parents only 1 time a year, except that a copy also shall be given to the parents:

(i) upon initial referral or parental request for evaluation;

(ii) upon the first occurrence of the filing of a complaint under subsection (b)(6); and

(iii) upon request by a parent.

(B) *Internet website.* A local educational agency may place a current copy of the procedural safeguards notice on its Internet website if such website exists.

(2) *Contents.* The procedural safeguards notice shall include a full explanation of the procedural safeguards, written in the native language of the parents, unless it clearly is not feasible to do so, and written in an easily understandable manner, available under this section and under regulations promulgated by the Secretary relating to:

(A) independent educational evaluation;

(B) prior written notice;

(C) parental consent;

(D) access to educational records;

(E) the opportunity to present and resolve complaints, including:

(i) the time period in which to make a complaint;

(ii) the opportunity for the agency to resolve the complaint; and

(iii) the availability of mediation;

(F) the child's placement during pendency of due process proceedings;

(G) procedures for students who are subject to placement in an interim alternative educational setting;

(H) requirements for unilateral placement by parents of children in private schools at public expense;

(I) due process hearings, including requirements for disclosure of evaluation results and recommendations;

(J) State-level appeals (if applicable in that State);

(K) civil actions, including the time period in which to file such actions; and

(L) attorneys' fees.

(e) Mediation

(1) *In general.* Any State educational agency or local educational agency that receives assistance under this subchapter shall ensure that procedures are established and implemented to allow parties to disputes involving any matter including matters arising prior to the filing of a complaint pursuant to subsection (b)(6) of this section, to resolve such disputes through a mediation process.

(2) *Requirements.* Such procedures shall meet the following requirements:

(A) The procedures shall ensure that the mediation process:

(i) is voluntary on the part of the parties;

(ii) is not used to deny or delay a parent's right to a due process hearing under subsection (f) of this section, or to deny any other rights afforded under this subchapter; and

(iii) is conducted by a qualified and impartial mediator who is trained in effective mediation techniques.

(B) *Opportunity to meet with a disinterested party.* A local educational agency or a State agency may establish procedures to offer to parents and schools that choose not to use the mediation process, an opportunity to meet, at a time and location convenient to the parents, with a disinterested party who is under contract with:

(i) a parent training and information center or community parent resource center in the State established under section 671 or 672; or

(ii) an appropriate alternative dispute resolution entity, to encourage the use, and explain the benefits, of the mediation process to the parents.

(C) *List of qualified mediators.* The State shall maintain a list of individuals who are qualified mediators and knowledgeable in laws and regulations relating to the provision of special education and related services.

(D) *Costs.* The State shall bear the cost of the mediation process, including the costs of meetings described in subparagraph (B).

(E) *Scheduling and location.* Each session in the mediation process shall be scheduled in a timely manner and shall be held in a location that is convenient to the parties to the dispute.

(F) *Written agreement.* In the case that a resolution is reached to resolve the complaint through the mediation process, the parties shall execute a legally binding agreement that sets forth such resolution and that:

(i) states that all discussions that occurred during the mediation process shall be confidential and may not be used as evidence in any subsequent due process hearing or civil proceeding;

(ii) is signed by both the parent and a representative of the agency who has the authority to bind such agency; and

(iii) is enforceable in any State court of competent jurisdiction or in a district court of the United States.

(G) *Mediation discussions.* Discussions that occur during the mediation process shall be confidential and may not be used as evidence in any subsequent due process hearing or civil proceeding.

(f) Impartial due process hearing

(1) *In general*

(A) *Hearing.* Whenever a complaint has been received under subsection (b)(6) or (k), the parents or the local educational agency involved in such complaint shall have an opportunity for an impartial due process hearing, which shall be conducted by the State educational agency or by the local educational agency, as determined by State law or by the State educational agency.

(B) *Resolution session*

(i) *Preliminary meeting.* Prior to the opportunity for an impartial due process hearing under subparagraph (A), the local educational agency shall convene a meeting with the parents and the relevant member or members of the IEP Team who have specific knowledge of the facts identified in the complaint:

(I) within 15 days of receiving notice of the parents' complaint;

(II) which shall include a representative of the agency who has decisionmaking authority on behalf of such agency;

(III) which may not include an attorney of the local educational agency unless the parent is accompanied by an attorney; and

(IV) where the parents of the child discuss their complaint, and the facts that form the basis of the complaint, and the local educational agency is provided the opportunity to resolve the complaint, unless the parents and the local educational agency agree in writing to waive such meeting, or agree to use the mediation process described in subsection (e).

(ii) *Hearing.* If the local educational agency has not resolved the complaint to the satisfaction of the parents within 30 days of the receipt of the complaint, the due process hearing may occur, and all of the applicable timelines for a due process hearing under this part shall commence.

(iii) *Written settlement agreement.* In the case that a resolution is reached to resolve the complaint at a meeting described in clause (i), the parties shall execute a legally binding agreement that is:

(I) signed by both the parent and a representative of the agency who has the authority to bind such agency; and

(II) enforceable in any State court of competent jurisdiction or in a district court of the United States.

(iv) *Review period.* If the parties execute an agreement pursuant to clause (iii), a party may void such agreement within 3 business days of the agreement's execution.

(2) *Disclosure of evaluations and recommendations*

(A) *In general.* Not less than 5 business days prior to a hearing conducted pursuant to paragraph (1), each party shall disclose to all other parties all evaluations completed by that date, and recommendations based on the offering party's evaluations, that the party intends to use at the hearing.

(B) *Failure to disclose.* A hearing officer may bar any party that fails to comply with subparagraph A from introducing the relevant evaluation or recommendation at the hearing without the consent of the other party.

(3) *Limitations on hearing*

(A) *Person condu cting hearing.* A hearing officer conducting a hearing prusuant to paragraph (1)(A) shall, at a minimum:

(i) not be:

(I) an employee of the State educational agency or the local educational agency involved in the education or care of the child; or

(II) a person having a personal or professional interest that conflicts with the person's objectivity in the hearing;

(ii) possess knowledge of, and the ability to understand, the provisions of this title, Federal and State regulations pertaining to this title, and legal interpretations of this title by Federal and State courts;

(iii) possess the knowledge and ability to conduct hearings in accordance with appropriate, standard legal practice; and

(iv) possess the knowledge and ability to render and write decisions in accordance with appropriate, standard legal practice.

(B) *Subject matter of hearing.* The party requesting the due process hearing shall not be allowed to raise issues at the due process hearing that were not raised in the notice filed under subsection (b)(7), unless the other party agrees otherwise.

(C) *Timeline for requesting hearing.* A parent or agency shall request an impartial due process hearing within 2 years of the date the parent or agency knew or should have known about the alleged action that forms the basis of the complaint, or, if the State has an explicit time limitation for requesting such a hearing under this part, in such time as the State law allows.

(D) *Exceptions to the timeline.* The timeline described in subparagraph (C) shall not apply to a parent if the parent was prevented from requesting the hearing due to:

(i) specific misrepresentations by the local educational agency that it had resolved the problem forming the basis of the complaint; or

(ii) the local educational agency's withholding of information from the parent that was required under this part to be provided to the parent.

(E) *Decision of hearing officer*

(i) *In general.* Subject to clause (ii), a decision made by a hearing officer shall be made on substantive grounds based on a determination of whether the child received a free appropriate public education.

(ii) *Procedural issues.* In matters alleging a procedural violation, a hearing officer may find that a child did not receive a free appropriate public education only if the procedural inadequacies:

(I) impeded the child's right to a free appropriate public education;

(II) significantly impeded the parents' opportunity to participate in the decisionmaking process regarding the provision of a free appropriate public education to the parents' child; or

(III) caused a deprivation of educational benefits.

(iii) *Rule of construction.* Nothing in this subparagraph shall be construed to preclude a hearing officer from ordering a local educational agency to comply with procedural requirements under this section.

(F) *Rule of construction.* Nothing in this paragraph shall be construed to affect the right of a parent to file a complaint with the State educational agency.

(g) Appeal

(1) *In general.* If the hearing required by subsection (f) is conducted by a local educational agency, any party aggrieved by the findings and decision rendered in such a hearing may appeal such findings and decision to the State educational agency.

(2) *Impartial review and independent decision.* The State educational agency shall conduct an impartial review of the

findings and decision appealed under paragraph (1). The officer conducting such review shall make an independent decision upon completion of such review.

(h) Safeguards. Any party to a hearing conducted pursuant to subsection (f) or (k) of this section, or an appeal conducted pursuant to subsection (g) of this section, shall be accorded:

(1) the right to be accompanied and advised by counsel and by individuals with special knowledge or training with respect to the problems of children with disabilities;

(2) the right to present evidence and confront, cross-examine, and compel the attendance of witnesses;

(3) the right to a written, or, at the option of the parents, electronic verbatim record of such hearing; and

(4) the right to written, or, at the option of the parents, electronic findings of fact and decisions:

(A) shall be made available to the public consistent with the requirements of section 617(b) (relating to the confidentiality of data, information, and records); and

(B) shall be transmitted to the advisory panel established pursuant to section 612(a)(21).

(i) Administrative procedures

(1) *In general*

(A) *Decision made in hearing.* A decision made in a hearing conducted pursuant to subsection (f) or (k) of this section shall be final, except that any party involved in such hearing may appeal such decision under the provisions of subsection (g) of this section and paragraph (2).

(B) *Decision made at appeal.* A decision made under subsection (g) of this section shall be final, except that any party may bring an action under paragraph (2).

(2) *Right to bring civil action*

(A) *In general.* Any party aggrieved by the findings and decision made under subsection (f) or (k) of this section who does not have the right to an appeal under subsection (g) of this section, and any party aggrieved by the findings and decision under this subsection, shall have the right to bring a civil action with respect to the complaint presented pursuant to this section, which action may be brought in any State court of competent jurisdiction or in a district court of the United States without regard to the amount in controversy.

(B) *Limitation.* The party bringing the action shall have 90 days from the date of the decision of the hearing officer to bring such an action, or, if the State has an explicit time limitation for bringing such action under this part, in such time as the State law allows.

(C) *Additional requirements.* In any action brought under this paragraph, the court:

(i) shall receive the records of the administrative proceedings;

(ii) shall hear additional evidence at the request of a party; and

(iii) basing its decision on the preponderance of the evidence, shall grant such relief as the court determines is appropriate.

(3) *Jurisdiction of district courts; attorneys' fees*

(A) *In general.* The district courts of the United States shall have jurisdiction of actions brought under this section without regard to the amount in controversy.

(B) *Award of attorneys' fees*

(i) *In general.* In any action or proceeding brought under this section, the court, in its discretion, may award reasonable attorneys' fees as part of the costs:

(I) to a prevailing party who is the parent of a child with a disability;

(II) to a prevailing party who is a State educational agency or local educational agency against the attorney of a parent who files a complaint or subsequent cause of action that is frivolous, unreasonable, or without foundation, or against the attorney of a parent who continued to litigate after the litigation clearly became frivolous, unreasonable, or without foundation; or

(III) to a prevailing State educational agency or local educational agency against the attorney of a parent, or against the parent, if the parent's complaint or subsequent cause of action was presented for any improper purpose, such as to harass, to cause unnecessary delay, or to needlessly increase the cost of litigation.

(ii) *Rule of construction.* Nothing in this subparagraph shall be construed to affect section 327 of the District of Columbia Appropriations Act, 2005.

(C) *Determination of amount of attorneys' fees.* Fees awarded under this paragraph shall be based on rates prevailing in the community in which the action or proceeding arose for the kind and quality of services furnished. No bonus or multiplier may be used in calculating the fees awarded under this subsection.

(D) *Prohibition of attorneys' fees and related costs for certain services*

(i) *In general.* Attorneys' fees may not be awarded and related costs may not be reimbursed in any action or proceeding under this section for services performed subsequent to the time of a written offer of settlement to a parent if:

(I) the offer is made within the time prescribed by Rule 68 of the Federal Rules of Civil Procedure or, in the case of an administrative proceeding, at any time more than 10 days before the proceeding begins;

(II) the offer is not accepted within 10 days; and

(III) the court or administrative hearing officer finds that the relief finally obtained by the parents is not more favorable to the parents than the offer of settlement.

(ii) *IEP Team Meetings.* Attorneys' fees may not be awarded relating to any meeting of the IEP Team unless such meeting is convened as a result of an administrative proceeding or judicial action, or, at the discretion of the State, for a mediation described in subsection (e).

(iii) *Opportunity to resolve complaints.* A meeting conducted pursuant to subsection (f)(1)(B)(i) shall not be considered:

(I) a meeting convened as a result of an administrative hearing or judicial action; or

(II) an administrative hearing or judicial action for purposes of this paragraph.

(E) *Exception to prohibition on attorneys' fees and related costs.* Notwithstanding subparagraph (D), an award of attorneys' fees and related costs may be made to a parent who is the prevailing party and who was substantially justified in rejecting the settlement offer.

(F) *Reduction in amount of attorneys' fees.* Except as provided in subparagraph (G), whenever the court finds that:

(i) the parent, or the parent's attorney, during the course of the action or proceeding, unreasonably protracted the final resolution of the controversy;

(ii) the amount of the attorneys' fees otherwise authorized to be awarded unreasonably exceeds the hourly rate prevailing in the community for similar services by attorneys of reasonably comparable skill, reputation, and experience;

(iii) the time spent and legal services furnished were excessive considering the nature of the action or proceeding; or

(iv) the attorney representing the parent did not provide to the local educational agency the appropriate information in the notice of the complaint described in subsection (b)(7)(A) of this section; the court shall reduce, accordingly, the amount of the attorneys' fees awarded under this section.

(G) *Exception to reduction in amount of attorneys' fees.* The provisions of subparagraph (F) shall not apply in any action or proceeding if the court finds that the State or local educational agency unreasonably protracted the final resolution of the action or proceeding or there was a violation of this section.

(j) Maintenance of current educational placement. Except as provided in subsection (k)(4) of this section, during the pendency of any proceedings conducted pursuant to this section, unless the State or local educational agency and the parents otherwise agree, the child shall remain in the then-current educational placement of the child, or, if applying for initial admission to a public school, shall, with the consent of the parents, be placed in the public school program until all such proceedings have been completed.

(k) Placement in alternative educational setting

(1) *Authority of school personnel*

(A) *Case-by-case determination.* School personnel may consider any unique circumstances on a case-by-case basis when determining whether to order a change in placement for a child with a disability who violates a code of student conduct.

(B) *Authority.* School personnel under this subsection may remove a child with a disability who violates a code of student conduct from their current placement to an appropriate interim alternative educational setting, another setting, or suspension, for not more than 10 school days (to the extent such alternatives are applied to children without disabilities).

(C) *Additional authority.* If school personnel seek to order a change in placement that would exceed 10 school days and the behavior that gave rise to the violation of the school code is determined not to be a manifestation of the child's disability pursuant to subparagraph (E), the relevant disciplinary procedures applicable to children without disabilities may be applied to the child in the same manner and for the same duration in which the procedures would be applied to children without disabilities, except as provided in section 612(a)(1) although it may be provided in an interim alternative educational setting.

(D) *Services.* A child with a disability who is removed from the child's current placement under subparagraph (G) (irrespective of whether the behavior is determined to be a manifestation of the child's disability) or subparagraph (C) shall:

(i) continue to receive educational services, as provided in section 612(a)(1), so as to enable the child to continue to participate in the general education curriculum, although in another setting, and to progress toward meeting the goals set out in the child's IEP; and

(ii) receive, as appropriate, a functional behavioral assessment, behavioral intervention services and modifications, that are designed to address the behavior violation so that it does not recur.

(E) *Manifestation determination.*

(i) *In general.* Except as provided in subparagraph (B), within 10 school days of any decision to change the placement of a child with a disability because of a violation of a code of student conduct, the local educational agency, the parent, and relevant members of the IEP Team (as determined by the parent and the local educational agency) shall review all relevant information in the student's file, including the child's IEP, any teacher observations, and any relevant information provided by the parents to determine—

(I) if the conduct in question was caused by, or had a direct and substantial relationship to, the child's disability; or

(II) if the conduct in question was the direct result of the local educational agency's failure to implement the IEP.

(ii) Manifestation. If the local educational agency, the parent, and relevant members of the IEP Team determine that either subclause (I) or (II) of clause (i) is applicable for the child, the conduct shall be determined to be a manifestation of the child's disability.

(F) *Determination that behavior was a manifestation.* If the local educational agency, the parent, and relevant members of the IEP Team make the determination that the conduct was a manifestation of the child's disability, the IEP Team shall:

(i) conduct a functional behavioral assessment, and implement a behavioral intervention plan for such child, provided that the local educational agency had not conducted such assessment prior to such determination before the behavior that resulted in a change in placement described in subparagraph (C) or (G);

(ii) in the situation where a behavioral intervention plan has been developed, review the behavioral intervention plan if the child already has such a behavioral intervention plan, and modify it, as necessary, to address the behavior; and

(iii) except as provided in subparagraph (G), return the child to the placement from which the child was removed, unless the parent and the local educational agency agree to a change of placement as part of the modification of the behavioral intervention plan.

(G) *Special circumstances.* School personnel may remove a student to an interim alternative educational setting for not more than 45 school days without regard to whether the behavior is determined to be a manifestation of the child's disability, in cases where a child:

(i) carries or possesses a weapon to or at school, on school premises, or to or at a school function under the jurisdiction of a State or local educational agency;

(ii) knowingly possesses or uses illegal drugs, or sells or solicits the sale of a controlled substance, while at school, on school premises, or at a school function under the jurisdiction of a State or local educational agency; or

(iii) has inflicted serious bodily injury upon another person while at school, on school premises, or at a school function under the jurisdiction of a State or local educational agency.

(H) *Notification.* Not later than the date on which the decision to take disciplinary action is made, the local educational agency shall notify the parents of that decision, and of all procedural safeguards accorded under this section.

(2) *Determination of setting.* The interim alternative educational setting in subparagraphs (C) and (G) of paragraph (1) shall be determined by the IEP Team.

(3) *Appeal*

(A) *In general.* The parent of a child with a disability who disagrees with any decision regarding placement, or the manifestation determination under this subsection, or a local educational agency that believes that maintaining the current placement of the child is substantially likely to result in injury to the child or to others, may request a hearing.

(B) *Authority of hearing officer*

(i) *In general.* A hearing officer shall hear, and make a determination regarding, an appeal requested under subparagraph (A).

(ii) *Change of placement order.* In making the determination under clause (i), the hearing officer may order a change in placement of a child with a disability. In such situations, the hearing officer may:

(I) return a child with a disability to the placement from which the child was removed; or

(II) order a change in placement of a child with a disability to an appropriate interim alternative educational setting for not more than 45 school days if the hearing officer determines that maintaining the current placement of such child is substantially likely to result in injury to the child or to others.

(4) *Placement during appeals.* When an appeal under paragraph (3) has been requested by either the parent or the local educational agency:

(A) the child shall remain in the interim alternative educational setting pending the decision of the hearing officer or until the expiration of the time period provided for in paragraph (1)(C), whichever occurs first, unless the parent and the State or local educational agency agree otherwise; and

(B) the State or local educational agency shall arrange for an expedited hearing, which shall occur within 20 school days of the date the hearing is requested and shall result in a determination within 10 school days after the hearing.

(5) *Protections for children not yet eligible for special education and related services*

(A) *In general.* A child who has not been determined to be eligible for special education and related services under this subchapter and who has engaged in behavior that violated a code of student conduct may assert any of the protections provided for in this subchapter if the local educational agency had knowledge (as determined in accordance with this paragraph) that the child was a child with a disability before the behavior that precipitated the disciplinary action occurred.

(B) *Basis of knowledge.* A local educational agency shall be deemed to have knowledge that a child is a child with a disability if:

(i) the parent of the child has expressed concern in writing to supervisory or administrative personnel of the appropriate educational agency, or a teacher of the child, that the child is in need of special education and related services;

(ii) the parent of the child has requested an evaluation of the child pursuant to section 614(a)(1)(B); or

(iii) the teacher of the child, or other personnel of the local educational agency, has expressed specific concerns about a pattern of behavior demonstrated by the child, directly to the director of special education of such agency or to other supervisory personnel of the agency.

(C) *Exception.* A local educational agency shall not be deemed to have knowledge that the child is a child with a disability if the parent of the child has not allowed an evaluation of the child pursuant to section 614 or has refused services under this part or the child has been evaluated and it was determined that the child was not a child with a disability under this part.

(D) *Conditions that apply if no basis of knowledge*

(i) *In general.* If a local educational agency does not have knowledge that a child is a child with a disability (in accordance with subparagraph (B)) prior to taking disciplinary measures against the child, the child may be subjected to disciplinary measures applied to children without disabilities who engaged in comparable behaviors consistent with clause (ii).

(ii) *Limitations.* If a request is made for an evaluation of a child during the time period in which the child is subjected to disciplinary measures under this subsection, the evaluation shall be conducted in an expedited manner. If the child is determined to be a child with a disability, taking into consideration information from the evaluation conducted by the agency and information provided by the parents, the agency shall provide special education and related services in accordance with the provisions of this subchapter, except that, pending the results of the evaluation, the child shall remain in the educational placement determined by school authorities.

(6) *Referral to and action by law enforcement and judicial authorities*

(A) *Rule of construction.* Nothing in this subchapter shall be construed to prohibit an agency from reporting a crime committed by a child with a disability to appropriate authorities or to prevent State law enforcement and judicial authorities from exercising their responsibilities with regard to the application of Federal and State law to crimes committed by a child with a disability.

(B) *Transmittal of records.* An agency reporting a crime committed by a child with a disability shall ensure that copies of the special education and disciplinary records of the child are transmitted for consideration by the appropriate authorities to whom it reports the crime.

(7) *Definitions.* In this subsection:

(A) *Controlled substance.* The term "controlled substance" means a drug or other substance identified under schedule I, II, III, IV, or V in section 202(c) of the Controlled Substances Act (21 U.S.C. 812(c)).

(B) *Illegal drug.* The term "illegal drug" means a controlled substance but does not include a controlled substance that is legally possessed or used under the supervision of a licensed health-care professional or that is legally possessed or used under any other authority under that Act or under any other provision of Federal law.

(C) *Weapon.* The term "weapon" has the meaning given the term "dangerous weapon" under section 930(g)(2) of title 18, United States Code.

(D) *Serious bodily injury.* The term "serious bodily injury" has the meaning given the term "serious bodily injury" under paragraph (3) of subsection (h) of section 1365 of title 18, United States Code.

(l) Rule of construction. Nothing in this chapter shall be construed to restrict or limit the rights, procedures, and remedies available under the Constitution, the Americans with Disabilities Act of 1990 (42 U.S.C. 12101 et seq.), title V of the Rehabilitation Act of 1973 (29 U.S.C. 791 et seq.), or other Federal laws protecting the rights of children with disabilities, except that before the filing of a civil action under such laws seeking relief that is also available under this subchapter, the procedures under subsections (f) and (g) of this section shall be exhausted to the same extent as would be required had the action been brought under this subchapter.

(m) Transfer of parental rights at age of majority

(1) *In general.* A State that receives amounts from a grant under this subchapter may provide that, when a child with a disability reaches the age of majority under State law (except for a child with a disability who has been determined to be incompetent under State law):

(A) the agency shall provide any notice required by this section to both the individual and the parents;

(B) all other rights accorded to parents under this subchapter transfer to the child;

(C) the agency shall notify the individual and the parents of the transfer of rights; and

(D) all rights accorded to parents under this subchapter transfer to children who are incarcerated in an adult or juvenile Federal, State, or local correctional institution.

(2) *Special rule.* If, under State law, a child with a disability who has reached the age of majority under State law, who has not been determined to be incompetent, but who is determined not to have the ability to provide informed consent with respect to the educational program of the child, the State shall establish procedures for appointing the parent of the child, or if the parent is not available, another appropriate individual, to represent the educational interests of the child throughout the period of eligibility of the child under this subchapter.

IDEA Regulations

As this book goes to press, the Department of Education is revising the regulations that interpret IDEA. The department has issued proposed new regulations, but these are only in draft form. The department has asked the public to comment on the proposed regulations; once it receives and considers these comments, and makes any revisions or changes to the proposed regulations it deems necessary, it will issue final

regulations. These final regulations will be legally binding, but the proposed regulations are not.

Until the final regulations are issued, the current IDEA regulations—those that were issued before the 2004 amendments to IDEA—are still in effect, to the extent they are consistent with the 2004 version of the law. Many of the regulations are not expected to change at all (although the citation numbers will change); some will be different, and some new regulations will be issued to address the new material in the 2004 amendments.

To read the current regulations, read the proposed regulations, and find out whether final new regulations have been issued yet, go to the website of the Department of Education's Office of Special Education and Rehabilitative Services, at www.ed.gov/osers.

Section 504 of the Rehabilitation Act of 1973 (Key Regulations)

Part 104—Nondiscrimination on the Basis of Handicap in Programs and Activities Receiving Federal Financial Assistance

Sec. 104.1 Purpose
The purpose of this part is to effectuate section 504 of the Rehabilitation Act of 1973, which is designed to eliminate discrimination on the basis of handicap in any program or activity receiving Federal financial assistance.

Sec. 104.2 Application
This part applies to each recipient of Federal financial assistance from the Department of Education and to each program or activity that receives or benefits from such assistance.

Sec. 104.3 Definitions
As used in this part, the term:

(a) The Act means the Rehabilitation Act of 1973, Pub. L. 93-112, as amended by the Rehabilitation Act Amendments of 1974, Pub. L. 93-516, 29 U.S.C. 794.

(b) Section 504 means section 504 of the Act.

(c) Education of the Handicapped Act means that statute as amended by the Education for all Handicapped Children Act of 1975, Pub. L. 94-142, 20 U.S.C. 1401 et seq.

(d) Department means the Department of Education.

(e) Assistant Secretary means the Assistant Secretary for Civil Rights of the Department of Education.

(f) Recipient means any state or its political subdivision, any instrumentality of a state or its political subdivision, any public or private agency, institution, organization, or other entity, or any person to which Federal financial assistance is extended directly or through another recipient, including any successor, assignee, or transferee of a recipient, but excluding the ultimate beneficiary of the assistance.

(g) Applicant for assistance means one who submits an application, request, or plan required to be approved by a

Department official or by a recipient as a condition to becoming a recipient.

(h) Federal financial assistance means any grant, loan, contract (other than a procurement contract or a contract of insurance or guaranty), or any other arrangement by which the Department provides or otherwise makes available assistance in the form of:

(1) Funds;

(2) Services of Federal personnel; or

(3) Real and personal property or any interest in or use of such property, including:

(i) Transfers or leases of such property for less than fair market value or for reduced consideration; and

(ii) Proceeds from a subsequent transfer or lease of such property if the Federal share of its fair market value is not returned to the Federal Government.

(i) Facility means all or any portion of buildings, structures, equipment, roads, walks, parking lots, or other real or personal property or interest in such property.

(j) Handicapped person—

(1) Handicapped persons means any person who (i) has a physical or mental impairment which substantially limits one or more major life activities, (ii) has a record of such an impairment, or (iii) is regarded as having such an impairment.

(2) As used in paragraph (j)(1) of this section, the phrase:

(i) Physical or mental impairment means (A) any physiological disorder or condition, cosmetic disfigurement, or anatomical loss affecting one or more of the following body systems: neurological; musculoskeletal; special sense organs; respiratory, including speech organs; cardiovascular; reproductive, digestive, genito-urinary; hemic and lymphatic; skin; and endocrine; or (B) any mental or psychological disorder, such as mental retardation, organic brain syndrome, emotional or mental illness, and specific learning disabilities.

(ii) Major life activities means functions such as caring for one's self, performing manual tasks, walking, seeing, hearing, speaking, breathing, learning, and working.

(iii) Has a record of such an impairment means has a history of, or has been misclassified as having, a mental or physical impairment that substantially limits one or more major life activities.

(iv) Is regarded as having an impairment means (A) has a physical or mental impairment that does not substantially limit major life activities but that is treated by a recipient as constituting such a limitation; (B) has a physical or mental impairment that substantially limits major life activities only as a result of the attitudes of others toward such impairment; or (C) has none of the impairments defined in paragraph (j)(2)(i) of this section but is treated by a recipient as having such an impairment.

(k) Qualified handicapped person means:

(1) With respect to employment, a handicapped person who, with reasonable accommodation, can perform the essential functions of the job in question;

(2) With respect to public preschool, elementary, secondary, or adult educational services, a handicappped person (i) of an age during which nonhandicapped persons are provided such services, (ii) of any age during which it is mandatory under state law to provide such services to handicapped persons, or (iii) to whom a state is required to provide a free appropriate public education under section 612 of the Education of the Handicapped Act; and

(3) With respect to postsecondary and vocational education services, a handicapped person who meets the academic and technical standards requisite to admission or participation in the recipient's education program or activity;

(4) With respect to other services, a handicapped person who meets the essential eligibility requirements for the receipt of such services.

(l) Handicap means any condition or characteristic that renders a person a handicapped person as defined in paragraph (j) of this section.

Sec. 104.4 Discrimination prohibited

(a) **General.** No qualified handicapped person shall, on the basis of handicap, be excluded from participation in, be denied the benefits of, or otherwise be subjected to discrimination under any program or activitiy which receives or benefits from Federal financial assistance.

(b) **Discriminatory actions prohibited.** (1) A recipient, in providing any aid, benefit, or service, may not, directly or through contractual, licensing, or other arrangements, on the basis of handicap:

(i) Deny a qualified handicapped person the opportunity to participate in or benefit from the aid, benefit, or service;

(ii) Afford a qualified handicapped person an opportunity to participate in or benefit from the aid, benefit, or service that is not equal to that afforded others;

(iii) Provide a qualified handicapped person with an aid, benefit, or service that is not as effective as that provided to others;

(iv) Provide different or separate aid, benefits, or services to handicapped persons or to any class of handicapped persons unless such action is necessary to provide qualified handicapped persons with aid, benefits, or services that are as effective as those provided to others;

(v) Aid or perpetuate discrimination against a qualified handicapped person by providing significant assistance to an agency, organization, or person that discriminates on the basis of handicap in providing any aid, benefit, or service to beneficiaries of the recipients program;

(vi) Deny a qualified handicapped person the opportunity to participate as a member of planning or advisory boards; or

(vii) Otherwise limit a qualified handicapped person in the enjoyment of any right, privilege, advantage, or opportunity enjoyed by others receiving an aid, benefit, or service.

(2) For purposes of this part, aids, benefits, and services, to be equally effective, are not required to produce the identical result or level of achievement for handicapped and nonhandicapped persons, but must afford handicapped persons equal opportunity to obtain the same result, to gain the same benefit, or to reach the same level of achievement, in the most integrated setting appropriate to the person's needs.

(3) Despite the existence of separate or different programs or activities provided in accordance with this part, a recipient

may not deny a qualified handicapped person the opportunity to participate in such programs or activities that are not separate or different.

(4) A recipient may not, directly or through contractual or other arrangements, utilize criteria or methods of administration (i) that have the effect of subjecting qualified handicapped persons to discrimination on the basis of handicap, (ii) that have the purpose or effect of defeating or substantially impairing accomplishment of the objectives of the recipient's program with respect to handicapped persons, or (iii) that perpetuate the discrimination of another recipient if both recipients are subject to common administrative control or are agencies of the same State.

(5) In determining the site or location of a facility, an applicant for assistance or a recipient may not make selections (i) that have the effect of excluding handicapped persons from, denying them the benefits of, or otherwise subjecting them to discrimination under any program or activity that receives or benefits from Federal financial assistance or (ii) that have the purpose or effect of defeating or substantially impairing the accomplishment of the objectives of the program or activity with respect to handicapped persons.

(6) As used in this section, the aid, benefit, or service provided under a program or activity receiving or benefiting from Federal financial assistance includes any aid, benefit, or service provided in or through a facility that has been constructed, expanded, altered, leased or rented, or otherwise acquired, in whole or in part, with Federal financial assistance.

(c) **Programs limited by Federal law.** The exclusion of nonhandicapped persons from the benefits of a program limited by Federal statute or executive order to handicapped persons or the exclusion of a specific class of handicapped persons from a program limited by Federal statute or executive order to a different class of handicapped persons is not prohibited by this part.

Sec.104.5 Assurances required

(a) **Assurances.** An applicant for Federal financial assistance for a program or activity to which this part applies shall submit an assurance, on a form specified by the Assistant Secretary, that the program will be operated in compliance with this part. An applicant may incorporate these assurances by reference in subsequent applications to the Department.

(b) **Duration of obligation**

(1) In the case of Federal financial assistance extended in the form of real property or to provide real property or structures on the property, the assurance will obligate the recipient or, in the case of a subsequent transfer, the transferee, for the period during which the real property or structures are used for the purpose for which Federal financial assistance is extended or for another purpose involving the provision of similar services or benefits.

(2) In the case of Federal financial assistance extended to provide personal property, the assurance will obligate the recipient for the period during which it retains ownership or possession of the property.

(3) In all other cases the assurance will obligate the recipient for the period during which Federal financial assistance is extended.

(c) **Covenants**

(1) Where Federal financial assistance is provided in the form of real property or interest in the property from the Department, the instrument effecting or recording this transfer shall contain a covenant running with the land to assure nondiscrimination for the period during which the real property is used for a purpose for which the Federal financial assistance is extended or for another purpose involving the provision of similar services or benefits.

(2) Where no transfer of property is involved but property is purchased or improved with Federal financial assistance, the recipient shall agree to include the covenant described in paragraph (b)(2) of this section in the instrument effecting or recording any subsequent transfer of the property.

(3) Where Federal financial assistance is provided in the form of real property or interest in the property from the Department, the covenant shall also include a condition coupled with a right to be reserved by the Department to revert title to the property in the event of a breach of the covenant. If a transferee of real property proposes to mortgage or otherwise encumber the real property as security for financing construction of new, or improvement of existing, facilities on the property for the purposes for which the property was transferred, the Assistant Secretary may, upon request of the transferee and if necessary to accomplish such financing and upon such conditions as he or she deems appropriate, agree to forbear the exercise of such right to revert title for so long as the lien of such mortgage or other encumbrance remains effective.

Sec.104.21 Discrimination prohibited

No qualified handicapped person shall, because a recipient's facilities are inaccessible to or unusable by handicapped persons, be denied the benefits of, be excluded from participation in, or otherwise be subjected to discrimination under any program or activity to which this part applies.

Sec.104.22 Existing facilities

(a) **Program accessibility.** A recipient shall operate each program or activity to which this part applies so that the program or activity, when viewed in its entirety, is readily accessible to handicapped persons. This paragraph does not require a recipient to make each of its existing facilities or every part of a facility accessible to and usable by handicapped persons.

(b) **Methods.** A recipient may comply with the requirements of paragraph (a) of this section through such means as redesign of equipment, reassignment of classes or other services to accessible buildings, assignment of aides to beneficiaries, home visits, delivery of health, welfare, or other social services at alternate accessible sites, alteration of existing facilities and construction of new facilities in conformance with the requirements of Sec. 104.23, or any other methods that result in making its program or activity accessible to handicapped persons. A recipient is not required to make structural changes in existing facilities where other methods are effective in achieving compliance with paragraph (a) of this section. In choosing among available methods for meeting the requirement of paragraph (a) of this section, a recipient shall give priority to those methods that offer programs and activities to handicapped persons in the most integrated setting appropriate.

(c) Small health, welfare, or other social service providers. If a recipient with fewer than fifteen employees that provides health, welfare, or other social services finds, after consultation with a handicapped person seeking its services, that there is no method of complying with paragraph (a) of this section other than making a significant alteration in its existing facilities, the recipient may, as an alternative, refer the handicapped person to other providers of those services that are accessible.

(d) Time period. A recipient shall comply with the requirement of paragraph (a) of this section within sixty days of the effective date of this part except that where structural changes in facilities are necessary, such changes shall be made within three years of the effective date of this part, but in any event as expeditiously as possible.

(e) Transition plan. In the event that structural changes to facilities are necessary to meet the requirement of paragraph (a) of this section, a recipient shall develop, within six months of the effective date of this part, a transition plan setting forth the steps necessary to complete such changes. The plan shall be developed with the assistance of interested persons, including handicapped persons or organizations representing handicapped persons. A copy of the transition plan shall be made available for public inspection. The plan shall, at a minimum:

(1) Identify physical obstacles in the recipient's facilities that limit the accessibility of its program or activity to handicappped persons;

(2) Describe in detail the methods that will be used to make the facilities accessible;

(3) Specify the schedule for taking the steps necessary to achieve full program accessibility and, if the time period of the transition plan is longer than one year, identify the steps of that will be taken during each year of the transition period; and

(4) Indicate the person responsible for implementation of the plan.

(f) Notice. The recipient shall adopt and implement procedures to ensure that interested persons, including persons with impaired vision or hearing, can obtain information as to the existence and location of services, activities, and facilities that are accessible to and usuable by handicapped persons.

Sec.104.23 New construction

(a) Design and construction. Each facility or part of a facility constructed by, on behalf of, or for the use of a recipient shall be designed and constructed in such manner that the facility or part of the facility is readily accessible to and usable by handicapped persons, if the construction was commenced after the effective date of this part.

(b) Alteration. Each facility or part of a facility which is altered by, on behalf of, or for the use of a recipient after the effective date of this part in a manner that affects or could affect the usability of the facility or part of the facility shall, to the maximum extent feasible, be altered in such manner that the altered portion of the facility is readily accessible to and usable by handicapped persons.

(c) Conformance with Uniform Federal Accessibility Standards

(1) Effective as of January 18, 1991, design, construction, or alteration of buildings in conformance with sections 3-8 of the Uniform Federal Accessibility Standards (UFAS) (Appendix A to 41 CFR subpart 101-19.6) shall be deemed to comply with the requirements of this section with respect to those buildings. Departures from particular technical and scoping requirements of UFAS by the use of other methods are permitted where substantially equivalent or greater access to and usability of the building is provided.

(2) For purposes of this section, section 4.1.6(1)(g) of UFAS shall be interpreted to exempt from the requirements of UFAS only mechanical rooms and other spaces that, because of their intended use, will not require accessibility to the public or beneficiaries or result in the employment or residence therein of persons with physical handicaps.

(3) This section does not require recipients to make building alterations that have little likelihood of being accomplished without removing or altering a load-bearing structural member. [45 FR 30936, May 9, 1980; 45 FR 37426, June 3, 1980, as amended at 55 FR 52138, 52141, Dec. 19, 1990]

Subpart D—Preschool, Elementary, and Secondary Education

Sec.104.31 Application of this subpart

Subpart D applies to preschool, elementary, secondary, and adult education programs and activities that receive or benefit from Federal financial assistance and to recipients that operate, or that receive or benefit from Federal financial assistance for the operation of, such programs or activities.

Sec.104.32 Location and notification

A recipient that operates a public elementary or secondary education program shall annually:

(a) Undertake to identify and locate every qualified handicapped person residing in the recipient's jurisdiction who is not receiving a public education; and

(b) Take appropriate steps to notify handicapped persons and their parents or guardians of the recipient's duty under this subpart.

Sec.104.33 Free appropriate public education

(a) General. A recipient that operates a public elementary or secondary education program shall provide a free appropriate public education to each qualified handicapped person who is in the recipient's jurisdiction, regardless of the nature or severity of the person's handicap.

(b) Appropriate education

(1) For the purpose of this subpart, the provision of an appropriate education is the provision of regular or special education and related aids and services that (i) are designed to meet individual educational needs of handicapped persons as adequately as the needs of nonhandicapped persons are met

and (ii) are based upon adherence to procedures that satisfy the requirements of Secs. 104.34, 104.35, and 104.36.

(2) Implementation of an individualized education program developed in accordance with the Education of the Handicapped Act is one means of meeting the standard established in paragraph (b)(1)(i) of this section.

(3) A recipient may place a handicapped person in or refer such person to a program other than the one that it operates as its means of carrying out the requirements of this subpart. If so, the recipient remains responsible for ensuring that the requirements of this subpart are met with respect to any handicapped person so placed or referred.

(c) Free education—

(1) *General.* For the purpose of this section, the provision of a free education is the provision of educational and related services without cost to the handicapped person or to his or her parents or guardian, except for those fees that are imposed on non-handicapped persons or their parents or guardian. It may consist either of the provision of free services or, if a recipient places a handicapped person in or refers such person to a program not operated by the recipient as its means of carrying out the requirements of this subpart, of payment for the costs of the program. Funds available from any public or private agency may be used to meet the requirements of this subpart. Nothing in this section shall be construed to relieve an insurer or similar third party from an otherwise valid obligation to provide or pay for services provided to a handicapped person.

(2) *Transportation.* If a recipient places a handicapped person in or refers such person to a program not operated by the recipient as its means of carrying out the requirements of this subpart, the recipient shall ensure that adequate transportation to and from the program is provided at no greater cost than would be incurred by the person or his or her parents or guardian if the person were placed in the program operated by the recipient.

(3) *Residential placement.* If placement in a public or private residential program is necessary to provide a free appropriate public education to a handicapped person because of his or her handicap, the program, including non-medical care and room and board, shall be provided at no cost to the person or his or her parents or guardian.

(4) *Placement of handicapped persons by parents.* If a recipient has made available, in conformance with the requirements of this section and Sec. 104.34, a free appropriate public education to a handicapped person and the person's parents or guardian choose to place the person in a private school, the recipient is not required to pay for the person's education in the private school. Disagreements between a parent or guardian and a recipient regarding whether the recipient has made such a program available or otherwise regarding the question of financial responsibility are subject to the due process procedures of Sec. 104.36

(d) Compliance. A recipient may not exclude any qualified handicapped person from a public elementary or secondary education after the effective date of this part. A recipient that is not, on the effective date of this regulation, in full compliance with the other requirements of the preceding paragraphs

of this section shall meet such requirements at the earliest practicable time and in no event later than September 1, 1978.

Sec. 104.34 Educational setting

(a) Academic setting. A recipient to which this subpart applies shall educate, or shall provide for the education of, each qualified handicapped person in its jurisdiction with persons who are not handicapped to the maximum extent appropriate to the needs of the handicapped person. A recipient shall place a handicapped person in the regular educational environment operated by the recipient unless it is demonstrated by the recipient that the education of the person in the regular environment with the use of supplementary aids and services cannot be achieved satisfactorily. Whenever a recipient places a person in a setting other than the regular educational environment pursuant to this paragraph, it shall take into account the proximity of the alternate setting to the person's home.

(b) Nonacademic settings. In providing or arranging for the provision of nonacademic and extracurricular services and activities, including meals, recess periods, and the services and activities set forth in Sec. 104.37(a)(2), a recipient shall ensure that handicapped persons participate with nonhandicapped persons in such activities and services to the maximum extent appropriate to the needs of the handicapped person in question.

(c) Comparable facilities. If a recipient, in compliance with paragraph (a) of this section, operates a facility that is identifiable as being for handicapped persons, the recipient shall ensure that the facility and the services and activities provided therein are comparable to the other facilities, services, and activities of the recipient.

Sec. 104.35 Evaluation and placement

(a) Preplacement evaluation. A recipient that operates a public elementary or secondary education program shall conduct an evaluation in accordance with the requirements of paragraph (b) of this section of any person who, because of handicap, needs or is believed to need special education or related services before taking any action with respect to the initial placement of the person in a regular or special education program and any subsequent significant change in placement.

(b) Evaluation procedures. A recipient to which this subpart applies shall establish standards and procedures for the evaluation and placement of persons who, because of handicap, need or are believed to need special education or related services which ensure that:

(1) Tests and other evaluation materials have been validated for the specific purpose for which they are used and are administered by trained personnel in conformance with the instructions provided by their producer;

(2) Tests and other evaluation materials include those tailored to assess specific areas of educational need and not merely those which are designed to provide a single general intelligence quotient; and

(3) Tests are selected and administered so as best to ensure that, when a test is administered to a student with impaired sensory, manual, or speaking skills, the test results accurately

reflect the student's aptitude or achievement level or whatever other factor the test purports to measure, rather than reflecting the student's impaired sensory, manual, or speaking skills (except where those skills are the factors that the test purports to measure).

(c) Placement procedures. In interpreting evaluation data and in making placement decisions, a recipient shall (1) draw upon information from a variety of sources, including aptitude and achievement tests, teacher recommendations, physical condition, social or cultural background, and adaptive behavior, (2) establish procedures to ensure that information obtained from all such sources is documented and carefully considered, (3) ensure that the placement decision is made by a group of persons, including persons knowledgeable about the child, the meaning of the evaluation data, and the placement options, and (4) ensure that the placement decision is made in conformity with Sec. 104.34.

(d) Reevaluation. A recipient to which this section applies shall establish procedures, in accordance with paragraph (b) of this section, for periodic reevaluation of students who have been provided special education and related services. A reevaluation procedure consistent with the Education for the Handicapped Act is one means of meeting this requirement.

Sec. 104.36 Procedural safeguards

A recipient that operates a public elementary or secondary education program shall establish and implement, with respect to actions regarding the identification, evaluation, or educational placement of persons who, because of handicap, need or are believed to need special instruction or related services, a system of procedural safeguards that includes notice, an opportunity for the parents or guardian of the person to examine relevant records, an impartial hearing with opportunity for participation by the person's parents or guardian and representation by counsel, and a review procedure. Compliance with the procedural safeguards of section 615 of the Education of the Handicapped Act is one means of meeting this requirement.

Sec. 104.37 Nonacademic services

(a) General

(1) A recipient to which this subpart applies shall provide nonacademic and extracurricular services and activities in such manner as is necessary to afford handicapped students an equal opportunity for participation in such services and activities.

(2) Nonacademic and extracurricular services and activities may include counseling services, physical recreational athletics, transportation, health services, recreational activities, special interest groups or clubs sponsored by the recipients, referrals to agencies which provide assistance to handicapped persons, and employment of students, including both employment by the recipient and assistance in making available outside employment.

(b) Counseling services. A recipient to which this subpart applies that provides personal, academic, or vocational counseling, guidance, or placement services to its students shall provide these services without discrimination on the basis of handicap. The recipient shall ensure that qualified handicapped students are not counseled toward more restrictive career objectives than are nonhandicapped students with similar interests and abilities.

(c) Physical education and athletics

(1) In providing physical education courses and athletics and similar programs and activities to any of its students, a recipient to which this subpart applies may not discriminate on the basis of handicap. A recipient that offers physical education courses or that operates or sponsors interscholastic, club, or intramural athletics shall provide to qualified handicapped students an equal opportunity for participation in these activities.

(2) A recipient may offer to handicapped students physical education and athletic activities that are separate or different from those offered to nonhandicapped students only if separation or differentiation is consistent with the requirements of Sec. 104.34 and only if no qualified handicapped student is denied the opportunity to compete for teams or to participate in courses that are not separate or different.

Sec. 104.38 Preschool and adult education programs

A recipient to which this subpart applies that operates a preschool education or day care program or activity or an adult education program or activity may not, on the basis of handicap, exclude qualified handicapped persons from the program or activity and shall take into account the needs of such persons in determining the aid, benefits, or services to be provided under the program or activity.

Sec.104.39 Private education programs

(a) A recipient that operates a private elementary or secondary education program may not, on the basis of handicap, exclude a qualified handicapped person from such program if the person can, with minor adjustments, be provided an appropriate education, as defined in Sec. 104.33(b)(1), within the recipient's program

(b) A recipient to which this section applies may not charge more for the provision of an appropriate education to handicapped persons than to nonhandicapped persons except to the extent that any additional charge is justified by a substantial increase in cost to the recipient.

(c) A recipient to which this section applies that operates special education programs shall operate such programs in accordance with the provisions of Secs. 104.35 and 104.36. Each recipient to which this section applies is subject to the provisions of Secs. 104.34, 104.37, and 104.38. ■

Appendix 2

Federal and State Departments of Education

Federal Department of Education Offices

The federal Department of Education, Office of Special Education, has the responsibility to ensure that all states meet the requirements of IDEA. For information on IDEA, contact the DOE at:

> U.S. Department of Education
> Office of Special Education and Rehabilitation
>   Services
> 400 Maryland Avenue, SW
> Washington, DC 20202
> 202-205-7468 (voice)
> www.ed.gov/osers

The federal Department of Education, Office for Civil Rights, is one place to file a complaint for IDEA violations. You can contact any of the following OCR offices.

Main Office

> U.S. Department of Education
> Office for Civil Rights
> 550 12th Street, SW
> Washington, DC 20202
> 800-421-3481 (voice)
> 877-521-2172 (TDD)
> 202-205-9862 (fax)
> www.ed.gov/ocr

Connecticut, Maine, Massachusetts, New Hampshire, Rhode Island, Vermont

> U.S. Department of Education
> Office for Civil Rights
> J. W. McCormack Post Office and Courthouse
> Room 701, 01-0062
> Boston, MA 02109
> 617-223-9662 (voice)
> 617-223-9695 (TDD)
> 617-223-9669 (fax)

New Jersey, New York

> U.S. Department of Education
> Office for Civil Rights
> 32 Old Slip, 26th Floor
> New York, NY 10005
> 646-428-3900 (voice)
> 212-637-0478 (TDD)
> 646-428-3890 (fax)

Delaware, Kentucky, Maryland, Pennsylvania, West Virginia

> U.S. Department of Education
> Office for Civil Rights
> 100 Penn Square East, Suite 515
> Philadelphia, PA 19107
> 215-656-8541 (voice)
> 215-656-8604 (TDD)
> 215-656-8605 (fax)

Alabama, Florida, Georgia, Tennessee

> Office for Civil Rights, Atlanta Office
> U.S. Department of Education
> 61 Forsyth Street SW, Suite 19T70
> Atlanta, GA 30303
> 404-562-6350 (voice)
> 404-331-7236 (TDD)
> 404-562-6455 (fax)

Arkansas, Louisiana, Mississippi, Texas

> U.S. Department of Education
> Office for Civil Rights
> 1999 Bryan Street, Suite 1620
> Dallas, TX 75201
> 214-661-9600 (voice)
> 214-880-2456 (TDD)
> 214-661-9587 (fax)

District of Columbia, North Carolina, South Carolina, Virginia

> U.S. Department of Education
> Office for Civil Rights
> 1100 Pennsylvania Avenue, NW, Rm. 316
> P.O. Box 14620
> Washington, DC 20044
> 202-208-2545 (voice)
> 202-208-7741 (TDD)
> 202-208-7797 (fax)

Illinois, Indiana, Iowa, Minnesota, North Dakota, Wisconsin

U.S. Department of Education
Office for Civil Rights
111 North Canal Street, Suite 1053
Chicago, IL 60606
312-886-8434 (voice)
312-353-2540 (TDD)
312-353-4888 (fax)

Michigan, Ohio

U.S. Department of Education
Office for Civil Rights
600 Superior Avenue East, Room 750
Cleveland, OH 44114
216-522-4970 (voice)
216-522-4944 (TDD)
216-522-2573 (fax)

Kansas, Missouri, Nebraska, Oklahoma, South Dakota

U.S. Department of Education
Office for Civil Rights
8930 Ward Parkway, Suite 2037
Kansas City, MO 64114
816-268-0550 (voice)
800-437-0833 (TDD)
816-823-1404 (fax)

Arizona, Colorado, New Mexico, Utah, Wyoming

U.S. Department of Education
Office for Civil Rights
Federal Building, Suite 310
1244 Speer Boulevard
Denver, CO 80204
303-844-5695 (voice)
303-844-3417 (TDD)
303-844-4303 (fax)

California

U.S. Department of Education
Office for Civil Rights
Old Federal Building
50 United Nations Plaza, Room 239
San Francisco, CA 94102
415-556-4275 (voice)
415-437-7786 (TDD)
415-437-7783 (fax)

Alaska, Hawaii, Idaho, Montana, Nevada, Oregon, Washington

U.S. Department of Education
Office for Civil Rights
915 Second Avenue, Room 3310
Seattle, WA 98174
206-220-7900 (voice)
206-220-7907 (TDD)
206-220-7887 (fax)

State Department of Education Offices

Your state department of education is the place to go to find legislation, curriculum material, or information on state special education programs as well as information about the IDEA and its requirements.

Alabama

Alabama Department of Education
Division of Special Education Services
(Gordon Persons Building)
P.O. Box 302101
Montgomery, AL 36130
334-242-8114 (voice)
334-242-9192 (fax)
www.alsde.edu/html

Alaska

Alaska Department of Education
Teaching and Learning Support
801 West 10th Street, Suite 200
Juneau, AK 99801
907-465-8693 (voice)
907-465-2806 (fax)
www.eed.state.ak.us

Arizona

Arizona Department of Education
Exceptional Student Services
1535 West Jefferson Street
Phoenix, AZ 85007
602-364-4000 (voice)
602-542-5404 (fax)
www.ade.az.us

Arkansas

Arkansas Department of Education
Special Education
Victory Building
1401 West Capitol Avenue, Suite 450
Little Rock, AR 72201
501-682-4221 (voice)
501-682-5159 (fax)
http://arkedu.state.ar.us

California

California Department of Education
Special Education Division
1430 N Street
Sacramento, CA 95814
916-445-4613 (voice)
916-327-3516 (fax)
www.cde.ca.gov

Colorado

Colorado Department of Education
Special Education Services Unit
201 East Colfax Avenue, Room 300
Denver, CO 80203
303-866-6694 (voice)
303-866-6811 (fax)
www.cde.state.co.us

Connecticut

Connecticut Department of Education
Bureau of Special Education and Pupil Services
P.O. Box 2219
Hartford, CT 06145
860-713-6910 (voice)
860-713-7153 (fax)
www.state.ct.us/sde

Delaware

Delaware Department of Education
Exceptional Children and Early Childhood
   Education
Townsend Building
P.O. Box 1402
Dover, DE 19903
302-739-4667 (voice)
302-739-2388 (fax)
www.doe.state.de.us

District of Columbia

District of Columbia
Division of Special Education
825 North Capitol Street, NE
Washington, DC 20002
202-471-4272 (voice)
202-442-5117 (fax)
www.K12.dc.us

Florida

Florida Department of Education
Bureau of Exceptional Education and Student
  Services
325 West Gaines Street
Tallahassee, FL 32399
850-245-0475 (voice)
850-921-8246 (fax)
www.fldoe.org

Georgia

Georgia Department of Education
Division for Exceptional Students
1870 Twin Towers East
Atlanta, GA 30334
404-656-3963 (voice)
404-651-6457 (fax)
www.doe.k12.ga.us

Hawaii

Hawaii Department of Education
Special Education Section
Building C, Room 102
637 18th Avenue
Honolulu, HI 96816
808-733-4400 (voice)
808-733-4841 (fax)
www.doe.k12.hi.us

Idaho

Idaho Department of Education
Bureau of Special Education
P.O. Box 83720
Boise, ID 83720
208-332-6910 (voice)
208-334-4664 (fax)
www.sde.state.id.us

Illinois

Illinois State Board of Education
Office of Special Education
100 North First Street
Springfield, IL 62777
217-782-5589 (voice)
217-782-0372 (fax)
www.isbe.state.il.us

Indiana

Indiana Department of Education
Division of Exceptional Learners
Room 229, State House
Indianapolis, IN 46204
317-232-0570 (voice)
317-232-0589 (fax)
www.doe.state.in.us

Iowa

Iowa Department of Education
Bureau of Children, Family and Community
  Services
Grimes State Office Building
Des Moines, IA 50319
515-281-3176 (voice)
515-242-6019 (fax)
www.state.ia.us/educate

Kansas

Kansas State Board of Education
Student Support Services
120 Southeast Tenth Avenue
Topeka, KS 66612
785-291-3097 (voice)
785-296-6715 (fax)
www.ksde.org

Kentucky

Kentucky Department of Education
Division of Exceptional Children Services
500 Mero Street, Eighth Floor
Frankfort, KY 40601
502-564-4970 (voice)
502-564-7371 (fax)
www.kde.state.ky.us

Louisiana

Louisiana Department of Education
Division of Special Populations
P.O. Box 94064
Baton Rouge, LA 70804
225-342-3633 (voice)
225-342-6965 (fax)
www.doe.state.la.us

Maine

Maine Department of Education
Office of Special Services
111 Sewall Street
Augusta, ME 04333
207-624-6650 (voice)
207-624-6651 (fax)
www.state.me.us/education

Maryland

Maryland State Department of Education
Division of Special Education
200 West Baltimore Street, 4th Floor
Baltimore, MD 21201
410-767-0261 (voice)
410-333-8165 (fax)
www.msde.state.md.us

Massachusetts

Massachusetts Department of Education
Director of Special Education
350 Main Street
Malden, MA 02148
781-338-3375 (voice)
781-338-3396 (fax)
www.doe.mass.edu

Michigan

Michigan Department of Education
Office of Special Education
608 West Allegan Street
Lansing, MI 48933
517-373-0923 (voice)
517-373-7504 (fax)
www.michigan.gov/mde

Minnesota

Minnesota Department of Education
Department of Children, Families and Learning
1500 Highway 36 West
Roseville, MN 55113
651-582-8200 (voice)
651-582-8729 (fax)
http://cfl.state.mn.us

Mississippi

Mississippi Department of Education
Office of Special Education
Central High School Building, Suite 335
Jackson, MS 39205
601-359-3498 (voice)
601-359-1829 (fax)
www.mde.k12.ms.us

Missouri

Missouri Department of Elementary and Secondary
  Education
Division of Special Education
P.O. Box 480
Jefferson City, MO 65102
573-751-5739 (voice)
573-526-4404 (fax)
www.dese.state.mo.us

Montana

Montana Office of Public Instruction
Division of Special Education
P.O. Box 202501
Helena, MT 59620
406-444-4429 (voice)
406-444-3924 (fax)
www.opi.state.mt.us

Nebraska

Nebraska Department of Education
Special Populations Office
P.O. Box 94987
301 Centennial Mall South
Lincoln, NE 68509
402-471-2295 (voice)
402-471-5022 (fax)
www.nde.state.ne.us

Nevada

Nevada Department of Education
Office of Special Education
700 East 5th Street
Carson City, NV 89701
775-687-9142 (voice)
775-687-9123 (fax)
www.doe.nv.gov

New Hampshire

New Hampshire Department of Education
Bureau for Special Education Services
101 Pleasant Street
Concord, NH 03301
603-271-3494 (voice)
603-271-1953 (fax)
www.ed.state.nh.us

New Jersey

New Jersey Department of Education
Office of Special Education Programs
P.O. Box 500
Trenton, NJ 08625
609-633-6833 (voice)
609-984-8422 (fax)
www.state.nj.us/education

New Mexico

New Mexico Public Education Department
Special Education Bureau
300 Don Gaspar Avenue
Sante Fe, NM 87501
505-827-1457 (voice)
505-954-0001 (fax)
www.ped.state.nm.us

New York

New York State Education Department
Office of Vocational and Educational Services for
  Individuals With Disabilities
One Commerce Plaza, Room 1624
Albany, NY 12234
518-474-2714 (voice)
518-474-8802 (fax)
http://usny.nysed.gov

North Carolina

North Carolina Department of Public Instruction
Division of Exceptional Children
6356 Mail Service Center
Raleigh, NC 27699
919-807-3969 (voice)
919-807-3243 (fax)
www.ncpublicschools.org

North Dakota

North Dakota Department of Public Instruction
Office of Special Education
600 East Boulevard Avenue, Dept. 201
Bismarck, ND 58505
701-328-2277 (voice)
701-328-4149 (fax)
www.dpi.state.nd.us

Ohio

Ohio Department of Education
Office for Exceptional Children
25 South Front Street
Columbus, OH 43215
614-466-2650 (voice)
614-728-1097 (fax)
www.ode.state.oh.us

Oklahoma

Oklahoma Department of Education
Special Education Services
2500 North Lincoln Boulevard
Oklahoma City, OK 73105
405-521-3301 (voice)
405-521-6205 (fax)
www.sde.state.ok.us

Oregon

Oregon Department of Education
Office of Special Education
255 Capitol Street, NE
Salem, OR 97310
503-378-3569 (voice)
503-378-5156 (fax)
www.ode.state.or.us

Pennsylvania

Pennsylvania Department of Education
Bureau of Special Education
333 Market Street, 7th Floor
Harrisburg, PA 17126
717-783-6913 (voice)
717-783-6139 (fax)
www.pde.state.pa.us

Rhode Island

Rhode Island Department of Education
Office of Special Needs
255 Westminster Street
Providence, RI 02903
401-222-3505 (voice)
401-222-6030 (fax)
www.ridoe.net

South Carolina

South Carolina Department of Education
Office of Exceptional Children
Rutledge Building 808
1429 Senate Street
Columbia, SC 29201
803-734-8224 (voice)
803-734-4824 (fax)
www.myscschools.com

South Dakota

South Dakota Department of Education
Office of Special Education
700 Governors Drive
Pierre, SD 57501
605-773-3678 (voice)
605-773-3782 (fax)
http://doe.sd.gov

Tennessee

Tennessee Department of Education
Division of Special Education
Andrew Johnson Tower, 5th Floor
710 James Robertson Parkway
Nashville, TN 37243
615-741-2851 (voice)
615-532-9412 (fax)
www.state.tn.us/education

Texas

Texas Education Agency
Division of Special Education
1701 North Congress Avenue
Austin, TX 78701
512-463-9414 (voice)
512-463-9560 (fax)
www.tea.state.tx.us

Utah

Utah State Office of Education
At-Risk and Special Education Services
P.O. Box 144200
250 East 500 South
Salt Lake City, UT 84114
801-538-7587 (voice)
801-538-7991 (fax)
www.usoe.k12.ut.us

Vermont

Vermont Department of Education
Student Support Services
State Office Building
120 State Street
Montpelier, VT 05620
802-828-2755 (voice)
802-828-0573 (fax)
www.state.vt.us/educ

Virginia

Virginia Department of Education
Division of Special Education & Student Services
P.O. Box 2120
Richmond, VA 23218
804-225-3252 (voice)
800-292-3820 (voice)
804-371-8796 (fax)
www.doe.virginia.gov

Washington

Washington Department of Public Instruction
Special Education Section
P.O. Box 47200
Olympia, WA 98504
360-725-6075 (voice)
360-586-0247 (fax)
www.k12.wa.us

West Virginia

West Virginia Department of Education
Office of Special Education
Building #6
1900 Kanawha Boulevard East, Room 304
Charleston, WV 25305
304-558-2696 (voice)
304-558-3741 (fax)
http://wvde.state.wv.us

Wisconsin

Wisconsin Department of Public Instruction
Division for Learning Support
P.O. Box 7841
125 South Webster Street
Madison, WI 53707
608-266-1781 (voice)
608-267-3746 (fax)
www.dpi.state.wi.us

Wyoming

Wyoming Department of Education
Special Programs Unit
Hathaway Building
2300 Capitol Avenue, 2nd Floor
Cheyenne, WY 82002
307-777-7417 (voice)
307-777-6221 (fax)
www.k12.wy.us

■

Appendix **3**

Support Groups, Advocacy Organizations, and Other Resources

General Resources on Special Education

Adapted Physical Education National Standards

SUNY Cortland
E224 Park Center
P.O. Box 2000
Cortland, NY 13045
888-APENS-EXAM (voice)
www.cortland.edu/APENS

Ensures that physical education instruction is provided for students with disabilities by qualified physical education instructors. The project has developed national standards for the profession and a national certification examination to measure knowledge of these standards.

American Council on Rural Special Education

Utah State University
2865 Old Main Hill
Logan, UT 84322-2865
435-797-3728 (voice)
http://extension.usu.edu/acres

Provides support and information to families of special education children living in rural America. ACRES publishes a national journal called the *Rural Special Education Quarterly*, and maintains an archive of article abstracts on its website. ACRES also publishes a bimonthly newsletter called "RuraLink."

Disability Resources Monthly

www.disabilityresources.org

Offers a monthly newsletter and many articles on disabilities. Provides numerous links to other Internet resources.

Education Development Center, Inc.

55 Chapel Street
Newton, MA 02458
617-969-7100 (voice)
617-964-5448 (TTY)
617-969-5979 (fax)
www.edc.org

Promotes the effective use of technology to enhance education for students with sensory, cognitive, physical, and social/emotional disabili-

ties, and offers articles and information on assistive technologies. The Center also has offices in New York and the District of Columbia—check their website for more information.

Family Fun

http://familyfun.go.com

An Internet site affiliated with Disney. Among other things, you can find articles on special education and children with disabilities.

Family Education Network

20 Park Plaza, 12th Floor
Boston, MA 02116
617-542-6500
http://familyeducation.com

Includes information on learning disabilities and children with special needs. Website features include a monthly column by a special education lawyer, "Ask the Expert"—what their expert has to say about learning issues, resources, and special education news.

Federal Resource Center for Special Education

1825 Connecticut Avenue, NW
Washington, DC 20009
202-884-8215 (voice)
202-884-8443 (fax)
202-884-8200 (TTY)
www.dssc.org/frc

Supports a nationwide special education technical assistance network (funded by the U.S. Department of Education's Office of Special Education and Rehabilitative Services), plans national meetings of education professionals, and links Regional Resource and Federal Centers with each other and with other technical assistance providers. The website includes the text of certain federal regulations, a list of links to disability organizations, publications (including the RRFC Links Online Newsletter), and proceedings of certain government conferences.

Internet Resources for Special Children

www.irsc.org

An Internet site that provides lists of links relating to the needs of children with disabilities for parents, family members, caregivers, friends, educators, and medical professionals. Categories are extensive, including almost every possible disability affecting children.

National Early Childhood Technical Assistance Center

Campus Box 8040,UNC-CH
Chapel Hill, NC 27599
919-962-2001 (voice)
919-843-3269 (TDD)
919-966-7463 (fax)
www.nectac.org

A program of the Child Development Center at the University of North Carolina at Chapel Hill, geared towards younger children (through age five). NECTAC has resources on childhood disabilities, the text of IDEA, and descriptions of programs developed under IDEA.

National Dissemination Center for Children With Disabilities

P.O. Box 1492
Washington, DC 20013
800-695-0285 (voice/TTY)
202-884-8441 (fax)
www.nichcy.org

Provides information on disabilities and disability-related issues for families, educators, and other professionals. The website contains contact information for local disability organizations, lists of disability organizations and government agencies by state, publications, and information on various disability topics, including how to prepare children with disabilities to make the transition from high school to the adult world.

School Psychology Resources Online

www.schoolpsychology.net

An Internet site with information on learning disabilities, ADHD, gifted children, autism, adolescence, parenting, psychological assessment, classroom management, and more. You can download handouts aimed at parents and teachers.

Special Education Resources From the Curry School of Education at University of Virginia

P.O. Box 400260
Charlottesville, VA 22904-4260
434-924-3334 (voice)
434-924-0747 (fax)
http://curry.edschool.virginia.edu/sped/projects/ose

This site offers information for parents and teachers on special education, including articles on learning disabilities and links to special education organizations and websites.

Special Education Resources on the Internet

www.seriweb.com

A collection of Internet-accessible information in the field of special education, including material on disabilities (including learning disabilities and ADD), transition resources, technology, and more.

TASH

29 West Susquehanna Avenue, Suite 210
Baltimore, MD 21204
410-828-8274 (voice)
www.tash.org

Provides information on current trends and issues in the field of disabilities, organizes conferences and workshops, advocates for legislative changes, distributes publications and videos, and disseminates information through electronic media.

Technical Perspectives, Inc.

1411 East Campbell Road, Suite 1900
Richardson, TX 75081
800-594-3779 (voice)
www.classplus.com/classplus

Publishes a software program called Classplus, which you can use to create an Individual Education Plan (IEP). Classplus allows you to develop comprehensive curricula, goals, and objectives for every subject and functional assessments.

On the website, you can see sample reports containing goals, sample progress reports, and IEP forms.

Parent Training and Information (PTI) Centers

The U.S. Department of Education, Office of Special Education Programs, funds organized parent-to-parent programs. The work is done locally through programs known as Parent Training and Information (PTI) Centers. PTI Centers enable parents to participate more effectively with professionals in meeting the educational needs of children with disabilities. You can contact a local PTI for information; PTI online information is available through the Department of Education's website.

Alabama

Special Education Action Committee, Inc.
P.O. Box 161274
Mobile, AL 36609
251-478-1208 (voice/TTY)
800-222-7322 (voice—Alabama only)
251-473-7877 (fax)

Alaska

PARENTS, Inc.
4743 East Northern Lights Boulevard
Anchorage, AK 99508
907-337-7678 (voice)
800-478-7678 (voice—Alaska only)
907-337-7629 (TTY)
907-337-7671 (fax)
www.parentsinc.org

Arizona

Pilot Parents of Southern Arizona
2600 North Wyatt Drive
Tucson, AZ 85712
520-324-3150 (voice)
877-365-7220 (voice)
520-324-3152 (fax)
www.pilotparents.org

Raising Special Kids
2400 North Central Avenue, Suite 200
Phoenix, AZ 85004
602-242-4366 (voice/TTY)
800-237-3007 (voice—Arizona only)
602-242-4306 (fax)
www.raisingspecialkids.org

Arkansas

Arkansas Disability Coalition
1123 South University Drive, Suite 225
Little Rock, AR 72204
501-614-7020 (voice/TTY)
800-223-1330 (voice—Arkansas only)
501-614-9082 (fax)
www.adcpti.org

FOCUS, Inc.
2809 Forest Home Road
Jonesboro, AR 72401
870-935-2750 (voice)
877-247-3843 (voice—Arkansas only)
870-931-3755 (fax)

California

Exceptional Parents Unlimited
4440 North First Street
Fresno, CA 93726
559-229-2000 (voice)
559-225-6059 (TTY)
559-229-2956 (fax)
www.exceptionalparents.org

Matrix: A Parent Network and Resource Center
94 Galli Drive, Suite C
Novato, CA 94949
415-884-3535 (voice)
415-884-3555 (fax)
www.matrixparents.org

Parents Helping Parents, Inc.
3041 Olcott Street
Santa Clara, CA 95054
408-727-5775 (voice)
866-747-4040 (voice)
408-727-0182 (fax)
www.php.com

Parents Helping Parents
4752 Mission Street, Suite 100
San Francisco, CA 94112
415-841-8820 (voice)
415-841-8824 (fax)

Rowell Family Empowerment of Northern California
1244-B Hartnell Avenue
Redding, CA 96002
530-226-5129 (voice)
877-227-3471 (voice)
530-226-5141 (fax)
www.rfenc.org

Support for Families of Children With Disabilities
2601 Mission Street, Suite 606
San Francisco, CA 94110
415-282-7494 (voice)
415-282-1226 (fax)
www.supportforfamilies.org

Team of Advocates for Special Kids, Inc. (TASK)
4550 Kearney Villa Road
San Diego, CA 92123
858-874-2386 (voice)
858-874-0123 (fax)
www.taskca.org

Team of Advocates for Special Kids, Inc. (TASK)
100 West Cerritos Avenue
Anaheim, CA 92805
714-533-8275 (voice)
866-828-8275 (voice—California only)
714-533-2533 (fax)
www.taskca.org

Colorado

PEAK Parent Center, Inc.
611 North Weber, Suite 200
Colorado Springs, CO 80903
719-531-9400 (voice)
800-284-0251 (voice)
719-531-9403 (TTY)
719-531-9452 (fax)
www.peakparent.org

Connecticut

Connecticut Parent Advocacy Center, Inc.
338 Main Street
Niantic, CT 06357
860-739-3089 (voice/TDD)
800-445-2722 (voice—Connecticut only)
860-739-7460 (fax)
www.cpacinc.org

Delaware

Parent Information Center
5570 Kirkwood Highway
Wilmington, DE 19808
302-999-7394 (voice)
888-547-4412 (voice—Delaware only)
302-999-7637 (fax)
www.picofdel.org

District of Columbia

Advocates for Justice and Education, Inc.
2041 MLK Avenue, SE, Suite 205
Washington, DC 20020
202-678-8060 (voice)
888-327-8060 (voice)
202-678-8062 (fax)
www.aje-dc.org

Florida

Family Network on Disabilities
2735 Whitney Road
Clearwater, FL 33760
727-523-1130 (voice)
800-825-5736 (voice—Florida only)
727-523-8687 (fax)
www.fndfl.org

Parent to Parent of Miami, Inc.
7990 Southwest 117 Avenue, Suite 201
Miami, FL 33173
305-271-9797 (voice)
305-271-6628 (fax)
www.ptopmiami.org

Georgia

Parents Educating Parents and Professionals
3680 Kings Highway
Douglasville, GA 30135
770-577-7771 (voice)
800-322-7065 (voice)
770-577-7774 (fax)
www.peppinc.org

Hawaii

AWARE (Assisting With Appropriate Rights in Education)
200 North Vineyard Boulevard, Suite 310
Honolulu, HI 96817
808-536-9684 (voice)
800-533-9684 (voice—Hawaii only)
808-536-2280 (TTY)
808-537-6780 (fax)
www.ldahawaii.org

Idaho

Idaho Parents Unlimited, Inc.
600 North Curtis, Suite 145
Boise, ID 83706
208-342-5884 (voice/TTY)
800-242-4785 (voice—Idaho only)
208-342-1408 (fax)
www.ipulidaho.org

Illinois

Designs for Change
29 East Madison, Suite 950
Chicago, IL 60602
312-236-7252 (voice)
312-857-1013 (TDD)
312-236-7927 (fax)
www.designsforchange.org

Family Matters
2505 South Veterans Drive
Effingham, IL 62401
217-347-5428 (voice)
866-436-7842 (voice—Illinois only/TTY)
217-347-5119 (fax)
www.fmptic.org

Family Resource Center on Disabilities
20 East Jackson Boulevard, Room 300
Chicago, IL 60604
312-939-3513 (voice)
800-952-4199 (voice—Illinois only)
312-939-3519 (TDD/TTY)
312-939-7297 (fax)
www.rcd.org

Indiana

Indiana Resource Center for Families With Special
  Needs
809 North Michigan Street
South Bend, IN 46601
574-234-7101 (voice)
800-332-4433 (voice—Indiana only)
574-234-7279 (fax)
www.insource.org

Iowa

Access for Special Kids
321 East Sixth Street
Des Moines, IA 50309
515-243-1713 (voice)
800-450-8667 (voice)
515-243-1902 (fax)
www.askresource.org

Kansas

Families Together, Inc.
3033 West Second, Suite 106
Wichita, KS 67203
316-945-7747 (voice)
888-815-6364 (voice—Kansas only)
316-945-7795 (fax)
www.familiestogetherinc.org

Keys for Networking, Inc.
1301 South Topeka Boulevard
Topeka, KS 66612
785-233-8732 (voice)
www.keys.org

Kentucky

FIND of Louisville
1146 South Third Street
Louisville, KY 40203
502-584-1239 (voice)
502-584-1261 (fax)
www.findoflouisville.org

Special Parent Involvement Network
10301-B Deering Road
Louisville, KY 40272
502-937-6894 (voice)
800-525-7746 (voice)
502-937-6464 (fax)
www.kyspin.com

Louisiana

Program of Families Helping Families of Greater
  New Orleans: Project PROMPT
4323 Division Street, Suite 110
Metairie, LA 70002
504-888-9111 (voice)
800-766-7736 (voice—Louisiana only)
504-888-0246 (fax)
www.projectprompt.org

Pyramid Community Parent Resource Center
2552 St. Phillip Street
New Orleans, LA 70119
504-827-0610 (voice)
504-827-2999 (fax)

Maine

Maine Parent Federation
P.O. Box 2067
Augusta, ME 04338
207-623-2144 (voice/TTY)
800-870-7746 (voice—Maine only)
207-623-2148 (fax)
www.mpf.org

Southern Maine Parent Awareness
886 Main Street, Suite 303
Sanford, ME 04073
207-324-2337 (voice)
800-564-9696 (voice—Maine only)
207-324-5621 (fax)
www.somepa.org

Maryland

Parents Place of Maryland
801 Cromwell Park Drive, Suite 103
Glen Burnie, MD 21061
410-768-9100 (voice/TTY)
410-768-0830 (fax)
www.ppmd.org

Massachusetts

Federation for Children With Special Needs
1135 Tremont Street, Suite 420
Boston, MA 02120
617-236-7210 (voice/TTY)
800-331-0688 (voice—Massachusetts only)
617-572-2094 (fax)
www.fcsn.org

Urban PRIDE
c/o The Boston Foundation
75 Arlington Street, 10th Floor
Boston, MA 02116
617-338-4508 (voice)
617-338-1604 (fax)
www.urbanpride.org

Michigan

Association for Children's Mental Health
2645 Woodlake Circle, Suite 140
Okemos, MI 48864
517-381-5125 (voice)
517-349-6FAX (fax)
www.acmh-mi.org

Citizens Alliance to Uphold Special Education
 (CAUSE)
6412 Centurion Drive, Suite 130
Lansing, MI 48917
517-886-9167 (voice)
800-221-9105 (voice—Michigan only)
517-886-9366 (fax)
www.causeonline.org

Minnesota

PACER Center, Inc.
8161 Normandale Boulevard
Minneapolis, MN 55437
952-838-9000 (voice)
888-537-2237 (voice)
952-838-0190 (TTY)
952-838-0199 (fax)
www.pacer.org

Mississippi

Project Empower
P.O. Box 1733
136 South Poplar Street
Greenville, MS 38702
662-332-4852 (voice)
800-337-4852 (voice)
662-332-1622 (fax)

Missouri

Missouri Parents Act (MPACT)
One West Armour, Suite 302
Kansas City, MO 64111
816-531-7070 (voice)
816-931-2992 (TDD)
816-531-4777 (fax)
www.ptimpact.com

Montana

Parents Let's Unite for Kids (PLUK)
516 North 32nd Street
Billings, MT 59101
406-255-0540 (voice)
800-222-7585 (voice—Montana only)
406-255-0523 (fax)
www.pluk.org

Nebraska

PTI Nebraska
3135 North 93rd Street
Omaha, NE 68134
402-346-0525 (voice)
800-284-8520 (voice)
402-934-1479 (fax)
www.pti-nebraska.org

Nevada

Nevada PEP
2355 Red Rock Street, #106
Las Vegas, NV 89146
702-388-8899 (voice)
800-216-5188 (voice)
702-388-2966 (fax)
www.nvpep.org

New Hampshire

Parent Information Center
P.O. Box 2405
Concord, NH 03302
603-224-7005 (voice/TTY)
800-232-0986 (voice—New Hampshire only)
603-224-4365 (fax)
www.parentinformationcenter.org

New Jersey

Statewide Parent Advocacy Network, Inc. (SPAN)
35 Halsey Street, 4th Floor
Newark, NJ 07102
973-642-8100 (voice)
800-654-SPAN (voice—New Jersey only)
973-642-8080 (fax)
www.spannj.org

New Mexico

Abrazos Family Support Services
P.O. Box 788
Bernalillo, NM 87004
505-867-3396 (voice)
505-867-3398 (fax)
www.abrazosnm.org

Parents Reaching Out (PRO)
1920B Columbia Drive, SE
Albuquerque, NM 87106
505-247-0192 (voice)
800-524-5176 (voice—New Mexico only)
505-247-1345 (fax)
www.parentsreachingout.org

New York

Advocacy Center
590 South Avenue
Rochester, NY 14620
585-546-1700 (voice)
800-650-4967 (voice—New York only)
585-546-7069 (fax)
www.advocacycenter.com

Advocates for Children of New York
151 West 30th Street, 5th Floor
New York, NY 10001
212-947-9779 (voice)
212-947-9790 (fax)
www.advocatesforchildren.org

Resources for Children With Special Needs
116 East 16th Street, 5th Floor
New York, NY 10003
212-677-4650 (voice)
212-254-4070 (fax)
www.resourcesnyc.org

Sinergia/Metropolitan Parent Center
15 West 65th Street, 6th Floor
New York, NY 10023
212-496-1300 (voice)
212-496-5608 (fax)
www.sinergiany.org

North Carolina

Exceptional Children's Assistance Center
907 Barra Row, Suites 102 & 103
Davidson, NC 28036
704-892-1321 (voice)
800-962-6817 (voice—North Carolina only)
704-892-5028 (fax)
www.ECAC-parentcenter.org

FIRST
P.O. Box 802
Asheville, NC 28802
828-277-1315 (voice)
877-633-3178 (voice)
828-277-1321 (fax)
www.firstwnc.org

Hope Parent Resource Center
300 Enola Road
Morganton, NC 28655
828-438-6540 (voice)
828-433-2821 (fax)

North Dakota

Pathfinder PTI
1600 Second Avenue, SW, Suite 30
Minot, ND 58701
701-837-7500 (voice)
701-837-7501 (TTY)
701-837-7548 (fax)
www.pathfinder.minot.com

Ohio

Ohio Coalition for the Education of Children With
   Disabilities
Bank One Building
165 West Center Street, Suite 302
Marion, OH 43302
740-382-5452 (voice/TTY)
800-374-2806 (voice)
740-383-6421 (fax)
www.ocecd.org

Oklahoma

Oklahoma Parents Center
4600 Southeast 29th Street, Suite 115
Del City, OK 73115
405-619-1500 (voice/TDD)
405-670-0776 (fax)
www.okparents.org

Oregon

Oregon PTI
2295 Liberty Street, NE
Salem, OR 97303
503-581-8156 (voice/TDD)
503-391-0429 (fax)
www.open.org/~orpti

Pennsylvania

Hispanics United for Special Needs Children
202 West Cecil B. Moore Avenue
Philadelphia, PA 19122
215-425-6203 (voice)
215-425-6204 (fax)
www.huneinc.org

Mentor Parent Program, Inc.
P.O. Box 47
Pittsfield, PA 16340
814-563-3470 (voice)
888-447-1431 (voice—Pennsylvania only)
814-563-3445 (fax)
www.mentorparent.org

Parent Education Network
2107 Industrial Highway
York, PA 17402
717-600-0100 (voice/TTY)
800-522-5827 (voice—Pennsylvania only)
717-600-8101 (fax)
www.parentednet.org

Rhode Island

Rhode Island Parent Information Network
175 Main Street
Pawtucket, RI 02860
401-727-4144 (voice)
800-464-3399 (voice—Rhode Island only)
401-727-4040 (fax)
www.ripin.org

South Carolina

PRO Parents
652 Bush River Road, Suite 218
Columbia, SC 29210
803-772-5688 (voice)
800-759-4776 (voice—South Carolina only)
803-772-5341 (fax)
www.proparents.org

South Dakota

South Dakota Parent Connection
3701 West 49th Street, Suite 102
Sioux Falls, SD 57106
605-361-3171 (voice/TDD)
800-640-4553 (voice—South Dakota only)
605-361-2928 (fax)
www.sdparent.org

Tennessee

Support & Training for Exceptional Parents (STEP)
712 Professional Plaza
Greenville, TN 37745
423-639-0125 (voice)
800-280-7837 (voice—Tennessee only)
423-639-8802 (TTY)
423-636-8217 (fax)
www.tnstep.org

Texas

Arc of Texas in the Rio Grande Valley
 Parents Supporting Parents Network
601 North Texas Boulevard
Weslaco, TX 78596
956-447-8408 (voice)
888-857-8688 (voice)
956-973-9503 (fax)
www.thearcoftexas.org

Special Kids, Inc.
5055 Bellfort
P.O. Box 266958
Houston, TX 77207
713-734-5355 (voice)
713-643-6291 (fax)

Partners Resource Network
1090 Longfellow Drive
Beaumont, TX 77630
409-898-4684 (voice/TTY)
800-866-4726 (voice—Texas only)
409-898-4869 (fax)
www.partnerstx.org

Utah

Utah Parent Center
2290 East 4500 South, Suite 110
Salt Lake City, UT 84117
801-272-1051 (voice/TTY)
800-468-1160 (voice—Utah only)
801-272-8907 (fax)
www.utahparentcenter.org

Vermont

Vermont Parent Information Center (VPIC)
600 Blair Park Road
Williston, VT 05495
802-876-5315 (voice/TTY)
800-639-7170 (voice—Vermont only)
802-658-5395 (fax)
www.vtpic.com

Virginia

PADDA, Inc.
813 Forrest Drive, Suite 3
Newport News, VA 23606
757-591-9119 (voice)
888-337-2332 (voice)
757-591-8990 (fax)
www.padda.org

Parent Educational Advocacy Training Center
6320 Augusta Drive, Suite 1200
Springfield, VA 22150
703-932-0010 (voice/TTY)
800-869-6782 (voice—Virginia only)
703-923-0030 (fax)
www.peatc.org

Washington

Parent to Parent Power
1118 South 142nd Street, Suite B
Tacoma, WA 98444
253-531-2022 (voice)
253-538-1126 (fax)
www.p2ppower.org

Rural Outreach
805 Southwest Alcora
Pullam, WA 99163
509-595-5440 (voice)

Washington PAVE
6316 South 12th Street, Suite B
Tacoma, WA 98465
253-565-2266 (voice/TTY)
800-572-7368 (voice—Washington only)
253-566-8052 (fax)
www.washingtonpave.com

West Virginia

West Virginia PTI
1701 Hamill Avenue
Clarksburg, WV 26301
304-624-1436 (voice/TTY)
800-281-1436 (voice—West Virginia only)
304-624-1438 (fax)
www.wvpti.org

Wisconsin

Family Assistance Center for Education, Training, and
   Support
2714 North Martin Luther King Drive
Milwaukee, WI 53212
414-374-4645 (voice)
877-374-4677 (voice)
414-374-4635 (TTY)
414-374-4655 (fax)
www.wifacets.org

Native American Family Empowerment Center
Great Lakes Inter-Tribal Council, Inc.
2932 Highway 47 North
P.O. Box 9
Lac du Flambeau, WI 54538
715-588-3324 (voice)
800-472-7207 (voice)
715-588-7900 (fax)
 www.glitc.org

Wyoming

Wyoming PIC
5 North Lobban
Buffalo, WY 82834
307-684-2277 (voice/TDD)
800-660-9742 (voice—Wyoming only)
307-684-5314 (fax)
www.wpic.org

Legal Resources on Special Education

American Bar Association Commission on Mental and Physical Disability Law

740 15th Street, NW, Ninth Floor
Washington, DC 20005
202-662-1570 (voice)
202-662-1012 (TTY)
202-662-1032 (fax)
www.abanet.org/disability

Puts out books, reporters, news updates, and
other publications to assist lawyers who
advocate for the rights of the disabled. The
Commission also maintains a library of
research materials and provides seminars and
workshops.

Bazelon Center

1101 15th Street, NW, Suite 1212
Washington, DC 20005
202-467-5730 (voice)
202-223-0409 (fax)
www.bazelon.org

A public interest law firm that conducts test
case litigation to defend the rights of people
with mental disabilities. The Bazelon Center
provides legal support to protection and
advocacy agencies, legal services offices, and
private attorneys, and monitors legislation and
regulations.

Center for Law and Education

1875 Connecticut Avenue, NW, Suite 510
Washington, DC 20009
202-986-3000 (voice)
202-986-6648 (fax)
www.cleweb.org

Assists local legal services programs and
litigates certain cases in matters concerning
education of low-income people. As a national
support center, CLE has developed enormous
expertise about the legal rights and responsibilities of students and school personnel as
well as about key education programs and
initiatives, including vocational education
programs and special education for students
with disabilities.

Children's Defense Fund

25 E Street, NW
Washington, DC 20001
202-628-8787 (voice)
www.childrensdefense.org

Assesses the adequacy of the screening,
diagnosis, and treatment programs for Medicaid-
eligible children.

Disability Rights Education and Defense Fund, Inc.

2212 Sixth Street
Berkeley, CA 94710
510-644-2555 (voice/TTY)
510-841-8645 (fax)
www.dredf.org

Dedicated to protecting and advancing the civil rights of people with disabilities through legislation, litigation, advocacy, technical assistance, and education and training of lawyers, people with disabilities, and parents of children with disabilities.

EDLAW

1310 Minor Avenue #207
Seattle, WA 98101
www.edlaw.net

The website includes information on newsletters, books, and conferences; a list of attorneys who specialize in special education; and full texts of special education statutes, regulations, and administrative interpretations. EDLAW also maintains a database of attorneys and advocates through COPAA (the Council of Parent Attorneys and Advocates).

LRP Publications

800-341-7874 (voice)
215-784-0860 (voice)
561-622-2423 (fax)
www.lrp.com

Has an extensive library of legal materials, including special education publications. The website includes access to over 65 special education documents, covering evaluations, behavior, IDEA, IEPs, Section 504, and much more. LRP also publishes the "Individuals With Disabilities Education Law Reporter."

Wrightslaw

www.wrightslaw.com

A website maintained by Pete and Pam Wright. Pete is an attorney who has represented special education children for more than 20 years. Pam is a psychotherapist who has worked with children and families in mental health centers, psychiatric clinics, schools, juvenile detention facilities, hospitals, and homes. Their website includes articles about special education advocacy; statutes, regulations, and cases; information on ordering their advocacy package; information about books, conferences, and other projects; and links to other useful information on the Internet.

Resources Concerning Specific Disabilities

Alexander Graham Bell Association

3417 Volta Place, NW
Washington, DC 20007
202-337-5220 (voice)
202-337-5221 (TTY)
202-337-8314 (fax)
www.agbell.org

Provides hearing-impaired children with information and special education programs, and acts as a support group for parents of deaf children.

American Association of the Deaf-Blind

8630 Fenton Street, Suite 121
Silver Spring, MD 20910
301-495-4403 (voice)
301-495-4402 (TTY)
301-495-4404 (fax)
www.aadb.org

Advocates for people who have combined hearing and vision impairments, and provides technical assistance to families, educators, and service providers of people who are deaf-blind.

American Council of the Blind

1155 15th Street, NW, Suite 1004
Washington, DC 20005
202-467-5081 (voice)
800-424-8666 (voice)
202-467-5085 (fax)
www.acb.org

Advocates for legislative changes, particularly to improve educational and rehabilitation facilities.

American Foundation for the Blind

11 Penn Plaza, Suite 300
New York, NY 10001
212-502-7600 (voice)
212-502-7777 (fax)
www.afb.org

Provides information on specialized services in education for sight-impaired children and works to improve the quality of educational services for children and youths with visual impairments.

American Society for Deaf Children

P.O. Box 3355
Gettysburg, PA 17325
717-334-7922 (voice/TTY)
717-334-8808 (fax)
www.deafchildren.org

Advocates for deaf or hard of hearing children's total quality participation in education, including use of signing for enhancing and broadening the social, personal, and educational aspects of deaf and hard of hearing children's lives. ASDC supports flexible, innovative, and effective strategies for facilitating deaf and hard of hearing children's education.

ARC

1010 Wayne Avenue, Suite 650
Silver Spring, MD 20910
301-565-3842 (voice)
301-565-3843 (fax)
http://thearc.org

Advocates and provides support for families of people with mental retardation and developmental disabilities.

A-T Children's Project

668 South Military Trail
Deerfield Beach, FL 33442
800-5-HELP-AT (voice)
954-725-1153 (fax)
www.atcp.org

Provides physicians, research scientists, families, and support providers with information about an inherited childhood disease called Ataxia-Telangiectasia.

Attention Deficit Information Network, Inc.

58 Prince Street
Needham, MA 02492
781-455-9895 (voice)
www.addinfonetwork.com

Offers support and information to families of children with ADD and provides training programs, conferences, and workshops for parents and professionals who work with individuals with ADD.

Autism Society of America

7910 Woodmont Avenue, Suite 300
Bethesda, MD 20814
301-657-0881 (voice)
800-328-8476 (voice)
www.autism-society.org

Monitors legislation and regulations affecting support, education, training, research, and other services for individuals with autism. ASA also offers referral services.

Blind Childrens' Center

4120 Marathon Street
Los Angeles, CA 90029
323-664-2153 (voice)
http://blindcntr.org

General information for parents of blind children.

Brain Injury Association of America

8201 Greensboro Drive, Suite 611
McLean, VA 22102
703-761-0750 (voice)
800-444-6443 (voice)
www.biausa.org

Provides information and support to families of people with brain injuries.

Children and Adults With Attention Deficit Disorder (CHADD)

8181 Professional Place, Suite 201
Landover, MD 20785
301-306-7070 (voice)
301-306-7090 (fax)
www.chadd.org

Provides a network for parents of children with ADD, provides a forum of education for parents of, and professionals who work with, people with ADD, and works to provide positive educational experiences for children with ADD. CHADD publishes a quarterly newsletter and educators' manual. The site offers fact sheets, information on IDEA, and scientific research and studies on ADD.

Council for Exceptional Children, Division for Learning Disabilities

1110 N. Glebe Road
Arlington, VA 22201
888-CEC-SPED (voice)
703-264-9494 (fax)
866-915-5000 (TTY)
www.cec.sped.org

Information and resources for teaching students with learning disabilities. The website includes information on the DLD's publications (*Learning Disabilities Research and Practice Journal*, "Thinking About Inclusion & Learning Disabilities," and "Research on Classroom Ecologies and DLD Times Newsletter"), information on upcoming conferences, links to other organizations and government agencies, fact sheets, and detailed articles on particular learning disabilities and instruction techniques.

Council for Learning Disabilities

P.O. Box 4014
Leesburg, VA 20177
571-258-1010 (voice)
571-258-1011 (fax)
www.cldinternational.org

An organization of and for professionals who represent diverse disciplines and who are committed to enhancing the education and life-span development of individuals with learning disabilities. The site offers fact sheets, information on research, and legislative updates.

Epilepsy Foundation of America

4351 Garden City Drive
Landover, MD 20785
800-332-1000 (voice)
www.epilepsyfoundation.org

Promotes research and treatment of epilepsy, disseminates information and educational materials, provides direct services for people with epilepsy, and makes referrals when necessary.

Families of Spinal Muscular Atrophy

P.O. Box 196
Libertyville, IL 60048
847-367-7620 (voice)
800-886-1762 (voice)
847-357-7623 (fax)
www.fsma.org

Promotes and funds research, provides families with the use of an equipment pool to help alleviate the high cost of medical equipment, promotes public awareness, and publishes a quarterly newsletter.

Federation of Families for Children's Mental Health

1101 King Street, Suite 420
Alexandria, VA 22314
703-684-7710 (voice)
703-836-1040 (fax)
www.ffcmh.org

Focuses on the needs of children with emotional, behavioral, or mental disorders, by providing information and advocating in several areas including family support, education, and transition services. The website includes publications, IDEA updates, and links to local organizations.

The International Dyslexia Association

The Chester Building, Suite 382
8600 LaSalle Road
Baltimore, MD 21286
410-296-0232 (voice)
800-222-3123 (messages)
410-321-5069 (fax)
www.interdys.org

Promotes effective teaching approaches and related clinical educational intervention strategies for people with dyslexia; supports research; and disseminates research through conferences, publications, and local and regional offices.

LD Online

www.ldonline.com

One of my favorites, this site offers lots of detailed articles for parents, teachers, and kids on learning disabilities, evaluations, methodologies, IEPs, IDEA, and much more. There's a special area of the site just for kids, as well as bulletin boards and lots of state-by-state links.

Learning Disabilities Association of America

4156 Library Road
Pittsburgh, PA 15234
412-341-1515 (voice)
412-344-0224 (fax)
www.ldaamerica.org

A nonprofit membership organization with state and local affiliates. Members receive a national newsletter along with state and local chapter newsletters and information on advocating for their children, state and federal laws, and support groups. The site offers fact sheets, news, and other resources. Click "State LDA Pages" for links to state and local chapters.

National Aphasia Association

351 Butternut Court
Millersville, MD 21108
800-922-4622 (voice)
www.aphasia.org

Promotes public education, research, rehabilitation, and support services to assist people with aphasia and their families. The site offers information, research, fact sheets, and access to support groups.

National Association of the Deaf

814 Thayer Avenue
Silver Spring, MD 20910
301-587-1788 (voice)
301-587-1789 (TTY)
301-587-1791 (fax)
www.nad.org

A consumer advocacy group promoting equal access to communication, education, and employment for people who are deaf or hard of hearing.

National Center for Learning Disabilities

381 Park Avenue South, Suite 1401
New York, NY 10016
212-545-7510 (voice)
888-575-7373 (voice)
212-545-9665 (fax)
www.ncld.org

Provides information on learning disabilities and resources available in communities nationwide to parents, professionals, and adults with learning disabilities. One of NCLD's areas of primary concern is early identification and intervention, as well as teacher preparation. The website includes links to other LD organizations and school testing organizations, and information on legal issues, gifted/learning disabilities, ADD/ADHD, and home schooling.

National Down Syndrome Congress

1370 Center Drive, Suite 102
Atlanta, GA 30338
770-604-9500 (voice)
800-232-6372 (voice)
www.ndsccenter.org

Offers support to parents of children with Down syndrome through annual seminars, fact sheets, pamphlets, booklets, newsletter, audiotapes, and other educational materials. NDSC maintains an advocate telephone helpline.

National Down Syndrome Society

666 Broadway, 8th Floor
New York, NY 10012
800-221-4602 (voice)
212-460-9330 (voice)
212-979-2873 (fax)
www.ndss.org

Helps families whose special education needs concern a child with Down syndrome.

National Federation of the Blind

1800 Johnson Street
Baltimore, MD 21230
410-659-9314 (voice)
410-685-5653 (fax)
www.nfb.org

Provides referrals and information on adaptive equipment, advocacy services, protection of civil rights, development and evaluation of technology, and support for blind people and their families. NFB has a special division called the National Organization of Parents of Blind Children.

National Fragile X Foundation

P.O. Box 190488
San Francisco, CA 94119
800-688-8765 (voice)
925-938-9315 (fax)
www.fragilex.org

Has information for educators on upcoming conferences and on support groups for parents and children, and maintains a family resource center.

National Spinal Cord Injury Association

6701 Democracy Boulevard, Suite 300-9
Bethesda, MD 20817
800-962-9629 (voice)
301-881-9817 (fax)
www.spinalcord.org

Provides information and support to people with spinal cord injuries and their families.

Schwab Learning

1650 South Amphlett Boulevard, Suite 300
San Mateo, CA 94402
650-655-2410 (voice)
650-655-2411 (fax)
www.schwablearning.org

The Schwab Foundation provides parents and educators in the San Francisco area quarterly educational programs, information and referrals, and guidance counseling. The site includes extensive resources about ADD, evaluations, dyslexia, homework, IEPs, learning disabilities, tutors, teaching methods, family issues, and much more.

Signing Exact English Center for the Advancement of Deaf Children

P.O. Box 1181
Los Alamitos, CA 90720
562-430-1467 (voice)
562-795-6614 (fax)
www.seecenter.org

Promotes the understanding of signing exact English to improve English skills for deaf children. SEE Center services include a telephone information service about deafness, workshops, videotapes, and a parent information packet containing questions for parents to ask, especially in the school setting.

Spina Bifida Association of America

4590 MacArthur Blvd., NW, Suite 250
Washington, DC 20007
202-944-3285 (voice)
800-621-3141 (voice)
www.sbaa.org

Offers educational programs and support services for people with spina bifida, their families, and concerned professionals; acts as a clearinghouse on information related to spina bifida; provides referral services; conducts seminars; and monitors legislation and regulations.

United Cerebral Palsy Association

1660 L Street, NW, Suite 700
Washington, DC 20036
800-872-5827 (voice)
202-973-7197 (TTY)
800-776-0414 (fax)
www.ucp.org

Assists individuals with cerebral palsy and other developmental disabilities and their families. UCPA provides parent education, early intervention information, family support, respite services, and information on assistive technology.

Williams Syndrome Association

P.O. Box 297
Clawson, MI 48017
800-806-1871 (voice)
248-244-2230 (fax)
www.williams-syndrome.org

Provides information for parents, teachers, and doctors of children with Williams Syndrome, a rare genetic condition that causes medical and developmental problems.

Appendix 4

Sample IEP Form

Every school district, in every state, has its own IEP form. While the forms vary, they must include the same information. We strongly recommend that you request a copy of your school's IEP form early in the process.

To get you familiar with IEP forms, we have included a sample here, reprinted with permission of the Marin County (California) Office of Education. (This is a draft version of their new IEP form, which has not yet been finalized.)

Individualized Education Program (IEP)

MARIN SELPA
IEP
Page 1
8/05

The IEP Team is not required to include: (1) additional information beyond what is explicitly required in IDEA and California Education Code and (2) information under one component of a student's IEP that is already contained under another component of the IEP.

Date _____

Outlined boxes are situational. All other areas must be addressed.

IDENTIFYING INFORMATION

Student _____ DOB _____ Age _____ Grade ____ ❑ M ❑ F

Parent/Guardian _____

Address _____ City _____ Zip _____   Cell _____

❑ LCI
Student's Address if different from parent's ❑ Foster Home _____   Work _____

District of Residence _____ School _____   Home _____

Home Language _____ If home language is other than English, is the student an English Language Learner? ❑ Yes ❑ No

DATES OF ANTICIPATED MEETINGS

Annual Review _____   AB 3632 6-Month Review _____   3-Yr. Reevaluation _____   Add'l. Review _____
        Month/Day/Year   Month/Day/Year   Month/Day/Year   Month/Day/Year

IEP MEETING INFORMATION

Purpose of the meeting: (*Check all that apply*)
❑ Initial ❑ Annual Review ❑ Review Based on 3-Yr. Reevaluation ❑ AB3632 6-Month Review ❑ Promotion/Retention
❑ Manifestation Determination   ❑ Transition ❑ Parent Request   ❑ Amend IEP dated _____
❑ Review assessments   ❑ Determine eligibility   ❑ Develop goals   ❑ Develop/review behavioral plan
❑ Recommend placement/service(s)   ❑ _____

REQUIRED TEAM MEMBERSHIP AND ATTENDANCE - *All of the identified roles of IEP team membership must be represented at the IEP meeting unless:*

The parent(s) and _____, representing _____ agree that

_____, a required IEP Team member (_____) does not have to attend this IEP meeting

❑ because the member's area of curriculum or related services is not being modified.

❑ even though this IEP meeting involves a modification or discussion of a required Team member's area of curriculum or related service and _____ has submitted written input into the the development of this IEP to the parent(s) and IEP Team **prior** to the meeting. _____

WHAT CONCERN(S) DOES THE PARENT WANT TO SEE ADDRESSED IN THIS IEP TO ENHANCE THE STUDENT'S EDUCATION?

Distribution: Original - Permanent File   Copy -Parent   Copies may be made for other team members

Student _____   Date of Meeting _____

**MARIN
SELPA**
IEP
Page 2
8/05

PRESENT LEVELS OF ACADEMIC ACHIEVEMENT AND FUNCTIONAL PERFORMANCE

The following assessment report(s) were reviewed. Report(s) include description(s) of the student's strengths, general education performance including STAR testing results and report cards, and achievement towards goals. (Please list name of report, examiner(s), and date of report)

ELIGIBILITY AS AN INDIVIDUAL WITH EXCEPTIONAL NEEDS

❏ **1. Meets eligibility criteria as indicated:**

❏ Mentally Retarded   ❏ Hard of Hearing   ❏ Visually Impaired   ❏ Orthopedically Impaired
❏ Language or Speech Disorder   ❏ Emotionally Disturbed   ❏ Traumatic Brain Injury   ❏ Deaf/Blind
❏ Autistic-Like Behaviors   ❏ Deaf   ❏ Multi-Handicapped _____
❏ Specific Learning Disability   ❏ Other Health Impaired *Specify Impairment* _____

❏ **2. Does not meet eligibility for handicaps considered:** _____
❏ **3. The IEP Team determined that no additional data are needed to confirm that the student continues to meet the eligibility criteria as a child with a disability**. *(Indicate in Section 1 the criteria the student has met)*

GOALS AND OBJECTIVES

❏ Draft IEP goals and ❏ objectives were reviewed, revised, and are recommended.
❏ IEP goals and ❏ objectives were recommended on _____ and are continued.*
❏ In addition to IEP goals and ❏ objectives continued from the meeting on _____,* additional goals
and ❏ objectives were reviewed, revised and are recommended.
At or after the Annual Review

STUDENT PROMOTION AND RETENTION (GRADES 2-8)

Promotion from grade ____ to grade ____ (current school year) and grade ___ to grade ___ (200__ - 200__ school year) shall be based on the following criteria:
❏ District adopted criteria for general education students
❏ Substantial progress on goals. Grades 2-3 require reading standards only; grades 4-8 require reading, language arts, and math. *List goal pages* _____
❏ _____
_____
_____

❏ **The student is at risk of retention, the IEP team considered the following:**
❏ Yes ❏ No Is the current IEP for the student's academic, linguistic, social and emotional, and behavioral needs appropriate?
❏ Yes ❏ No Is the manner of assessment, including any accommodations and modifications, identified in the IEP appropriate?
❏ Yes ❏ No Were all the services required by the student to make progress in the general education curriculum appropriately identified in the student's IEP?
❏ Yes ❏ No Did the student receive all the services identified in the IEP?
❏ Yes ❏ No Was the assessment conducted consistent with the IEP?
❏ Yes ❏ No Was the student's promotion standard appropriate and clarified in the IEP?
See page _____ for IEP Team recommendations

Distribution: Original - Permanent File   Copy -Parent   Copies may be made for other team members

Student _____   Date of Meeting _____

MARIN SELPA
IEP
Page 3
8/05

TEAM DETERMNATION OF ELIGIBILITY FOR A SPECIFIC LEARNING DISABILITY   ❑ Initial Evaluation
❑ 3-Year Reevaluation

I.   Presence of a Severe Discrepancy (Select either A or B and then complete items II through IV)
  ❑ A. The IEP Team finds a severe discrepancy (18.5 points or more) between measures of intellectual ability and one
       or more of the following areas of achievement:
       ❑ Written Expression   ❑ Basic Reading Skills   ❑ Reading Comprehension
       ❑ Mathematics Calculation   ❑ Mathematics Reasoning   ❑ Listening Comprehension ❑ Oral Expression
       Measure of Intellectual Ability_____ Score(s) _____
       Test(s) of Academic Achievement/Scores(s) _____
       _____
       Discrepancy between Intellectual Ability and Academic Achievement _____

  ❑ B. Standard measures do not reveal a severe discrepancy, but the IEP team finds a severe discrepancy does exist
       based upon the additional documentation provided in the attached report. (Complete and attach "Specific
       Learning Disability Discrepancy" documentation-See page 4)

II. The discrepancy identified in Item 1 (above) is directly related to a processing disorder. ❑ Yes ❑ No
     Check the appropriate area(s): ❑ Sensory Motor Skills   ❑ Visual Processing ❑ Auditory Processing
                         ❑ Attention ❑ Cognitive Abilities (including asssociation, conceptualization, and expression)
     Name of Test _____ Score _____

III. If any of the items below (A-E) are checked "Yes", the student may not be identified as having a specific learning
     disability.
     A. The discrepancy is primarily a result of a visual, hearing, or motor impairment.   ❑ Yes ❑ No
     B. The discrepancy is primarily a result of mental retardation or emotional disturbance.   ❑ Yes ❑ No
     C. The discrepancy is primarily a result of environmental, cultural, or economic disadvantage.   ❑ Yes ❑ No
     D. The discrepany is primarily a result of limited school experience or poor school attendance.   ❑ Yes ❑ No
     E. This discrepancy can be corrected through other general or categorical services offered within
        the general instructional program.   ❑ Yes ❑ No

IV. The student has a specific learning disability. ❑ Yes ❑ No

I agree with the conclusions stated above:

School Psychologist/Date _____   Administrator/Designee/Date_____

Resource Specialist/Date _____   Teacher/Date _____

Speech/Language Specialist/Date _____   Nurse/Date _____

Parent/Guardian/Date _____   Other/Date _____

My assessment of this student differs from the above report as follows: *(Attach a statement)*
Name, Title/Date _____

Distribution: Original - Permanent File   Copy -Parent   Copies may be made for other team members

▬▬▬▬▬▬▬▬▬▬

Student _____   Date of Meeting _____   🌳 **MARIN SELPA**
IEP
Page 4
8/05

SPECIFIC LEARNING DISABILITY DISCREPANCY DOCUMENTATION REPORT

This form is to be completed in order to document the presence of a Specific Learning Disability in instances when the student does not exhibit a severe discrepancy between ability and achievement as measured by standardized tests. (Ed. Code 3030 (j)(C))

1. Data from assessment instruments (ability and achievement): _____
_____
_____
_____
_____

2. Information provided by parent: _____
_____
_____
_____
_____

3. Information provided by the student's present teacher: _____
_____
_____
_____
_____

4. Summary of the student's classroom performance:
   a. Observations: _____
   _____
   _____

   b. Work Samples: _____
   _____
   _____

   c. Group Test Scores: _____
   _____
   _____

5. Consideration of the student's age: _____
_____
_____
_____

6. Additional Relevant Information: _____
_____
_____
_____

Distribution: Original - Permanent File   Copy -Parent   Copies may be made for other team members

Student _____ Date of Meeting _____

MARIN SELPA
IEP
Page 5
8/05

TEAM DETERMINATION OF ELIGIBILITY FOR LANGUAGE OR SPEECH DISORDER

❏ Initial Evaluation
❏ 3-Year Reevaluation

Must Meet One or More of Criteria 1-5 and Criteria 6 and 7.

❏ 1. **Articulation Disorder -** Such that the student's production of speech significantly interferes with communication and attracts adverse attention. Significant interference in communication occurs when the student's production of single or multiple speech sounds on a developmental scale of articulation competency is below that expected for his or her chronological age or developmental level.

    Chronological Age or Developmetal Level _____

    Articulation Test _____ Age Equivalent, Standard Score or %ile _____

❏ 2. **Abnormal Voice -** A studentl has an abnormal voice which is characterized by persistent, defective voice quality, pitch or loudness. (Student must have medical clearance for voice therapy.)

❏ 3. **Fluency Disorders -** A student has a fluency disorder when the flow of verbal expression including rate and rhythm adversely affects communication between the student and listener.

❏ 4. **Language or Speech Disorder** - Which is the result of a hearing loss.

❏ 5. **Language Disorder** - *The student has an expressive or receptive language disorder when he or she meets one of the following criteria:*

    ❏ A. The student scores at least 1.5 standard deviations (22.5 points) below the mean or below the 7th percentile, for his or her chronological age or developmental level on *two or more* standardized tests in one or more of the following areas of language development. *Check appropriate area(s):*

      ❏ Morphology   ❏ Syntax   ❏ Semantics   ❏ Pragmatics

      Chronological Age or Developmental Level _____

      Standardized Test _____ Discrepancy _____ %ile _____

      Standardized Test _____ Discrepancy _____ %ile _____

    ❏ B. The student scores at least 1.5 standard deviations below the mean or the score is below the 7%ile for his or her chronological age or developmental level on one or more standardized tests in one of the areas listed above *AND* displays inappropriate or inadequate usage of expressive or receptive language as measured by a representative spontaneous or elicited language sample of fifty utterances. *Check appropriate area(s):*

      ❏ Morphology   ❏ Syntax   ❏ Semantics   ❏ Pragmatics

      Chronological Age or Developmental Level _____

      Standardized Test: _____ Discrepancy _____ %ile _____

      Language Sample Results _____

❏ 6. **Adversely affects educational performance.**

❏ 7. **Cannot be corrected without special education and related services.**

TEAM DETERMINATION OF ELIGIBILITY FOR CHILDREN BETWEEN THE AGES OF THREE AND FIVE YEARS

❏ Initial Evaluation
❏ 3-Year Reevaluation

Must Meet Criteria I and II

I. Meets eligibility criteria as indicated:

❏ Mentally Retarded   ❏ Hard of Hearing   ❏ Multi-Handicapped   ❏ Visually Impaired

❏ Orthopedically Impaired   ❏ Other Health Impaired *Specific Impairment* _____

❏ Deaf/Blind   ❏ Autistic-Like Behaviors ❏ Traumatic Brain Injury   ❏ Deaf

❏ Specific Learning Disability   ❏ Language or Speech Disorder   ❏ Emotionally Disturbed

or

❏ Has an established medical disability, which is defined as a disabling medical condition or congenital syndrome which the IEP team determines has a high predictability of requiring intensive special education and services.

    Specify medical condition: _____

II. If any of the items below (A-D) are checked "Yes", the child may not be eligible for special education and services if his or her educational needs are due primarily to:

    A. Unfamiliarity with the English Language   ❏ Yes ❏ No

    B. Temporary physical disabilities   ❏ Yes ❏ No

    C. Social maladjustment   ❏ Yes ❏ No

    D. Environmental, cultural, or economic factors   ❏ Yes ❏ No

III. Needs cannot be met with modification of regular environment   ❏ Yes ❏ No

Distribution: Original - Permanent File   Copy -Parent   Copies may be made for other team members

Transition Services

Beginning no later than the first IEP to be in effect when the student is 16 and updated annually

**MARIN
SELPA**
IEP
Page 6
8/05

Student _____   Date of Meeting _____

DESCRIBE HOW THE STUDENT PARTICIPATED IN THE PROCESS - *Check all that apply*

❑ IEP Team Meeting   ❑ Interview ❑ Observation   ❑ Transitional Planning Assessment   ❑ Pre-IEP Planning Activities
❑ _____

PARENTAL RIGHTS AND AGE OF MAJORITY - *Check all that apply*

❑ If the student will be age 17 during this IEP, the student was informed of parental rights that will transfer to him/her at age 18.
❑ The student has turned age 18 and there is a guardian established by court order. The guardian is _____ .

CULMINATION GOAL

A student's right to FAPE is terminated upon graduation with a high school diploma or exceeding the age eligibility
❑ The student is working toward a diploma and the anticipated date of graduation is _____ .
    1. The California High School Exit Exam (CAHSEE) has been passed: ❑ Math ❑ Reading and Writing
    2. The student has completed a course with the content equivalent of Algebra I ❑ Yes ❑ No
    3. The student must complete the district's prescribed course of study. The student must earn _____ credits.
       The student has earned _____ credits. The student needs to earn _____ credits. ❑ The District's course
       requirements are attached.
    4. ❑ The District also requires the following in order to receive a diploma: _____
       _____
       _____
       ❑ The District does not have any additional requirements.

❑ The student is working toward a certificate of attendance/completion and the anticipated date of culmination is _____ .
       ❑ The District's requirements are attached.

DESIRED OUTCOMES - *What is the vision for the student in these areas?*

Transition Field *If the field is not applicable to the student at this time, provide details that support this conclusion.*	**Action Plan** *What steps will the general education and special education personnel, family and/or others take to help the student be successful in this area? (Document courses or training the student will need, agencies that must be contacted, a timeline for completion, etc.)* *If the field is not applicable to the student at this time, provide details that support this conclusion.*	**Measurable Transition Goal** *Are there skills (disability related) necessary for the student to achieve the outcome? If so, identify the IEP goal which will address this area of assessed need. For each step identified in the Action Plan, indicate if an IEP goal has been developed.* **If an IEP goal has been developed, indicate the page number.**
Course of Study - Consider the following: ❑ Apprenticeship program ❑ Vocational college ❑ Technical institute ❑ Community College ❑ 4-year College ❑ GED Program ❑ _____		

Distribution: Original - Permanent File   Copy -Parent   Copies may be made for other team members

Student _____ Date of Meeting _____

DESIRED OUTCOMES - *What is the vision for the student in these areas?*

Transition Field *If the field is not applicable to the student at this time, provide details that support this conclusion.*	Action Plan *What steps will the general education and special education personnel, family and/or others take to help the student be successful in this area? (Document courses or training the student will need, agencies that must be contacted, a timeline for completion, etc.)* *If the field is not applicable to the student at this time, provide details that support this conclusion.*	Measurable Transition Goal *Are there skills (disability related) necessary for the student to achieve the outcome? If so, identify the IEP goal which will address this area of assessed need. For each step identified in the Action Plan, indicate if an IEP goal has been developed.* **If an IEP goal has been developed, indicate the page number.**
Related Services - *If the student will require related services, indicate the services.* ❑ Mental Health Services ❑ Speech Therapy ❑ Physical Therapy ❑ Vocational Counseling ❑ _____		
Employment **Desired job/occupation** _____ ❑ Competitive employment without support ❑ Competitve employment with time-limited support ❑ Competitive employment with long-term support ❑ Supported employment ❑ Sheltered employment ❑ Military ❑ _____		
Community Experiences **Housing** ❑ Live alone without supports ❑ Live alone with support ❑ Live with family/relative ❑ Live with roommate(s) ❑ Group home-specialized training ❑ Supervised apartment ❑ Residential/nursing facility ❑ _____ **Social and Leisure** ❑ Independent recreation and leisure ❑ Family supported recreation and leisure ❑ Specialized recreation ❑ Community-supported recreation program ❑ _____		

Distribution: Original - Permanent File   Copy -Parent   Copies may be made for other team members

Student _____   Date of Meeting _____

DESIRED OUTCOMES - *What is the vision for the student in these areas?*

Transition Field	Action Plan	Measurable Transition Goal
If the field is not applicable to the student at this time, provide details that support this conclusion.	*What steps will the general education and special education personnel, family and/or others take to help the student be successful in this area? (Document courses or training the student will need, agencies that must be contacted, a timeline for completion, etc.)* *If the field is not applicable to the student at this time, provide details that support this conclusion.*	*Are there skills (disability related) necessary for the student to achieve the outcome? If so, identify the IEP goal which will address this area of assessed need. For each step identified in the Action Plan, indicate if an IEP goal has been developed.* ***If an IEP goal has been developed, indicate the page number.***

Daily Living Skills

Income/Resources
❑ Earned wages
❑ Social Security benefits
❑ Special Needs Trust
❑ _____

Medical Considerations
❑ Insurance
   ❑ Family insurance
   ❑ Individual insurance
   ❑ Medi-Cal
❑ Requires assistance for monitoring medical needs
❑ _____

Support Services
❑ Conservatorship
❑ Counseling services
❑ Day Program(s)
❑ Lifetime support/assistance/planning
❑ _____

Adult Responsibilities
❑ Voter registration
❑ Selective service registration
❑ Parenting
❑ Volunteerism
❑ Family Planning
❑ California Identification Card
❑ Money management
❑ Consumer Skills
❑ _____

Transportation
❑ Driver's license
❑ Public transportation
❑ Specialized transportation
❑ Family transportation
❑ _____

Self-Care
❑ Personal grooming
❑ Meal planning and preparation
❑ Home management
❑ _____

Distribution: Original - Permanent File   Copy -Parent   Copies may be made for other team members

Behavioral Intervention Plan

For behavior interfering with student's learning or that of others.
Note: Numbers correspond to the scoring system on the
Behavior Support Plan (BSP) Quality Evaluation Guide

MARIN
SELPA
IEP
Page 9
8/05

Student _____   Date of Meeting _____

1. The behavior impedes learning is *(describe what it looks like)*

2. It impedes learning because

3. The need for a Behavior Intervention Plan ❑ early stage intervention ❑ moderate ❑ serious ❑ extreme

4. Frequency or intensity or duration of behavior

   reported by _____ and/or observed by _____

PREVENTION - PART 1 ENVIRONMENTAL FACTORS AND NECESSARY CHANGES

Observation & Analysis

What are the predictors for the behavior? *(Situations in which the behavior is likely to occur: people, time, place, subject, etc.)*
5.

What supports the student using problem behavior? (What is missing in the environment/curriculum or what is in the environment curriculum that needs changing?)
6.

Remove the student's need to use the problem behavior

Intervention

What environmental changes, structures and supports are needed to remove the student's need to use this behavior? *(Changes in Time/Space/Materials/Interactions to remove likelihood or behavior)*
7.

Who wil establish?
Who will monitor?
Frequency?

ALTERNATIVES - PART 2 FUNCTIONAL FACTORS AND NEW BEHAVIORS TO TEACH AND SUPPORT

Observation & Analysis

Team believes the behavior occurs because: *(Function of behavior in terms of getting, protesting, or avoiding something)*
8.

Accept a replacement behavior that meets same need

What does the team believes the student should do **instead** of the problem behavior? *(How should the student escape/protest, avoid or get his/her need met in an acceptable way?)*
9.

Distribution: Original - Permanent File   Copy -Parent   Copies may be made for other team members

Behavioral Intervention Plan

Student _____   Date of Meeting _____

ALTERNATIVES - PART 2 CONTINUED

Intervention

What teaching strategies/necessary curriculum/materials are needed? *(List successive teaching steps for student to learn replacement behavior(s))?*
10.

Who will establish?
Who will monitor?
Frequency?

What are reinforcement procedures to use for establishing, maintaining, and generalizing the replacement behavior(s)?
11.

Selection of reinforcer based on:

❑ Reinforcer for using replacement behavior   ❑ Reinforcer for general increase in positive behaviors

By whom?   Frequency?

EFFECTIVE REACTION - PART 3 REACTIVE STRATEGIES

What strategies will be employed if the problem behavior occurs again? *(1. Prompt student to switch to the replacement behavior 2. Describe how staff should handle the problem if the behavior occurs again 3. Positive discussion with student after behavior ends 4. Any necessary further classroom or school consequences?)*
12.

Personnel?

OUTCOME - PART 4 BEHAVIORAL GOALS

Behavioral Goal(s)
13. ❑ Goal page(s) _____
❑ The above behavioral goal(s) are to: Increase use of replacement behavior and may also include:
❑ Develop new general skills that remove student's need to use the problem behavior
❑ Reduce frequency of problem

Observation and analysis conclusion:
Are curriculum accommodations or modifications also necessary?   ❑ Yes ❑ No
Wher are they described?   ❑ IEP Page 17   ❑ IEP Page 18 ❑ IEP _____
Are environmental support/changes necessary?   ❑ Yes ❑ No
Is reinforcement of replacement behavior alone enough (no new teaching is necessary?)   ❑ Yes ❑ No
Are both teaching of new replacement behavior and reinforcement needed?   ❑ Yes ❑ No
Is this BIP to be coordinated with agency's service plans?   ❑ Yes ❑ No
Person responsible for contact between agencies _____

COMMUNICATION - PART 5 COMMUNICATION PROVISIONS

Manner and content of communication
14.
Between?   Frequency?

Distribution: Original - Permanent File   Copy -Parent   Copies may be made for other team members

Positive Behavior Intervention Plan (Hughes Bill)

Student _____ Date of Meeting _____

SUMMARY OF FUNCTIONAL ANALYSIS ASSESSMENT

OBJECTIVE AND MEASURABLE DESCRIPTION OF TARGETED MALADAPTIVE AND REPLACEMENT BEHAVIORS

Targeted maladaptive behavior(s)

Replacement positive behavior(s)

STUDENT'S GOALS SPECIFIC TO THE BEHAVIORAL INTERVENTION PLAN

DESCRIPTION OF INTERVENTIONS TO BE USED AND CIRCUMSTANCES FOR USE

Distribution: Original - Permanent File   Copy -Parent   Copies may be made for other team members

MARIN
SELPA
IEP
Page 12
7/05

Student _____   Date of Meeting _____

RECORDING SCHEDULES

Frequency of use of interventions

Frequency of data collection (targeted and replacement behavior(s)

Criteria for discontinuing use of interventions due to lack of effectiveness

Criteria for phasing out or less intense/frequent schedules or techniques

EXTENT TO WHICH INTERVENTIONS WILL BE CARRIED OUT IN OTHER SETTINGS (WORK, COMMUNITY, HOME, ETC.)

DATES FOR PERIODIC REVIEW BY IEP TEAM TO DETERMINE EFFICACY OF PROGRAM

Manifestation Determination

**MARIN
SELPA**
IEP
Page 13
8/05

Student _____ Date of Present Meeting _____

DESCRIPTION OF BEHAVIOR SUBJECT TO DISCIPLINARY ACTION

THE IEP TEAM CONSIDERED ALL THE RELEVANT INFORMATION IN THE STUDENT'S FILE INCLUDING

Relevant Information Provided by the Parents

Teacher Observation of the Student

Student's IEP

Student _____ Date of Meeting _____

THE IEP TEAM HAS DETERMINED

❏ Yes ❏ No   1. The conduct in question was caused by, or had a direct and substantial relationship to, the student's
                   disability

OR

❏ Yes ❏ No   2. The conduct in question was the direct result of the local educational agency's failure to implement the
                   IEP.

Check the appropriate box:

❏   The behavior was not a manifestation of the student's disability. Proceed with disciplinary proceedings
      and continue to provide a free appropriate public education.

❏   The behavior is a manifestation of the student's disability, no further disciplinary proceedings shall occur.
      The IEP Team shall:
      ❏ Conduct a functional behavioral assessment, and implement a behavioral intervention plan for the
         student
      OR
      ❏ Review the existing behavioral intervention plan and modify it, as necessary, to address the behavior

      AND
      ❏ Return the student to the placement from which he/she was removed
      OR
      ❏ Change the student's placement as agreed upon by the parent and the District (See page 16 of the
         IEP)

SPECIAL CIRCUMSTANCES

The student:
❏ Carried or possessed a weapon to or at school, on school premises, or to or at a school function
❏ Knowingly possessed or used illegal drugs, or sold or solicited the sale of a controlled substance, while at a school, on
   school premises, or at a school function
❏ Inflicted serious bodily injury upon another person while at school, on school premises, or at a school function

and the District is removing the student to an interim alternate educational setting, _____,

for not more than 45 school days.

Distribution: Original - Permanent File   Copy -Parent   Copies may be made for other team members

Student _____   Date of Meeting _____

MARIN
SELPA
IEP
Page 15
8/05

DISTRICT JUSTIFICATION FOR EDUCATIONAL PLACEMENT

RECOMMENDED EDUCATIONAL PLACEMENT	CORRESPONDING PLACEMENT
IEP services can be provided solely in the general education classroom	❏ General Education Classroom
Some IEP services should be provided outside the general education classroom	❏ Some services outside the General Education classroom
All IEP services should be provided outside the general education classroom.	❏ Special Day Class
All IEP services should be provided outside the general education classroom and separately from a school that also serves students without disabilities.	❏ Special Day Class on an isolated site ❏ Non Public School - Day Program
IEP services require a 24-hour educational program.	❏ AB 3632 Residential Placement
Home-based IEP services for a student who is 3 to 5 years of age.	❏ Home-based Early Childhood Program
IEP services provided in a program outside of the home for a student who is 3 to 5 years of age.	❏ Center-based Early Childhood Program
A mix of IEP services that are not provided in primarily school-based settings.	❏ Other

JUSTIFICATION FOR NON PARTICIPATION IN GENERAL EDUCATION

Is the student removed from the general education classroom at any time? ❏ Yes ❏ No
Percent of time out of general education classroom? _____%
If "yes", why is removal considered critical to the student's program?

1. ❏ Small group instruction is necessary for this student to acquire skills specified in the IEP.
2. ❏ The student's needs as addressed in IEP goals cannot be satisfactorily achieved in the general educational/ preschool environment even with the provision of supplemental aids and services.
3. ❏ Additional individualized instruction is required to facilitate his/her learning.
4. ❏ Behavioral intervention plan, strategies, and/or behavioral goals recommended in the student's IEP require a degree of structure which cannot be implemented in a general education classroom.
5. ❏ Student's behavior significantly impairs his/her ability to learn in a large group setting, as well as impairing the learning of other students in a large group setting.
6. ❏ Based upon individual needs and goals in the student's IEP, the general curriculum/appropriate preschool activities would need to be completely restructured.
7. ❏ Student requires utilization of the Severely Handicapped Modified Alternative Curriculum in a highly structured environment to acquire skills specified in his/her IEP.
8. ❏ _____
_____

TYPE OF PHYSICAL EDUCATION

❏ Regular Physical Education   ❏ Modified Physical Education   ❏ Adaptive Physical Education
❏ Medical Waiver   ❏ Completed District PE Course Requirements

Distribution: Original - Permanent File   Copy -Parent   Copies may be made for other team members

Student _____ Date of Meeting _____

**MARIN
SELPA**
IEP
Page 16
8/05

PLACEMENT, SERVICES, AND EQUIPMENT CONSIDERED AND RECOMMENDED

Dates
Unless otherwise specified, services
will be for the regular school year.

Location
Please check appropriate box(es) and specify location

❑ Special Day Class From_____ To _____   ❑ Public-Home School _____
   ❑ Day ❑ Residential ❑ Pursuant to AB 3632   ❑ Public-Other Than Home School*_____
                                                 ❑ Certified Non Public School* _____
                                                 ❑ _____ *

*If not home school, rationale: ❑ Public Preschool ❑ Student would benefit from program available on an isolated site.
❑ Needs cannot be met at home school ❑ Student would benefit from program available at site other than home school

Dates (Month/Day/Year)
Services checked below will be provided until the next
annual review excluding holidays, non-student days,
and all vacations unless otherwise specified.

Frequency

Location
Please identify the specific location(s)
of the program(s)/service(s) and
indicate

R = Room Other Than Gen. Ed. or SDC

❑ Resource Specialist From_____ To _____ _____ _____ ❑ C ❑ R
                       ❑ Direct   ❑ Consult

❑ Language/Speech From_____ To _____ _____ _____ ❑ C ❑ R
                   ❑ Direct   ❑ Consult

❑ Occupational   From_____ To _____ _____ _____ ❑ C ❑ R
   Therapy   ❑ Direct   ❑ Consult

❑ CCS Services From_____ To _____ _____ _____ ❑ C ❑ R
                ❑ Direct   ❑ Consult   ❑ Monitor   ❑ Occupational Therapy   ❑ Physical Therapy

❑ Home/Hospital From_____ To _____ _____ _____ ❑ C ❑ R
                 ❑ Direct   ❑ Consult

❑ Add. Classroom From_____ To _____ _____ _____ ❑ C ❑ R
   Support

❑ Community Mental From_____ To _____ _____ _____ ❑ C ❑ R
   Health

❑ _____ From_____ To _____ _____ _____ ❑ C ❑ R
               ❑ Direct   ❑ Consult

❑ _____ From_____ To _____ _____ _____ ❑ C ❑ R
               ❑ Direct   ❑ Consult

❑ Transportation _____

❑ Specialized equipment/services _____

EXTENDED SCHOOL YEAR

❑ Does not require special education and related services in excess of the regular academic year.
❑ Recommended based upon unique or severe needs.

Program/DIS Service	Dates (Month/Day/Year)	Frequency	Location
❑ Special Day Class	From_____ To _____		
_____	From_____ To _____	_____	_____ ❑ C ❑ R
_____	From_____ To _____	_____	_____ ❑ C ❑ R
_____	From_____ To _____	_____	_____ ❑ C ❑ R
	From_____ To _____	_____	_____ ❑ C ❑ R
Transportation	From_____ To _____	_____	

Distribution: Original - Permanent File   Copy -Parent   Copies may be made for other team members

Student_____   Date of Meeting _____

ACCOMMODATIONS, MODIFICATIONS, AND GRADING

These are to assist the student in attaining the annual goals stated on the IEP as well as increasing the student's involvement and progress in the general curriculum.

Accommodations are adjustments for students with disabilities in instruction or student output that minimize the impact of the disability but do not fundamentally alter or lower course standards or expectations.

Modifications are adjustments for students with disabilities in instruction or student output that minimize the impact of the disability but fundamentally alter or lower course standards or expectations. **Grades** may be modified or a course description may be modified to reflect modified curriculum.

ACCOMMODATIONS for Courses and Classroom or District Tests

	List Specific Courses/District Tests		List Specific Courses/District Tests
1. Highlighted Texts		14. Preferential Seating	
2. Taped Texts		15. Reduced Paper/Pencil Tasks	
3. Note-Taking Assistance		16. Repeated Review/Drill	
4. Taped Lectures		17. Alternative Setting	
5. Peer Buddy		18. Assistive Technology	
6. Peer Tutor		19. Reader Services	
7. Assignment Notebooks		20. Calculator	
8. Extended Time		21. Study Sheets	
9. Shortened Assignments		22. Braille	
10. Frequent Breaks		23. Large Type	
11. Directions Given in a Variety of Ways		24. Alternative/Oral Tests	
12. Increased Verbal Response		25. Short Answer Tests	
13. Alternative Materials/ Assignments		26.	

SUPPORTS FOR SCHOOL PERSONNEL

❏ Yes ❏ No   Are supports for school personnel needed for the student to advance appropriately toward attaining the annual goals, participate in the general curriculum, and be educated and participate with others in educational activities? If yes, specify what supports are needed._____

Distribution: Original - Permanent File   Copy -Parent   Copies may be made for other team members

Student _____   Date of Meeting _____

MODIFICATIONS - *Use the codes below or use an additional page to describe modifications per course or content area*

CONTENT AREAS	CODE	DESCRIPTION OF MODIFICATION OF CURRICULUM
Reading		
Math		
Social Science/History		
Science		
Language Arts		
Physical Education		
Classroom or District Tests Other Than Statewide		

CODES
1. Out of Level Curriculum
2. Partial Curriculum (specify which concepts and standards are covered and which are omitted).
3. Individualized Curriculum, adapting standards to student's ability (attach description of curriculum concepts/ standards to be covered and expectations of student).

EFFECTS OF MODIFIED CURRICULUM - *Check all those that apply*

❏ Student participates in STAR Testing with modifications.
❏ Student participates in the California Alternate Performance Assessment (CAPA).
❏ Student has individualized promotion standards developed by the IEP team(See IEP page 2)
❏ Student is working towards a certificate of completion/attendance*(for secondary students only)*.
❏ Student may not complete diploma requirements *(for secondary students only).*
❏ Student may not be able to pass the California High School Exit Exam (CAHSEE) *(for secondary students only).*
❏ _____

GRADES - *Required if grade or course is to be modified*

Which of the courses will result in a modified grade?

How is a modified grade indicated on the student's report card?

On the student's transcript?

Does it affect honor roll or academic awards? ❏ Yes ❏ No

Does it affect class ranking? ❏ Yes ❏ No

Reason for Modified Curriculum/Grade:
❏ Student requires utilization of SH Modified Alternative Curriculum in a highly structured environment to acquire skills specified in his/her IEP.
❏ _____

Distribution: Original - Permanent File   Copy -Parent   Copies may be made for other team members

Student _____ Date of Meeting _____

PARTICIPATION IN STATEWIDE ASSESSMENT OF STUDENT ACHIEVEMENT

❏ **Student's grade placement is exempt from statewide testing (before grade 2 and after grade 11)**
❏ **Student can participate in the statewide achievement testing program without variations/accommodations/ modifications.**
❏ **Student will participate in the California Alternate Performance Assessment (CAPA):**
    ❏ at the level corresponding to his/her grade level placement.*
    ❏ at Level 1 because he/she:
        • is between the ages of seven and sixteen (grades 2-11) as of December 2 **and**
        • has severe, pervasive disabilities **and**
        • functions at the sensorimotor developmental stage, approximately 24 months or less.

*Eligibility for the CAPA is based on a student's Individualized Education Program (IEP), which reflects an emphasis on functional life skills. To be eligible for participation in CAPA, the response to each of the statements below must be "Agree". If the answer to any of these questions is "Disagree", then the team **should consider** including the student in the STAR assessments.*

Circle "Agree" or "Disagree" for each item:

Agree	Disagree	The student requires extensive instruction in multiple settings to acquire, maintain, and generalize skills necessary for application in school, work, home, and community environments.
Agree	Disagree	The student demonstrates academic/cognitive ability and adaptive behavior that require substantial adjustments to the general curriculum. That student may participate in many of the same activities as their non-disabled peers; however, their learning objectives and expected outcomes focus on the functional applications of the general curriculum.
Agree	Disagree	The student cannot address the performance level assessed in the statewide assessment, even with accommodations or modifications.
Agree	Disagree	The decision to participate in the alternate assessment is **not** based on the amount of time the student is receiving special education services.
Agree	Disagree	The decision to participate in the alternate assessment is **not** based on excessive or extended absences.
Agree	Disagree	The decision to participate in the alternate assessment is **not** based on language, cultural or economic differences.
Agree	Disagree	The decision to participate in the alternate assessment is **not** based deafness/blindness, visual, auditory, and/or motor disabilities.
Agree	Disagree	The decision to participate in the alternate assessment is **not** primarily based on a specific categorical label.
Agree	Disagree	The decision for alternate assessment is an IEP team decision, rather than an administrative decision.

❏ **Student can participate in the statewide achievement testing program with the following ❏ variations ❏ accommodations ❏ modifications.**

✔	Test Variation	STAR		CAHSEE	Physical Fitness
		CAT/6	CST		
	Hear the test directions printed in the test administration manual translated into the student's primary language. Ask clarifying questions about the test directions in the student's primary language.	Variation Allowed	Variation Allowed	Variation Allowed	Variation Allowed
	Additional supervised breaks within a testing day or following each section (STAR) within a test part provided that the test section is completed within a testing day. A test section is identified by a "STOP" at the end of it.	Variation Allowed	Variation Allowed	Variation Allowed	Variation Allowed
	English Learners (ELs) may have the opportunity to be tested separately with other ELs provided that the student is directly supervised by an employee of the school who has signed the test security affidavit and the student has been provided such a flexible setting as part of their regular instruction or assessment.	Variation Allowed	Variation Allowed	Variation Allowed	Variation Allowed
	Access to translation glossaries/word lists (English-to-primary language). Glossaries/word lists shall not include definitions or formulas.	Not Allowed	Variation Allowed Not Allowed ELA	Variation Allowed	Not Applicable

Because the CELDT and SABE/2 are tests specifically for English learners, there are no separate guidelines for administering these two test to this population.

Distribution: Original - Permanent File   Copy -Parent   Copies may be made for other team members

MARIN SELPA
IEP
Page 19 b
8/05

Student _____ Date of Meeting _____

ACCOMMODATIONS/MODIFICATIONS FOR CALIFORNIA STATEWIDE ASSESSMENTS

✔ Accommodation/Modification	STAR			CAHSEE	CELDT	Physical Fitness
	CAT/6	CST	SABE/2			
Test administration directions that are simplified or clarified (does not apply to test questions)	All	All	All	All	All	All
Test individual student separately provided that a test examiner directly supervises the student	1	1	1	1	1	1
Visual magnifying equipment	1	1	1	1	1	Not Applicable
Audio amplification equipment	1	1	1	1	1	1
Noise buffers (e.g. individual corral or study enclosure)	1	1	1	1	1	Not Applicable
Special lighting or acoustics; special or adaptive furniture	1	1	1	1	1	Not Applicable
Colored overlay, mask, or other means to maintain visual attention	1	1	1	1	1	Not Applicable
Manually Coded English or American Sign Language to present directions for administration (does not apply to test questions)	1	1	1	1	1	1
Student marks in test booklet (other than responses)	2	All	2	All	All	Not Applicable 1
Student marks responses in test booklet and responses are transferred to a scorable answer document by an employee of the school, district, or nonpublic school	2	2	2	2	2	Not Applicable
Responses dictated (orally or in Manually Coded English or American Sign Language) to a scribe for selected-response items (multiple-choice questions)	2	2	2	2	2	Not Applicable
Word processing software with spell and grammar check tools turned off on the essay responses (writing portion of the test)	Not Applicable	2	Not Applicable	2	2	Not Applicable
Essay responses dictated orally or in Manually Coded English to a scribe, audio recorder, or speech to text converter and the student provides all spelling and language conventions	Not Applicable	2	Not Applicable	2	2	Not Applicable
Assistive device that does not interfere with the independent work of the student on the multiple-choice and/or essay responses (writing portion of the test)	2	2	2	2	2	Not Applicable
Braille transcriptions provided by the test contractor	2	2	Not Applicable	2	2	Not Applicable
Large print versions Test items enlarged if font larger than required on large print versions.	2	2	2	2	2	Not Applicable

Distribution: Original - Permanent File   Copy -Parent   Copies may be made for other team members

Student _____   Date of Meeting _____

MARIN SELPA
IEP

ACCOMMODATIONS/MODIFICATIONS FOR CALIFORNIA STATEWIDE ASSESSMENTS - CONTINUED

Page 19c
8/05

| ✔ Accommodation/Modification | STAR | | | CAHSEE | CELDT | Physical Fitness |
	CAT/6	CST	SABE/2			
Extra time on a test within a testing day	2	All	2	All	All	All
Test over more than one day for a test or test part to be administered in a single setting	2	2	2	2	2	Not Applicable
Supervised breaks within a section of the test	2	2	2	2	2	Not Applicable
Administration of the test at the most beneficial time of day to the student	2	2	2	2	2	2
Test administered at home or in hospital by a test examiner.	2	2	2	2	2	2
Dictionary	3	3	3	3	3	Not Applicable
Manually Coded English or American Sign Language to present test questions	2 / 3	2 / 3	2 / 3	2 / 3	2 / 3	Not Applicable
Questions or items read aloud to student/audio presentation	2 / 3	2 / 3	2 / 3	2 / 3	2 / 3	Not Applicable
Calculators on the mathematics or science tests	3	3	3	Not Applicable	Not Applicable	Not Applicable
Arithmetic table on the mathematics or science tests	3	3	3	3	Not Applicable	Not Applicable
Math manipulatives on the mathematics or science tests	3	3	3	3	Not Applicable	Not Applicable
Word processing software with spell and grammar check tools enabled on the essay responses (writing portion of the test)	Not Applicable	3	Not Applicable	3	3	Not Applicable
Essay responses dictated orally, in Manually Coded English, or in American Sign Language to a scribe, (audio recorder, or speech-to-text converter); scribe provides spelling, grammar, and language conventions	Not Applicable	3	Not Applicable	3	3	Not Applicable
Assisted device that interferes with the independent work of the student on the multiple-choice and/or essay responses	3	3	3	3	3	Not Applicable
Unlisted Accommodation or Modification						

All =   These test variations may be provided to all students.
Test Variation (1) =   Eligible students may have testing variations if regularly used in the classroom.
Accommodation 2) =   Eligible students shall be permitted to take the California statewide assessments with **accommodations** if specified in the eligible student's IEP or Section 504 plan.
Modification (3) =   Eligible students shall be permitted to take the California statewide assessments with **modifications** if specified in the eligible student's IEP or Section 504 Plan for use on the examination, standardized testing, or for use during classroom instruction and assessment.

For the STAR Program and CELDT, eligible students shall be permitted to take the tests with modifications if specified in the eligible student's IEP or 504 plan.

Distribution: Original - Permanent File   Copy -Parent   Copies may be made for other team members

MARIN
SELPA
IEP
Page 20
8/05

Student _____   Date _____

PLAN TO TRANSITION FROM NPS OR SDC TO GENERAL ED. CLASS PROGRAM

Activity	*Time Spent Each Day or Week*
❑ Provide general education assignments to student while still in special education class.	_____ ❑ Day ❑ Week
❑ Special education teacher, parent, and/or student visit the general education/special day class.	_____ ❑ Day ❑ Week
❑ General education class routine reviewed with student.	_____ ❑ Day ❑ Week
❑ Gradual transition into general education/special day class beginning on _____.	_____ ❑ Day ❑ Week
❑ Peer monitor from general education class assists student.	_____ ❑ Day ❑ Week
❑ Training for general ed. teacher and/or other staff. Topic:_____	_____ Date(s)
❑ Conference with parents and service providers to talk about the special needs of student.	Date(s)
❑ Discussion with students in the general educations class. Topic:_____	_____ Date(s)
❑ _____	_____

SPECIAL FACTORS - *If "yes", indicate where the need is addressed in the IEP*

Does the student's behavior impede his/her learning or that of others?   ❑ Yes ❑ No
    ❑ Behavior Intervention Plan (BIP) pages 9 and 10 OR ❑ Postive Behavior Intervention Plan (PBI) included on pages 11 and 12
    AND ❑ IEP Goal page(s) _____
    ❑ _____

Does the student have limited English proficiency?   ❑ Yes ❑ No
    ❑ IEP Page _____ ❑ IEP Goal page(s) _____

Does the student require any assistive technology devices or services in order to be involved, and to progress in the general curriculum or to be educated in a less restrictive environment?   ❑ Yes ❑ No
    ❑ Needs addressed on IEP Page _____

Does the student who is blind or visually impaired require instruction in Braille?   ❑ Yes ❑ No ❑ NA
    ❑ Braille instruction addressed on IEP page(s)_____ ❑ IEP Goal page(s) _____

Does the student have any special communication needs? (In the case of a student who is deaf or hard of hearing consider the student's language and communication needs, opportunities for direct communications with peers and professional personnel in the student's language and communication mode, academic level, and full range of needs, including opportunities for direct instruction in the student's language and communication mode.) ❑ Yes ❑ No
    ❑ Services addressed on IEP page(s)_____ ❑ IEP Goal page(s) _____

REFERRALS AND ACTIONS FOLLOWING THE IEP TEAM MEETING

Action	*Responsible Personnel and Position*	*By When*
❑ Transportation		
❑ Additional Assessment for _____		
❑ Additional Assessment for _____		
❑ Referral for AB 3632 Assessment		
❑ Copy of IEP to All Service Providers		
❑		

Distribution: Original - Permanent File   Copy -Parent   Copies may be made for other team members

Student: _____ Date of Meeting _____

MARIN SELPA
IEP
Page 21____
8/05

REFERRALS AND/OR ADDITIONAL RECOMMENDATIONS/COMMENTS

MARIN
SELPA
IEP
Page 22
8/05

Student _____ Date of Meeting _____

This IEP document contains the following pages:
1❑ 2❑ 3❑ 4❑ 5❑ 6❑ 7❑ 8❑ 9❑ 10❑ 11❑ 12❑ 13❑ 14❑ 15❑ 16❑ 17❑ 18❑
19a❑ 19b❑ 19c❑ 20❑ 21____ to ____❑ 22❑ 23❑ and Goals pages _____ through _____ .

TEAM MEMBERS - *The following persons affirm that they participated in the development of this IEP. It does not indicate consent. Parent/Guardian or adult student (age 18 or older) consent is on page 23.*

Administrator _____	Parent _____
Administrator _____	Parent _____
Administrator _____	Resource Specialist _____
Agency Rep _____	SDC Teacher _____
Community Mental Health _____	Speech/Language Specialist _____
District Representative _____	Student _____
Guidance Counselor _____	Teacher _____
Hearing Impaired Specialist _____	Teacher _____
Nurse _____	Translator/Interpreter _____
Psychologist _____	_____
Occupational Therapist _____	_____
Orientation/Mobility/VI Instructor _____	_____

❑ Parents were provided with their annual copy of the *Notice of Procedural Safeguards.*
❑ Parents were given a copy of the IEP at no cost.
❑ Parents were given a copy of the ❑ evaluation report(s) ❑ eligibility determination ❑ Summary of Performance, if appropriate, at no cost.

PRIOR WRITTEN NOTICE OF IEP AND PLACEMENT DECISION

The school district proposes to implement this IEP as written. This proposed IEP will allow the student to receive a free appropriate public education in the least restrictive environment. This decision is based upon a review of current records, current assessments, and the student's performance as documented in *Present Level of Academic Achievement and Functional Performance* section on page 2. Other options considered, if any, and the reasons for their rejection are attached or can be found in the *Placement, Services, and Equipment Considered and Recommended* on page 16. Additionally, other factors, if any, that are relevant to this proposal are attached.

A copy of procedural safeguards must be provided to the parent of a student with a disability once per year unless the student is initially referred for an evaluation, the parent requests an additional copy, or the parent initiates a due process complaint.

Please contact the Special Education Administrator at the phone number listed below for your school district if you:
- Would like an additional copy of the Notice of Procedural Safeguards
- Need assistance in understanding the provisions of your rights and safeguards
- Require a translation, orally or by other means, in a different language, or other mode of communication.

Contact Person _____ Phone _____

If you need additional assistance, you may contact the Marin Special Education Local Plan Area (SELPA) at (415) 499-5850.

Distribution: Original - Permanent File   Copy - Parent   Copies may be made for other team members

Student _____ Date of Meeting _____

**MARIN
SELPA**
IEP
Page 23
8/05

ADDENDUMS OR MODIFICATIONS TO THE IEP

The parent(s) and _____, representing _____ ❑ agree ❑ disagree

that in making changes to the student's IEP between the annual meetings, the parent and the district may choose not to convene a meeting, and instead, develop a written document to amend the student's IEP.

ACKNOWLEDGMENT

I have been fully informed of all information relevant to the proposed actions specified in this notice. I understand the actions proposed. I understand my rights (*Notice of Procedural Safeguards*). _____

CONSENT

❑ I was notified of the IEP meeting and was able to attend; I have reviewed the IEP and consent to it.

❑ I was notified of the IEP meeting and was able to attend; I choose not to make a decision at this time. I have received a copy of the IEP and a copy of "Notification of IEP Recommendations".

❑ I agree and give my consent for the above recommendations to be implemented with the exception of:
     ❑ assessment   ❑ eligibility   ❑ goals   ❑ services   ❑ location
_____

❑ I acknowledge that my son/daughter is not an individual with exceptional needs and thus not eligible for special ed. services.

❑ I disagree and wish to schedule: ❑ an IEP meeting ❑ informal meeting ❑ local mediation
                                      ❑ state mediation   ❑ state due process hearing

❑ I decline the services offered.

❑ I agree that the District has offered my son/daughter a free appropriate public education. However, I am voluntarily placing my son/daughter in a private school.

PARENT REQUESTS

❑ I request a copy of the IEP to be provided in my primary language or alternative format (braille or tape recording).

❑ I would like to receive notices by electronic mail communication (e-mail).
   My e-mail address is _____

_____   _____
Signature of Parent/Guardian/Adult Student /Authorized Representative   Date

_____   _____
Signature of Parent/Guardian/Authorized Representative   Date

Distribution: Original - Permanent File   Copy -Parent   Copies may be made for other team members

**MARIN
SELPA**
Page 1
8/05

Addendum to the IEP

This form is not to be used for an Initial IEP, Annual Review, or a 3-Year Reevaluation

Date _____

IDENTIFYING INFORMATION

Student _____ Birthdate _____ Age _____ Grade _____ ❑ M ❑ F

Parent/Guardian _____

Address _____ City _____ Zip _____ Cell _____

❑ LCI
Student's Address if different from parent's ❑ Foster Home _____ Work _____

District of Residence _____ School_____ Home———————

REQUIRED TEAM MEMBERSHIP AND ATTENDANCE - *All of the identified roles of IEP team membership must be represented at the IEP meeting unless:*

The parent(s) and _____, representing _____ agree that

_____, a required IEP Team member (_____) was excused from attending this IEP meeting

❑ because the member's area of curriculum or related services is not being modified.

❑ even though this IEP meeting involves a modification or discussion of a required team member's area of curriculum or related service and _____ has submitted written input into the the development of this IEP to the parent(s) and IEP Team **prior** to the meeting. _____

IEP ADDENDUM INFORMATION - *Please check the area(s) amended at today's IEP, complete the corresponding pages and include them with pages 1,2, and 3 of the Addendum to the IEP.*

❑ Parental Concerns - Page 1
❑ Assessment Reports - Page 2
❑ Eligibility as an Individual With Exceptional Needs - Page 2
❑ Student Promotion and Retention - Page 2
❑ Determination of Eligibiilty for SLD - Page 3
❑ SLD Documentation Report - Page 4
❑ Determination of Eligibiilty for SLI - Page 5
❑ Documentation of Eligibiilty Between the Ages of Three and Five Years - Page 5
❑ Transition Services - Pages 6, 7, and 8
❑ Parental Rights and Age of Majority - Page 6
❑ Culmination Goal- Page 6
❑ Behavior Intervention Plan - Pages 9 and 10
❑ Behavior Intervention Plan (Hughes Bill) - Pages 11 and 12
❑ Manifestation Determination - Pages 13 and 14
❑ District Justification for Educational Placement - Page 15
❑ Justification for Non Participation in General Education - Page 15
❑ Type of Physical Education - Page 15

❑ Placement, Services, and Equipment Considered and Recommended - Page 16
❑ Extended School Year - Page 16
❑ Accommodations - Page 17
❑ Supports for School Personnel - Page 17
❑ Modifications - Page 18
❑ Effects of Modified Curriculum - Page 18
❑ Grades - Page 18
❑ Participation in STAR Testing - Page 19a
❑ Accommodations/Modifications for California Statewide Assessments - Pages 19b and19c
❑ Plan to Transition From NPS or SDC to General Class Program - Page 20
❑ Special Factors - Page 20
❑ Referrals and/or Actions Required Following the IEP - Page 20
❑ Referrals and/or Additional Recommendations/Comments - Page 21
❑ Goals - Page(s)_____
❑ Other (please specify)_____

Distribution: White - Permanent File   Canary - Parent   Copies may be made for other team members

**MARIN
SELPA**
Addendum
Page 2
8/05

Student _____ Date _____

*The IEP developed on_____ and the amended sections developed today and on
the previous dates (if any) _____ comprise the complete, current IEP.*

This document contains pages 1 and 2 of the Addendum to the IEP and the following amended pages :
1❑ 2❑ 3❑ 4❑ 5❑ 6❑ 7❑ 8❑ 9❑ 10❑ 11❑ 12❑ 13❑ 14❑ 15❑ 16❑ 17❑ 18❑
19a❑ 19b❑ 19c❑ 20❑ 21__ through __❑ 22❑ 23❑ Goal(s) pages _____ through _____❑.

DATES OF ANTICIPATED MEETINGS

Annual Review _____ AB 3632 6 Month Review _____ 3-Yr. Reevaluation _____ Add'l. Review _____
          Month/Day/Year   Month/Day/Year   Month/Day/Year   Month/Day/Year

TEAM MEMBERS - *The following persons affirm that they participated in the development of this IEP. It does not indicate
consent. Parent/Guardian/Adult student (age 18 or older) consent is on page 3.*

Administrator_____   Occupational Therapist _____

Administrator_____   Orientation/Mobility/VI Instructor _____

Administrator_____   Parent _____

Agency Rep. _____   Parent _____

Community Mental Health _____   Resource Specialist _____

District Representative _____   SDC Teacher _____

Guidance Counselor _____   Speech/Language Specialist _____

Hearing Impaired Specialist _____   Student _____

Nurse _____   Teacher _____

Psychologist _____   _____

❑ Parents were provided with their annual copy of the *Notice of Procedural Safeguards.*
❑ Parents were given a copy of the IEP at no cost.
❑ Parents were given a copy of the ❑ evaluation report(s) ❑ eligibility determination ❑ Summary of Performance, if
    appropriate, at no cost.

PRIOR WRITTEN NOTICE OF IEP AND PLACEMENT DECISION

The school district proposes to implement this IEP as written. This proposed IEP will allow the student to receive a free appropriate
public education in the least restrictive environment. This decision is based upon a review of current records, current assessments, and
the student's performance as documented in *Present Level of Academic Achievement and Functional Performance* section on IEP page
2. Other options considered, if any, and the reasons for their rejection are attached or can be found in the *Placement, Services, and
Equipment Considered and Recommended* on page 16. Additionally, other factors, if any, that are relevant to this proposal are attached.

A copy of procedural safeguards must be provided to the parent of a student with a disability once per year unless the student is initially
referred for an evaluation, the parent requests an additional copy, or the parent initiates a due process complaint.

Please contact the Special Education Administrator at the phone number listed below for your school district if you:
          • Would like an additional copy of the Notice of Procedural Safeguards
          • Need assistance in understanding the provisions of your rights and safeguards
          • Require a translation, orally or by other means, in a different language, or other mode of communication.

Contact Person _____ Phone _____

If you need additional assistance, you may contact the Marin Special Education Local Plan Area (SELPA) at 499-5850.

MARIN SELPA
Addendum
Page 3
8/05

Student _____   Date of Meeting _____

ACKNOWLEDGMENT

I have been fully informed of all information relevant to the proposed actions specified in this notice. I understand the actions proposed. I understand my rights (*Notice of Procedural Safeguards*). _____

CONSENT

❏ I was notified of the IEP meeting and was able to attend; I have reviewed the IEP and consent to it.

❏ I was notified of the IEP meeting and was able to attend; I choose not to make a decision at this time. I have received a copy of the IEP and a copy of "Notification of IEP Recommendations".

❏ I agree and give my consent for the above recommendations to be implemented with the exception of:
   ❏ assessment   ❏ eligibility   ❏ goals   ❏ services   ❏ location
   _____

❏ I acknowledge that my son/daughter is not an individual with exceptional needs and thus not eligible for special ed. services.

❏ I disagree and wish to schedule: ❏ an IEP meeting   ❏ informal meeting   ❏ local mediation
                                     ❏ state mediation   ❏ state due process hearing

❏ I decline the services offered.

❏ I agree that the District has offered my son/daughter a free appropriate public education. However, I am voluntarily placing my son/daughter in a private school.

PARENT REQUESTS

❏ I request a copy of the IEP to be provided in my primary language or alternative format (braille or tape recording).

❏ I would like to receive notices by electronic mail communication (e-mail).
   My e-mail address is _____

_____   _____
Signature of Parent/Guardian/Adult Student /Authorized Representative   Date

_____   _____
Signature of Parent/Guardian/Authorized Representative   Date

Appendix 5

Tear-Out Forms

Request for Information on Special Education

Request to Begin Special Education Process and Evaluation

Request for Child's School File

Request to Amend Child's School File

Special Education Contacts

IEP Journal

Monthly IEP Calendar

IEP Blueprint

Letter Requesting Evaluation Report

Request for Joint IEP Eligibility/Program Meeting

Progress Chart

Program Visitation Request Letter

Class Visitation Checklist

Goals Chart

IEP Material Organizer Form

IEP Meeting Participants

IEP Meeting Attendance Objection Letter

IEP Preparation Checklist

Letter Confirming Informal Negotiation

Letter Requesting Due Process

Request for Information on Special Education

Date: _____

To: _____

_____

_____

_____

Re: _____

I am writing to you because my child is experiencing difficulties in school. I understand there is a special process for evaluating a child and determining eligibility for special education programs and services. Please send me any written information you have about that process. Please also send me information about how I can contact other parents and local support groups involved in special education.

Thank you very much for your kind assistance. I look forward to talking with you further about special education.

Sincerely,

_____

_____

_____

_____

Request to Begin Special Education Process and Evaluation

Date: _____

To: _____

         _____

         _____

         _____

Re: _____

I am writing to you because my child is experiencing difficulties in school. _____

_____

_____

_____

_____

_____ .

I am formally requesting that the school immediately begin its special education process, including initial evaluation for eligibility. I understand that you will send me an evaluation plan explaining the tests that may be given to my child. Because I realize the evaluation can take some time, I would appreciate receiving the evaluation plan within ten days. Once you receive my approval for the evaluation, would you please let me know when the evaluation will be scheduled?

I would also appreciate any other information you have regarding the evaluation, how eligibility is determined, and the general IEP process.

Thank you very much for your kind assistance. I look forward to working with you and your staff.

Sincerely,

_____

_____

_____

_____

_____

Request for Child's School File

Date: _____

To: _____

_____

_____

_____

Re: _____

I would like a copy of my child's records, including all tests, reports, evaluations, grades, notes by teachers or other staff members, memoranda, photographs—in short, *everything* in my child's school file. I understand I have a right to these files under _____

_____

_____

_____

_____ .

I would greatly appreciate having these files within the next five days. I would be happy to pick them up. I will call you to discuss how and when I will get copies.

Thank you for your kind assistance.

Sincerely,

_____

_____

_____

_____

_____

Request to Amend Child's School File

Date: _____

To: _____

_____

_____

_____

Re: _____

I recently reviewed a copy of my child's file and would like to have a portion of the file amended, specifically:

_____

_____

_____

_____

_____

_____ .

IDEA provides that I have the right to request that all information that is "inaccurate or misleading, or violates the privacy of [my] child" be amended. I feel that this is just such a case. Therefore, I request that you immediately rectify the situation.

Please notify me in writing as soon as possible of your decision regarding this matter. Thank you.

Sincerely,

_____

_____

_____

_____

_____

Special Education Contacts

School Staff

_____

_____

_____

_____

_____

_____

Outside Professionals

_____

_____

_____

_____

_____

_____

Other Parents

_____

_____

_____

_____

_____

Support Groups

_____

_____

State Department of Education

_____

_____

Other

_____

_____

_____

_____

IEP Journal

Date: _____ **Time:** _____ a.m./p.m.

Action: ☐ Phone Call _____ ☐ Meeting _____

☐ Other: _____

Person(s) Contacted: _____

Notes: _____

_____

_____

_____

_____

_____

_____

_____

_____

_____

_____

_____

■ ■

IEP Journal

Date: _____ **Time:** _____ a.m./p.m.

Action: ☐ Phone Call _____ ☐ Meeting _____

☐ Other: _____

Person(s) Contacted: _____

Notes: _____

_____

_____

_____

_____

_____

_____

_____

_____

_____

_____

Monthly IEP Calendar

Month and Year: _____

1	2	3	4	5	6	7
8	9	10	11	12	13	14
15	16	17	18	19	20	21
22	23	24	25	26	27	28
29	30	31				

IEP Blueprint

The IEP blueprint represents the ideal IEP for your child. Use it as a guide to make and record the educational desires you have for your child.

Areas of the IEP	Preferred Situation for Your Child
1. Classroom Setting and Peer Needs— issues to consider:	
☐ regular versus special education class	
☐ partially or fully mainstreamed	
☐ type of special education class	
☐ number of children in the classroom	
☐ ages and cognitive ranges of children in class	
☐ kinds of students and behaviors that might or might not be appropriate for your child, and	
☐ language similarities.	
2. Teacher and Staff Needs—issues to consider:	
☐ number of teachers and aides	
☐ teacher-pupil ratio	
☐ experience, training, and expertise of the teacher, and	
☐ training and expertise of aides.	
3. Curricula and Teaching Methodology— be specific. If you don't know what you *do* want, specify what you *don't* want.	

Areas of the IEP	Ideal Situation for Your Child

4. Related Services—issues to consider:

☐ specific needed services

☐ type of services

☐ frequency of services, and

☐ length of services.

5. Identified Programs—specify known programs that you think would work for your child and the school that offers them.

6. Goals—your child's academic and functional aims.

7. Classroom Environment and Other Features—issues to consider:

☐ distance from home

☐ transition plans for mainstreaming

☐ vocational needs

☐ extracurricular and social needs, and

☐ environmental needs.

Areas of the IEP	Ideal Situation for Your Child

8. **Involvement in the General Curriculum/ Other**—to what extent will your child be involved in regular programs and curriculum, and what help will your child need to do it?

☐ current academic level in reading, writing, social skills, etc., and

☐ statewide assessment exams: Will your child take them? Will accommodations be necessary?

Letter Requesting Evaluation Report

Date: _____

To: _____

_____

_____

_____

Re: _____

I appreciate your involvement in my child's evaluation and look forward to your report. Would you please:

1. Send me a copy of a draft of your report before you finalize it. As you can imagine, the process can be overwhelming for parents. It would be most helpful to me to see your report, because the proposed tests are complicated and I need time to evaluate the results.

2. Send me your final report at least four weeks before the IEP meeting.

Again, thank you for your kind assistance.

Sincerely,

_____

_____

_____

_____

_____

Request for Joint IEP Eligibility/Program Meeting

Date: _____

To: _____

_____

_____

_____

Re: _____

I believe there is sufficient information for us to discuss both my child's eligibility for special education and the specifics of my child's IEP at the same meeting. I would appreciate it if you would plan enough time to discuss both those important items at the _____ IEP meeting. I would also like to see any and all reports and other written material that you will be introducing at the IEP meeting, at least two weeks before the meeting.

Thanks in advance for your help. I hope to hear from you soon.

Sincerely,

_____

_____

_____

_____

_____

Progress Chart

Student: _____

Class: _____

Date: _____

Key Goals	Current Status	Comments

Math

Progressing appropriately?

☐ yes   ☐ no

_____

_____

_____

Reading

Progressing appropriately?

☐ yes   ☐ no

_____

_____

_____

Writing

Progressing appropriately?

☐ yes   ☐ no

_____

_____

_____

Spelling

Progressing appropriately?

☐ yes   ☐ no

_____

_____

_____

Social-behavioral

Progressing appropriately?

☐ yes   ☐ no

_____

_____

_____

Language development

Progressing appropriately?

☐ yes   ☐ no

_____

_____

_____

Motor development

Progressing appropriately?

☐ yes   ☐ no

_____

_____

_____

Other

Progressing appropriately?

☐ yes   ☐ no

_____

_____

_____

_____

Program Visitation Request Letter

Date: _____

To: _____

_____

_____

_____

Re: _____

I appreciate the concerns you have and realize that you can't know which programs are appropriate for my child until after the IEP meeting. Nonetheless, I think it would be very helpful for me to see existing programs so I can be a more effective member of the IEP team. I do not feel I can make an informed IEP decision without seeing, firsthand, all possible options. I want to assure you that I understand that by giving me the names of existing programs, you are not stating an opinion as to their appropriateness for my child.

I assure you that I will abide by all rules and regulations for parental visits. If those rules and regulations are in writing, please send me a copy.

Thanks in advance for your help. I hope to hear from you soon.

Sincerely,

_____

_____

_____

_____

_____

Class Visitation Checklist

Date: _____ Time: _____ a.m./p.m.

School: _____

Class: _____

Student Description:

Total students: _____ Gender range: _____

Age range: _____

Cognitive range: _____

_____

_____

Language/communication range: _____

_____

_____

_____

Disability range: _____

_____

_____

_____

Behavioral range: _____

_____

_____

_____

Other observations: _____

_____

_____

_____

Staff Description:

Teachers: _____

_____

_____

_____

Aides: _____

_____

_____

_____

Other observations: _____

_____

_____

_____

Curricula/Classroom Strategies:

Curricula: _____

_____

_____

_____

_____

Strategies: _____

_____

_____

_____

_____

_____

Classroom Environment:

Description: _____

_____

_____

_____

_____

_____

Related Services:

_____

_____

_____

Other Comments:

_____

_____

_____

_____

_____

_____

How This Program Relates to IEP Blueprint:

_____

_____

_____

_____

_____

_____

Goals Chart

Skill Area	Annual Goal	Present Performance Level	How Progress Measured	Date of Completion
Reading				
Math				
Emotional and psychological				

Skill Area	Annual Goal	Present Performance Level	How Progress Measured	Date of Completion
Social-behavioral				
Linguistic and communication				
Self-help and independent living skills (transition services)				

Goals Chart

NOLO
△△ www.nolo.com

IEP Material Organizer Form

Use this form to track documents and people that provide support for or opposition to your goals.

Issue: _____

Document or Witness* Name(s):	Binder Location (if applicable)	Helps You	Hurts You	Key Supportive or Oppositional Information	Rebuttal Document or Witness Name(s) (if hurts) (If none, what will you say at meeting?)

* A "witness" is someone (teacher, doctor, evaluator, tutor, psychologist) who gives an oral or written opinion regarding your child's needs at the IEP meeting.

NOLO

IEP Meeting Participants

Name	Position/Employer	Purpose for Attending	Point of View

IEP Meeting Attendance Objection Letter

Date: _____

To: _____

_____

_____

_____

Re: _____

I understand that _____,

will be at _____ IEP meeting. _____

knows nothing about _____ and appears to have no knowledge that

might be of use to the IEP team. I am formally requesting that _____

not attend, unless there is some clear reason that makes _____

attendance appropriate and necessary for the development of _____

IEP plan. As you know, IEP meetings can be particularly difficult for parents. We are already anxious about ours and would prefer that you not take action that will heighten our stress level.

If you insist on _____ attending without any reason, then we will file a complaint with the state and federal departments of education.

I will call you in a few days to find out your decision on this issue. Thank you for considering my request.

Sincerely,

_____

_____

_____

_____

_____

IEP Preparation Checklist

☐ Find out the date, time, and location.

☐ Get a copy of the school's agenda.

☐ Make your own agenda.

☐ Prepare your IEP material organizer.

☐ Draft IEP plan.

☐ Find out who is attending on behalf of school district.

☐ Invite and prepare your own IEP participants.

☐ Give the school a copy of the following:

　　☐ independent evaluations

　　☐ documents such as reports and work samples

　　☐ names and titles of people attending IEP, and

　　☐ notice of intent to tape record IEP meeting (if applicable)

☐ Create a meeting reminder list of items you want to be sure to remember.

Letter Confirming Informal Negotiation

Date: _____

To: _____

_____

_____

_____

Re: _____

I appreciated the chance to meet on _____ and discuss

_____. I also appreciated your

point of view and the manner in which we solved the problem.

I want to confirm our agreement that _____

_____

_____

_____ .

I greatly appreciate the manner in which you helped solve this problem. _____

_____

_____

_____ .

Thank you.

Sincerely,

_____

_____

_____

_____

_____

Letter Requesting Due Process

Date: _____

To: _____

_____

_____

_____

Re: _____

_____

_____

We are formally requesting due process, beginning with mediation. We believe _____

_____

_____

_____ .

We believe an appropriate solution would include, but should not be limited to, the following:

_____

_____

_____

_____

_____ .

Please contact us at once to schedule the mediation.

Sincerely,

_____

_____

_____

_____

_____

Index

CATALOG

...more from Nolo

	PRICE	CODE
BUSINESS		
Becoming a Mediator: Your Guide to Career Opportunities	$29.99	BECM
Business Buyout Agreements (Book w/CD-ROM)	$49.99	BSAG
The CA Nonprofit Corporation Kit (Binder w/CD-ROM)	$69.99	CNP
California Workers' Comp: How to Take Charge When You're Injured on the Job	$34.99	WORK
The Complete Guide to Buying a Business	$24.99	BUYBU
The Complete Guide to Selling Your Business	$24.99	SELBU
Consultant & Independent Contractor Agreements (Book w/CD-ROM)	$29.99	CICA
The Corporate Records Handbook (Book w/CD-ROM)	$69.99	CORMI
Create Your Own Employee Handbook (Book w/CD-ROM)	$49.99	EMHA
Dealing With Problem Employees	$44.99	PROBM
Deduct It! Lower Your Small Business Taxes	$34.99	DEDU
Effective Fundraising for Nonprofits	$24.99	EFFN
The Employer's Legal Handbook	$39.99	EMPL
Federal Employment Laws	$49.99	FELW
Form Your Own Limited Liability Company (Book w/CD-ROM)	$44.99	LIAB
Home Business Tax Deductions: Keep What You Earn	$34.99	DEHB
How to Create a Noncompete Agreement (Book w/CD-ROM)	$44.95	NOCMP
How to Form a California Professional Corporation (Book w/CD-ROM)	$59.99	PROF
How to Form a Nonprofit Corporation (Book w/CD-ROM)—National Edition	$49.99	NNP
How to Form a Nonprofit Corporation in California (Book w/CD-ROM)	$49.99	NON
How to Form Your Own California Corporation (Binder w/CD-ROM)	$59.99	CACI
How to Form Your Own California Corporation (Book w/CD-ROM)	$34.99	CCOR
How to Get Your Business on the Web	$29.99	WEBS
How to Run a Thriving Business: Strategies for Success & Satisfaction	$19.99	THRV

Prices subject to change.

	PRICE	CODE
How to Write a Business Plan	$34.99	SBS
Incorporate Your Business	$49.99	NIBS
The Independent Paralegal's Handbook	$34.99	PARA
Legal Guide for Starting & Running a Small Business	$34.99	RUNS
Legal Forms for Starting & Running a Small Business (Book w/CD-ROM)	$29.99	RUNSF
LLC or Corporation?	$24.99	CHENT
The Manager's Legal Handbook	$39.99	ELBA
Marketing Without Advertising	$20.00	MWAD
Mediate, Don't Litigate	$24.99	MEDL
Music Law (Book w/CD-ROM)	$34.99	ML
Negotiate the Best Lease for Your Business	$24.99	LESP
Nolo's Guide to Social Security Disability	$29.99	QSS
Nolo's Quick LLC	$29.99	LLCQ
Nondisclosure Agreements (Book w/CD-ROM)	$39.95	NAG
The Partnership Book: How to Write a Partnership Agreement (Book w/CD-ROM)	$39.99	PART
The Performance Appraisal Handbook	$29.99	PERF
The Small Business Start-up Kit (Book w/CD-ROM)	$29.99	SMBU
The Small Business Start-up Kit for California (Book w/CD-ROM)	$24.99	OPEN
Starting & Running a Successful Newsletter or Magazine	$29.99	MAG
Tax Savvy for Small Business	$36.99	SAVVY
Workplace Investigations: A Step by Step Guide	$39.99	CMPLN
Working for Yourself: Law & Taxes for Independent Contractors, Freelancers & Consultants	$39.99	WAGE
Working With Independent Contractors (Book w/CD-ROM)	$29.99	HICI
Your Crafts Business: A Legal Guide (Book w/CD-ROM)	$26.99	VART
Your Limited Liability Company: An Operating Manual (Book w/CD-ROM)	$49.99	LOP
Your Rights in the Workplace	$29.99	YRW

CONSUMER

	PRICE	CODE
How to Win Your Personal Injury Claim	$29.99	PICL
Nolo's Encyclopedia of Everyday Law	$29.99	EVL

	PRICE	CODE
Nolo's Guide to California Law	$24.99	CLAW

ESTATE PLANNING & PROBATE

	PRICE	CODE
8 Ways to Avoid Probate	$19.99	PRAV
Estate Planning Basics	$21.99	ESPN
The Executor's Guide: Settling a Loved One's Estate or Trust	$34.99	EXEC
How to Probate an Estate in California	$49.99	PAE
Make Your Own Living Trust (Book w/CD-ROM)	$39.99	LITR
Nolo's Simple Will Book (Book w/CD-ROM)	$36.99	SWIL
Plan Your Estate	$44.99	NEST
Quick & Legal Will Book	$16.99	QUIC
Special Needs Trust: Protect Your Child's Financial Future	$34.99	SPNT

FAMILY MATTERS

	PRICE	CODE
Building a Parenting Agreement That Works	$24.99	CUST
The Complete IEP Guide	$34.99	IEP
Divorce & Money: How to Make the Best Financial Decisions During Divorce	$34.99	DIMO
Do Your Own California Adoption: Nolo's Guide for Stepparents and Domestic Partners (Book w/CD-ROM)	$34.99	ADOP
Every Dog's Legal Guide: A Must-Have for Your Owner	$19.99	DOG
Get a Life: You Don't Need a Million to Retire Well	$24.99	LIFE
The Guardianship Book for California	$39.99	GB
A Legal Guide for Lesbian and Gay Couples	$34.99	LG
Living Together: A Legal Guide (Book w/CD-ROM)	$34.99	LTK
Living Wills and Powers of Attorney in California (Book w/CD-ROM)	$21.99	CPOA
Nolo's IEP Guide: Learning Disabilities	$29.99	IELD
Prenuptial Agreements: How to Write a Fair & Lasting Contract (Book w/CD-ROM)	$34.99	PNUP
Using Divorce Mediation: Save Your Money & Your Sanity	$29.99	UDMD

	PRICE	CODE

GOING TO COURT

	PRICE	CODE
Beat Your Ticket: Go To Court & Win! (National Edition)	$21.99	BEYT
The Criminal Law Handbook: Know Your Rights, Survive the System	$34.99	KYR
Everybody's Guide to Small Claims Court (National Edition)	$26.99	NSCC
Everybody's Guide to Small Claims Court in California	$29.99	CSCC
Fight Your Ticket & Win in California	$29.99	FYT
How to Change Your Name in California	$34.99	NAME
How to Collect When You Win a Lawsuit (California Edition)	$29.99	JUDG
The Lawsuit Survival Guide	$29.99	UNCL
Nolo's Deposition Handbook	$29.99	DEP
Represent Yourself in Court: How to Prepare & Try a Winning Case	$34.99	RYC
Win Your Lawsuit: A Judge's Guide to Representing Yourself in California Superior Court	$29.99	SLWY

HOMEOWNERS, LANDLORDS & TENANTS

	PRICE	CODE
California Tenants' Rights	$27.99	CTEN
Deeds for California Real Estate	$24.99	DEED
Every Landlord's Legal Guide (National Edition, Book w/CD-ROM)	$44.99	ELLI
Every Landlord's Tax Deduction Guide	$34.99	DELL
Every Tenant's Legal Guide	$29.99	EVTEN
For Sale by Owner in California	$29.99	FSBO
How to Buy a House in California	$34.99	BHCA
The California Landlord's Law Book: Rights & Responsibilities (Book w/CD-ROM)	$44.99	LBRT
The California Landlord's Law Book: Evictions (Book w/CD-ROM)	$44.99	LBEV
Leases & Rental Agreements	$29.99	LEAR
Neighbor Law: Fences, Trees, Boundaries & Noise	$26.99	NEI
The New York Landlord's Law Book (Book w/CD-ROM)	$39.99	NYLL
New York Tenants' Rights	$27.99	NYTEN
Renters' Rights (National Edition)	$24.99	RENT

	PRICE	CODE
The Inventor's Notebook	$24.99	INOT
License Your Invention (Book w/CD-ROM)	$39.99	LICE
Nolo's Patents for Beginners	$29.99	QPAT
Patent, Copyright & Trademark	$39.99	PCTM
Patent It Yourself	$49.99	PAT
Patent Pending in 24 Hours	$29.99	PEND
Patenting Art & Entertainment: New Strategies for Protecting Creative Ideas	$39.99	PATAE
The Public Domain	$34.99	PUBL
Trademark: Legal Care for Your Business and Product Name	$39.99	TRD
Web and Software Development: A Legal Guide (Book w/ CD-ROM)	$44.99	SFT
What Every Inventor Needs to Know About Business & Taxes (Book w/CD-ROM)	$21.99	ILAX

RESEARCH & REFERENCE

Legal Research: How to Find & Understand the Law	$39.99	LRES

SENIORS

Long-Term Care: How to Plan & Pay for It	$21.99	ELD
Social Security, Medicare & Goverment Pensions	$29.99	SOA

SOFTWARE

**Call or check our website at www.nolo.com
for special discounts on Software!**

	PRICE	CODE
Incorporator Pro	89.99	STNC1
LLC Maker—Windows	$89.95	LLP1
Patent Pending Now!	$199.99	PP1
PatentEase—Windows	$349.00	PEAS
Personal RecordKeeper 5.0 CD—Windows	$59.95	RKD5
Quicken Legal Business Pro 2006—Windows	$109.99	SBQB6
Quicken WillMaker Plus 2006—Windows	$79.99	WQP6

Special Upgrade Offer

Save 35% on the latest edition of your Nolo book

Because laws and legal procedures change often, we update our books regularly. To help keep you up-to-date, we are extending this special upgrade offer. Cut out and mail the title portion of the cover of your old Nolo book and we'll give you **35% off** the retail price of the NEW EDITION of that book when you purchase directly from Nolo. This offer is to individuals only.

Call us today at 1-800-728-3555

Prices and offer subject to change without notice.

Order Form

Name

Address

City

State, Zip

Daytime Phone

E-mail

Item Code	Quantity	Item	Unit Price	Total Price

Method of payment

☐ Check ☐ VISA ☐ MasterCard
☐ Discover Card ☐ American Express

Subtotal	
Add your local sales tax (California only)	
Shipping: RUSH $9, Basic $5 (See below)	
"I bought 3, ship it to me FREE!"(Ground shipping only)	
TOTAL	

Account Number

Expiration Date

Signature

Shipping and Handling

Rush Delivery—Only $9

We'll ship any order to any street address in the U.S. by UPS 2nd Day Air* for only $9!

* Order by noon Pacific Time and get your order in 2 business days. Orders placed after noon Pacific Time will arrive in 3 business days. P.O. boxes and S.F. Bay Area use basic shipping. Alaska and Hawaii use 2nd Day Air or Priority Mail.

Basic Shipping—$5

Use for P.O. Boxes, Northern California and Ground Service.

Allow 1-2 weeks for delivery. U.S. addresses only.

For faster service, use your credit card and our toll-free numbers

**Call our customer service group
Monday thru Friday 7am to 7pm PST**

Phone	1-800-728-3555
Fax	1-800-645-0895
Mail	**Nolo**
	950 Parker St.
	Berkeley, CA 94710

**Order 24 hours a day @
www.nolo.com**

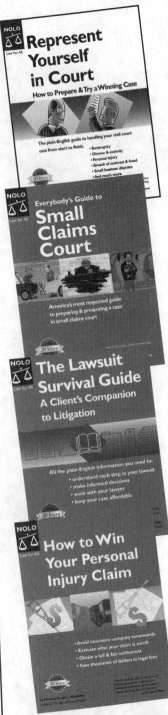